Publisher
Marie Butler-Knight

Product Development Manager
Faithe Wempen

Managing Editor
Elizabeth Keaffaber

Acquisitions Manager
Barry Pruett

Copy Editor
San Dee Phillips

Cover Designer
Jay Corpus

Designer
Barbara Webster

Indexers
Jennifer Eberhardt
Greg Eldred

Production Team
Gary Adair, Brad Chinn, Kim Cofer, Meshell Dinn, Mark Enochs,
Stephanie Gregory, Jenny Kucera, Beth Rago, Marc Shecter, Kris Simmons,
Greg Simsic, Carol Stamile, Robert Wolf

Special thanks to C. Herbert Feltner
for ensuring the technical accuracy of this book.

CONTENTS

INTRODUCTION

"There aren't enough hours in the day." It's a common complaint. Time is a commodity everyone can use more of. The Microsoft Corporation has packaged five of their most powerful and useful software products into one impressive package called Microsoft Office. These programs run with the help of a sixth package, Microsoft Windows. With these software products, you can save time as you create impressive business documents, financial statements, and presentations, and use electronic mail for fast, convenient communication with colleagues.

Windows 3.1 is a graphical user interface (GUI) that allows you to organize and run your software packages in a graphical operating environment, instead of using prompts and obscure commands (DOS). Windows comes with several useful applications, including a word processor (Write), a graphics painting program (Paintbrush), and a communications program (Terminal). It also features many accessories, such as a clock, a calendar, and a card file, that will help organize and simplify your work.

The five software packages in Microsoft Office are:

- **Word for Windows 6.0**   Arguably the best Windows-based word processing program on the market. Word has features to let you create a one-page memo, a newsletter with graphics, or even a 500-page report.

- **Excel 5.0**   A powerful yet easy-to-maneuver spreadsheet program. Excel can be used to generate impressive financial statements, charts and graphs, and databases, and to share the information with other software packages.

- **PowerPoint 4.0**   An easy-to-use presentation program that lets you create impressive slides and overheads or print out presentations.

- **Mail 3.0**   An electronic mail program that lets you share information (data and files) and exchange electronic mail with colleagues.

- **Access 2.0**   A database program that's quickly become a leader in the industry because of its powerful capabilities and ease of use. Access is included only in the Professional edition of Office.

Using This Book

Microsoft Office 6 in 1 is designed to help you learn these six programs quickly and easily. You don't have to spend any time figuring out what to learn. All of the most important tasks are covered in this book. There's no need for long classes or thick manuals. Learn the skills you need in short, easy-to-follow lessons.

The book is organized into six parts—one for each software package—with 20–30 lessons in each part. Because each of these lessons takes 10 minutes or less to complete, you can quickly master the basic skills needed to navigate Windows, create documents, financial statements, or slide shows, or send and reply to mail messages.

A bonus section discusses the sharing of information from one software package to another. This sharing is called Object Linking and Embedding (OLE).

If this is the first time you've ever used Windows or a Windows product, begin with the Windows part of this book. What you learn in this part will help you navigate your way through the other software packages.

Conventions Used in This Book

Each of the short lessons in this book includes step-by-step instructions for performing specific tasks. The following icons are included to help you quickly identify particular types of information:

Icons (small graphic symbols) indicate ways you can save time when you're using any of the Microsoft Office products.

Icons offer easy-to-follow definitions that you'll need to know in order to understand how to use a software package.

Icons help you avoid making mistakes.

In addition to the above icons, the following conventions are also used:

On-screen text	On-screen text will appear in boldface type.
What you type	Information you type will appear in boldface type.
Items you select	Items you select or keys you press will appear in boldface type.

Acknowledgments

Alpha Books would like to acknowledge the contributing authors of this book: Peter Aitken, Jennifer Fulton, Joe Kraynak, Kate Miller, Steve Poland, Michelle Shaw, and Carl Townsend. Thanks to Michelle Shaw for coordinating the second edition of this book, and Kelly Oliver, Liz Keaffaber, and Faithe Wempen for extra editorial assistance.

And finally, thanks to our hard-working Alpha production team: Gary Adair, Brad Chinn, Kim Cofer, Meshell Dinn, Jennifer Eberhardt, Greg Eldred, Mark Enochs, Stephanie Gregory, Jenny Kucera, Beth Rago, Marc Shecter, Kris Simmons, Greg Simsic, Carol Stamile, and Robert Wolf.

WINDOWS™ 3.1

Starting Windows

In this lesson, you will learn what Windows is, how to start Windows, how to interpret what you see, and how to make a quick escape.

The What and Why of Windows

If you've spent any time at the DOS prompt, you know how frustrating it can be to use DOS cryptic commands to communicate with your computer. Working with your computer is much easier when you allow Microsoft Windows to be the interpreter between you and DOS. Windows is a program that sets up an "environment" for you to work in, based on colorful pictures (called *icons*) and menus. This friendly environment is called a *Graphical User Interface (GUI)*.

Graphical User Interface A GUI (pronounced "GOO-ey") is a picture-based way of interacting with your computer. Instead of typing commands, you select from menus and pictures to tell the computer what you want.

Windows comes with many useful applications, including a no-frills word processor (Write), a graphics program (Paintbrush), and a communication program (Terminal). It also provides several handy accessories, such as Calendar, Calculator, and Notepad. Some users never need more features than these simple applications provide.

Application Another word for a computer program that does something useful, like help you compose a letter (Word) or create a spreadsheet (Excel). Sometimes, the small applications that come with Windows (such as Clock and Calendar) are called "applets."

3

Since this book is about Microsoft Office, we'll assume that you have purchased the more powerful Windows-based Microsoft Office applications, which do everything the simple programs do and more. That's why we won't attempt to cover applications like Write in this book; we'll assume you're using the Microsoft Office products instead. If you are interested in learning more about Write, Paintbrush, and the other free Windows applications, check out *The Complete Idiot's Guide to Windows* (Alpha Books).

Why Use Windows?

This book covers Windows first because so many features are consistent from one Windows application to the next. Knowing how to use Windows itself gives you a tremendous advantage when learning how to use any Windows-based application. After reading the Windows lessons, you will be much better equipped to tackle Word, Excel, PowerPoint, Mail, and Access.

Why have so many major companies, including Microsoft, focused their time and money on developing Windows-based applications? Here are some benefits Windows applications provide:

- You can work on more than one file at a time within a single application. This allows you to copy information from one file to the other without wasting time retyping information.

- You can work in more than one application at a time. By choosing a simple menu command, you can switch between applications without having to close one to open the other. You can also copy information from one application to the other.

- Windows' graphical user interface is easy to figure out and remember, so you'll be up and running quickly. Once you get started, you'll be surprised how quickly your "educated guesses" become correct ones.

- All applications designed for Windows use similar keyboard and mouse operations to select objects and choose commands. To a great extent, when you've learned one application, you've learned part of them all.

Windows' GUI provides a common approach to using a variety of applications for your computer. With just a little effort, Windows is fast, easy, and fun to learn.

Starting Windows

To start Windows, follow these steps:

1. Begin at the **C:** prompt (or the prompt for the drive where Windows is installed). If you are not at the correct prompt, type the drive designation (such as **C:**), and press **Enter**.

2. Once you are at the correct prompt, type **win** and press **Enter**.

If Nothing Happens If you type **win** and get message like **Bad command or file name**, Windows may not be installed on your computer. Consult the appendix at the back of this book to learn how to install Windows.

Once you have successfully started Windows, the Windows title screen (including the version number) briefly appears. Next, Program Manager appears (see Figure 1.1).

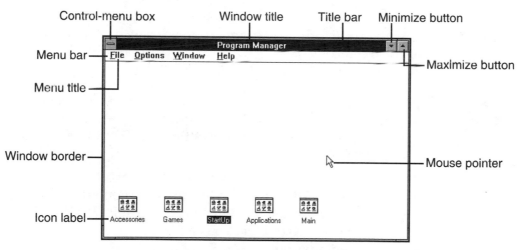

Figure 1.1 The Program Manager window.

The Program Manager Window

As you can see in Figure 1.1, the Program Manager Window is made up of several components. These components are used throughout Windows and Windows applications to make it easy for you to get your work done.

The components of the Program Manger window include:

Border   Identifies the edge of the window.

Window Title   Identifies the window and (often) suggests the use of the window.

Title Bar   Gives added information, such as a document name if you are working with a document in the window.

Desktop   This is the area outside the window.

Mouse Pointer   The pointer (usually an arrow) on-screen that allows you to select items and choose commands. Move the mouse pointer and select items by clicking the mouse button. See Lesson 2 for more information about using the mouse.

Minimize and Maximize Buttons   Click on these buttons to make the active window smaller or larger. Once the window is full-screen size, a button called the *Restore button* allows you to restore the window to its previous (smaller) size.

Group Icons   The Application Manager uses two types of icons. The first type is called a *group icon* (see Figure 1.1). When you select a group icon, a program group appears containing a group of program icons.

Program Group   A window containing a collection of related program icons. Program groups can be shrunk down to group icons to get them out of the way. (You'll learn to do this later.)

Program icons   These are displayed in program group windows. Program icons represent applications (Microsoft Excel, WordPerfect, and so on) that you can run. When you select the icon, the program runs.

Control-Menu Box   Used to access the Control menu, from which you may change the size of the window, close a window, or switch to another window.

Menu Bar   Displays the menu titles you select to access the commands contained in the menu. Each application might have different menu titles, but you access the menus in the same fashion. For more on menus, see Lesson 4. Figure 1.2 shows the menu commands available in the File menu.

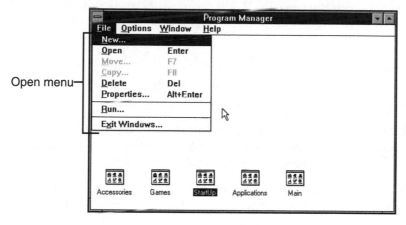

Figure 1.2   The Program Manager File menu.

More About Icons

An icon is a small picture in Windows that may represent:

- A document, directory, or disk drive.

- An application (such as Word for Windows or Excel).

- A program group window (such as Accessories).

Most icons have labels (some are more descriptive than others). Figure 1.3 shows the window that appears after opening the Games group icon. Notice that there are program-item icons for two games: Solitaire and Minesweeper. To play either game, open the appropriate icon.

How Windows Is Organized

It is no accident that the Program Manager appears when you start Windows. The Program Manager is the heart of Windows. From here, you may access any of the applications that came with Windows or any applications you have installed.

Program icons are stored in program groups that act as a filing system to group related program icons together. When you first install Windows, several groups are created automatically. The Main group contains the following Windows applications:

Control Panel   Contains the controls for the Windows environment. From the Control Panel, you can change the colors of the screen, control the sensitivity of the mouse and keyboard, and access many other features of Windows.

File Manager   Helps you manage the files and directories on your disk. You can use File Manager to move or copy files to a different directory or disk, delete files, open applications, and print files.

Print Manager   Acts as the middleman between your application and the printer. When you print a file in Windows, it is sent to the Print Manager, which in turn sends it to the printer.

Windows Setup   Allows you to add components to Windows that were not included when Windows was installed. Setup also allows you to add applications to run in Windows.

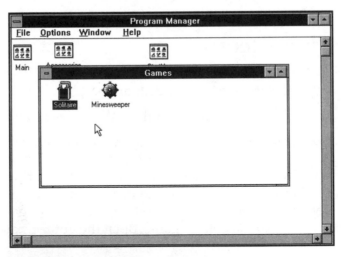

Figure 1.3   Game icons and their labels.

Tutorial   Offers a guided tour of Windows. This icon will be present only if you chose to install the Tutorial when you installed Windows.

PIF Editor   PIF files contain information used by Windows to run non-Windows applications. This includes file names, memory requirements, and so on. Windows 3.1 provides PIF files for more non-Windows programs than ever before, and the PIF Editor allows you to configure them.

Clipboard Viewer   Allows you to view and save Clipboard images. The Clipboard serves as a temporary storage area when you copy something from one application to be pasted into another.

Other groups include Accessories, Games, and StartUp. If you have installed other programs, you may have other groups, too, such as Applications or Microsoft Office.

Leaving So Soon?

Just in case you want to take a break before starting Lesson 2, here is how you can exit Windows. From the Program Manager window (see Figure 1.1), press and hold down the **Alt** key, and press **F4**. Windows will ask you to confirm that you want to exit the application. Press **Enter** to confirm and exit, or press **Esc** to cancel and remain in Windows.

Other Exits   There are lots of other ways to exit Windows. You'll learn about them in lesson 6.

In this lesson, you learned how to start Windows, and you learned the major components of the opening screen. In the next lesson, you'll learn how to use the mouse.

Navigating the Desktop with a Mouse

In this lesson, you will learn how to select windows and icons, and to move windows around on the desktop, using a mouse.

Mouse Basics

Most people prefer to use a mouse when working with Windows. You can use the mouse to select objects, change the appearance of the screen, and choose commands for Windows to perform, all with a quick point-and-click.

You don't *have* to use a mouse; most mouse operations have keyboard equivalents. However, throughout most of this book, we will be covering only the mouse operations, except when there is a keyboard shortcut that you might find easier. Diehard keyboard users can check out Lesson 3 for instructions that apply through the rest of the book in lieu of using the mouse.

You'll see certain terms used throughout this chapter as well as the remainder of the book (such as *point, drag,* and *click*). Now is the time to become thoroughly familiar with these terms.

Point and Click to Select

You can use the mouse to quickly select an icon, window, or menu command. This is a two-step process:

Step 1: Point. Move the mouse across your desk or mouse pad so the mouse cursor (usually a pointer) touches the object. You may have to pick up the mouse and reposition it if you run out of room on your desk.

Simply pointing at an object doesn't give Windows enough information to do anything. To select an object or choose a command, click the left mouse button on the object you are pointing at.

Step 2: Click. Quickly press and release the left mouse button once. If the object is an icon or window, it will become highlighted. If you click on a menu title, the menu will open.

For practice, click once on the **Control-menu** box in the upper left corner of the Program Manager window. You'll see menu options for sizing the Program Manager window, closing the Program Manager, and switching applications. You can make the menu disappear by clicking outside the menu.

Double-Click to Open or Close

Double-clicking an object is a shortcut to opening a group window or starting a program from an icon. Double-clicking on a **Control-menu** box is a shortcut to closing a window.

Double-Click   As the name suggests, a double-click is simply two clicks of the left mouse button in rapid succession.

For example, point at the **Accessories** group icon, and double-click. If you do it correctly, the Accessories icon opens into the Accessories window. Once it's open, double-click on the **Clock** program icon. The Clock program starts, and a clock appears on your desktop.

When you're finished looking at the clock, close it by double-clicking on its window's **Control-menu** box, or click once on the **Control-menu** box, and then click on the **Close** command on the menu that appears.

Quitting Windows   If you double-click on the Program Manager's **Control-menu** box, a dialog box will appear asking if you want to exit Windows. If this happens, and you don't want to exit windows, click on **Cancel**, or press the **Esc** key.

Dragging Objects Around On-Screen

You can also use the mouse to *drag* an object (usually a window, dialog box, or icon) to a new position on-screen.

To drag an object to a new location on-screen, point to the object. If you're dragging a window, you must point to its title bar. (You can point to any part of an icon.) Hold down the left mouse button, and move the mouse pointer to a new location. The object is dragged along with the mouse cursor. When the pointer reaches the right location, release the left mouse button.

You can also drag the borders of windows to resize them. Try it now, or skip ahead to Lesson 8 to get the full story.

Using Scroll Bars

Scroll bars appear when text, graphics, or icons in a window take up more space than the area shown. Using scroll bars, you can move up, down, left, or right in a window.

If you don't see scroll bars on your Program Manager window, drag one of the group icons as far as it will go into the corner of the Program Manager window. Scroll bars will appear. Figure 2.1 shows a Program Manager window with both vertical and horizontal scroll bars.

Figure 2.1   Scroll bars.

To scroll the window's view so you can see hidden portions, click on the scroll arrow that points in the direction you want to move the view. For instance, to see what's below the bottom border, click on the scroll arrow that points down. Click once to move a small amount, or click and hold to move farther.

You can also drag the scroll box to move quickly to a distant area (top or bottom) of the window. To drag a scroll box:

1. Point to the scroll box in the scroll bar, and hold down the mouse button.

2. Drag the scroll box to the new location on the scroll bar.

3. Release the mouse button.

Window by Window You can move the contents of a window one windowful at a time. To do so, just click in the scroll bar on either side of the scroll box.

Empty Window? Don't worry if text or graphics don't appear in a window. Use the scroll bars to bring the text or graphic into view.

In this lesson, you learned how to navigate the Windows desktop using the mouse. In the next lesson, you will learn how to navigate the desktop using the keyboard.

Navigating the Desktop with the Keyboard

In this lesson, you will learn how to use the keyboard to select objects and to move objects on the screen.

Keyboard Basics

As discussed in the previous chapter, most people prefer using the mouse to navigate Windows. Some, however, prefer using the keyboard. You will soon discover which is easier for you. Even if you decide that you prefer the mouse, there may be times when you are forced to use the keyboard (if your mouse goes on the blink). This lesson may then be your saving grace.

The rest of the book focuses on mouse actions, but the keyboard skills you learn in this lesson can be used instead wherever steps call for mouse use.

Opening Windows and Running Programs

You must open program group windows to get access the program icons that run programs. To open a group icon and run a program in it with the keyboard, follow these steps:

1. From the Program Manager window, press **Ctrl+Tab** as needed to select the group icon you want to open. The icon label appears highlighted when it's selected.

2. Press **Enter** to open the group window. See Figure 3.1.

3. Use the arrow keys to select the appropriate program icon within the group window.

4. Press **Enter** to run the program.

Program Manager
Control-menu box

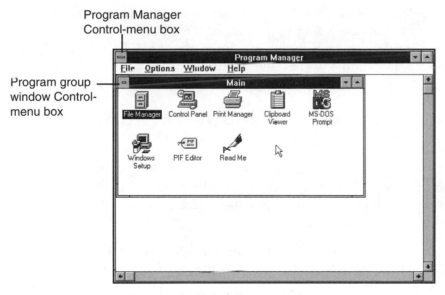

Program group
window Control-
menu box

Figure 3.1   After opening the Main icon.

Active Window or Icon   The active window (or icon) is the one with the highlighted title bar (or label). Any commands you select will affect the active window or icon.

Closing a Window

To close the window with the keyboard:

1. Make sure the window you want to close is active. If it's not, press **Alt+Esc** until it becomes the active window.

2. Press **Alt+hyphen** to open the window's **Control menu** if the window is a program group window, or **Alt+Spacebar** if the window is an application that's running (such as Excel).

3. Press **C** to choose the **Close** command to close the window.

Don't Close Program Manager!   If the active window is not an application, and you press Alt+Spacebar and choose Close, Windows assumes you want to close "the active application"—that is, Program Manager itself. That's probably not what you want at this point.

The Quick Close Using the Keyboard   To close a group or file window using the keyboard, press **Ctrl+F4**. If the window is an application window, press **Alt+F4** to quit the application and close the window.

Moving or Resizing Windows with the Keyboard

You can use the keyboard to move and resize windows. These operations can be performed more quickly using the mouse, but you have more control using the keyboard. To use the keyboard to move a window to a new location on the screen:

1. Open the window's **Control** menu (by pressing **Alt+hyphen** or **Alt+Spacebar**, depending on which type of window it is).

2. Press **M** to choose the **Move** command. The mouse pointer turns into a four-headed arrow (see Figure 3.2) positioned over the title bar.

3. Use the arrow keys to move the window to a new location.

4. Press **Enter** to accept the new location. **Esc** cancels the operation and returns the window to its original location.

Control Menu Options Unavailable   The Control Menu Move and Size commands are not active if the window is at its maximum size (maximized). The Size command is also unavailable if the window is reduced to an icon (minimized). You'll learn more about maximized and minimized windows in Lesson 8.

You can also resize a window using the keyboard. Resizing is covered in Lesson 8, but only the mouse method, which is by far the easiest. The keyboard method is rather tedious, but is presented here in case you might need it.

1. Open the window's **Control** menu.

2. Press **S** to choose the **Size** command. The mouse pointer will turn into a four-headed arrow.

3. Use the arrow keys to move the mouse pointer to the border or corner of the window you want to resize. The four-headed arrow becomes a two-headed arrow, indicating the directions you can move the border.

4. Use the arrow keys to resize the window.

5. Press **Enter** to accept the new window size. **Esc** cancels the operation and returns the window to its original size.

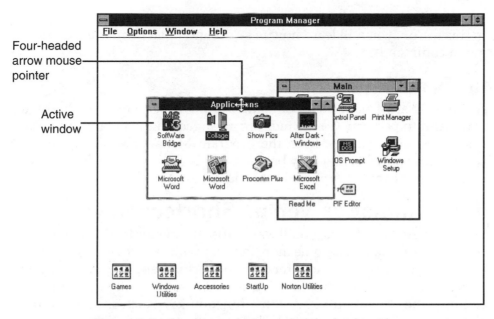

Figure 3.3 Moving a window using the keyboard.

In this lesson, you learned how to manipulate the Windows environment using the keyboard. In the next lesson, you'll learn how to make selections with the menus.

Using Menus

In this lesson, you will learn how to select and open menus, and choose menu commands.

What Is a Menu?

A menu is a list of related commands from which you can choose a command to perform. Commands are arranged on the menus in logical categories. For example, from the Program Manager window, all the commands related to files may be accessed via the File menu. The names of the menus available appear in the menu bar.

Menu Commands Versus Shortcut Keys

When you first get started, you'll want to use the menus to view and select commands. Once you become more familiar with Windows, you'll probably want to use shortcut keys for often-used commands. They allow you to access a command without using the menus. Shortcut keys typically combine the Ctrl or Shift key with a function key (such as Alt+F1). If a shortcut key is available, it will be listed on the menu, to the right of the command.

For example, Figure 4.1 shows the File menu from the Program Manager. You can open the **File** menu and select **Properties**, or press the shortcut key combination **Alt+Enter**, to view the properties of a group or program-item icon. Either method accomplishes the same result.

> **TIP** **Choosing Menu Commands** This book often uses the format *menu title, menu command* to tell you what menu commands to choose. In the above example, "choose **File Properties**" is equivalent to "open the **File** menu and select the **Properties** command."

Menu
command

Shortcut key

Figure 4.1   The Program Manager File menu.

Choosing Menu Commands

To choose a menu command, click on the menu's name in the menu bar. The menu opens to display the available commands. To choose a particular command, click on it with the mouse pointer.

You can also select menu commands with the keyboard if you prefer. Hold down the **Alt** key and type the underlined letter (the *selection letter*) in the menu name. The menu opens. To select a command, type the underlined letter in the command's name.

Here's an example. To see the Help options available for the Program Manager, just click on the word **Help** in the Program Manager menu bar, or press **Alt+H**. The menu drops down (see Figure 4.2). To see a table of contents for Help, choose **Contents** by either clicking on it or typing **C**. The Program Manager Help window shown in Figure 4.3 appears.

Notice that when the mouse pointer is positioned over a specific Help topic, it becomes a pointing finger. You can move the finger to any option and click on that option for specific Help information.

To close this or any window, double-click on its **Control-menu** box. To close a menu without selecting anything from it, click outside the menu, or press **Esc**.

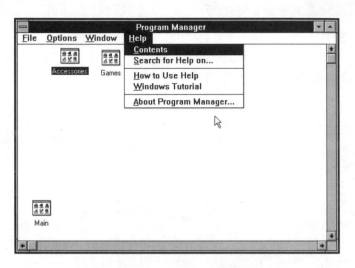

Figure 4.2   The Help menu.

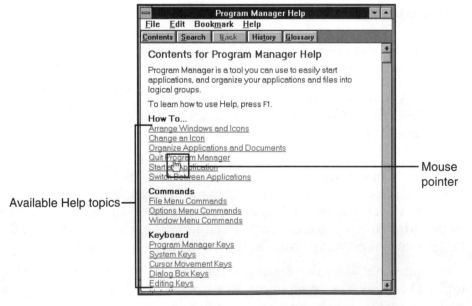

Figure 4.3   The Program Manager Help window.

Reading a Menu

There are some features common to every menu, as shown in Figure 4.4.

- Selection letters (letters you press to choose a command) are underlined.

- Shortcut keys (where available) are listed to the right of the command. Use these to bypass menus.

- An ellipsis after a command indicates that more information is needed before the command is completed. Windows usually employs a *dialog box* to gather this information from you. For more on dialog boxes, see Lesson 5.

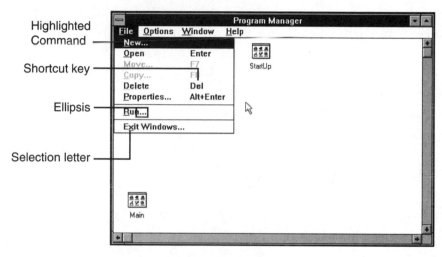

Figure 4.4   The Program Manager File menu.

Unavailable Commands   Some commands may appear grayed-out. These commands can be used only under certain circumstances. For example, you cannot copy an icon before you first select one to be copied.

For example, suppose you want to exit Windows. Follow these steps. (Notice the ellipsis following the Exit Windows command.)

1. Open the **File** menu.

2. Choose **Exit Windows**. A dialog box appears.

3. If you want to exit Windows, click on the **OK** command button, or press **Enter**. To abort the exit process, click on the **Cancel** command button, or press **Esc**.

Another common menu symbol is the check mark. The check mark indicates that a menu option is currently active. Each time you choose the menu command, the option is turned on or off (like a light switch).

In this lesson, you learned how to choose menu commands and how to read a menu. In the next lesson, you will learn how to use dialog boxes.

Using Dialog Boxes

In this lesson, you will learn how to use dialog boxes to access and enter information.

What Is a Dialog Box?

Windows uses dialog boxes to exchange information with you. Most often, dialog boxes ask you to provide more information so that an operation can be completed. A menu command followed by an ellipsis (...) indicates that a dialog box will be used to gather more information.

Dialog boxes are also used to warn you about a problem (for example, **File already exists, Overwrite?**) or to confirm that an operation should take place (for example, the Exit Windows dialog box).

Components of a Dialog Box

Dialog boxes vary in complexity. Some ask you to confirm an operation before it is executed, for example, a dialog box that asks you if you want to format a disk. In this case, you would select **OK** to confirm or **Cancel** to abort the operation. Other dialog boxes are quite complex, asking you to specify several options.

The following list briefly explains the components of a dialog box. The following sections describe the components and how to use them in greater detail.

Text Box   A text box allows you to type in an entry; for example, a name for a file you want to save or a label for an icon you've just added to a group.

List Box   A list box presents a list of possible choices from which you may choose. Scroll bars often allow you to scroll through the list. Often, a text box is associated with a list box. The list item that you select appears in the text box.

Drop-Down List Box   A single-line list box that opens to display a list of choices when you click on the down-arrow button on the right side of the list box.

Option Buttons   Option buttons present a group of related choices from which you may choose one. Option buttons are sometimes referred to as radio buttons, because when you select a button, the currently selected button deselects, or "pops out," such as on a car radio. You cannot select more than one option at a time.

Check Boxes   Check boxes present a single option or group of related options. The option is active if an **X** appears in the check box next to it. Unlike with option buttons, more than one check box can be selected at a time.

Command Buttons   Command buttons carry out the command displayed on the button (Open, Quit, Cancel, OK, and so on). If there is an ellipsis on the button (for example, Options...), choosing it will open another dialog box.

Text Box

A text box allows you to enter information needed to complete a command. This is typically a file name or directory name. Figure 5.1 shows the Move dialog box from File Manager, which contains a text box.

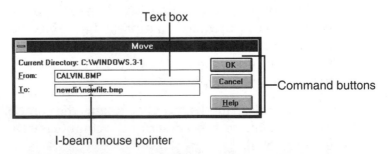

Figure 5.1   The Move dialog box from the Windows File Manager.

To activate a text box:

1. Point at the text box you want to activate. Notice that the mouse pointer changes to an I-beam when you point at the text box.

2. Click on the left mouse button to activate the text box. A vertical line, called an insertion point, appears to mark where text you type will be inserted.

3. Type the text you want to enter into the text box.

Tab to It   Instead of clicking in a text box to activate it, you can press the **Tab** key. Pressing **Tab** cycles through each of the elements in the dialog box, making each one in turn the "active" element.

List Boxes

A list box enables you to make a selection from a list of available options. For example, the list box displayed in the Browse dialog box (shown in Figure 5.2) enables you to select a file to open. Notice the scroll bar along the right side of the list box. You can use the scroll bar to bring items in the list into view, as you learned in Lesson 2.

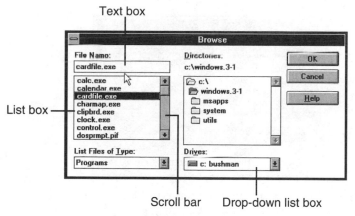

Figure 5.2   The Browse dialog box.

To select an item from a list box, click on the appropriate list item. Notice that in the Browse list box, the item you select is automatically displayed in the linked text box above the list box. Click on **OK** or press **Enter** to accept the selection; click on **Cancel** or press **Esc** to close the dialog box without making the selection.

To select an item from a drop-down list box, open the list box by clicking on the down arrow button, and then click on the appropriate list item.

Keyboard Tips   If you want to use the keyboard instead of the mouse, just think "**Tab** and **down**." Use the **Tab** key to make the list box active, and then press the down arrow key to scroll through the list (and to open the drop-down list if needed).

Option Buttons

Option buttons enable you to make a single choice from a list of possible command options. For example, the Print Range options displayed in Figure 5.3 allow you to select which pages of your document to print. The active option is indicated by the small, filled-in circle. To select an option button, click on the circle for the option you want.

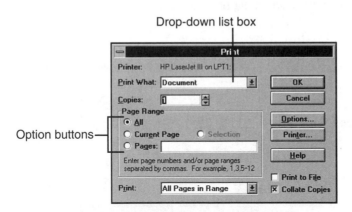

Figure 5.3   The Print dialog box from Word for Windows.

More Keyboard Hints   For option buttons and check boxes, think "Tab, arrow, and space." Activate the section with **Tab**, switch between options with the arrow keys, and then make your selection with the Spacebar. This goes for both options buttons and check boxes.

Check Boxes

Command options you can select (activate) or deselect (deactivate) are usually presented as check boxes. When a check box is selected, an **X** appears in the box, and the associated command option is active (see Figure 5.4).

To select or deselect a check box option, click on its box with the mouse pointer.

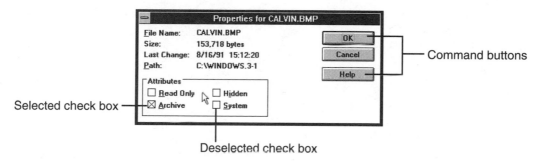

Figure 5.4 The Properties dialog box from File Manager.

Command Buttons

Command buttons are used to perform operations. In Figure 5.4, three common command buttons appear. The **OK** command button is used to accept the information you have entered or verify an action and close the dialog box. **Cancel** is used to leave the dialog box without executing the information you provided in the dialog box. **Help** is another common command button that provides you with help specific to the dialog box you are working in.

Keyboard Commands Pressing **Esc** is the keyboard equivalent to selecting the **Cancel** button. Pressing **Enter** is equivalent to selecting the **OK** button. **F1** will bring up Help.

Accidents Happen If you accidentally select the **Cancel** command button, don't worry. You can always re-enter the dialog box and continue. Be careful when you select **OK**. The instructions you have entered in the dialog box are executed.

In this lesson, you learned how to use dialog boxes. In the next lesson, you will learn how to exit Windows and, perhaps more importantly, what to do before you exit.

Exiting Windows

In this lesson, you will learn the various ways to exit Windows.

Methods of Exiting Windows

Three methods are available to quit Windows:

- Through the Program Manager File menu.
- With a shortcut key.
- Through the Program Manager Control menu.

Exit Using the File Menu

Follow these steps to exit Windows using the File menu (see Figure 6.1):

1. Choose **File Exit Windows** from the Program Manager window.

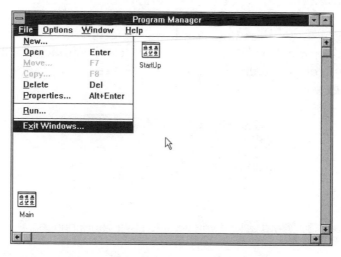

Figure 6.1 Using the File menu to exit Windows.

2. Select the **OK** command button in the Exit Windows dialog box (see figure 6.2).

Figure 6.2   The Exit Windows dialog box.

Exit Using a Shortcut Key

A quick alternative to selecting Exit Windows from the File menu is to press **Alt+F4**. You'll get the same confirmation dialog box as you do with the menu steps, as shown in Figure 6.2.

Exit Using the Control Menu

To exit Windows using the Control menu, double-click the Program Manager **Control-menu** box, or single-click on it, and then select **Close** from the menu that appears. Again, the same Figure 6.2 dialog box will confirm your decision.

Windows Protects You

Because you can work with several documents and applications at one time, you may get carried away and forget to save a document before you exit Windows. Fear not; Windows protects you. For example, if you are working on a Word document and try to exit Windows without saving the document, the dialog box shown in Figure 6.3 prompts you to save your changes.

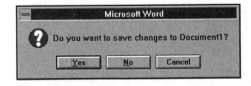

Figure 6.3   Word asks if you want to save your changes.

Select **Yes** to save the changes, **No** to discard any changes you made, or **Cancel** to stop exiting Windows. This dialog box helps you avoid losing document changes.

Forget to Save? This message is your only warning. If you accidently respond **No** to saving current changes, the changes made in the document are lost.

Leaving Applications Before Exiting Windows

Even though Windows provides the protection described, it is safest to get in the habit of closing documents and applications yourself before quitting Windows.

In most Windows applications, choose **File Save** to save a document. Then, exit the application. If it is a Windows application, you can exit just as you would exit Windows (press **Alt+F4**, or choose **File Exit**).

The Way Things Were

If you've made any changes to the Program Manager window during your Windows session, you may want to save them so they will appear the next time you start Windows. The changes might include moving icons around within group windows, moving windows around within the Program Manager window, or even changing which windows will be open when you next start Windows.

To activate this option, choose **Options Save Settings on Exit**. A check mark appears when this option is active.

In this lesson, you learned several ways to exit Windows. In the next lesson, you'll learn how to start and exit Windows applications.

Starting and Exiting Applications

In this lesson, you will learn how to start and exit Windows applications, and how to open and close document windows in a Windows application.

Starting Windows Applications

A Windows application is a program designed specifically to run under Windows—it won't run any other way. All of the Microsoft programs covered in this book are Windows applications. The procedure for starting and exiting all Windows applications is the same.

There are two main ways to start a Windows application:

- Using the program icon associated with the application.
- Using the Program Manager **File Run** command.

You can also start a program using File Manager, as you'll learn in Lesson 17.

Using the Program Icon

You most often will use the program icon to start an application. When you install a Windows application, a program icon for it is created in a Program Manager group. To run the program, you simply select the icon.

Before you can use the program icon, however, you must discover which program group it is located in. Sometimes, this is easy to figure out. For example, Word is probably located in the Microsoft Office program group, because it's part of Microsoft Office. Other times, it may be more difficult. For instance, would a program such as Clipboard Viewer be in Main or Accessories? It would seem to fit logically in either. For the answer, see Figure 7.1.

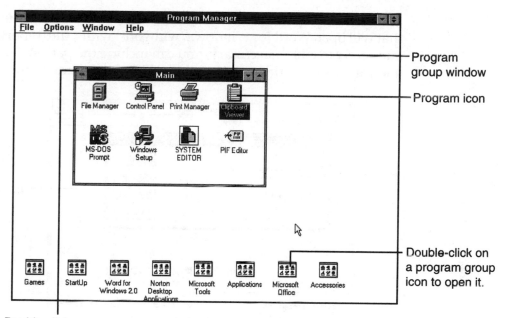

Program group window

Program icon

Double-click on a program group icon to open it.

Double-click a program group window's control-menu box to close it.

Figure 7.1   You may have to open several program groups to find the program icon you're seeking.

You may have to open several program groups before you find the program icon you want. Just double-click on a program group's icon to open it, and double-click on its Control-menu box to close it.

To start an application from a program icon, follow these steps:

1. Open (double-click on) the program group icon that contains the program icon you want.

2. Double-click on the program-item icon for the application. The application runs.

Using the Run Command

You can also use the Program Manager **File Run** command to start applications. Using the **Run** command enables you to enter command parameters or options that change the way the application is started. For example, most word processors can be started so that a file you specify is automatically opened and ready to edit. Figure 7.2 displays the command that will open Word for Windows (winword) with a file (report.doc) open and ready to edit. If necessary, you can include the path statement (drive and directory) for the program file and/or the document file.

Command line
Browse button

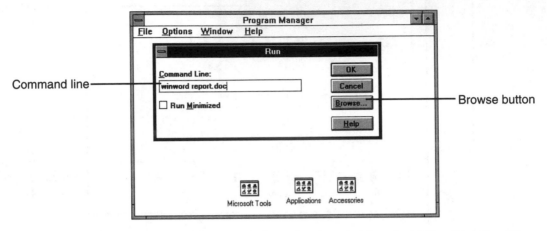

Figure 7.2 Loading Word for Windows and a document file using the Windows File Run command.

What Are Your Options? Check the documentation that comes with each application for the start-up options available. You may want to jot down special start-up commands you plan on using often.

To use the Run command, follow these steps:

1. From the Program Manager window, choose **File Run**. The Run command dialog box appears (see Figure 7.3).

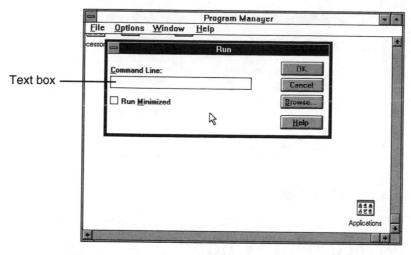

Text box ──

Figure 7.3 The Run dialog box ready for your command.

2. Type the command in text box. Examples of possible commands are as follows:

WINWORD

C:\WINWORD\WINWORD

C:\WINWORD\WINWORD REPORT.DOC

C:\WINWORD\WINWORD C:\MYFILES\REPORT.DOC

3. When the command is complete, select **OK**. (If you decide not to use the Run command, select **Cancel**.)

What's the Name? Suppose you don't remember the command that will run the application. Select the **Browse** button on the Run dialog box. The Browse dialog box shown in Figure 7.4 appears. From it, you can see files that may be selected.

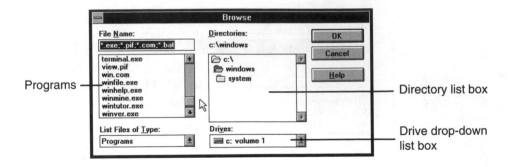

Programs

Directory list box

Drive drop-down list box

Figure 7.4   The Browse dialog box.

Using a Document Window

When you open an application, it appears in a window. Within that window, a *document window* (a blank work area) appears in which you can enter your data. You can have several document windows open at once in an application.

The terminology changes a bit for each application. In Excel, document windows are called Worksheets. In Access, they're called tables. But the principle is the same, so for now let's refer to them as document windows.

Creating and Opening a Document Window

When you start up an application, a new document window is created for you. If you want to open a second document window, you may choose the **File New** command from that application's menu bar. A new window is created. (The original document window is still available too; open the **Window** menu, and you'll see a list of all the open document windows from which to choose.)

Save Your Work   Always save your documents using the **File Save** command before you exit an application. You should give each document file a unique name. That way, you can use the **File Open** command later to open the document file and continue working.

Closing a Document Window

When you are done with a document, you should close the document window to get it out of the way. First, save the document if you entered any data worth saving: choose **File Save**, and enter a unique name for it. Then choose **File Close**, or simply double-click on the document window's **Control-menu** box. This ensures the document will not be lost or damaged accidentally.

Exiting Windows Applications

Before you exit an application, make sure all open documents for that application are saved and closed through the **File** menu.

Forget to Save Your Changes?   If you attempt to close a document window or exit an application before you save changes, Windows will ask you if you want to save before closing. This is a safety feature built into Windows. To save your work, click on the **Yes** command button. To exit without saving your work, click on the **No** command button. To remain in the application, click on the **Cancel** command button.

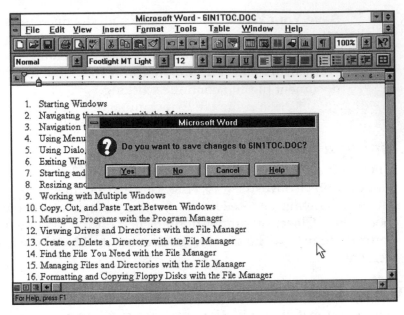

Figure 7.5   The Microsoft Word Save Changes dialog box.

Just like in Windows itself, there are three ways to exit a Windows application:

- With the Control menu.
- With the application's Exit command.
- With the shortcut key.

Close or Exit?   The term *close* is used in reference to document windows. When you are finished working on a document, save your changes, and close the document window. The application will still be open. The **Exit** command will close your document window(s) *and* exit the application.

Take Your Pick

To exit an application using its Control menu, double-click on the **Control-menu** box, or single-click on the box, and then choose **Close** from the menu that appears.

To exit an application using the Exit command, choose **File Exit**.

The quick route to exiting is to use the shortcut key. Press **Alt+F4**, and you're on your way.

In this lesson, you learned how to start and exit applications, and you learned common methods for opening and closing a document window. In the next lesson, you will learn how to resize and move windows.

Resizing and Moving Windows

In this lesson, you will learn more about moving windows and changing their size.

Sizing with Maximize, Minimize, and Restore

You may want to increase the size of a window to see its full contents. Or you may want to decrease the size of a window (even down to icon form) to make room for other windows. One way to resize a window is to use the **Maximize**, **Minimize**, and **Restore** commands, located on the right side of the window title bar. Table 8.1 displays the Maximize, Minimize, and Restore buttons and defines the purpose of each one.

Table 8.1   Window Sizing Command Buttons

Command Button	Description
▲	**Maximize** button: enlarges the window to its maximum size.
▼	**Minimize** button: reduces the Window to its icon form.
⬍	**Restore** button: returns a window to the size it was before it was maximized. (Available only in maximized windows).

To maximize, minimize, or restore a window, click on the appropriate button.

Figure 8.1 shows the Program Manager window maximized. Notice that the Minimize and Restore buttons are available. Figure 8.2 displays the Program Manager window "restored," with the Minimize and Maximize buttons available.

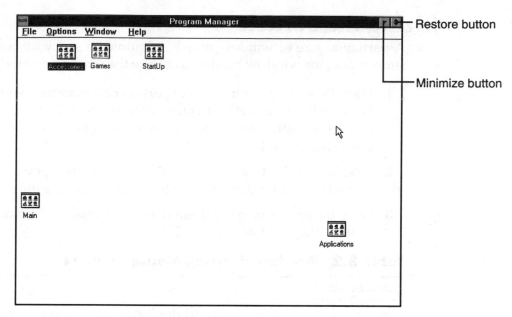

Figure 8.1 The Program Manager window maximized to full-screen size.

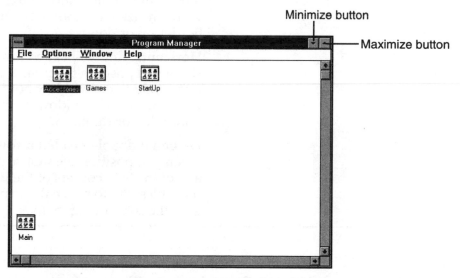

Figure 8.2 Program Manager window at less than maximum size.

Sizing the Borders

A particular size of window may be required to suit your needs. If so, simply drag the window border to change the size of the window:

1. Place the mouse pointer on the portion of the border (vertical, horizontal, or corner) that you want to resize. When the mouse pointer is positioned correctly, it will change into one of the shapes displayed in Table 8.2.

2. Drag the border to the new position. A faint line appears to show you where the border will be when you release the mouse button.

3. Once the border is in the desired location, release the mouse button. The window is resized.

Table 8.2   Window Resizing Mouse Pointers

Mouse Pointer	Description
↕	**Vertical** double-headed arrow: appears when you position the mouse pointer over either the top or bottom window border. It enables you to resize the window by dragging the border up or down.
↔	**Horizontal** double-headed arrow: appears when you position the mouse pointer over either side of the window border. It enables you to resize the window by dragging the border left or right.
⤢	**Diagonal** double-headed arrow: appears when you position the mouse pointer over any of the four corners of the window border. It enables you to resize the window by dragging the corner diagonally.

Missing Some Icons?   When you reduce the size of a window, you might not be able to see all the window contents at once. Remember that you can use the scroll bars to see the contents of the window.

Moving a Window

When you start working with multiple windows, moving a window becomes as important as sizing one. You will want to move windows to make room for other work on your desktop. To move a window, point at the Windows title bar, and drag it to a new location.

In this lesson, you learned how to change the appearance of your desktop by changing the size of or moving a window. In the next lesson, you will learn how to open, arrange, and move among multiple windows.

Working with Multiple Windows

In this lesson, you will learn how to open and arrange multiple windows. You will also learn how to move between windows.

Multiple Windows

Windows allows you to use more than one application at a time, and each Windows application supports multiple document windows. As you can imagine, opening multiple applications with multiple windows can make your desktop pretty busy! That's why it's important to be able to arrange and switch between windows easily.

As you learned in Lesson 7, you can open an application by double-clicking on the program icon or using the **Run** command. To open a new document window within an application, choose the **File New** command associated with the application.

Arranging Windows

Once you have multiple open windows, you can use the commands under the **Window** menu to arrange the windows. Figure 9.1 shows several windows open at the same time. These are windows created from the group icons on the Program Manager screen, but they could be various program-item or document windows as well. The screen is confusing and, as you'll see, one window is hidden by the others. Cascading and tiling the windows can help make sense of the mess.

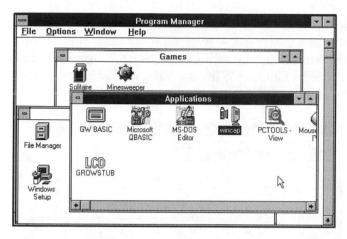

Figure 9.1   The Program manager with multiple windows open.

Cascading Windows

A good way to get control of a confusing desktop is to choose the **Window Cascade** command. Choosing this command causes Windows to lay all the open windows on top of each other so the title bar of each is visible. The resulting cascaded window arrangement is shown in Figure 9.2.

Cascade Quickly   Press the shortcut key combination **Shift+F5** to cascade your windows without using the **Window** menu.

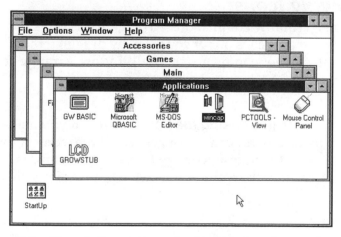

Figure 9.2   The windows after selecting Window Cascade.

Tiling Windows

Another arrangement is referred to as *tiled*. When you choose this command, Windows resizes and moves each open window so they appear side-by-side. Choose **Window Tile**, and an arrangement similar to that shown in Figure 9.3 appears.

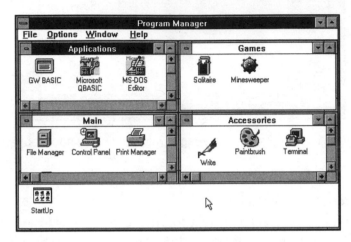

Figure 9.3   The windows after selecting Window Tile.

Timely Tiling   Press the shortcut key combination **Shift+F4** to tile your windows without using the **Window** menu.

Arranging Icons

Another **Window** command is **Arrange Icons**. This command is handy after you move icons out of your way by dragging them with the mouse. When things get confusing, choose **Window Arrange Icons** to clean up after yourself.

Instead of Using the Scroll Bars   If you make a window smaller and can no longer see all the icons in the window, select **Window Arrange Icons**. This optimizes the arrangement of the icons in the new window dimensions.

Moving Between Windows

Another common dilemma when using multiple windows is how to move between windows. The application (and document window if available) currently in use has a highlighted title bar. That's how you know which window is active.

Now Where Was I?   The window currently in use is called the active window. Moving to a new window means you are changing the window that is active.

To move to a different window, click on any part of the window you want to use (make active). The title bar is highlighted, and you may work in the window.

Another way to move between various windows is to select the window you want from the Window menu, as shown in Figure 9.4. The advantage to this method is that you can select a window that isn't currently visible on-screen.

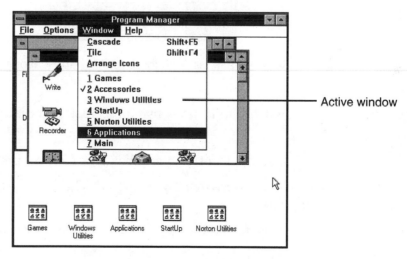

Active window

Figure 9.4   The Program Manager's Window menu.

Moving Between Applications

Remember that Windows allows you to have multiple windows open within an application *and* have multiple applications open at the same time. The last section taught you how to move between windows in the same application. This section will tell you how to move between applications.

Using the Task List

The Task List dialog box can be used to switch between applications. A sample Task List dialog box is shown in Figure 9.5. There are three applications running. Notice that the entry for Write (Windows word processor application) is followed by the name of the active document window (RPT2.WRI).

Figure 9.5   The Task List with three running applications.

To switch applications using the Task List dialog box, follow these steps:

1. Click on the **Control-menu** box. The Control menu appears.

2. Click on the **Switch To** command. The Task List dialog box appears.

3. Double-click on the application you wish to switch to.

Quick Switch   Rather than using the Control menu, you can access the Task List quickly by either double-clicking on an open space on your Windows desktop or pressing **Ctrl+Esc**. Then, just double-click on the application you want.

For switching tasks (applications), there are some shortcuts you might find helpful.

One shortcut is to use **Alt+Tab**. Hold down the **Alt** key, and press the **Tab** key. (Keep the **Alt** key down.) A box displays the name of an open application. Each time you press the **Tab** key, a different open application's name appears. When you see the application you want, release the **Alt** key, and you will switch to that application.

Another shortcut is to press **Alt+Esc** to toggle through all the open applications. If an application's window is minimized, press **Enter** to reopen the window after highlighting with **Alt+Esc**.

In this lesson, you learned how to control your desktop by opening and arranging windows. You also learned how to move between multiple windows and applications. In the next lesson, you will learn how to move information between windows with the **Cut**, **Copy**, and **Paste** commands.

Moving and Copying Text Between Windows

In this lesson, you will learn how to move information between windows using Copy, Cut, and Paste in conjunction with the Clipboard.

What Is the Clipboard?

One of the handiest features of the Windows environment is that information (both text and graphics) can be copied or moved from one window to another. This includes windows (documents) in the same application as well as between applications. When information is copied or cut, it is placed in an area called the *Clipboard*.

The Clipboard holds only the most recent information copied or cut. When you copy or cut something else, it replaces what was previously on the Clipboard. You can paste the contents of the Clipboard into any Windows program as many times as you want: Pasting does not erase the information on the Clipboard.

Cut, Copy, and Paste   When you *cut* information, it is removed from its original location and placed on the Clipboard. When you *copy* information, it is copied to the Clipboard without disturbing the original. When you *paste*, the information on the Clipboard is duplicated at the location you specify, without disturbing the copy on the Clipboard.

You can see the contents of the Clipboard at any time by following these steps:

1. Open the **Main** group icon.

2. From the Main window, open the **Clipboard Viewer** program icon.

3. The contents of the Clipboard appears in the Clipboard Viewer window. In Figure 10.1, an address was copied or cut to the Clipboard.

Figure 10.1 The contents of the Clipboard seen through the Clipboard Viewer.

Without a Trace When you turn off your computer or exit Windows, the content of the Clipboard is lost.

Take a look at the contents of your Clipboard. Unless you have recently cut or copied information, the Clipboard will be empty.

Selecting Text

Before you can cut or copy text, you must identify which text is to be cut or copied. This is called *selecting* text. You can select anything to cut or copy, not just text, as you'll learn later.

Selected text is highlighted so you can quickly distinguish it. Figure 10.2 illustrates selected text in a Word document.

To select text:

1. Position the mouse pointer at the first character of the text to be selected.

2. Hold down the left mouse button, and drag the mouse pointer to the last character to be selected.

3. Release the mouse button. The selected text is highlighted.

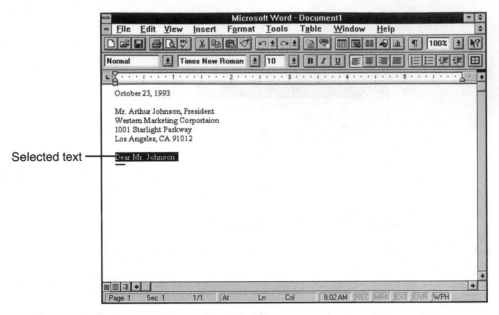

Selected text ——

Figure 10.2   Selected text in a Word document.

Deselecting Text   To get rid of the highlight on the selection, click anywhere in the document with the mouse.

Text Selection Shortcuts   To select a single word using the mouse, double-click on the word. To select text word-by-word (instead of character-by-character), hold down both the **Shift** and **Ctrl** keys while using the arrow keys.

Selecting Graphics

The procedure for selecting graphics depends on the Windows application program you are using. Since it varies, we will cover this topic under the appropriate applications later in the book.

Using Copy, Cut, and Paste Between Windows

Once you have selected the text or graphics, the procedures for cutting, copying, and pasting are the same in all Windows applications. To cut or copy and paste information between windows of the same application as well as between windows of different applications:

1. Select the text or graphic to cut or copy (following the instructions earlier in this lesson).

2. Choose **Edit Copy** to keep the original selection in place or **Cut** to remove the original selection. The selected material is placed in the Clipboard.

3. Position the cursor (insertion point) where you want to insert the selection. You may need to open another application or document.

4. Choose **Edit Paste**. The selection is copied from the Clipboard to your document. A copy remains on the Clipboard until you cut or copy something else.

> **TIP**
>
> **Multiple Copies**   Because items remain on the Clipboard until you cut or copy again, you can paste information from the Clipboard multiple times. You can also perform other tasks before you paste.

Try it. Enter your address in Word, and select it. Choose **Edit Copy** to copy it to the Clipboard. Choose **File New** to open a new Word window. Then, choose **Edit Paste** to paste the address in the new window. When you're done, choose **File Exit** to exit the Word program.

In this lesson, you learned how to copy, cut, and paste information between windows. In the next lesson, you will learn how to manage your programs using Program Manager.

Managing Programs with Program Manager

In this lesson, you will learn to manage program groups to keep track of your applications.

What Is a Program Group?

Imagine how it would be if all the icons for all of your programs were contained in one program group window. You would have to search through them all every time you wanted to run a program! Luckily, Windows enables you to group your applications into logical categories.

A program group is a window within the Program Manager window. When it's closed, it appears as a program group icon on the desktop; when it's open, it reveals program icons for various applications you can run.

Windows sets up several useful groups for you automatically, such as Accessories, Main, and Games. You are not stuck with just these, however; you can create your own groups, move program icons to different groups, delete icons, and even delete groups.

Creating a Group

As you begin to use Windows, you may find that you want additional groups. For example, if there are a few applications that you use every day, you may want to set up a group for them. You may also want to create separate groups for Windows and non-Windows applications.

To create a group, follow these steps:

1. From the Program Manager window, choose **File New**. The New Program Object dialog box appears (see Figure 11.1).

2. Make sure **Program Group** is selected.

3. Select **OK**. The Program Group Properties dialog box appears.

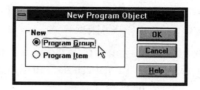

Figure 11.1   The New Program Object dialog box.

4. Type the **Description** (which will become the group icon label and the group window title).

5. Select **OK**. The group window is now created. A window with the description you entered appears.

Try creating a group window for your own application. Once the group window is created, you can either drag applications into it from other groups or add applications to it using the procedure outlined in the next section.

Adding an Application to a Group

Applications Must Be Installed   Adding an application to a group is *not* the same as installing the application on your computer. The application must already be installed on your computer before you can add it to a group.

Adding an application to a group links the application to a program icon displayed in the group. When you add an application to a group, you really do two things:

- Set up a program icon to launch the application.
- Tell Windows what file to execute when the icon is opened.

Applications may be added to any group, including the ones that were created when Windows was installed. Follow these steps:

1. Open the group window that you want the new program icon to reside in.

2. From Program Manager, choose **File New**. The New Program Object dialog box appears.

3. Select the **Program Item** option button, and then select **OK**. The Program Item Properties dialog box appears (see Figure 11.2).

4. Enter a Description for the icon. This description will appear as the icon label and the group window title.

5. Enter the Command Line to the executable file including the path. For example, if you're adding Word for Windows 6.0 from the C:\WINWORD6 directory, type **C:\WINWORD6\WINWORD.EXE**.

What's an Executable File? The *executable file* is a file that will execute, or run (that is, a program file). Executable files usually end in .EXE. You can select the **Browse** command button to open the Browse dialog box. From here, you can search for and select the executable file you want included as the Command line.

6. If you want a different default directory while you're running the application, enter a **Working Directory**. In most cases, you can skip this step.

7. To start the application as a desktop icon (instead of in a window), check **Run Minimized**.

8. Select **OK** when the Program Item Properties dialog box is complete.

Figure 11.2 illustrates a completed Program Item Properties dialog box. This is to set up an application called Collage Plus Version 3.2 within the Screen Utilities group.

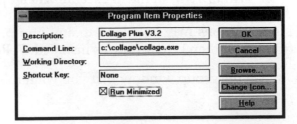

Figure 11.2   The completed Program Item Properties dialog box.

Figure 11.3 shows the Screen Utilities group window with the program icon just created. In this case, the icon was supplied by the application manufacturer and referenced in the COLLAGE.EXE file. If an icon is not found by Windows, it assigns an icon for you.

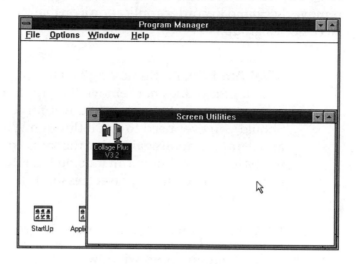

Figure 11.3 The Screen Utilities group window with the Collage Plus program icon.

Changing Icons If you don't like the looks of a program icon, you can assign a different one to the application. Choose **File Properties** from the Program Manager window. Select the **Change Icon** command button, and specify a new icon file. Windows 3.1 provides a host of new icons; the file MORICONS.DLL in the Windows directory contains these icons.

After you have added an application, test it by double-clicking on the program icon to run the application. If it works, you're ready to move on. If it doesn't, Windows will tell you what is wrong. Go back and try the steps again, making sure that the path and executable file name are correct.

Removing a Program Icon from a Group

In rearranging the groups to best meet your needs, you may want to remove a program icon from a group. For example, if your system doesn't have any sound recording or playback capabilities, you may want to remove the Sound Recorder application icon that Windows installed in the Accessories group.

What Am I Really Removing?   Deleting a program icon from a group does not remove that application from your computer—it just makes Windows forget that it's there. Should you ever need to run it through Windows, you can add the application again using the steps you learned earlier in this lesson or simply run it using the **File Run** command or from the File Manager (see Lesson 17).

To delete a program icon from a program group, follow these steps:

1. Open the program group window.

2. Select the program icon for the application you want to delete.

3. Choose **File Delete**. A message appears asking you to confirm the deletion (see Figure 11.4).

4. Select **Yes** to delete the application or **No** to cancel.

Figure 11.4   The Delete program icon confirmation dialog box.

Deleting a Program Group

You can also delete a whole program group and all its associated program icons. When you do, the applications related to those program icons remain on your computer—Windows just forgets where they are located.

To delete a program group, follow these steps:

1. From the Program Manager screen, select the program group icon you want to delete. If the program group window is open, close it so only the icon appears.

2. Choose **File Delete**. A message (similar to Figure 11.4) appears asking for confirmation.

3. Select **Yes** to delete the group or **No** to cancel.

In this lesson, you learned how to manage program groups in Program Manager. In the next lesson, you'll learn how to view drives and directories with the File Manager.

Viewing Drives and Directories with File Manager

In this lesson, you will learn how to control disk drives and directories with File Manager. You'll learn some basics about drives, directories, and files, and you'll learn how to manipulate them through the File Manager program.

What Are Drives?

A *drive* is the hardware that reads from and writes to a disk. A hard disk and its drive are considered one inseparable unit, while a floppy disk can easily be removed from its drive and replaced with a different disk.

Drives are given letter names. Drives A and B for most computers are floppy disk drives, used to store and retrieve data from diskettes. The designation for the hard disk inside the computer is typically drive C. (Since hard disks and their drives are not easily separated, the terms *disk* and *drive* are often used interchangeably when referring to hard disks.) If the computer has more than one hard disk, or if the hard disk has been divided into multiple partitions, or *logical drives*, the additional drives are usually labeled D, E, F, and so on.

What Are Directories?

Because so much information can be stored on a disk, hard disks are usually divided into directories. For example, drive C typically has a separate directory for DOS (the disk operating system), a directory for Windows, and so on. Floppy disks can contain directories too, but usually don't. (Because of their limited capacity, it is easy to keep track of files on a floppy disk without using directories.)

Disk space is not set aside for individual directories; in fact, directories take up hardly any disk space at all. If you think of a disk as a file drawer full of papers, directories are like tabbed folders used to organize the papers into manageable groups.

What Are Files?

Directories hold files, just as folders hold pieces of paper. A file may contain the instructions for the computer to perform (typically called *program* or *executable files*). Or a file may contain a text document that you can read (often referred to as a *document file*).

Regardless of the type of file, you can use the Windows File Manager to view and control them.

Starting File Manager

To start File Manager, follow these steps:

1. Open the **Main** program group from the Program Manager window.

2. Run the **File Manager** program by double-clicking on its program icon. File Manager appears.

Figure 12.1 shows the File Manager window. The directory window's title bar shows the drive for the information displayed (in this case, drive C).

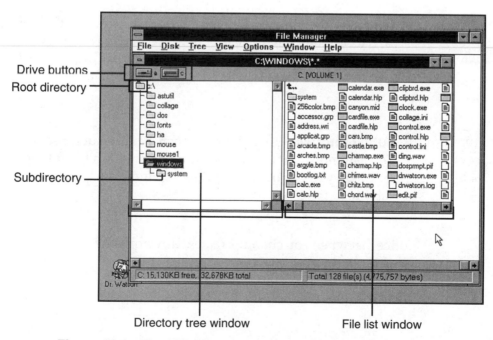

Figure 12.1 The File Manager window displaying a directory window.

The Directory Tree

The left side of the directory window contains the directory tree, a graphical representation of the directories and subdirectories on your system. (The directory tree on your screen will probably contain different directories from the one shown in Figure 12.1.)

In Figure 12.1, you can see that drive C contains a directory called *windows*. The Windows directory has a subdirectory: *system*. The right side of the window contains a list of the files in the directory currently highlighted on the directory tree. Notice that the folder icon next to the Windows directory (highlighted directory) appears as an open folder. In this example, the files in the Windows directory appear in the right half of the File manager window.

Changing Directories

When you change directories using the directory tree, it shows you the files in each directory. This is helpful if you are searching for a particular file to open, move, or copy.

To change the directory, point to the directory you want, and click.

The Root Directory   The directory that leads to all other directories (much like the root of a tree leads to all branches and leaves) is the *root directory*. In Figure 12.1, the root directory is shown as **C:**.

Subdirectories   Any directory can have a subdirectory. You can think of it as having file folders within file folders; they help you organize your files. In Figure 12.1, *system* is a subdirectory of *windows*.

Notice that when you change to a new directory, the names of the files in the directory appear.

Expanding and Collapsing Directory Levels

As you noticed before, the directory tree shows the subdirectory of the Windows directory. You can *collapse* (decrease the detail of) the directory tree, so that the subdirectory does not appear. You can also *expand* (increase the detail of) the directory tree, so that subdirectories many levels deep will *all* show.

- To expand a directory, double-click on the directory icon.

- To collapse a directory, double-click on the directory icon

Expand and Collapse Quickly Use the File Manager **Tree** menu to speed expanding and collapsing of multiple directories. Select **Tree Expand Branch** to expand all levels for the selected directory. Select **Tree Expand All** to expand the entire tree. Select **Tree Collapse Branch** to collapse the levels for the selected directory.

It's Only for Show Collapsing and expanding affects only this display; it doesn't alter your directories in any way.

Changing Drives

You can change drives to see the directories and files contained on a different disk. To change drives, click on the drive icon in the upper left corner of the Directory Tree window. For a keyboard shortcut, press **Ctrl+***drive letter* (for example, press **Ctrl+A** for Drive A).

Can't Change Drives? Make sure there is a disk in the drive you are selecting. If there is not, a warning message will appear instructing you to try again.

Returning to Program Manager

Each directory window can be minimized and maximized within File Manager, or closed altogether (except for the last one remaining open, which cannot be closed). If you have more than one directory window open at once, you may want to minimize all but the one you're working with.

You can also minimize or close the File Manager window itself to return to Program Manager. If you're not going to use File Manager again right away, it is better to close it rather than minimize it, to conserve system resources.

To close File Manager, double-click on the **Control-menu** box, or close it in any of the other ways you learned to close applications in Lesson 7.

In this lesson, you learned how to view the contents of drives and directories using File Manager. In the next lesson, you'll learn how to create and delete directories with File Manager.

Creating and Deleting Directories with File Manager

In this lesson, you will learn how to create and delete directories to organize your files.

Creating a Directory

There are several reasons you may want to create a directory. Many application installation programs create a directory when you install the application on your computer. If one of your application installation programs does not, you will want to create a directory for the application.

A more common reason to create a directory is to store document files. For example, you may want to create a directory to store documents you create with Word. That way, the document files will not be scattered among the more than a hundred Windows program files in the Windows directory. Having a separate directory for Word documents can make it much easier to find and manipulate the documents you create.

To create a directory, follow these steps:

1. Open **File Manager** by double-clicking on its program icon in the Main program group. The directory window appears showing the directory tree and the files in the highlighted directory.

2. Highlight the directory under which you want the new directory to reside. (The directory you create will be a subdirectory of the directory you highlight.) If you don't want the new directory to be a subdirectory of another directory, highlight the root directory (**C:**).

3. Choose **File Create Directory**. The Create Directory dialog box appears.

4. Type the Name of the new directory, up to eight characters.

5. Select **OK**. The new directory is created.

Figure 13.1 illustrates the Create Directory dialog box for a new directory called WRITEDOC, a subdirectory of the WINDOWS directory. Figure 13.2 shows the WRITEDOC directory added to the directory tree.

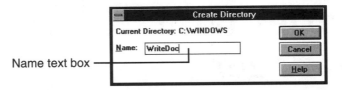

Figure 13.1 The Create Directory dialog box for the WRITEDOC directory.

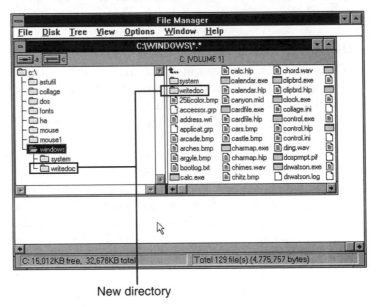

Figure 13.2 The WRITEDOC directory is added.

Deleting a Directory

You may need to delete a directory. For example, you may create a directory in the wrong spot on the directory tree. Or you may want to remove the directory for an application you no longer use. You can delete a directory with File Manager.

To delete a directory, follow these steps:

1. Make sure you have the necessary copies of any files in the directory you are going to delete. (The files must be deleted before the directory can be deleted.)

2. From the File Manager directory tree, highlight the directory you want to delete.

3. Choose **File Delete**. The Delete dialog box appears.

4. Make sure the directory shown is correct. Select **OK**.

5. A Confirm Directory Delete dialog box appears. Check the directory again, and then select **OK**.

6. If files are in the directory, a Confirm File Delete dialog box appears for each file. You must select **OK** to delete each file before the directory can be deleted.

Do I Have to Confirm Every File?   The Delete Confirmation dialog box provides you with a **Yes to All** command button to confirm the deletion of all files at once. Use this feature with caution.

I Hate When That Happens!   Be very careful any time you delete a directory. Make doubly certain you are deleting the correct directory.

In this lesson, you learned how to create and delete directories. In the next lesson, you will learn how to find specific files within directories.

Finding Files with File Manager

In this lesson, you will learn how to locate files quickly with the directory window and the Search command.

Opening and Closing a Directory Window

More than one directory window can be open at a time. This is useful when you are looking for files and even more useful when you want to copy or move files from one directory to another. (Copying and moving files are covered in Lesson 15.)

To open a new directory window, choose **Window New Window** from File Manager. A window appears that is identical to the previous window except for the title on the window's title bar. Notice that each window's title now has a colon and a number following the name (see Figure 14.1). If you change the selected directory, the number disappears.

> **TIP**   **Shortcut to Creating a New Directory Window**   If you want the new window to display the contents of another disk drive, simply double-click on that drive's icon. Single-clicking the icon displays the drive's contents in the current window; double-clicking opens a new window to display the contents of the drive.

> **TIP**   **Arranging Windows**   Remember, you can arrange your windows using **Window Cascade** or **Window Tile**. The **Window** menu also lists the windows, placing a check mark in front of the active window.

Window #1

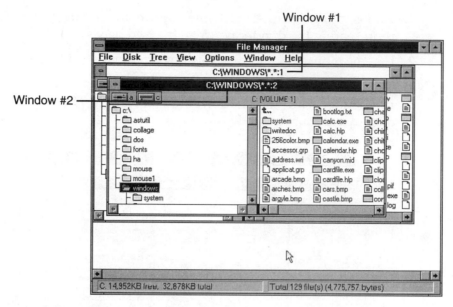

Window #2

Figure 14.1 When a second window is opened, File Manager attaches a colon and a number (:1, :2) to each window title.

When you're finished with a directory window, close it by double-clicking on the **Control-menu** box or by pressing **Ctrl+F4**.

Changing the Display

File Manager's View menu controls how the directory window displays information.

In the examples you've seen, the directory tree and the list of files were both shown. You can choose to show only one or the other, and you can change the way each is shown.

To show only the tree, choose **View Tree Only**; to show only the list of files (the *directory*), choose **View Directory Only**. To show them both again, choose **View Tree and Directory**.

If you elect to display both the tree and directory, you can change the amount of window space allotted to each. For example, you may want to see more files and less white space around the tree. Follow these steps to change the way the window space is divided between the panes.

1. Choose **View Split**. A black line appears in the directory window, representing the divider between the two panes.

2. Use the mouse pointer or arrow keys to move the black line to the desired location (as shown in Figure 14.2).

3. Press **Enter** when the line is where you want it. The window display is changed (see Figure 14.3).

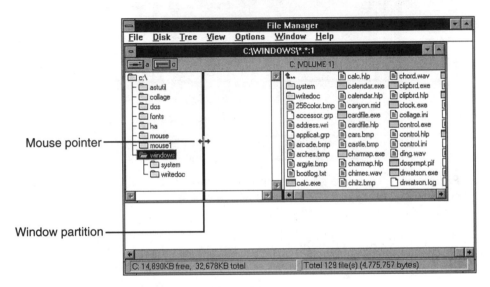

Figure 14.2 The line to select the split.

In Figure 14.3, only file names and icons are shown in the directory. File Manager can display more information about each file if you desire. Choose **View All File Details**; to display the following information about each file:

- Size in bytes

- Last modification date

- Last modification time

- File attributes (to identify whether a file is hidden, system, archive, or read only)

Or choose **View Partial Details** to identify which of the above information you want displayed.

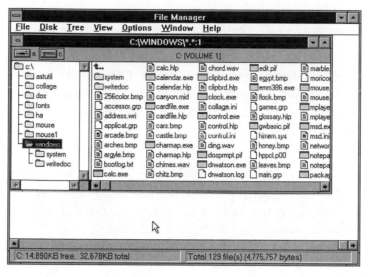

Figure 14.3 The completed split.

Controlling the Order of the Display

As shown in Figure 14.3, the files in the directory are in alphabetical order by file name. You may also sort the directory display by the following methods:

- **View Sort by Type** arranges files alphabetically by extension. For example, *sample.doc* would come before *file.txt*, which would come before *budget.wri*.

- **View Sort by Size** arranges files by size from largest to smallest.

- **View Sort by Date** arranges files by date from newest to oldest.

- **View By File Type** opens a dialog box that allows you to select certain types of files to include or exclude in the listing (program files, document files, directories, and so on).

After experimenting with these arrangements, you can restore the default setting by choosing **View Sort by Name**.

Updating a Directory Window

Most often, when you create, change, or delete a file, the directory window is updated immediately. If it is not (as is the case with some networks), you

71

can update the directory window yourself. Simply choose **Window Refresh** (**F5** is the keyboard shortcut to refresh a window).

If you add or delete directories from the DOS prompt (either outside of Windows or from Windows' DOS shell), it may be necessary to use **Windows Refresh** to get File Manager to see a directory or file that you created from the DOS prompt, or to realize that the one you deleted using DOS is gone.

Searching for a File

As you create more files, the ability to find a specific file becomes more critical. You can search for either a single file or a group of files with similar names using the **File Search** command. To search for a group of files, use the wild card * (asterisk) with a partial file name to narrow the search. Table 14.1 shows some search examples and their potential results.

Table 14.1   Search Results Examples

Characters Entered for Search	*Sample Search Results*
rpt1.doc	rpt1.doc
rpt*.doc	rpt1.doc, rpt2.doc, rpt11.doc
c*.exe	calc.exe, calendar.exe
*.exe	calc.exe, calendar.exe, notepad.exe
c*.*	calc.exe, calendar.exe, class.wri

To search for a file, follow these steps:

1. From File Manager, choose **File Search**. The Search dialog box appears (see Figure 14.4).

2. In the **Search For** text area, enter the characters to search for. Use wild cards to identify unknown characters.

3. If you want to search the entire drive, type **C:** in the **Start From** text box and make sure the **Search All Subdirectories** check box is active.

   If you would like to search only a certain directory and its subdirectories, type it in the **Start From** text box.

To search a single directory (no subdirectories), type it in the **Start From** text box, and make sure the **Search All Subdirectories** check box is not active.

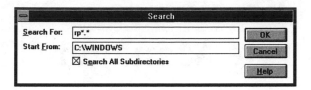

Figure 14.4   The completed Search dialog box.

4. Select **OK** to begin the search. The Search Results window appears, showing the files that were found (see Figure 14.5).

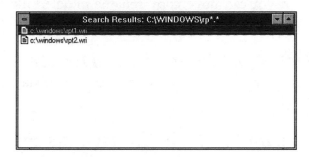

Figure 14.5   The search results.

In this lesson, you learned how to open and close directory windows, change the display and the order of the files shown, and update a directory window. You also learned how to search for a file through one or more directories. In the next lesson, you will learn how to move, copy, rename, and delete files and directories.

Managing Files and Directories with File Manager

In this lesson, you will learn how to move, copy, rename, and delete files and directories.

Selecting and Deselecting Files or Directories

Before you can move, copy, rename, or delete files or directories, you must identify, or *select*, the ones you want. The following sections tell you how.

Selecting a Single File or Directory

To select a single file or directory from File Manager's directory window, just click on it.

Selecting Multiple Contiguous Files or Directories

Selecting a single file is useful, but to really speed up operations, you will want to select multiple files and then execute commands that will affect the entire group. For example, you may want to select several files to be copied to a disk. Copying them all at once is much faster than copying each file individually.

It is easy to select multiple files or directories that are displayed contiguously in the File Manager directory window. Figure 15.1 illustrates a selection of contiguous files.

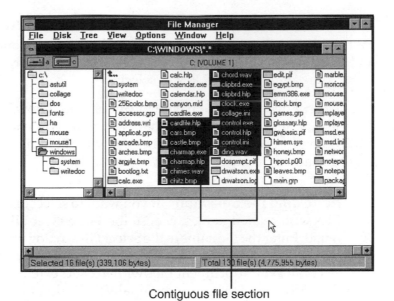

Figure 15.1 Selecting contiguous files.

Contiguous Files When the files that you want to select are listed together in File Manager, without any files that you *don't* want between them, they are *contiguous*.

To select contiguous files or directories:

1. Click on the first file or directory that you want to select. When you click on it, it is highlighted.

2. Hold down the **Shift** key, and click on the last file or directory that you want to select. All the items between the first and last selections are highlighted (including the first and last selections themselves).

To deselect a contiguous group of files or directories, click on a file or directory outside the selected items.

Selecting Noncontiguous Files or Directories

Often, the files or directories you want to select are not contiguous but separated by several files that you do not want. However, this is not a problem. You can use the **Ctrl** key to select them.

To select or deselect an item with the mouse, hold down the **Ctrl** key while you click on the file or directory. The item you click on will be highlighted, and any other items you click on (while holding down the **Ctrl** key) will remain highlighted, too.

Narrowing the Selection If you want to select or deselect files with related names, choose the **File Select Files** command. Enter the file name in the Select Files dialog box. Then, choose **Select** or **Deselect**. For example, you may want to select all Word document files with a .DOC extension, then deselect a few of the files individually if you don't want them all for your activity.

Figure 15.2 shows multiple noncontiguous files selected.

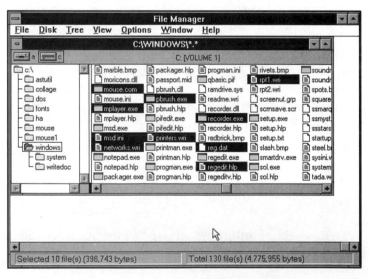

Figure 15.2   Selecting multiple noncontiguous files.

Moving or Copying Files or Directories

To move or copy files or directories through File Manager, you *drag and drop*; that is, you select the items you want from your *source* directory, drag them to the *destination* directory, and then drop them there. You'll learn this technique in more detail in the steps that follow.

Move vs. Copy   *Move* means the file or directory is no longer in the original spot but is in the new location. *Copy* means the original file or directory remains in the original spot, and a new copy of the file or directory is in a second location.

Before you move or copy, make sure the source directory window is visible, so you can highlight the file(s) that you're going to drag. Also, make sure that the destination drive or directory is visible, either as an open window or as an icon.

If you're copying between two directories, you can open both directory windows and then choose **Window Tile**. Figure 15.3 shows a tiled display of the WORD directory window (the *source* directory), and the WINWORD directory (the *destination* directory) ready for file copying.

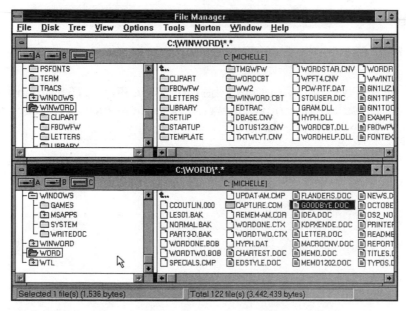

Figure 15.3   Two windows ready for moving or copying files.

Copying Files and Directories

With the mouse, use this procedure to copy:

1. Select the files or directories to copy.

2. Press the **Ctrl** key, and drag the files or directories to the destination drive, window, or icon.

3. Release the mouse button and the **Ctrl** key.

4. A dialog box appears asking you to confirm the copy. Click on **OK**.

   Here's an alternative procedure for copying:

1. Select the files or directories to copy.

2. Choose **File Copy**. The Copy dialog box appears.

3. The selected files are listed in the From text box. Type the desired destination in the To text box, including the path to the destination drive and directory. Figure 15.4 shows a completed Copy dialog box.

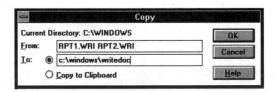

Figure 15.4   The Copy dialog box completed.

4. Select **OK** by pressing the **Enter** key. Figure 15.5 illustrates the result of the copy. The Write document files have been copied into the WriteDoc directory.

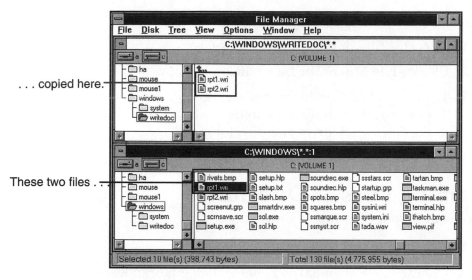

. . . copied here.

These two files . . .

Figure 15.5 The completed copy operation.

CAUTION

The File Is Already There If you attempt to copy a file or directory to a location where an identical file or directory exists, Windows lets you know with a message.

Moving Files and Directories

With the mouse, use these steps to complete a move:

1. Select the files or directories to move.

2. Drag the files or directories to the drive, window, or icon.

3. Release the mouse button.

4. A dialog box appears asking you to confirm the move. Click on **OK**.

Here's an alternate method:

1. Select the files or directories to move.

2. Choose **File Move**. The Move dialog box appears.

3. The selected files or directories are listed in the From text box. Type the desired destination in the To text box, including the path to the destination drive and directory.

4. Select **OK** by pressing the **Enter** key.

Renaming Files or Directories

To rename your files, follow these steps:

1. Select the file or directory to rename.

2. Choose **File Rename**. The Rename dialog box appears.

3. In the To text box, type in the new name for the file or directory.

4. Select **OK**.

It Worked Yesterday   Don't rename program files. Many applications will not work if their files have been renamed.

Deleting Files or Directories

You can delete files or directories, but be careful. Before you delete anything, it is a good idea to make a backup copy of any files or directories you might need later.

Better Safe Than Sorry   A common use for the delete command is to delete the original after a file has been copied. Moving the file would accomplish the same result, but it's safer to copy, because you still have the original in case anything goes wrong.

To delete, follow these steps:

1. Select the file or directory to delete.

2. Choose **File Delete**. The Delete dialog box appears, indicating what will be deleted.

3. Check the Delete dialog box carefully to make certain you are deleting what you intended to delete.

4. Select **OK**. You will be asked to confirm the deletion. If you are deleting a directory and there are files that must be deleted first, you will be asked to confirm each file deletion.

In this lesson, you learned how to copy, move, rename, and delete files and directories. In the next lesson, you will continue to enhance your skills with File Manager by using it to format and copy floppy disks.

Formatting and Copying Floppy Disks with File Manager

In this lesson, you will learn how to format and copy a floppy disk using File Manager.

Formatting a Floppy Disk

When you buy a box of floppy disks, the floppy disks are usually unformatted. (You can buy formatted disks, but they're more expensive.) They're sold unformatted because some computers use operating systems other than DOS, and such systems need to format the floppy disks in their own format.

Therefore, before you can use a new floppy disk, you must format it to work with your computer's operating system. Formatting prepares the floppy disk by organizing its space into *sectors* and creating a *file allocation table* (*FAT*) to keep track of the data stored in each sector.

Recycled Disks   You can format and reformat a floppy disk as often as you want. When you format a previously used floppy disk, any files that were on the floppy disk are lost. Before formatting a used floppy disk, be certain the floppy disk does not contain files you want to keep.

Disks can be formatted from the DOS command line, but you may find it more convenient to format disks from within File Manager. Follow these steps to format a floppy disk:

1. Insert the floppy disk into the drive.

2. From File Manager, choose **Disk Format Disk**. The Format Disk dialog box appears (see Figure 16.1).

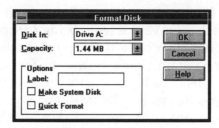

Figure 16.1 The Format Disk dialog box.

3. From the Format Disk dialog box, use the **Disk In** drop-down list to select the drive the floppy disk is in.

4. Use the drop-down list to select the **Capacity**. Refer to Table 16.1 for a list of capacity choices.

5. Select **OK**.

6. A confirmation box appears. Carefully check the information.

7. Once you are certain the information for formatting is correct, select **OK**. The disk drive lights up during formatting, and a message appears on your screen identifying how much of the formatting process is complete.

8. When the process is over, the Format Complete dialog box appears, listing the amount of space available on the newly formatted floppy disk and asking if you want to format another floppy disk. Select **Yes** to format another or **No** to stop formatting.

Table 16.1   Floppy Disk Capacity to Specify When Formatting

Disk Diameter	Disk Density	Capacities Available
3 1/2-inch	Double	720KB
3 1/2-inch	High	1.44MB
5 1/4-inch	Double	360KB
5 1/4-inch	High	360KB or 1.2MB

High-density 5 1/4-inch floppy disks can be formatted at either 360KB or 1.2MB capacity, but high-density 3 1/2-inch floppy disks can be formatted at only one capacity: 1.44MB.

Your Floppy Disk Won't Format   If the floppy disk has errors that prevent it from being formatted, Windows will tell you. Throw out any floppy disks that cannot be formatted or have problems during the formatting process. If the floppy disk is a high-density 3 1/2-inch floppy disk, make sure you format it at 1.44MB capacity; if you try to format a high-density 3 1/2" floppy disk at 720KB capacity, Windows will (falsely) report that the floppy disk has errors.

It is always a good idea to keep several formatted floppy disks available in case you need to move or copy files in a hurry.

Making System Disks

What Is a System Disk?   A system disk contains operating system files you need to start your computer in the event your hard disk fails. With it, you can start your computer from the floppy disk drive.

You should always have at least one system disk on hand in case something goes wrong. A hard disk problem can lock you out of your system unless you have a system disk (so can an error in your CONFIG.SYS or AUTOEXEC.BAT file). With a system disk, you can boot from the floppy drive, bypassing the hard drive (*and* the error) until the problem can be found and corrected.

More Than One Drive   If you have two floppy disk drives (A and B) of differing sizes (5 1/4-inch and 3 1/2-inch), your system disk must be the kind that fits on drive A (usually the 5 1/4-inch one). This is because when your computer boots, it checks drive A first for a disk, and if it finds none, it boots from the hard disk. It never checks drive B when booting, so you can't boot from there.

You can create a system disk when you format the floppy disk by checking the **Make System Disk** check box in the Format Disk dialog box. Or to make a formatted floppy disk into a system disk, follow these steps:

1. From File Manager's directory window, select the icon for your hard disk. (This is where the operating system files reside.)

2. Insert a formatted floppy disk into drive A.

3. Choose **Disk Make System Disk**. The Make System Disk dialog box appears for you to verify the drive.

4. Once you have verified the drive, select **Yes**. A message appears telling you that the system disk is being created. When the message disappears, the system disk is created.

Create a system disk for your computer, and store it in a safe place. Someday, you'll be glad that you took this precaution.

Copying a Floppy Disk

If you want to copy *all* the files on one floppy disk to another, rather than each one individually, you can do it easily with File Manager. The only condition is that both floppy disks must be of the same capacity. For example, if the source floppy disk is 1.44MB (high density), the destination floppy disk must also be 1.44MB.

Which Is Which?   The *source* floppy disk is the one you are copying from. The *destination* floppy disk is the one you are copying to.

Proceed with Caution   When you copy a floppy disk, all files previously on the destination floppy disk are lost.

Follow these steps to copy a floppy disk:

1. Place the source floppy disk in the drive to copy *from*. If you have two drives of the same size and capacity, place the destination floppy disk in the drive to copy *to*.

2. From File Manager, select the drive of the source floppy disk.

3. Choose **Disk Copy Disk**.

4. A message appears reminding you that all the files on the destination floppy disk will be erased. Select **Yes** to go on.

5. The Copy Disk dialog box appears. If you are using two drives, the floppy disk will be copied without your having to swap floppy disks. If you are using one drive, Windows will instruct you when to swap the source and destination floppy disks. Follow the instructions.

In this lesson, you learned how to format disks and how to copy an entire floppy disk. You also learned how to create a system disk. The next lesson will conclude your work with File Manager. You will learn how to start an application from File Manager.

Starting an Application from File Manager

In this lesson, you will learn how to start an application from within File Manager.

Using the Run Command

In Lesson 7, you learned how to start an application using the application icon or the File Run command from the Program Manager window. You can't select application icons from File Manager, but you can still use the File Run command.

There are several advantages to using the Run command from File Manager:

- You can sort the files using **View Sort by Type**, which lets you see all the *executable* (.EXE) files grouped together. This allows you to quickly find the file that starts the program you want to use.

- No typing is required to start the application. You select the directory from the directory tree and the file from the directory window. Then, when you use the File Run command, all the information is already entered in the appropriate blanks. Figure 17.1 shows the Run dialog box with the .EXE file for the Solitaire game ready to be run.

Figure 17.1 The Run dialog box with the Solitaire game .EXE file ready to run.

- You can specify start-up parameters for the application, just as you can from the DOS command line. (The manual for the application describes different start-up options.)

To use the File Run command, follow these steps:

1. To reduce typing, select the appropriate directory and executable file from the File Manager directory tree and window.

2. From the File Manager window, choose **File Run**. The Run dialog box appears.

3. When the command and any start-up options are entered, select **OK**.

Executable Files   Applications are started from executable files. These typically end in .EXE. Some applications are started from executable files that end in .COM, or from batch files (which end in .BAT), but this is less common.

Selecting the File to Run

There are other ways to start an application from File Manager. You can locate the executable file and double-click on it. More importantly, Windows 3.1 allows you to open an application by double-clicking on a document created by the application.

Starting an Application from the Executable File

You can double-click on an executable file to start the application, rather than use the File Run command. Note that you cannot add start-up parameters to the command. The advantage is that you can start an application from the directory window and bypass the Run command dialog box.

Starting an Application from an Associated File

There are three common types of file icons displayed by File Manager. The one that looks like a miniature window indicates that this file is an executable file. This icon will appear next to all .EXE, .COM, and .BAT files.

The other icons (which look like pieces of paper with a corner turned down) indicate that the file is a document file. Some of these icons are blank, and some have lines on them. The lines indicate that Windows knows what application created the document file. If you double-click on one of these icons, the *associated application* will open with the file you chose in a document window.

File association is a very powerful feature of Windows 3.1. It allows you to drag a document icon to different applications for processing. For instance, you can print an associated file simply by dragging its icon from File Manager and dropping it into the Print Manager icon. This allows you to print a document (for example, a Write document) without having to open the application first.

Using Drag and Drop to Create Program Icons

In Lesson 11, you learned how to add program icons to program groups. You can also add program icons to program groups using File Manager. This procedure will likely test your ability to work with multiple open windows, but once you get the hang of it, you'll be on your way to becoming a Windows power user.

To create a new program icon using File Manager, follow these steps:

1. Open File Manager, and locate the executable file that you want to appear as a program icon in a program group.

Give Yourself Room to Work   You know that you will have to be able to see both the Program Manager window and the File Manager window to be able to complete this task. When you start File Manager, resize the window to allow room on-screen for the Program Manager window (see Figure 17.2).

File Manager window

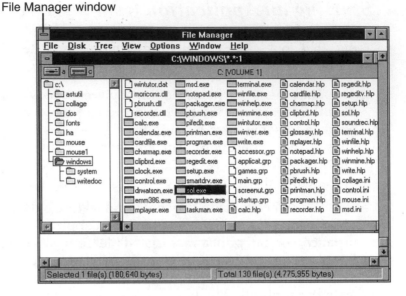

Figure 17.2   Dragging a file from File Manager to a program group.

2. Switch Tasks back to Program Manager. Resize the Program Manager window so that you are able to see both the File Manager window and Program Manager window. You should also be able to see the program group icon or window to which you want to add the program icon.

To View All Your Groups in One Window   The easiest way to see all your program groups (especially in a small Program Manager window) is to iconize (minimize from a window to an icon) all the program groups. Once all your program groups are iconized, choose **Window Arrange Icons** to bring all the program group icons into view.

3. Drag the file in question from File Manager to the program group to which you want to add the program icon.

4. When the mouse pointer is positioned over the appropriate program group window or icon, drop (release the mouse button) the file into the group. A new program icon appears in the group.

Notice that as you drag the file between File Manager and Program Manager, the mouse pointer appears as a circle with a line through it (like a no-smoking sign). This indicates that you cannot drop the file where the pointer is located (if you do, nothing will happen). When the mouse pointer is positioned over a program group window or icon, it turns into the familiar arrow pointer and a document icon with a plus sign in it (see Figure 17.2). This indicates that you can drop the file here.

As you can see, you can drag-and-drop executable files into a program group, and they become program icons. Windows 3.1 allows you to do this with associated document files as well. For example, if you have a document that you work with regularly (for instance, Journal of Customer Service Calls), you can drag it to Program Manager and drop it into a group. The new program will take the icon of the associated application. You can double-click on the icon to open the application and the document at the same time.

In this lesson, you learned how to start your applications in File Manager. In the next lesson, you will learn how to get ready to print.

Getting Ready to Print

In this lesson, you will learn how to get ready to print, and how to set up any special typefaces.

Checking the Printer Installation

When you installed Windows, you configured the printer and the link to the printer. This is important because almost all Windows applications print using the Print Manager and the default printer defined through it. Before you attempt to print, you need to check Windows to make sure the settings are correct.

To check the print setup from Windows, go to the Printers dialog box using the following steps:

1. From Program Manager, open the **Main** group icon.

2. Open the **Control Panel** program-item icon from the Main group window.

3. Open the **Printers** icon. The Printers dialog box appears (see Figure 18.1).

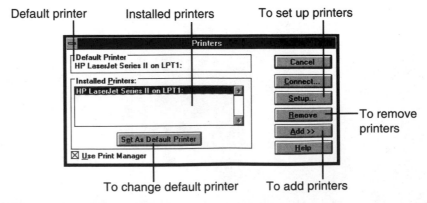

Figure 18.1   The Printers dialog box.

Default vs. Installed Printer   The Printers dialog box identifies the Default Printer and the Installed Printers. The Default Printer is the one that the computer assumes is connected to your computer unless you select another printer. The Installed Printers are those for which special instructions (called *Printer Drivers*) are available on your computer. You can select an Installed Printer and then select the **Set As Default Printer** button to make it the Default Printer.

From the Printers dialog box, you can select the following buttons to check the settings.

- The Connect button opens the Connect dialog box. On it, you can see the port (connection) to which your printer is attached. This port is usually LPT1 (for parallel printers) or COM1 (for serial printers).

- The Connect dialog box allows you to check or change the settings that control the time-out periods for the Print Manager. Time-outs define the length of time the Print Manager will wait to inform you of a printing problem.

Printer Port   The printer port is the connection on your computer to which the cable to your printer is attached. If the port description indicates **Not Present**, this means Windows does not detect that port on your computer. Check your printer manual to see whether your printer is parallel or serial and, therefore, will use the parallel or serial port.

- The Setup button allows you to enter information about your printer setup (see the dialog box in Figure 18.2). You can define the following:

The Resolution in dots per inch (the more dots, the finer the resolution).

The Paper Size, the Paper Source.

The amount of Memory in your printer (check your printer manual if you are not sure).

The Orientation to either Portrait (the short side of the paper is at the top) or Landscape (the long side of paper is at the top).

The number of Copies to print.

- The Add button lets you add new printers to the Installed Printers list. Just select the name of the printer, and then select the Install button.

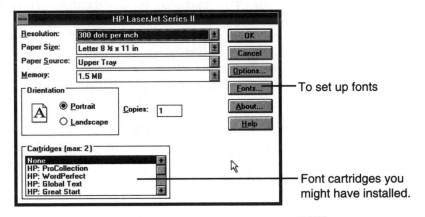

To set up fonts

Font cartridges you might have installed.

Figure 18.2   The dialog box for setting up your printer.

What Disk?   When you install new features to your Windows environment, have your installation diskettes close at hand. In the example above, Windows will probably ask you to insert one of the disks containing the printer drivers before it can carry out your instructions.

Once you have all the setup options in place, you may return to the Control Panel.

In addition to making sure Windows is ready for printing, you'll want to check your equipment. Things to double-check include:

- Is the cable between the computer and the printer securely attached on each end?

- Is the printer turned on?

- Is the printer ready for the computer's transmission with the ON LINE light on?

- Is paper loaded in the printer?

Working with Fonts

Many printers can print more than one character style or typeface (called a *font*). Check your printer manual to see if it is capable of printing multiple fonts. If it is, you will want to check the font setup in Windows before printing.

Where Are These Fonts?   Fonts may be stored on disks or on cartridges that slide into the printer.

When you set up Windows, the fonts for your printer were identified. The dialog box shown in Figure 18.3 refers to an HP LaserJet Series II printer. Cartridges are commonly sold for this printer. The cartridge B:Times Proportional 1 has been selected. A maximum of two cartridges may be selected for this printer at one time.

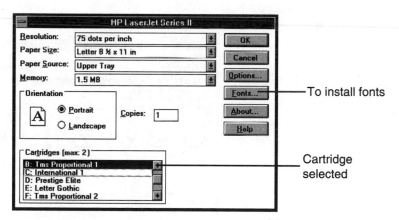

Figure 18.3   Font cartridge selected.

Use the **Fonts** button on the dialog box shown in Figure 18.3 to open the Font Installer dialog box. You can determine which fonts are installed from this dialog box.

To check the font setup:

1. From the Program Manager Main group window, open the **Control Panel**.

2. Open the **Printers** icon.

3. Select **Setup** on the Printers dialog box.

4. If your fonts are stored on cartridges, highlight the cartridge(s) you will use (based on the maximum number identified in the dialog box).

5. If your fonts are stored on floppy disk, select the **Fonts** button. The Font Installer dialog box appears. You may select the font you want from the list of available fonts.

Installing TrueType Fonts

Windows 3.1 comes with a number of TrueType fonts. These are fonts that appear in your printed document exactly as they do on your screen. The information your printer needs to print TrueType fonts is downloaded to your printer each time you print a document containing them.

Figure 18.4 shows the Fonts Installer dialog box with a number of TrueType fonts installed.

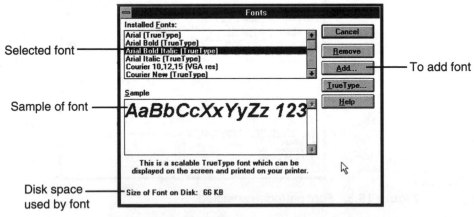

Figure 18.4   The Fonts dialog box.

To add fonts, follow these steps:

1. From Program Manager, open the **Control Panel**.

2. Open the **Fonts** icon. The Fonts dialog box, shown in Figure 18.4, appears.

3. Select **Add** from the Fonts dialog box.

4. From the Add Font File dialog box, select the directory where the font file is located, select the font to add, and select **OK**.

5. Once the font is added, you may add another font or close the dialog box.

Removing a Font from Memory or Disk

Fonts take up space in active memory as well as your hard disk. You may want to delete fonts you do not use to free memory or remove them entirely from your disk. To remove fonts, follow these steps:

1. From Program Manager, open the **Control Panel**.

2. Open the **Fonts** icon. The Fonts dialog box appears.

3. Select the font to remove, and then select the **Remove** button.

4. A message appears for you to verify the removal. If you leave the Delete Font File from Disk box unchecked, the font is only removed from active memory. Check the box, and the font file is removed from the hard disk as well.

In this lesson, you learned how to prepare to print. In the next lesson, you will learn how to print with the Print Manager.

Printing with the Print Manager

In this lesson, you will learn how to print through the Print Manager and check the status of your print jobs.

Purpose of the Print Manager

The Print Manager acts as the middleman between your printer and the application you are printing from. When you choose **File Print** from most Windows applications, the font and file information is handed off to the Print Manager. The Print Manager then feeds the information to the printer. This allows you to continue working in your application while your job is printing.

Print Jobs   A *print job* (or simply *job*) is created when you choose the **Print** command from the application in which you are working.

Checking the Print Queue

When you print a document, the printer usually begins processing the job immediately. What happens if the printer is working on another job, sent by you, or in the case of a network printer, someone else? In this case, the Print Manager acts as a print queue and holds the job until the printer is ready for it.

Print Queue   The *print queue* is a holding area for jobs that have to be printed. If you were to list the contents of the queue, the jobs would appear in the order they were sent to the Print Manager.

Figure 19.1 illustrates the document NETWORKS.WRI in the print queue. As you can see, the percent of the document that has been printed is shown (34% of 63KB) along with the time and date the document was sent to print. Notice also that the printer is shown to be printing. This indicates the document was just sent to the queue and is beginning to print.

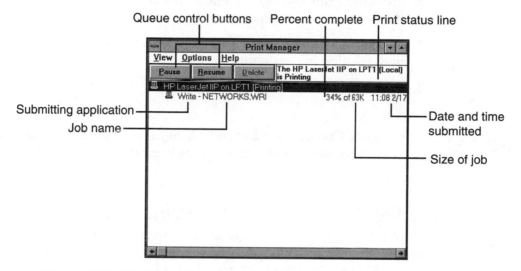

Figure 19.1 The Print Manager print queue window.

To display the print queue, follow these steps:

1. From Program Manager, open the **Main** group icon.

2. Open the **Print Manager** icon (see Figure 19.1).

3. The Print Manager window appears with a list of *queued* documents. If no documents are waiting to print, a message tells you the printer is idle.

Controlling the Print Job

You can control print jobs once they are in the queue. This includes changing the order in which the jobs print, pausing and resuming the print job, or deleting a job before it prints.

Reordering Jobs in the Queue

To use the mouse to change the order of a job in the queue, drag the job entry to a new position in the list. To use the keyboard to reposition a job in the queue:

1. From the Print Manager window, use the arrow keys to highlight the document to be repositioned.

2. Hold down **Ctrl**, and use the arrow keys to move the job to the new position in the queue.

3. Release the **Ctrl** key.

First Come, First Served   You cannot reorder or place a job before the job that is currently printing.

Pausing and Resuming the Print Queue

You may want to pause the queue and then resume printing later. For example, the paper in the printer may be misaligned. Pausing the print queue will give you time to correct the problem.

To pause the print queue, select the **Pause** button while in the Print Manager window. To resume printing, select the **Resume** button.

Printer Stalled   Your printer may stall while it is processing your print job. If it does, **stalled** will appear in the printer status line. Select the **Resume** button to start printing again. Chances are that a problem somewhere along the line caused the printer to stall, the queue will stall again, and you will have to solve the problem.

Delete a Print Job

Sometimes, you'll send a document to be printed and then change your mind. For example, you may think of other text to add to the document or realize you forgot to spell check your work. In such a case, deleting the print job is easy. Follow these steps:

1. From the Print Manager window, select the job to delete.

2. Select the **Delete** button.

3. A message appears for you to confirm the deletion.

4. Select **OK**.

Clear the Queue!   To delete all the files in the print queue, choose **View Exit** from the Print Manager menu bar, or double-click on the **Control-menu** box. Select **OK** from the Print Manager dialog box.

In this lesson, you learned how to print using the Print Manager and to check the status of your print jobs. In the next lesson, you will learn how to use the Control Panel to control your windows.

Controlling Windows with the Control Panel

In this lesson, you will learn how to change the look and performance of Windows by using the Control Panel.

The Control Panel is an application in the Main group that allows you to control many aspects of Windows (see Figure 20.1). Those discussed in this lesson include:

- Colors displayed on-screen.

- What appears on your desktop.

- International language and display support.

Controls the appearance of your desktop

Controls the color of Windows elements

Controls how Windows displays dates, currency, and other nation-dependent items

Figure 20.1   The Windows Control Panel.

Setting Colors

You can change the color of many components of Windows with the Control Panel. This can be important if you have a monochrome or LCD screen. These screens may not have the capability to display certain colors. This could cause a real problem if the color chosen to display command buttons cannot be displayed by your screen. Windows comes with several predefined color schemes for users with monochrome or LCD screens. The ability to control the color of certain Windows elements can also help you learn to use Windows faster. This is because you are able to look for a particular color and shape, instead of just a shape. Finally, you can adjust the colors displayed on your color monitor just for a change of pace.

Change colors with these steps:

1. From Program Manager, open the **Main** group icon, and then open the **Control Panel**.

2. Open the **Color** program-item. The Color dialog box appears.

3. Open the **Schemes** drop-down list box by clicking on the down arrow button. The predefined options appear (see Figure 20.2).

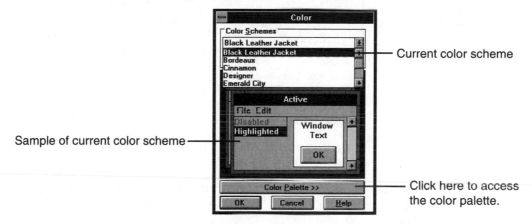

Figure 20.2   The Black Leather Jacket color scheme selected on the Color dialog box.

4. Use the arrow keys to scroll through the color scheme options. The display below Color **S**chemes illustrates the current selection.

5. Press **Enter** to select your choice.

TIP

Test Your Artistic Aptitude   After you become more comfortable with Windows, go into the Color dialog box and create your own color scheme. Select the **Show Palette** button. A new section of the Color dialog box appears. This will allow you to assign different colors to the various Windows components (title bar, buttons, menus, and so on). You can then save your creation as a Windows color scheme.

Changing the Desktop

Many visual and performance elements of your desktop can be changed through the Control Panel. The Desktop dialog box shown in Figure 20.3 has the following options.

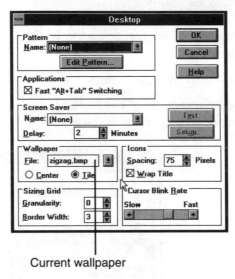

Current wallpaper

Figure 20.3   Desktop dialog box with Zigzag Wallpaper selected.

Pattern Name   Select the pattern that is displayed on the desktop. This is a simple, two-color pattern (defined in the Color dialog box).

Applications   Identify the speed at which windows cycle when you press **Alt+Tab**. This is the fast task-switching that Windows 3.1 offers.

Screen Saver   If the same image remains on your screen for an extended period of time, you could damage your monitor. By selecting a screen saver, when your computer is inactive for the default time, Windows will automatically blank the screen and run a pattern across your screen. To continue working, press a key or move the mouse.

Wallpaper   More elaborate than the Pattern selection, the Wallpaper option allows you to display .BMP files on your desktop. Windows comes with some very attractive wallpapers, or you can use Paintbrush to create your own.

Icons Determine icon Spacing and whether icon titles are wrapped to another line or cut off.

Sizing Grid Identify the setting of the magnetic grid that aligns windows and icons. Granularity determines the precision of the grid, and Border Width sets the size of the border of windows.

Cursor Blink Rate Set how fast the cursor (your marker in text boxes) blinks.

¿Habla Usted Español?

Most readers will be using Windows in the United States. But if you do work in an international setting, you may want to make some changes on the International dialog box. Figure 20.4 shows the dialog box with these settings:

- **Country** Windows has a number of standard country settings on how units are displayed, page setup defaults, and so on. Use this option to choose the Country settings you want to use.

- **Language** Some Windows applications provide foreign language support. Use this option to choose which language you want to work with.

- **Keyboard Layout** Windows supports a number of keyboard layouts. This controls the way keys are mapped to the special characters associated with the Language you have chosen to work with.

- **Measurement** Use this drop-down list to choose which measurement system you want to work with: English or Metric.

- **List Separator** In this text box, enter the character with which you want to separate elements of a list.

- **Date Format** Use this command button to change the way long and short dates are displayed.

- **Currency Format** Use this command button to change the way positive and negative currency values are displayed.

- **Time Format** Use this command button to change the way time values are displayed.

- **Number Format** Use this command button to change the way numbers are displayed.

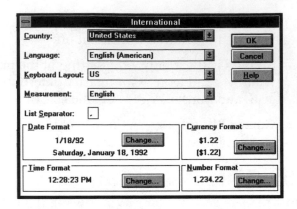

Figure 20.4   The International dialog box.

To control the international settings, follow these steps:

1. From the Control Panel window, open the **International** icon. The International dialog box appears.

2. Make the selections for the changes you want.

3. Select **OK**. The changes take effect.

In this lesson, you learned how to set colors, change the desktop appearance, and give Windows an international flavor. In the next lesson, you will learn how to use the Control Panel to control hardware settings.

Controlling Hardware Settings with the Control Panel

In this lesson, you will learn to use the Control Panel to control hardware settings for ports, mouse, keyboard, date/time, drivers, and sound. Figure 21.1 displays the Control Panel and points out the icons you will be using in this lesson.

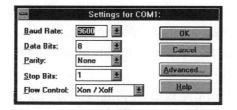

Figure 21.1   The Windows Control Panel.

Altering the Date and Time

The system date and time is set in your computer. This is used to time-stamp files as they are created or modified. Also, many application programs allow you to automatically insert the date and time on-screen or when you print. Always make sure the date and time are correct.

To check or set the date and time, follow these steps:

1. From the Control Panel, open the **Date/Time** icon. The Date & Time dialog box appears (see Figure 21.2).

2. Use the **Tab** key or the mouse to move between digits in the date and time. Enter the appropriate date and time. To use the mouse, click on the portion of the date or time you want to change, and click on the up or down arrow button to increment or decrement the value accordingly.

3. Select **OK** or press **Enter** to accept the changes you have made. Press **Esc** or select **Cancel** to close the dialog box without saving changes.

Modifying Mouse Settings

You can modify the settings for your mouse. The following settings can be changed:

- The speed of mouse tracking (how fast/far the pointer moves when you move the mouse).

- The speed of the double-click (the time allowed between the first and second click so that your action is recognized as a double-click and not just two single-clicks).

- The use of the left and right buttons can be swapped (for you lefties out there).

- A trail of mouse pointers that follow the pointer movement can be turned on or off. This will drive an unsuspecting user up the wall.

Figure 21.2　The Date & Time dialog box.

Try It, You'll Like It　Always use the TEST area to try new settings before leaving the screen. For example, if you set the Double Click Speed all the way to **Fast**, you may not be able to double-click fast enough for it to register.

To modify these settings, follow these steps:

1. From the Control Panel, open the **Mouse** icon. The Mouse dialog box appears.

2. Enter the settings as desired, and test them in the TEST area.

3. Select **OK** or press **Enter** to accept the changes you have made. Press **Esc** or select **Cancel** to close the dialog box without saving changes.

Changing Keyboard Settings

You can change how long it takes for a key to be repeated and how fast a key repeats when it is held down. Follow these steps to change the response of the keyboard:

1. From the Control Panel, open the **Keyboard** icon. The Keyboard dialog box appears.

2. Enter the settings as desired, and test them out in the Test area.

3. Select **OK** or press **Enter** to accept the changes you have made. Press **Esc** or select **Cancel** to close the dialog box without saving changes.

Sound Control

Controlling sounds associated with actions or events can be simple or complex. At the simplest level, you can control the warning beep when you make an error or perform an action Windows does not recognize. If you have a sound card in your computer, you can set sounds for a variety of events in Windows.

To affect sound, follow these steps:

1. From the Control Panel, open the **Sound** icon. The Sound dialog box appears.

2. If you do not have a sound card in your computer, the Events and Files selections are grayed-out and unavailable. To turn off the warning beep, leave the Enable System Sounds box blank. To enable the warning beep, make sure that box is checked.

3. If you have a sound card, you can select the different Events and, for each, assign a Files sound. Use Test to test out your sound selection. Also, make sure Enable System Sounds is checked.

4. Select **OK** or press **Enter** to accept the changes you have made. Press **Esc** or select **Cancel** to close the dialog box without saving changes.

Changing Ports

If you will be communicating with another computer or installing a new printer, you may need to change the settings for the port to which the modem or printer will be connected.

Through the Port icon, you can set the Baud Rate, Data Bits, Parity, Stop Bits, and Flow Control. Most manuals for communications software and hardware specify the settings that must be used. If you have trouble, contact the manufacturer or support line for the product(s) involved. To change port settings, follow these steps:

1. From the Control Panel, open the **Ports** icon.

2. Select the port designation (COM1 through COM4) assigned to the port you will use.

3. The dialog box appears containing the settings for that port.

4. Enter the settings as instructed by the manual or technical support person.

5. Select **OK** or press **Enter** to accept the changes you have made. Press **Esc** or select **Cancel** to close the dialog box without saving changes.

In this lesson, you learned how to change the time, hardware settings, mouse and keyboard, and sound.

This Windows section has prepared you for your journey into the world of Microsoft applications. You are now ready to tackle Word, Excel, PowerPoint, Mail, and Access in whatever order you want. If at any point, you find you have forgotten something like how to work with dialog boxes, or how to cut and paste, please refer to the appropriate Windows lesson for a quick brush up.

WORD 6

Getting Started with Word

In this lesson, you'll start Word for Windows, learn the parts of the Word for Windows screen (including the toolbars), and learn how to quit the program.

About Word for Windows

Microsoft Word for Windows 6.0 is one of the most powerful word processing programs available. It combines advanced features that you may need to use only occasionally with simple-to-use, basic word processing features that you will need to use on a daily basis. Its accessible toolbars and shortcut menus, combined with its extensive on-line help system, make Word for Windows both easy to learn and fun to use.

Starting Word for Windows

If you haven't yet installed Word for Windows, please refer to the Appendix at the back of this book for instructions. After you install Word for Windows, your Windows Program Manager screen will include a Microsoft Office program group. Double-click on the program group icon to open the program group window. That window will contain a Microsoft Word 6.0 icon. To start the program, double-click on the **Word 6.0** icon.

Parts of the Screen

When you start Word for Windows, you will see an opening logo for a few seconds and then the main screen with a blank document that's ready for your input will appear. Depending on how your system is set up, it may also display a Tip of the Day box containing a brief, useful tip about the Word for Windows program. Press **Enter**, or click on **OK** to close the Tip of the Day box.

Tip of the Day   You can learn a lot from this small window in Word's opening screen, but if it becomes a nuisance just turn it off by clicking on the Show Tips at Startup box. If you change your mind later, select **Tip of the Day** from the **Help** menu.

Take a moment to familiarize yourself with the Word for Windows screen. It contains a number of useful components, which are labeled in Figure 1.1.

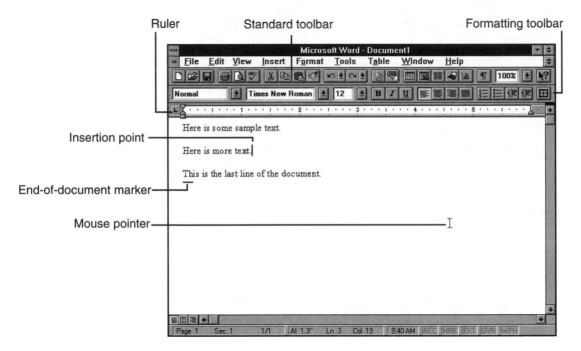

Figure 1.1   Components of the Word for Windows screen.

- The *Standard toolbar* displays buttons that you can select to perform commonly needed editing tasks. The toolbar works only with your mouse.

- The *Formatting toolbar* is used to select character and paragraph formatting commands. It, too, is accessed only with the mouse.

- The *Ruler* controls margins, indents, and tab stops.

- The *insertion point* is the blinking vertical line that marks the location where text you type will be inserted and where the editing actions will occur.

- The *end-of-document* marker is the horizontal line that marks the end of the document. In an empty document, the insertion point and the end-of-document marker share the same location.

The Toolbars

The Toolbars contain buttons that allow you to quickly perform the most commonly needed tasks. For example, the far left button on the Standard toolbar represents the File New command, and the button next to it represents the File Open command. If you position the mouse pointer on a toolbar button (without clicking), its name appears in a small yellow box next to your mouse pointer, as shown in Figure 1.2.

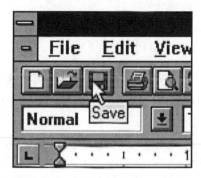

Figure 1.2 When you point at a tool, its name appears.

You'll probably find that clicking on a toolbar button is quicker and more convenient than entering the entire command sequence. Lesson 2 teaches you more about the toolbar buttons and their functions.

Toolbar Tip If you find that there are buttons on your Standard toolbar that you never use, and there are other features that you *do* use more often, you can customize your toolbar by deleting nonessential buttons and adding your own. See Lesson 30 to learn how to create custom toolbars.

Entering Text

To enter text, simply type on the keyboard. As you type, the text is inserted, and the insertion point moves to the right. When the line reaches the right edge of the screen, you don't need to press Enter (or Return) as you do on a typewriter, Word for Windows automatically moves to the start of the next line; this is called *wrapping*. Press **Enter** only when you want to start a new paragraph. As you enter more lines than will fit on the screen, Word for Windows automatically scrolls previously entered text upward to keep the insertion point in view.

Leave It to Word Wrap Press **Enter** only when you want to start a new paragraph.

Deleting Text

It is as simple to delete text as it is to enter it. You can delete single characters or large blocks of text.

- To delete the character to the right of the insertion point, press **Del**.

- To delete the character to the left of the insertion point, press **Backspace**.

- To delete a block of text, select the text, and then press **Del** or **Backspace**. You will get a message in your status line asking if you really want to delete the block of text. Press **Y** for yes.

If you make a mistake when deleting, you can recover deleted text with the **Edit Undo** command. This command appears on the Edit menu as either Undo Typing or Undo Clear, depending on how you deleted the text. In either case, the effect is the same: the deleted characters are replaced in their original position. You must select this command immediately after deleting and before performing any other action. You can also click on the **Undo** button on the toolbar, or press the shortcut key **Ctrl+Z** to undo the deletion.

Quitting Word for Windows

When you're done using Word for Windows, first save and close any open documents by choosing **File Save** and double-clicking on the document's **Control-menu** box. You can then quit Word by double-clicking on the

Control-menu box, choosing **File Exit**, or pressing **Alt+F4**. The program terminates, and you're returned to the Program Manager screen.

In this lesson, you learned how to start and exit Word for Windows and were introduced to the Word screen. In the next lesson, you'll learn more about the Word toolbars.

Getting to Know the Toolbars

In this lesson, you'll learn about the Formatting and Standard toolbars.

The toolbars in Word for Windows give you quick access to the most commonly used commands. You'll probably find that using a toolbar button is quicker and more convenient than selecting the command through the menu system.

Toolbars can be used only with a mouse. To select a button on a toolbar, just click on it. If you're not sure about a tool's function, position the mouse pointer on a toolbar button (without clicking). The name of the tool appears just under the button, and a description of the tool's function appears in the status bar at the bottom of the screen.

The Standard toolbar contains tools that you use most frequently during document creation, file handling, and printing. The Formatting toolbar contains the most common formatting tasks, such as font selection, alignment, and applying bold and italic. The Tables 2.1 and 2.2 introduce you to the tools you'll find on these two toolbars.

TIP

Toolbar Tip   If you find that there are buttons on your toolbars that you never use, and there are other features that you *do* use more often, you can customize your toolbar by deleting nonessential buttons and adding your own. See Lesson 30 to learn how to create custom toolbars.

Table 2.1 Standard Toolbar

Icon	Name	What It Does
	New	Creates a new document.
	Open	Opens an existing file.
	Save	Saves the current document.
	Print	Prints the current document.
	Print Preview	Displays document in print preview mode.
	Spelling	Checks spelling.
	Cut	Cuts selection to Clipboard.
	Copy	Copies selection text to Clipboard.
	Paste	Pastes from the Clipboard.
	Format Painter	Copies formatting from the selection.
	Undo	Undoes the last editing action.
	Redo	Reverses the last undo command.
	AutoFormat	Automatically formats a document.
	Insert AutoText	Creates or inserts an autotext entry.
	Insert Table	Creates a table.
	Insert Microsoft Excel Worksheet	Inserts a Microsoft Excel spreadsheet.

continues

119

Table 2.1 Continued

Icon	Name	What It Does
	Columns	Changes column format.
	Drawing	Displays the drawing toolbar.
	Insert Chart	Inserts a Microsoft Graph chart.
	Show/Hide ¶	Displays or hides nonprinting characters.
100%	Zoom Control	Scales the editing view.
	Help	Gives help on a command or screen region.

Table 2.2 Formatting Toolbar

Icon	Name	What It Does
Normal	Style	Applies an existing style or records a style by example.
Times New Roman	Font	Changes the font of the selection.
12	Font Size	Changes the font size of the selection.
B	Bold	Makes the selection bold (toggle).
I	Italic	Makes the selection italic (toggle).
U	Underline	Formats the selection with a continuous underline (toggle).
	Align Left	Aligns the paragraph at the left indent.

Icon	Name	What It Does
	Center	Centers the paragraph between the left and right indents.
	Right Align	Aligns the paragraph at the right indent.
	Justify	Aligns the paragraph at both the left and the right indent.
	Numbering	Creates a numbered list based on the current defaults.
	Bullets	Creates a bulleted list based on the current defaults.
	Decrease	Decreases indent or promotes Indent the selection one level.
	Increase	Increases indent or demotes the Indent selection one level.
	Borders	Shows or hides the Borders toolbar.

Getting Help

When you need help using a tool, click on the **Question Mark (?)** tool, if available, and then click on the tool you want help with. If the ? tool is not visible, press **Shift+F1**, and click on a tool. A Help window will appear to show you how to use the tool. Double-click on the Help window's Control-menu box to close the Help window.

Hiding Toolbars

You may find that the toolbars take up too much room on your screen. To hide a toolbar you can:

- Click on the toolbar with the right mouse button to display the toolbar shortcut menu. Displayed toolbars appear with a check mark. Click on the name of the displayed toolbar that you want hidden.

OR

- Choose **View Toolbars** to get the Toolbars dialog box. Click on the toolbar that you don't want displayed. Its check mark will disappear. Choose **OK**.

If you want to make the toolbar reappear later or display a different toolbar:

1. Choose **View Toolbars** to display the Toolbars dialog box.

2. Select the toolbar that you want to display.

3. Choose **OK**.

If another toolbar is currently displayed when you want to show a new one, you can:

1. Click with the right mouse button in the displayed toolbar to open a shortcut menu.

2. Click on the name of the toolbar you want to display.

In this lesson, you learned how to use the Standard and Formatting toolbars, to get help with the tools, and to hide toolbars that you don't want on-screen. In the next lesson, you'll learn how to use Word's help system.

The Help System

In this lesson, you'll learn how to use the Word for Windows on-line help system.

The Help Menu

Word for Windows has an extensive on-line help system that is easy to use. One way to access the help system is via the **Help** command on the main menu. Figure 3.1 shows you the commands available on the Help pull-down menu.

Figure 3.1   The Help menu.

- **Contents**   Displays the main Help table of contents.

- **Search for Help on**   Lets you search through Help for information relating to a specific keyword.

- **Index**   Calls up the main help system index.

- **Quick Preview**   Lists introductory lessons for getting started with Word.

- **Examples and Demos**   Lists the lessons available in the Word tutorial.

- **Tip of the Day**   Displays a brief, helpful tip about the Word for Windows program.

- **WordPerfect Help**   Displays help for users of the WordPerfect word processing program.

- **Technical Support**   Displays information about support that is available for Microsoft Word.

- **About Microsoft Word**   Lists information about the Word for Windows program, such as the program version number and the license number.

Some of these commands, such as Contents, Index, and Search for Help on work the same as in Program Manager, covered in the first part of this book, so we won't cover them again here. However, there are some Help features unique to Word, too.

Examples and Demos

When you select **Examples and Demos** from the **Help** menu, the screen in Figure 3.3 appears, listing many of the most common tasks that beginners need to accomplish. Click on the button next to the topic you want to see, or click on **Close** to return to Word.

Tip of the Day

As you saw in Lesson 1, a Tip of the Day appears automatically when you start Word unless you suppress it. Select **Tip of the Day** now from the **Help** menu to open its window. If you want to see a tip every time you start Word, make sure the Show Tips at Startup check box is selected. (If not, make sure it's deselected, without an X.)

To read more tips, click on the **Next Tip** button. To see an index of all the available tips, so you can search for a particular topic, click on the **More Tips** button. When you're finished, click on the **OK** button to return to Word.

Quick Preview

If you've used Word 2.0 or WordPerfect for Windows before, you may find the Quick Preview helpful. It takes you on a brief tour of Word, explains what features have changed since version 2.0, and provides some help for users switching over from WordPerfect.

After selecting Quick Preview from the Help menu, you'll see the screen shown in Figure 3.2. Click on the button next to the topic that interests you, and follow the instructions on-screen. You can return to Word by clicking on the **Return to Word** button in the bottom right corner of the screen.

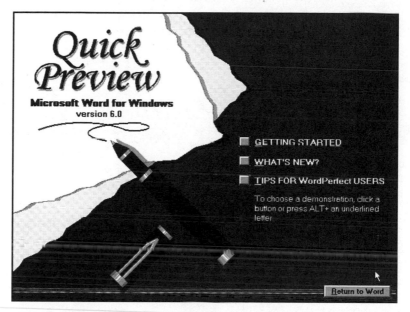

Figure 3.2   The Quick Preview takes you on a quick tour.

WordPerfect Help

One way to get general WordPerfect assistance, as you already have seen, is to select **Quick Preview** from the **Help** menu. But for more detailed help on converting your WordPerfect knowledge to Word skills, select **WordPerfect Help** from the **Help** menu instead.

A dialog box appears listing many common tasks in the left column, such as underlining and centering. When you select a task on the list, the instructions for performing the task appear in the right column.

Context-Sensitive Help

The Word for Windows help system is context-sensitive, just like Windows itself. This means that if you are selecting a menu command or entering information in a dialog box, pressing **F1** will automatically display help information on your current task. Once the Help window is displayed, you can use all of its features to access additional information. When you close the Help window, you are returned to your task right where you left off.

In this lesson, you learned how to use the Word for Windows help system. In the next lesson, you'll learn how to control the way Word displays documents on your screen.

Controlling the Screen Display

In this lesson, you'll learn how to control the Word for Windows screen display to suit your working style.

Document Display Modes

Word for Windows offers four different modes in which you can display your document.

Normal Mode

Most often, you'll probably want to work in normal mode. This is Word for Windows' default display. Figure 4.1 shows a document in normal mode. As you can see, all special formatting is visible on-screen. Different font sizes, italics, boldface, and other enhancements are displayed on the screen much as they will appear on the printed page. Certain aspects of the page layout, however, are simplified in order to speed editing. For example, headers and footers are not displayed. Normal mode is fine for most editing tasks.

Select **View Normal** to switch to normal view. In the View menu, the currently selected mode has a dot displayed next to it.

Outline Mode

Use outline mode to create outlines and to examine the structure of a document. Figure 4.2 shows the sample document in outline mode. Here you can choose to view your document headings only, hiding all subordinate text. Document headings, along with subordinate text, can quickly be promoted, demoted, or moved to a new location. In order for this to be of much use, you need to assign heading styles to the document headings, a technique you'll learn more about in Lesson 19.

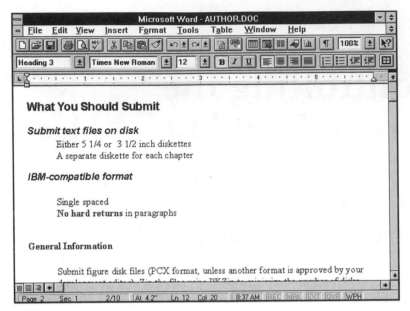

Figure 4.1   A document displayed in normal mode.

Select **View Outline** to switch to outline view.

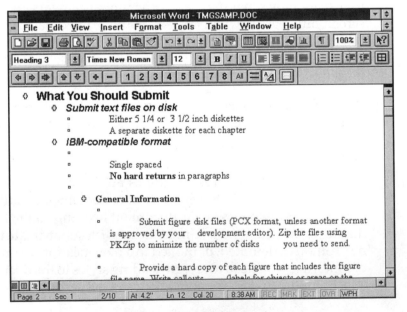

Figure 4.2   A document displayed in outline mode.

Page Layout Mode

Page layout mode displays your document exactly as it will be printed. Headers, footers, and all the details of page layout are displayed on-screen. You can perform editing in page layout mode; in fact, this mode is ideal when you are fine-tuning the details of page composition. Be aware, however, that the additional computer processing that's required makes display changes relatively slow in page layout mode, particularly when you have a complex page layout. Figure 4.3 shows the sample document in page layout mode.

Select **View Page Layout** to switch to page layout view.

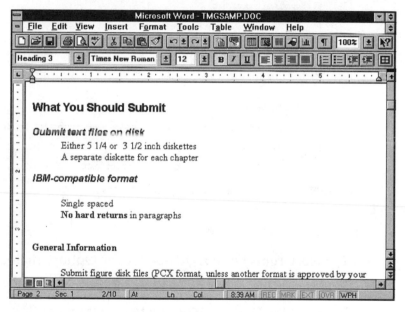

Figure 4.3   A document displayed in page layout mode.

TIP

View It First!   Use page layout mode to see what your document will look like when it is printed.

Draft Font Mode

Draft font mode is a display option that can be applied in both normal and outline views. As Figure 4.4 illustrates, a single generic font is used for screen display, and special formatting such as italics and boldface are indicated by underlining. Draft font mode provides the fastest editing and screen display, and is ideal when you are concentrating on the contents of your document more than on its appearance.

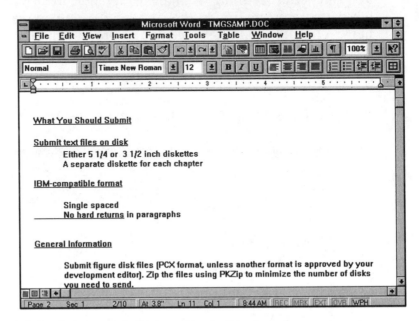

Figure 4.4   A document displayed in draft font mode.

To turn draft font mode on or off:

1. Select **Tools Options** to display the Options dialog box.

2. If necessary, click on the **View** tab to display the View options.

3. Select the **Draft Font** option to turn it on or off.

4. Select **OK**.

Full Screen Display

To see the maximum amount of text on the screen, select **View Full Screen**. In full screen mode, the title bar, menu, toolbars, status line, and all other Word elements are hidden, and the full screen is devoted to text. You can enter and edit text in this mode, and can select from the menus using the usual keyboard commands. To turn off full screen mode, select **View Full Screen** again, or click on the **Full** icon that is displayed in the lower right corner of the screen.

Ruler and Toolbar Display

The Word for Windows default is to display the Ruler, Standard toolbar, and Formatting toolbar at the top of the editing screen. At times, however, you may want to hide one or more of these items to give yourself a larger work area and a less cluttered screen. Of course, you will not have access to the editing features of the item(s) you have hidden.

To control the screen display of the Ruler, select **View** to display the View menu, and then select **Ruler** to toggle the Ruler display between on and off. To control the toolbars, select **View Toolbars** to display the Toolbars dialog box. Turn the Standard and Formatting options on or off as desired, and then select **OK**.

The Whole Picture Hide the Ruler and toolbars when you need to display the maximum amount of text but don't want to use full screen mode.

Zooming the Screen

The View Zoom command lets you control the size of your document as displayed on the screen. You can enlarge the size to facilitate reading small fonts, or decrease the size to view an entire page at one time. When you select **View Zoom**, the dialog box in Figure 4.5 is displayed.

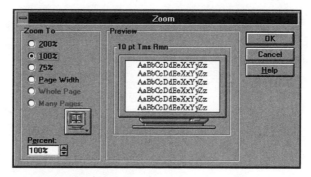

Figure 4.5   The Zoom dialog box.

In this dialog box, you have the following options. As you make selections, the Preview section of the dialog box shows you what the selected zoom setting will look like.

- Under **Zoom To**, select the desired page magnification. 200% is twice normal size, 75% is three-quarters normal size, and so on. In the Percent box, you can enter a custom magnification in the range 10–200%.

- Select **Page Width** to have Word for Windows automatically scale the display to fit the entire page width on the screen.

- Select **Whole Page** to have Word for Windows automatically scale the display to fit the entire page on the screen.

- Select **Many Pages** to display two or more pages at the same time. Click on the monitor button under the **Many Pages** option, and then drag to specify how many pages to display.

Note that the Whole Page and Many Pages options are available only if you are viewing the document in page layout mode.

In this lesson, you learned how to control the Word for Windows screen display. In the next lesson, you'll learn how to save documents.

Saving Documents

In this lesson, you'll learn how to name your document, save it to disk, and enter summary information.

Saving a Document for the First Time

When you create a new document in Word for Windows, it is stored temporarily in your computer's memory under the default name Document*n*, where *n* is a number that increases by one for each new unnamed document. The computer only "remembers" your document until you quit the program or the computer is turned off. Then, it forgets everything you told it. To save the document permanently so you can retrieve it later, you must save it to disk. This is done with the **File Save** command, or by selecting the **File Save** button on the toolbar.

When you save a document for the first time, you must assign it another name. When you select **File Save** for an unnamed document (or **File Save As** for any document), Word for Windows displays the Save As dialog box, as shown in Figure 5.1.

In the **File Name** text box, enter the name you want to assign to the document file. The name can be one to eight characters long and should be descriptive of the document's contents. Then select **OK**. Word for Windows automatically adds the .DOC extension when the file is saved.

What's an Extension?   The extension is the one- to three-letter part of a file name to the right of the period.

Current directory

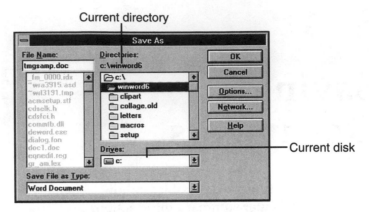

Current disk

Figure 5.1   The Save As dialog box.

What happens next depends on the setting of the Prompt for Summary Info option. To set this option, select **Tools Options**, click on the **Save** tab, and then select the **Prompt for Summary Info** box. If the option is turned off, Word immediately saves your document. If the option is turned on, Word displays the Summary Info dialog box, which is shown in Figure 5.2. This figure shows typical summary information that you might want to use. You can ignore this dialog box, or you can enter information here that will later be useful in keeping track of your documents.

- **Title**   Enter the title of the document. This is not the same as the document's file name.

- **Subject**   Enter a phrase describing the subject of the document.

- **Author**   Word automatically fills this field with the user name you entered when installing the program. You can change it if you like.

- **Keywords**   Enter one or more words related to the document contents.

- **Comments**   Enter any information you want saved with the document.

- **Statistics**   Click on the **Statistics** button to display information about the document, such as the number of words, last date edited, and so on.

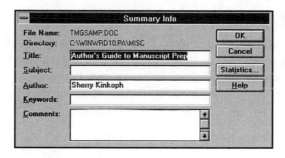

Figure 5.2 The Summary Info dialog box.

Summary Info Box Doesn't Appear? Select **Summary Info** from the **File** menu to display it.

Viewing Statistics At any time, select **File Summary Info Statistics** to view a document's statistics.

After entering any summary information, click on **OK**. Word for Windows saves the document, along with the summary information you entered, in a file with the name you specified. You are then returned to the document screen, with the newly assigned file name displayed in the title bar.

Saving a Named Document

As you work on a document, you should save it often to minimize possible data loss in the event of a power failure or other system problem. Once you have assigned a name to a document, the **File Save** command saves the current document version under its assigned name; no dialog boxes are displayed.

Don't Forget! Save your document regularly as you work on it.

Changing a Document Name

You may want to save a named document under a new name. For example, you might want to keep the old version under the original name and the revised version under a new name. To change a document name, select **File Save As**. The Save As dialog box is displayed, showing the current document name in the File Name text box. Then take the following steps:

1. Change the file name to the desired new name.

2. (Optional) Select a directory in the Directories list box to save the document in a different directory.

3. (Optional) Select a drive from the Drives drop-down box to save the document on a different disk drive.

4. Select **OK**. The document is saved under the new name.

Changing Summary Information

You can change the summary information associated with a document at any time. Select **File Summary Info**, and the Summary Info dialog box will be displayed. Make the desired changes, and select **OK**. The new information will be registered with the document the next time you save the file.

In this lesson, you learned how to save a document, change a document name, and enter document summary information. In the next lesson, you'll learn how to retrieve a document from disk.

Opening Documents

In this lesson, you'll learn how to retrieve a document from disk into Word for Windows, how to search for a specific file, and how to open documents that were created with other programs.

Opening a Word for Windows Document

You can open any document created with Word for Windows for further editing, printing, and so on. To do so, select **File Open**, or click on the **File Open** button on the toolbar. The Open dialog box will be displayed, as shown in Figure 6.1.

File template

File Name list box

Directories list box

Drives

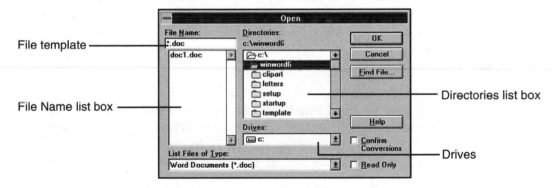

Figure 6.1   The File Open dialog box.

Opening a Document   Use **File Open** to retrieve a document that you saved earlier.

137

In the File Name text box, the current file template is listed. By default this is ***.doc**, meaning that the dialog box will list all files with the .DOC extension (the default extension for Word for Windows files). The File Name list box lists all files in the current directory that match that description.

File Template   A *file template* tells Word for Windows the types of file names to list according to their file name extensions.

- To retrieve a file, double-click on its name in the File Name list box. The file will be read from disk and displayed for editing.

- To retrieve a file from a different directory, select the desired directory from the Directories list box.

- To retrieve a file from a different disk, select the desired disk from the Drives drop-down box.

- To open a file in read-only mode, select the **Read Only** check box before retrieving the file. If you modify a read-only file, you can save it only under a new name using the **File Save As** command; you cannot save modifications under the existing name.

Finding a File

If you cannot remember the full name or location of the file that you want to retrieve, use the **Find File** button in the Open dialog box to find it by name, contents, and summary information. When you select **Find File**, Word for Windows displays the Search dialog box, shown in Figure 6.2. Make entries in this dialog box as described in these steps:

1. Pull down the File Name list to select the type of file to search for, or enter your own specification in the File Name text box. For example, to find all Word documents whose names start with C, enter the specification **C*.DOC**.

2. Pull down the Location list to specify the disk to be searched, or type in the path of the subdirectory to search.

3. (Optional) Check the **Rebuild File List** check box if you want the file list resulting from your search to replace the list from an earlier search.

4. (Optional) Check the **Include Subdirectories** check box if you want Word to search subdirectories.

5. (Optional) Select **Advanced Search**, and then make selections in the dialog box to have Word base the search on the file's summary information or its time and date of creation.

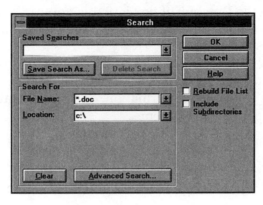

Figure 6.2 The Search dialog box.

6. Once the dialog box entries are complete, select **OK**. Word searches the specified disk/directory and displays the Find File dialog box shown in Figure 6.3.

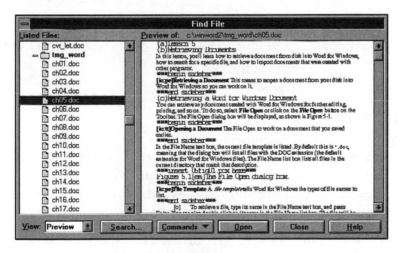

Figure 6.3 The Find File dialog box.

The Find File dialog box is split into these two areas:

- The **Listed Files** box lists the names of all the matching files, sorted by subdirectory and name. You can scroll through this list to find your missing file.

- The **Preview of** box displays the contents of the highlighted file. When the **Preview of** box is active you can scroll using the keyboard or mouse to view more of the file's contents.

The **View** pull-down list in the lower left corner lets you control what's displayed in the Preview of section. You can display the highlighted file's summary information, or a more detailed file list, instead of a preview of the file's contents.

The buttons at the bottom of the Find File dialog box offer the following options:

- Select **Open** to retrieve the highlighted file into Word.

- Select **Search** to start another search.

- Select **Close** to close the dialog box and return to Word.

- Select **Commands** for a list of other actions from which you can choose: Open Read Only, Print, Summary, Delete, Copy, and Sorting.

Memory Helper   Use the Find File window to locate a file whose name you've forgotten.

Importing Documents

You can import documents that were created with other applications, converting them to Word for Windows format. For example, you could import a document that was created with WordPerfect 6.1, retaining all of its special formatting and fonts. Word for Windows can import from a wide variety of programs. To import a file, follow these steps:

1. Select **File Open**, or click on the **File Open** button on the toolbar. The Open dialog box will be displayed.

2. Open the List Files of Type drop-down box. Select **All files (*.*)** to include files with extensions other than .DOC on the File Name list.

3. Change drives or directories as needed so that the file you want to open appears in the File Name list.

4. Select the file to import, or type its name directly into the File Name box.

5. (Optional) Select the **Confirm Conversions** check box if you want to verify the type of file being converted. Otherwise, if Word can determine what type of file it is, Word will not ask for confirmation.

6. Select **OK**. If the **Confirm Conversions** option was checked, Word for Windows asks you to confirm the type of file being imported.

7. If asked to confirm, select **OK**. The file is imported and converted to Word for Windows format.

In this lesson, you learned how to retrieve a document from disk into Word for Windows, how to search for a specific file, and how to import documents that were created with other programs. In the next lesson, you'll learn how to print your document.

Printing Your Document

In this lesson, you'll learn how to print your document.

Quick Printing

To print a Word for Windows document, you must have installed and selected the printer you are going to use in Windows. The printer must be turned on and on-line. If you need help with this, see the Windows section of this book.

Once your printer is ready, follow these steps to print the entire document:

1. Select **File Print**, or press **Ctrl+P**. The Print dialog box is displayed (see Figure 7.1).

2. Select **OK**. The document is printed.

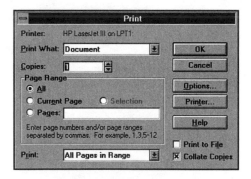

Figure 7.1   The Print dialog box.

Speedy Printing   To print one copy of the entire document without going to the Print dialog box, click on the **Print** button on the Toolbar.

Printer Not Working?   Refer to your Microsoft Windows and printer documentation for help.

Printing Part of a Document

You can print a single page of a document or a range of pages. This can be useful for checking the results of your formatting and other document components. To print specific pages, follow these steps:

1. (Optional) If you want to print a single page, position the insertion point anywhere on the page to be printed. Or if you want to print only specific paragraphs, select the paragraphs you want to print.

2. Select **File Print**, or press **Ctrl+P**. The Print dialog box is displayed.

3. Select the appropriate option button under Page Range:

   Select **All** to print every page.

   Select **Current Page** to print the page the insertion point is on.

   Select **Selection** to print the text you selected. (This option is unavailable if you did not select any text in step 1.)

   Select **Pages** to print a range of pages, and then enter the beginning and ending page numbers, separated by a dash, in the box (for example, 2–6). If you want to print specific noncontiguous pages, enter the page numbers separated by a comma (for example, 1,3).

4. Select **OK**. The selected page(s) or text is printed.

Setting Up the Page

If you don't change it, Word for Windows formats printer output for 8¹/₂-by-11-inch paper in portrait orientation. You can modify these settings if needed (if you want to print on 8 ¹/₂-by-14-inch legal paper, for example).

Orientation   Orientation refers to the way in which your text is printed on the page. *Portrait* orientation is the default and prints text parallel to the short edge of the paper. *Landscape* orientation prints text parallel to the long edge of the paper.

To change the print orientation or the paper size:

1. Select **File Page Setup**. The Page Setup dialog box is displayed.

2. Click on the **Paper Size** tab.

3. Select **Paper Size** to open the drop-down box. Word for Windows lists several common paper sizes.

4. Select the desired paper size.

5. If you select **Custom Size**, use the **Height** and **Width** boxes to specify the actual paper size.

6. Under Orientation, select **Portrait** or **Landscape**.

7. Select **OK**. The new settings will be in effect for your document and will be used the next time it is printed.

Previewing the Print Job

You can view a screen display that previews exactly what your document will look like when printed. To do so, follow these steps:

1. Select **File Print Preview**. The current page is displayed in preview mode (see Figure 7.2).

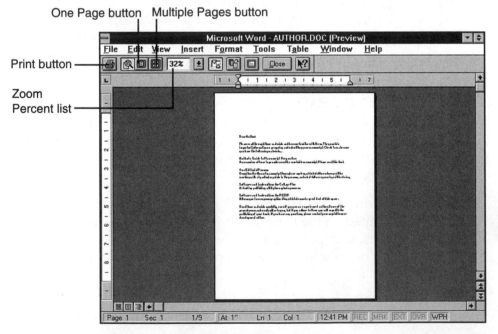

Figure 7.2 The Print Preview screen.

2. Press **PgUp** or **PgDn**, or use the scroll bar to view other pages.

3. Click on the **Multiple Pages** button, and then drag over the page icons to preview more than one page at once. Click on the **One Page** button to preview a single page.

4. Pull down the **Zoom Percent** list, and select a magnification to preview the document at different magnifications.

5. Click on the **Print** button to print the document.

6. Click on **Close** or press **Esc** to end Print Preview display.

Using Print Options

There are several printing options available that you may find useful. To use these options:

1. Select **File Print**, or press **Ctrl+P**. The Print dialog box is displayed.

2. Select **Options**. The Options dialog box (shown in Figure 7.3) is displayed.

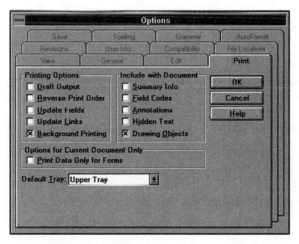

Figure 7.3   The Options dialog box.

3. Under Printing Options, select one or more of the following:

- **Draft Output**   Produces draft output that prints faster but may lack some graphics and formatting (depending on your specific printer).

- **Reverse Print Order**   Prints pages in last-to-first order. This setting produces collated output on printers that have face-up output.

- **Update Fields**   Automatically updates all document fields (except locked ones) before printing.

4. Select **OK**. You are returned to the Print dialog box.

5. Select **OK** to begin printing.

In this lesson, you learned how to print all or part of your documents. In the next lesson, you'll learn how to move and copy text.

Moving and Copying Text

In this lesson, you'll get a refresher course on moving and coping text, plus learn special ways to move and copy text in your Word document.

Selecting Text

You learned how to select text, in order to move it or copy it, back in the Windows section of this book. To summarize:

1. Click and hold down the left mouse button at the beginning of the text you want to select.

2. Drag the mouse over the text, highlighting (selecting) as you move.

3. Release the mouse button when all of the desired text is selected.

Moving and Copying Text

As you may remember from the Windows section of the book, the difference between moving and copying is that when you move text, it gets deleted from its original location and inserted at a new location. When you copy text, the original text remains in place, and you insert a duplicate of it in a new location.

When you move or copy, the text is saved temporarily to the Clipboard from which you may then paste it into the document in a new location.

- To move text, select **Edit Cut**.

- To copy text, select **Edit Copy**.

- To paste text, select **Edit Paste**.

Save Your Fingers   Copying text can save you typing. For example, copy a paragraph to a new location when you need to modify it slightly.

147

Again and Again You can paste the same text from the Clipboard more than once. The text remains there, throughout your work session, until it is replaced with new text.

Moving and Copying with the Toolbar

In addition to the standard moving and copying procedures just explained, Word provides a few moving and copying shortcuts. Here's how to use the Standard toolbar to move or copy:

1. Select the text.

2. Click on either the **Cut** or **Copy** button on the Standard toolbar (see Figure 8.1).

3. Click on the **Paste** button.

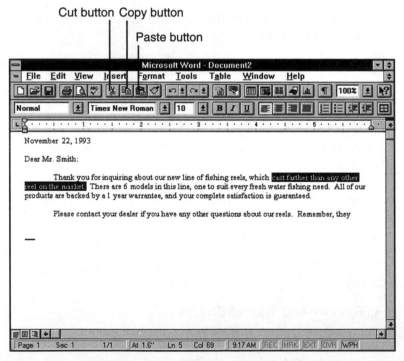

Figure 8.1 Select the text, and then select the Cut or Copy button to move or copy the text to the Clipboard.

A Copying Shortcut with the Keyboard

Here's another copying shortcut, one that uses the keyboard rather than the toolbar:

1. Select the text to be copied.

2. Point at the location where you want the text copied.

3. Press and hold **Ctrl+Shift**, and click on the right mouse button. The text is copied to the new location.

Moving Text by Dragging It

Just as you can drag icons from place to place in Windows' Program Manager, you can drag text from one location to another in your document. Follow these steps:

1. Select the text to be moved.

2. Point at the selected text, and press and hold the left mouse button.

3. Drag to the new location. As you drag, a dotted vertical line indicates where the text will be inserted.

4. Position the dotted line at the desired insertion point, and release the mouse button. The text is moved.

Copying Text That You Just Typed

You can quickly insert a copy of text that you just typed at a different document location:

1. At one document location, type the text to be copied.

2. Move the insertion point to the second location for the text.

3. Select **Edit Repeat Typing**, or press **F4**.

In this lesson, you learned how to move and copy text. In the next lesson, you'll learn how to format paragraphs.

Formatting Your Document

This lesson introduces you to the concept of *formatting*, or changing the appearance of your document, and also tells you where in the book to turn for information on specific kinds of formatting.

What Is Formatting?

The term *formatting* refers to changes you make in your document's appearance. Whenever you underline a word, set a paragraph off with italics, display a list as a table, or change the page margins, you are working with formatting.

Formatting is an important part of many documents. An attractive and well-formatted document has a definite edge in clarity and impact over another document that has the same content but is poorly formatted. Most of the remaining lessons in this book deal with formatting; this brief lesson serves as a general introduction.

How Is Formatting Applied?

There are two methods for applying most of Word's formatting commands. The difference depends on whether you want to format text that already exists in the document, or text that you are about to type:

- To format existing text, you first select the text, and then issue the formatting command. The format change affects only the selected text.

- To format new text, move the insertion point to the location where the text is to be placed, and then issue the formatting command. The format change will affect all text that you type until you turn off or change the Format command.

Where Do I Turn Next?

If it's possible, you should continue working through the book's lessons in their order. If you need to find information on a particular formatting topic right away, use Table 9.1 as a guide.

Table 9.1   Formatting Topics for Further Reading

For Information on	Turn to
Using fonts, underlining, boldface, and italics	Lesson 10
Changing the page margins and line spacing	Lesson 11
Using and setting tabs	Lesson 12
Modifying text alignment	Lesson 13
Adding page numbers, headers, and footers	Lesson 16
Creating numbered and bulleted lists	Lesson 18
Arranging text in columns	Lesson 19
Using Word's automatic formatting	Lesson 22

Formatting Characters

In this lesson, you'll learn how to apply special formatting to characters.

What Is Character Formatting?

The term *character formatting* refers to attributes that apply to individual characters in a document. Font, type size, underlining, italics, and boldface are examples of character formatting. A character format can apply to anything from a single letter to the entire document.

Using Fonts

What Is a Font?   A font is a set of letters and characters of a particular style and size.

The style of a font is denoted by a name, such as Times Roman or Courier. The size of a font is specified in terms of points (there are 72 points in an inch). As you enter text in a document, the Formatting toolbar displays the font name in the Font box and the point size in the Font Size box. For example, in Figure 10.1, Courier 12-point is the current font.

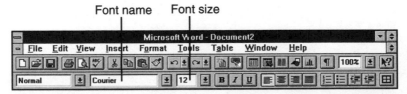

Figure 10.1   The Formatting toolbar displays the name and size of the current font.

Changing the Font or Size of Existing Text

You can change the font style and size of any portion of your document, from a single character to the entire text. The exact fonts and sizes you have available will depend on your Windows installation and on the printer you are using. To change font and size, follow these steps:

1. Select the text to change. If your selection currently contains only a single font and size, they are displayed on the Formatting toolbar. If it contains more than one font or size, the boxes on the toolbar will be blank.

2. To change the font, click on the down arrow next to the Font drop-down box on the Formatting toolbar. Click on the font name you want.

3. To change the point size, click on the down arrow next to the Font Size drop-down box on the Formatting toolbar. Click on the desired point size.

Fast Selection!   Remember that you can quickly select an entire document by pressing **Ctrl+5** (on the numeric keypad).

If you are in page layout view or in normal view with draft mode off, the screen display will immediately be updated to show the new font. In draft mode, different fonts are not displayed on-screen, but the Formatting toolbar will display the name and size of the current font.

Fast Scrolling!   In documents with many different fonts, use draft display mode to speed up screen scrolling.

Changing the Font or Size of New Text

You can change the font that will be used for new text that you type by following these steps:

1. Move the insertion point to the location where you will type the new text.

2. To change the font, click on the down arrow next to the Font drop-down box on the Formatting toolbar. Click on the font name you want.

3. To change the point size, click on the down arrow next to the Font Size drop-down box on the Formatting toolbar. Click on the desired point size.

4. Type the new text. It will appear in the newly specified font. Other text in your document will not be affected.

Bold, Underline, and Italics

The attributes boldface, italics, and underlining can be applied alone or in combination to any text in your document. These attributes are controlled by the toggle buttons marked **B**, *I*, and <u>U</u> on the Formatting toolbar (see Figure 10.2).

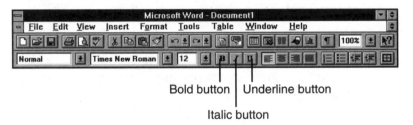

Bold button | Underline button

Italic button

Figure 10.2 The bold, italic, and underline buttons on the Formatting toolbar are toggle buttons—either on or off.

Toggle Buttons These are buttons that, when selected, turn the corresponding attribute on, if it was off, and off, if it was on.

To apply bold, italic, or underline attributes to new text that you type:

1. Move the insertion point to the location of the new text.

2. Click on the Formatting toolbar button(s) for the desired formatting.

3. Type the text.

4. To turn off the attribute, click on the button again, or press the corresponding key combination.

To apply these attributes to existing text, follow these steps:

1. Select the text.

2. Click on the Formatting toolbar button(s) for the desired formatting.

Keyboard Shortcuts Instead of clicking on the buttons on the toolbar, you can press shortcut key combinations instead. Press **Ctrl+B** for bold, **Ctrl+I** for italics, or **Ctrl+U** for underlining.

In this lesson, you learned how to format characters. In the next lesson, you'll learn how to set page margins and line spacing.

Setting Margins and Line Spacing

In this lesson, you'll learn how to set page margins and line spacing.

Setting Margins with the Ruler

The Ruler displayed across the top of the Word for Windows work area makes setting margins easy. You can work visually rather than thinking in terms of inches or centimeters. The Ruler is designed to be used with a mouse.

To set margins with the Ruler, you must be in page layout view, and the Ruler must be visible. To display the Ruler, select **Ruler** from the **View** menu. If you do not see a ruler running along the left edge of the document, you are not yet in page layout view—select **Page Layout** from the **View** menu.

Margins The left and right margins are the distances, respectively, between the text and the left and right edges of the page. The top and bottom margins are the distances between the text and the top or bottom edges of the page.

Margin settings affect the entire document. The white bar on the Ruler shows the current margin settings (see Figure 11.1). To change a margin, you drag the end of the white bar. Follow these steps:

1. On either the vertical or horizontal Ruler, point at the end of the white bar on the Ruler. The mouse pointer will change into a two-headed arrow.

2. Drag the end of the white bar to a new position. Do not drag the square or the triangles on the Ruler; these are indent markers, and change the indentation for single paragraphs.

Drag here to change the right margin; be careful not to drag the triangles or square.

Mouse pointer changes to double-headed arrow.

Drag here to change the top margin

Dotted line appears as you drag the margin.

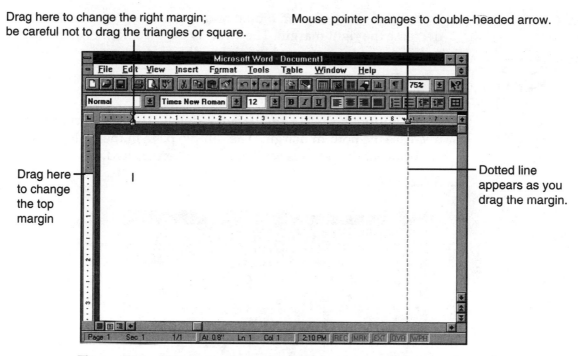

Figure 11.1 The Ruler displays a white bar to show the current margin settings.

Changing Margins To change the margins for only a portion of a document, change the left and/or right indent (covered in Lesson 12).

Setting Margins with a Dialog Box

If you prefer to not use the Ruler, or want to enter specific values for the margins, you can set the margins using the Page Setup dialog box. Using this method gives you more precise control over the margin settings.

1. Select **File Page Setup**, and then click on **Margins** tab to display the Margin options (see Figure 11.2).

2. In the **Left** box, click on the up or down arrows to increase or decrease the left margin. The numerical value is the distance between the left edge of the page and the left edge of text. The sample page in the dialog box shows what the settings will look like when printed.

3. In the **Right** box, click on the up or down arrows to increase or decrease the right margin. The value is the distance between the right edge of the page and the right edge of text.

4. In the **Top** box, click on the up or down arrows to increase or decrease the top margin.

5. In the **Bottom** box, click on the up or down arrows to increase or decrease the bottom margin. The sample page in the dialog box shows what the settings will look like when printed.

6. Select **OK**.

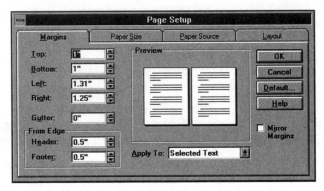

Figure 11.2 The Page Setup dialog box with the Margins tab displayed.

Header and Footer Margins Top and bottom margins do not affect the position of headers and footers.

Changing Line Spacing

Word offers a variety of line spacing options. Unlike changes to margins, changes to line spacing do not affect the entire document at once. They affect only the paragraph in which the insertion point lies, or text that is selected when the line spacing change command is issued.

Follow these steps to change line spacing:

1. Position the insertion point in the paragraph for which you want to change the line spacing, or select all the paragraphs that you want to affect.

2. Select **Format Paragraph** to display the Paragraph dialog box. If necessary, click on the **Indents and Spacing** tab (see Figure 11.3).

3. Pull down the Line Spacing list, and select the desired spacing. The Single, 1.5 Lines, and Double settings are self-explanatory. The other settings are:

   Exactly Space between lines will be exactly the value, in points, that you enter in the At box.

   At Least Space between lines will be at least the value you enter in the At box; Word will increase the spacing as needed if the line contains large characters.

   Multiple Sets spacing for more than one line. In the At box, enter the spacing you want, making sure it accommodates the largest letters.

4. After you have made your line spacing selections, click on **OK** to close the dialog box.

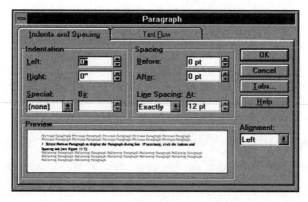

Figure 11.3 The Paragraph dialog box with the Indents and Spacing options displayed.

In this lesson, you learned how to set page margins and line spacing. The next lesson shows you how to use and set tabs.

Setting Tabs

In this lesson, you'll learn how to use and set tabs.

What Are Tabs?

Tabs provide a way for you to control the indentation and vertical alignment of text in your document. When you press the **Tab** key, Word inserts a tab in the document, which moves the cursor (and any text to the right of it) to the next tab stop. By default, Word has tab stops at half-inch intervals across the width of the page. You can modify the location of tab stops, and can also control the way that text aligns at a tab stop.

Types of Tab Stops

There are four types of tab stops, each of which aligns text differently:

- **Left-aligned**   The left edge of text aligns at the tab stop. Word's default tab stops are all left-aligned.

- **Right-aligned**   The right edge of text aligns at the tab stop.

- **Center-aligned**   Text is centered at the tab stop.

- **Decimal-aligned**   The Decimal point (period) is aligned at the tab stop (used for aligning columns of numbers).

Figure 12.1 illustrates the effects of the four tab alignment options. This figure also shows the four different symbols that are displayed on the Ruler to indicate the position of tab stops.

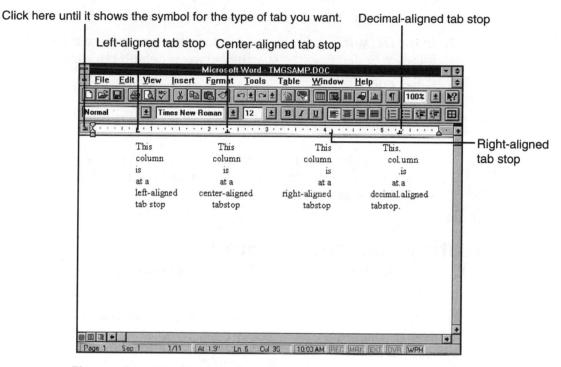

Figure 12.1   The four tab stop alignment options.

Default Tab Stops

If you don't set any custom tab stops in a document, Word uses the default ones. When you set custom tab stops in a document, however, the default tab stops disable themselves so they won't get in the way of the ones you set. For example, if you set tab stops at 1-inch and 3-inch, all the default tab stops up to the 3-inch mark disappear. But if you don't set any more past the 3-inch mark, the default tab stops will still be present at 3 1/2-inch, 4-inch, 4 1/2-inch, and so on.

Changing the Default Tab Stops

You cannot delete the default tab stops, but you can change the spacing between them. For instance, you can set them to occur every 1-inch instead of every 1/2-inch. Here are the steps to follow:

1. Select **Format Tabs** to display the Tabs dialog box.

2. In the **Default Tab Stops** box, click on the up or down arrow to increase or decrease the spacing between default tab stops.

3. Select **OK**.

The default tab stop spacing affects the entire document.

Getting Around It To effectively "delete" the default tab stops, set the spacing between them to a value larger than the page width.

Creating Custom Tab Stops

If the default tab stops are not suited to your needs, you can add custom tab stops.

1. Select the paragraphs for which you want to set custom tabs. If no text is selected, the new tabs will affect text that you type at the insertion point.

2. Click on the tab symbol at the left end of the Ruler until it displays the symbol for the type of tab you want to insert (see Figure 12.1).

3. Point at the approximate tab stop location on the Ruler, and press and hold the left mouse button. A dashed vertical line will extend down through the document showing the tab stop position relative to your text.

4. Move the mouse to the left or right until the tab stop is at the desired location.

5. Release the mouse button. A tab stop marker appears on the Ruler.

Where's the Ruler? If your Ruler is not displayed, select **View Ruler**.

When you add a custom tab stop, all of the default tab stops to the left are temporarily hidden. This ensures that the custom tab stop will take precedence.

Moving and Deleting Custom Tab Stops

Follow these steps to move a custom tab stop to a new position:

1. Point at the tab stop symbol on the Ruler.

2. Press and hold the left mouse button.

3. Drag the tab stop to the new position.

4. Release the mouse button.

To delete a custom tab stop, follow the same steps, except in step 3 drag the tab stop symbol off the Ruler.

Using Tab Leader Characters

A *tab leader character* is a character that is displayed in the blank space to the left of text that has been positioned using a tab. Typically, periods or hyphens are used for leader characters to create effects like that shown in Figure 12.2. This menu was created by setting a decimal-aligned tab stop at the 5.25" position with a dot leader character.

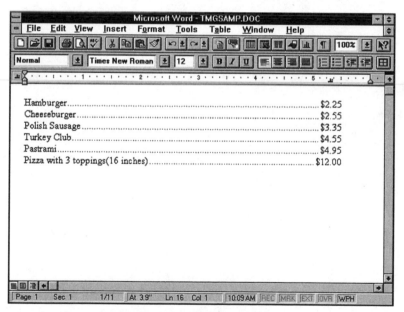

Figure 12.2   Using tabs with a leader character.

To change the leader character for a custom tab stop:

1. Point at the tab stop symbol on the Ruler, and double-click. Word will display the Tabs dialog box.

2. Under Leader, select the desired leader character.

3. Select **OK**.

In this lesson, you learned how to set and use tabs. The next lesson shows you how to align text.

Aligning Text

In this lesson, you'll learn how to use indents and justification in your documents. These features help to further customize the overall flow and appearance of your text.

Indenting Paragraphs

Word for Windows allows you to individually set the *indent* for the left edge, the right edge, and the first line of a paragraph.

What Is Indentation? Indentation refers to the distance between the edges of a paragraph and the page margins.

Setting Indents with the Ruler

The easiest way to set indents is with the Ruler and the mouse. (If the Ruler is not displayed, select **View Ruler**.) The Ruler is calibrated in inches from the left margin. The Ruler elements that you use to set indents are illustrated in Figure 13.1.

Figure 13.1 The Ruler can be used to set indentation.

To change indent positions, drag the indent symbols to the desired positions:

- To indent the first line of a paragraph, drag the **First Line** indent symbol.

- To indent all lines of a paragraph except the first one, drag the **Other Lines** indent symbol (this is called a hanging indent).

- To indent all lines of a paragraph, drag the **All Lines** indent symbol.

- To indent the right edge of the paragraph, drag the **Right Indent** symbol.

If you select one or more paragraphs first, the new indents will apply only to the selected paragraphs. If you don't select any paragraphs, the new indents will apply only to the paragraph in which the insertion point lies, and to new paragraphs typed at that location.

Quick Tab   To quickly increase or decrease the left indent for the current paragraph or selected paragraphs, click on the **Indent** button or the **Outdent** button on the Formatting toolbar.

Displaying the Formatting Toolbar   If the Formatting toolbar is not displayed, select **View Toolbars**, and then select the Formatting option.

Setting Indents with a Dialog Box

If you prefer, you can set indents using a dialog box:

1. Select **Format Paragraph** to display the Paragraph dialog box, and then click on the **Indents and Spacing** tab, if necessary, to display the indents and spacing options (Figure 13.2).

2. Under Indentation, click on the up and down arrows in the **Left** or **Right** boxes to increase or decrease the indentation settings. For a first line or a hanging indent, select the indent type in the **Special** pull-down list, and then enter the indent amount in the **By** box.

The sample page in the dialog box illustrates how the current settings will appear.

3. Select **OK**. The new settings are applied to any selected paragraphs or to new text.

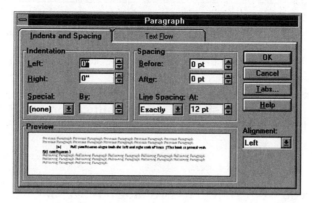

Figure 13.2 Setting Indents in the Paragraph dialog box.

Justifying Text

Word for Windows offers four justification options:

- **Left justification**   Aligns the left ends of lines.

- **Right justification**   Aligns the right ends of lines.

- **Full justification**   Aligns both the left and right ends of lines. (This book is printed with full justification.)

- **Center justification**   Centers lines between the left and right margins.

To change the justification for one or more paragraphs, first select the paragraphs to change. Then click on one of the justification buttons on the Formatting toolbar, as shown in Figure 13.3.

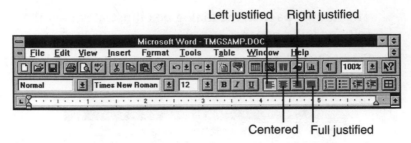

Figure 13.3 Click on these buttons to set text justification.

What Is Justification? Justification refers to the way in which lines on the page are aligned with the lines above and below them.

If you would rather use a dialog box to change justification, select the paragraphs, and then:

1. Select **Format Paragraph** to display the Paragraph dialog box.

2. Open the **Alignment** drop-down box.

3. Select the desired alignment.

4. Select **OK**.

Changing Justification If you change justification without selecting any paragraphs, the new justification will apply only to any new paragraphs that you type.

In this lesson, you learned how to set indentation and justification in your documents. In the next lesson, you'll learn how to search for and replace text.

Searching for and Replacing Text

In this lesson, you'll learn how to search for specific text in your document, and how to automatically replace each occurrence of it with new text.

Searching for Text

You can have Word for Windows search through your document to find occurrences of specific text. The default is to search the entire document. If there is text selected, the search will be limited to the selection.

To search for text, follow these steps:

1. Select **Edit Find**. The Find dialog box will be displayed, as shown in Figure 14.1.

2. In the **Find What** text box, enter the text to find. This is the search template.

Search Template   The search template is a model of the text you want to find.

3. (Optional) Select **Find Whole Words Only** to match whole words only. With this option off, a search template of "light" would match light, lightning, and so on. With this option on, it would match only light.

169

Figure 14.1   The Edit Find dialog box.

4. (Optional) Select **Match Case** to require an exact match for upper- and lowercase letters. If this option is not selected, Word searches for text of either case.

5. In the Search box, select **All** to have Word search the entire document. You can also select **Down** to have Word for Windows search from the insertion point to the end of the document, or from the beginning of the selected text to the end. Select **Up** to search in the opposite direction.

6. Select **Find Next**. Word for Windows looks through the document for text that matches the search template. If it finds matching text, it highlights it in the text and stops with the Find dialog box still displayed.

7. You now can do one of two things:

   - Select **Find Next** to continue the search for another instance of the template.

   - Press **Esc** to close the dialog box and return to the document. The found text remains selected.

If, after searching only part of the document, Word for Windows reaches the start of the document (for an upward search) or the end of the document (for a downward search), you are given the option of continuing the search from the other end of the document. Once the entire document has been searched, a message to that effect is displayed.

Finding and Replacing Text

The Edit Replace command is used to search for instances of text, and to replace them with new text. The Edit Replace dialog box is shown in Figure 14.2.

Figure 14.2 The Replace dialog box.

Make entries in this dialog box as follows:

1. In the **Find What** text box, enter the target text that is to be replaced.

2. In the **Replace With** text box, enter the replacement text.

3. If desired, select the **Find Whole Words Only**, **Match Case**, and **Search** options, as explained earlier in this lesson.

4. Select **Replace All** to have Word for Windows go through the entire document, replacing all instances of the target text with the replacement text. You can also select **Find Next** to highlight the first instance of the target text.

Deleting Text To delete the target text, leave the **Replace With** box blank.

If you selected **Find Next**, you now have three options:

- Select **Replace** to replace the highlighted text with the replacement text and then find the next instance of the target text.

- Select **Find Next** to leave the highlighted text unchanged and then find the next instance of the target text.

- Select **Replace All** to find and replace all remaining instances of the target text.

Saving Time To save typing, use abbreviations for long words and phrases, and then later use the Replace feature to change them to final form.

Recovery! If you make a mistake replacing text, you can recover with the **Edit Undo Replace** command. For this to work, you must use the Undo command immediately after the mistake (before you perform any other action).

In this lesson, you learned how to search for and optionally replace text. In the next lesson, you'll learn how to use Word for Windows templates.

Using Templates and Wizards

In this lesson, you'll learn how to use and create templates.

What Is a Template?

You may not be aware of it, but every Word for Windows document is based on a *template*. A template is a model, or pattern, that contains the features used for a specific type of document. A template can contain boilerplate text, graphics, and formatting. It can also contain styles, glossary entries, and macros (all of which are covered in later lessons). Any document that is based upon a given template automatically contains all the elements of that template.

Recycle It! Word for Windows contains some templates for your use or modification, or you can create your own from scratch. Speed up your work by creating a specialized template for document types that you use frequently.

For example, let's say you write a lot of business letters. You could create a business letter template that contains your company's name and address, logo, a salutation, and a closing. Every time you need to write a business letter, you create a new document based on the template. Such a template is shown in Figure 15.1.

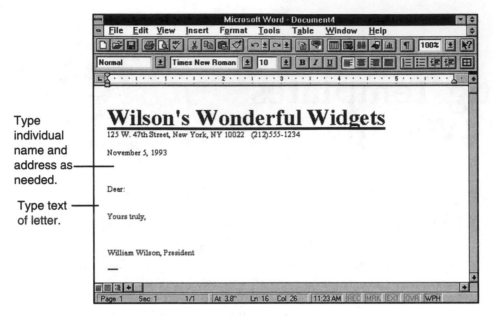

Type individual name and address as needed.

Type text of letter.

Figure 15.1 A business letter template.

By default, Word for Windows bases new documents on the NOR-MAL template, which is supplied with your Word for Windows package. This is a bare-bones template that contains only a few basic styles. Other Word templates are suitable for various business and personal uses. Templates are stored with a .DOT extension in the Word directory.

Using a Template

When you create a new document with the **New** button on the toolbar, a new document based on the NORMAL template opens. When you start a new document with the **File New** command, however, you have an opportunity to select which template to base your document upon.

When you installed Word, several templates were installed with it (unless you chose through the installation program not to install them). The templates that come with Word include several letter and memo variations as well as templates for resumes and reports. To use a template:

1. Select **File New**. The New dialog box is displayed (Figure 15.2).

2. Under Template, select the name of the template you want to use.

3. Select **OK**. The new document is created based on the selected template.

Figure 15.2 The New dialog box lists available templates.

Template Confusion? If you're not sure which template to use, select **NORMAL**.

Once the document is created you can modify any aspect of it, including portions that originated in the template.

Make It Quick! To quickly create a new document based on the NORMAL template, click on the **New Document** button on the Standard toolbar.

Creating a New Template

You can create new templates to suit your specific word processing needs. To create a new template:

1. Select **File New**. The New dialog box is displayed.

2. Under New, select the **Template** option.

3. Under Template, be sure that **NORMAL** is selected.

4. Select **OK**. A blank document editing screen appears with a default name, such as **TEMPLATE1**.

5. Enter the boilerplate text and other items that you want to be part of the template.

6. Select **File Save**. The Save As dialog box is displayed.

7. In the File Name text box, enter a name of one to eight characters for the template.

8. Select **OK**. The template is saved under the specified name, with the .DOT extension added. The new template is now available for use each time you start a new document.

Boilerplate   This is text that appears the same in all documents of a certain type.

Modifying an Existing Template

You can retrieve any existing template from disk and modify it. You can then save it under the original name or a new name. To modify a template:

1. Select **File Open**. The Open dialog box is displayed.

2. Open the List Files of Type drop-down box, and select **Document Templates**.

3. If necessary, select a different drive and directory in the Drives and Directories lists (templates are usually stored in the C:\WINWORD\TEMPLATE directory).

4. Under File Name, select the template that you want to modify.

5. Make the desired modifications and additions to the template.

6. To save the modified template under its original name, select **File Save**. To save the modified template under a new name, select **File Save As**, and enter a new template name.

If you modify the text in a template, those changes will not be reflected in documents that were based on the template as it was before the changes were made.

In this lesson, you learned about Word for Windows templates. In the next lesson, you'll learn how to create and use page numbers, headers, and footers.

Page Numbers, Headers, and Footers

In this lesson, you'll learn how to add page numbers, headers, and footers to your documents.

Adding Page Numbers

Many documents, particularly long ones, benefit from having numbered pages. Word for Windows offers complete flexibility in the placement and format of page numbers. To add page numbers to your document:

1. Select **Insert Page Numbers**. The Page Numbers dialog box is displayed, as shown in Figure 16.1.

Figure 16.1 The Page Numbers dialog box.

2. Pull down the Position list, and select the desired position on the page: **Top of Page** (Header) or **Bottom of Page** (Footer).

3. Pull down the Alignment list, and select **Left**, **Center**, or **Right**. You can also select **Inside** or **Outside** if you're printing two-sided pages and want the page numbers positioned near (Inside) or away from (Outside) the binding.

4. The default number format is Arabic numerals (1, 2, 3, and so on). To select a different format (for example, Roman: i, ii, iii), select **Format**, and select the desired format.

5. Select **OK**.

When you add a page number using the above procedure, Word for Windows makes your selection part of the document's header or footer. Headers and footers are explained next.

What Are Headers and Footers?

A *header* or *footer* is text that is printed at the top (a header) or bottom (a footer) of every page of a document. A header or footer can be as simple as the page number, or it can contain chapter titles, authors' names, or any other information you desire. Word for Windows offers several header/footer options:

- The same header/footer on every page of the document.

- One header/footer on the first page of the document and a different header/footer on all other pages.

- One header/footer on odd-numbered pages and a different header/footer on even-numbered pages.

Headers and Footers   The header is at the top of the page, and the footer is at the bottom.

Adding or Editing a Header or Footer

To add a header or footer to your document, or to edit an existing header or footer, follow these steps:

1. Select **View Header and Footer**. Word displays the current page's header, enclosed by a nonprinting dashed line (Figure 16.2). Regular document text is dimmed, and the Header and Footer toolbar is displayed. On the toolbar, click on the **Switch** button to switch between the header and footer.

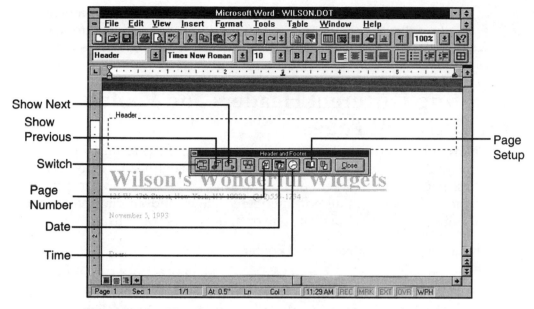

Show Next

Show Previous

Switch

Page Number

Date

Time

Page Setup

Figure 16.2 The Header and Footer toolbar is displayed when you select View Header and Footer.

2. Enter the header or footer text and formatting using the regular Word editing techniques.

3. If you want the date, time, or page number inserted, click on the appropriate button on the toolbar.

4. Click on the **Show Next** and **Show Previous** buttons on the Header and Footer toolbar to switch between the various sections. As you edit, each header or footer will be labeled (for example, **First Page Header**, **Odd Page Footer**, and so on).

5. When you are finished, click on the **Close** button on the toolbar to return to the document.

TIP

Deleting a Header or Footer   To delete a header or footer, follow the previous steps for editing the header or footer. Select all of the text in the header or footer, and press **Del**.

Creating Different Headers and Footers for Different Pages

Normally, Word displays the same header and footer on all pages of a document. However, you can tell Word to print one header or footer on the first page and a different one on all other pages. Or you can print one header or footer on all odd-numbered pages and another on all even-numbered pages. To activate one or both of these options:

1. Select **View Header and Footer**.

2. Click on the **Page Setup** button on the Header and Footer toolbar. Word will display the Page Setup dialog box. Click on the **Layout** tab, if necessary, to display the page layout options (Figure 16.3).

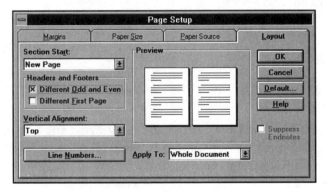

Figure 16.3   The Page Setup dialog box.

3. In the Headers and Footers section of the dialog box, turn on the **Different Odd and Even** option and/or the **Different First Page** option.

4. Select **OK** to close the Page Setup dialog box.

In this lesson, you learned how to add page numbers, headers, and footers to a document. The next lesson shows you how to proof and improve your document using the Speller and Thesaurus features.

Proofing Your Document

In this lesson, you'll learn to use Word for Windows Speller and Thesaurus utilities to help proof your document.

Using the Spelling Checker

The spelling checker lets you verify and correct the spelling of words in your document. Word for Windows checks words against a standard dictionary and lets you know when it encounters an unknown word. You then can ignore it, change it, or add it to a *supplemental dictionary* (a list of nonstandard words you have designated the spelling checker to consider correct).

To check spelling in a portion of your document, select the text to check. To check the entire document, first move the insertion point to the start of the document by pressing **Ctrl+Home**. Then:

1. Click on the **Spelling** button on the Standard toolbar. The spelling check begins. If a word is found in the document that is not in the dictionary, it is highlighted in the text and the Spelling dialog box is displayed (see Figure 17.1).

Figure 17.1 The Spelling dialog box.

2. In the Spelling dialog box, the **Not in Dictionary** box displays the word that was not found in the dictionary. If the spelling checker has found any likely replacements, they are listed in the **Suggestions** list box. In the dialog box, you have the following options:

- To ignore the highlighted word and continue, select **Ignore**.

- To ignore the highlighted word and any other instances of it in the document, select **Ignore All**.

- To change the highlighted word, type the new spelling in the Change To box, or highlight the desired replacement word in the Suggestions list box. Then select **Change** (to change the current instance of the word) or **Change All** (to change all instances of this word in the document).

- To add the word to the dictionary, select **Add**.

3. The spelling checker proceeds to check the rest of the document. When it is finished checking, it displays a message to that effect. To cancel spell checking at any time, select **Cancel** in the Spelling dialog box.

TIP

Fast Check! To check the spelling of a single word, double-click on the word to select it, and then click on the **Spelling** button on the toolbar, or press **F7**.

Using the Thesaurus

A thesaurus provides you with synonyms (words with similar meaning) and antonyms (words with opposite meaning) for words in your document. Using the thesaurus can help you avoid repetition in your writing (and can also improve your vocabulary). To use the Thesaurus:

1. Place the insertion point on the word you want to check.

2. Select **Tools Thesaurus**, or press **Shift+F7**. The Thesaurus dialog box opens (Figure 17.2). This dialog box has several components.

- **Looked Up** Displays the word of interest.

- **Meanings box** Lists alternative meanings for the word. If the word was not found, Word displays an Alphabetical List box instead; this list contains a list of words with spellings similar to the selected word.

- If the Thesaurus found one or more meanings for the word, the dialog box displays the **Replace with Synonym** list showing synonyms for the currently highlighted meaning of the word. If meanings were not found, the dialog box displays a **Replace with Related Word** list.

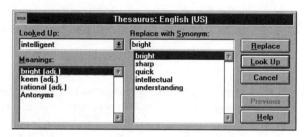

Figure 17.2 The Thesaurus dialog box.

3. While the Thesaurus dialog box is displayed, there are several actions you can take:

   - To find synonyms for the highlighted word in the Replace with Synonym list or the Replace with Related Words list (depending on which one is displayed), select **Look Up**.

   - To find synonyms for a word in the Meanings list, select the word, and then select **Look Up**.

   - For some words, the thesaurus will display the term **Antonyms** in the Meanings list. To display antonyms for the selected word, highlight the term **Antonyms**, and then select **Look Up**.

4. To replace the word in the document with the word that is highlighted in the Replace with Synonym list or the Replace with Related Word list, select **Replace**.

5. To close the thesaurus without making any changes to the document, select **Cancel**.

TIP

Prevent Repetition   Use the Thesaurus to avoid repeating words in your document.

In this lesson, you learned how to use the Speller and Thesaurus to proof your document. The next lesson shows you how to create numbered and bulleted lists.

Creating Numbered and Bulleted Lists

In this lesson, you'll learn how to create numbered and bulleted lists in your document.

Why Use Numbered and Bulleted Lists?

Numbered and bulleted lists are useful formatting tools for setting off lists of information in a document; you've seen plenty of both in this book! Word for Windows can create these elements automatically. Use bulleted lists for items of information that are related, but are not in any particular order. Use numbered lists for items that are in a specific order. Figure 18.1 shows examples of numbered and bulleted lists.

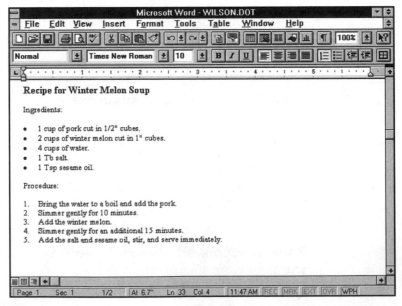

Figure 18.1 Word can automatically create numbered and bulleted lists.

When you create a list, each paragraph is considered a separate list item and receives its own number or bullet.

Creating a Numbered or Bulleted List

To create a numbered or bulleted list from existing text, follow these steps:

1. Select the paragraphs that you want in the list.

2. Select **Format Bullets and Numbering** to display the Bullets and Numbering dialog box.

3. Depending on the type of list you want, click on the **Bulleted** tab or the **Numbered** tab. Figure 18.2 shows the Numbered style options, and Figure 18.3 shows the Bulleted style options.

4. Click on the bulleting or numbering option that you want.

5. Select **OK**.

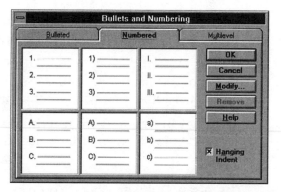

Figure 18.2 List numbering style options displayed in the Bullets and Numbering dialog box.

To create a numbered or bulleted list as you type:

1. Move the insertion point to the location for the list. Press **Enter**, if necessary, to start a new paragraph.

2. Select **Format Bullets and Numbering** to display the Bullets and Numbering dialog box.

3. Depending on the type of list you want, click on the **Bulleted** tab or the **Numbered** tab.

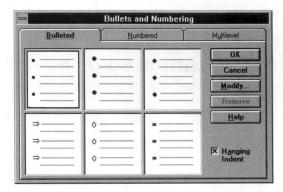

Figure 18.3 List bulleting style options displayed in the Bullets and Numbering dialog box.

4. Click on the bulleting or numbering style that you want.

5. Select **OK**.

6. Type in the list elements, pressing **Enter** at the end of each paragraph. Each paragraph will be automatically numbered or bulleted as it is added.

7. At the end of the last paragraph, press **Enter**. Word will insert an extra, empty list item that will be removed in the next step.

8. Select **Format Bullets and Numbering** to display the Bullets and Numbering dialog box, and then select **Remove**.

There's a Quicker Way You can create a numbered or bulleted list quickly, in the default style, by highlighting the paragraphs and clicking on the **Numbering** button or **Bullets** on the Standard toolbar.

Undoing a Numbered or Bulleted List

Follow these steps to remove bullets or numbers from a list:

1. Select the paragraphs from which you want to remove bullets or numbering. This can be the entire list or just part of it.

2. Select **Format Bullets and Numbering** to display the Bullets and Numbering dialog box.

3. Select **Remove**.

Adding Items to Numbered and Bulleted Lists

You can add new items to a numbered or bulleted list by following these steps:

1. Move the insertion point to the location in the list where you want the new item.

2. Press **Enter** to start a new paragraph. Word automatically inserts a new bullet or number and renumbers the list items as needed.

3. Enter the new text.

4. Repeat as many times as needed.

This lesson showed you how to use numbered and bulleted lists. In the next lesson, you'll learn how to arrange text in columns.

Arranging Text in Columns

In this lesson, you'll learn how to use columns in your documents.

Why Use Columns?

Columns are commonly used in newsletters, brochures, and similar documents. The shorter lines of text provided by columns are easier to read, and also provide greater flexibility in formatting a document with graphics, tables, and so on. Word for Windows makes it easy to use columns in your documents. Figure 19.1 shows a document formatted with three columns.

Figure 19.1   A document formatted with three columns.

Note that the Word for Windows columns feature creates *newspaper* style columns, in which the text flows to the bottom of one column and then continues at the top of the next column on the page. For side-by-side paragraphs, such as you would need in a resume or a script, use Word's Table feature, covered in Lesson 23.

Creating Columns

Word for Windows has four predefined column layouts:

- Two equal width columns

- Three equal width columns

- Two unequal width columns with the wider column on the left

- Two unequal width columns with the wider column on the right

You can apply any of these column formats to all or part of a document, to selected text or from the insertion point onward. Here are the steps to follow:

1. If you want only a part of the document in columns, select the text that you want in columns, or move the insertion point to the location where you want columns to begin.

2. Select **Format Columns** to display the Columns dialog box (Figure 19.2).

3. Under Presets, click on the column format that you want.

4. Pull down the Apply To list, and specify the extent to which the columns should apply.

5. Turn on the **Line Between** option to display a vertical line between columns.

6. Select **OK**.

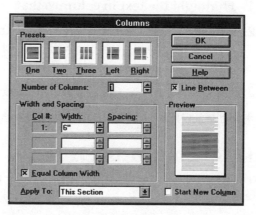

Figure 19.2   The Columns dialog box.

Toolbar Shortcut To display selected text or the entire document in one to six equal width columns, click on the **Columns** button on the Standard toolbar, and then drag over the desired number of columns.

If none of the Preset column types suit your needs, you can select your own column setups manually in the Columns dialog box. Change the Number of Columns to the number of columns desired, up to 12. Change the width of each column in the Width and Spacing section of the dialog box.

Pinstriped columns You can "pinstripe" your document by making a vertical line appear between the columns. Simply select the **Line Between** check box.

Screen Display of Columns

To view columns on-screen while you are editing, you must be working in page layout mode. In normal mode, Word displays only a single column at a time. To switch to page layout mode, select view page layout.

Modifying Columns

Here are the steps to follow to modify existing columns:

1. Highlight the text in columns that you want to modify.

2. Select **Format Columns** to display the Columns dialog box. The options in the dialog box will reflect the current settings for the selected columns.

3. Make changes to the column settings as desired.

4. Select **OK**.

Turning Columns Off

To convert multiple-column text back to normal one-column text, follow these steps:

1. Select the text that you want to change from multiple to a single column.

2. Select **Format Columns** to display the Columns dialog box.

3. Under Presets, select the **One style** option.

4. Select **OK**.

This lesson showed you how to arrange text in columns. The next lesson shows you how to use styles.

Using Styles

In this lesson, you'll learn how to use styles in your documents.

Understanding Styles

A style is a collection of formatting specifications that has been assigned a name and saved. You can quickly apply a style to any text in any Word for Windows document. Applying a style is a lot faster than manually applying each individual formatting element, and has the added advantage of assuring consistency. If you later modify a style's formatting, all paragraphs in the document to which that style has been assigned will automatically change to reflect the new definition.

What Is a Style?   A *style* is a named grouping of paragraph and character formatting that can be reused.

Word has two types of styles:

- *Paragraph* styles apply to entire paragraphs, and can include all aspects of formatting that affect a paragraph's appearance: font, line spacing, indents, tab stops, borders, and so on.

- *Character* styles apply to any text, and can include any formatting that applies to individual characters: font name and size, underlining, boldface, and so on—in other words, any of the formats that are assigned via the Font command on the Format menu.

Word for Windows comes with several predefined paragraph and character styles. You can use these styles as they are, or you can modify them to suit your needs and create your own new styles. These topics are covered in this lesson and the next one.

Viewing Style Names

The Style box at the left end of the Formatting toolbar displays the current style name. If there is text selected or if the insertion point is in text that has a character style applied, the Style box displays the character style name. Otherwise, it displays the paragraph style of the current paragraph.

Default Style   Every paragraph in a Word document has a paragraph style applied to it; the default is Word's pre-defined Normal style.

Word for Windows can also display the name of the paragraph style assigned to each paragraph in your document. This is shown in Figure 20.1. Style names can be displayed only in normal or outline view.

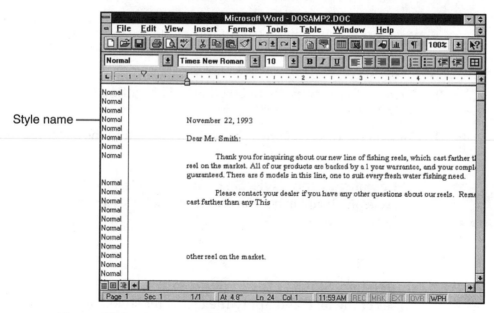

Figure 20.1   A screen with paragraph style names displayed.

To display the style name area:

1. Select **Tools Options**. Then, if necessary, click on the **View** tab to display the view options.

2. In the Window section, find the **Style Area Width** box. Click on the up arrow to set a positive width for the style name area. A setting of 0.5" is good for most situations. To hide the style name area, enter a width of 0.

3. Select **OK**. The screen now displays paragraph style names to the left of the text.

> **TIP**
>
> **Use Your Mouse**   While the Style Name Area is displayed, you can point at its right border with the mouse and drag it to a new width.

Assigning a Style

To assign a style to text:

1. To assign a paragraph style to multiple paragraphs, select the paragraphs. For a single paragraph, place the insertion point anywhere inside the paragraph. To assign a character style, select the text.

2. Open the Style drop-down box on the Formatting toolbar. The box lists all available styles.

3. Click on the desired style. The style is applied to the specified text.

> **TIP**
>
> **Looking at the Style Box**   In the Style box, paragraph styles are listed in boldface, and character styles are listed in normal text.

> **TIP**
>
> **Deleting Styles**   To remove a character style from text, select the text, and apply the character style **Default Paragraph Font**.

In this lesson, you learned how to use paragraph and character styles to format your document. The next lesson shows you how to create your own styles.

Creating Your Own Styles

In this lesson, you'll learn how to create your own styles and how to modify existing styles.

Creating a New Style

In the previous lesson, you learned how useful styles can be for formatting your documents. You also learned the difference between paragraph styles (which apply to entire paragraphs) and character styles (which apply to any section of text). You can use Word's predefined styles, or you can create your own.

Follow these steps to create a new paragraph style:

1. Find a paragraph to which you want the new style applied.

2. Format the paragraph in the new style that you want to apply to other paragraphs later on.

3. With the insertion point anywhere in the paragraph, click on the Style box.

4. Enter the new style name, and press **Enter**.

In step 4, be sure not to enter the name of an existing style. If you do, that style's formatting will be applied to the paragraph and the formatting changes that you made will be lost. (If you do this accidentally, you can recover the formatting by issuing the **Edit Undo** command immediately.)

Here's how to create a new character style:

1. Select **Format Style** to display the Style dialog box.

2. In the dialog box select **New**. The New Style dialog box is displayed (Figure 21.1).

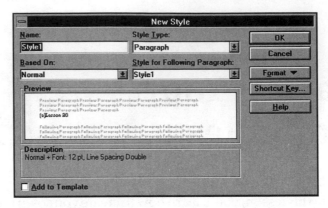

Figure 21.1 The New Style dialog box.

3. Pull down the Style Type list, and select **Character**.

4. Select the Name box, and type in the name for the new style.

5. Click on the **Format** button, and select **Font**. Word displays the Font dialog box.

6. Specify the formatting that you want the new style to have, and then select **OK** to return to the New Style dialog box.

7. Select **OK**, and then select **Close**.

Modifying a Style

You can change the formatting associated with any paragraph style. When you do so, all text in the document that has the style assigned will be modified. Follow these steps to modify an existing style:

1. To modify a paragraph style, select a paragraph formatted with the style. To modify a character style, select text (at least one character) that has that style assigned. The style name will be displayed in the Style box on the Formatting toolbar.

2. Make the desired changes to the text's formatting.

3. Be sure that the original text or paragraph is still selected.

4. Click on the Style box on the Formatting toolbar, and then click anywhere in the document window.

5. Word for Windows displays the Reapply Style dialog box. Select the option **Redefine the style using the selection as an example?** if it is not already selected.

6. Select **OK**. The style is redefined with the new formatting.

You can also modify an existing style using dialog boxes. To do so, follow these steps:

1. Select **Format Style** to display the Style dialog box, shown in Figure 21.2

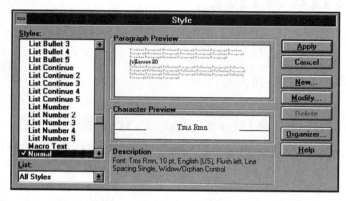

Figure 21.2 The Style dialog box.

2. In the Styles list, highlight the name of the style you want to modify.

3. Select **Modify** to display the Modify Style dialog box.

4. Select **Format**. From the list that is displayed, select the type of formatting you want to modify. The number of formatting types available on the list depends on whether you are modifying a Paragraph style or a Character style.

5. Word will display the appropriate formatting dialog box. Make the desired changes, and then select **OK**. You will return to the Modify Style dialog box.

6. Repeat steps 4 and 5 as many times as necessary to make all the desired modifications to the style's formatting.

7. From the Modify Styles dialog box, select **OK**. You return to the Style dialog box.

8. Select **Close**.

In this lesson, you learned how to create and modify styles. The next lesson shows you how to use automatic formatting.

Using Automatic Formatting

In this lesson, you'll learn how to have Word format your document automatically.

What Is Automatic Formatting?

Automatic formatting refers to Word's capability to analyze the structure of a document and recognize certain common elements, such as body text, headings, bulleted lists, and quotations. Word will then apply appropriate styles to the various text elements to create an attractively formatted document (for information on styles, refer to Lessons 20 and 21). You can accept or reject all or part of the automatically applied format, and can later make any desired modifications to the document. In addition to applying styles, Automatic Formatting can remove extra "returns" between paragraphs, create bulleted lists, and more.

Applying Automatic Formatting

You can apply automatic formatting to all or part of a document:

1. To format part of a document, select the text. Otherwise, position the insertion point anywhere in the document.

2. Select **Format AutoFormat**, and select **OK**. Word analyzes and reformats the document, and displays the AutoFormat dialog box shown in Figure 22.1.

3. Use the vertical scroll bar to scroll through the document and examine the new formatting. The dialog box will remain displayed; grab its title bar, and drag it to another location if it is blocking your view of the document.

Figure 22.1 Use the AutoFormat dialog box to accept or reject the formatting applied by the AutoFormat command.

4. Select **Reject All** to undo all formatting changes and return the document to its original state. Select **Accept** to accept all the changes. Select **Review Changes** if you want to review the changes and accept or reject them individually (described in detail in the following section).

Reviewing the Formatting Changes

If you select **Review Changes** from the AutoFormat dialog box, you can scroll through the document, examine each formatting change, and then either accept it or reject it. The Review AutoFormat Changes dialog box will be displayed during this procedure, as shown in Figure 22.2. Scroll through the document using the vertical scroll bar. Word indicates the changes that were made using the marks shown in Table 22.1.

Figure 22.2 Accept or reject individual formatting changes in the Review AutoFormat Changes dialog box.

Table 22.1 Word Indicates Formatting Changes Made

Change Made	Mark Displayed
New style applied to the paragraph	Blue paragraph mark
Paragraph mark deleted	Red paragraph mark
Text or spaces deleted	Strikethru
Characters added	Underline
Text or formatting changed	Vertical bar in left margin

As you examine the document, make selections in the Review AutoFormat Changes dialog box as follows:

- Select **Find** → or ← **Find** to highlight the next or previous change.

- Select **Reject** to undo the highlighted change.

- Select **Undo Last** to reverse the last Reject command (restoring the rejected change).

- Select **Hide Marks** to display the document as it would appear if all remaining changes were accepted. Select **Show Marks** to return to revisions display.

- Turn on the **Find Next after Reject** option to have Word automatically find the next revision after you reject the current one.

- Select **Cancel** to accept the remaining revisions and return to the AutoFormat dialog box.

Setting the AutoFormat Options

The AutoFormat feature has a number of settings that control which document elements it will modify. You can change these options to suit your preferences:

1. Select **Tools Options** to display the Options dialog box.

2. Click on the **AutoFormat** tab to display the AutoFormat options (Figure 22.3).

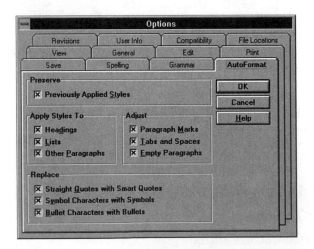

Figure 22.3 Use the Options screen to set Word's AutoFormat options.

3. Turn options on or off to control which document elements the AutoFormat command will affect.

4. Select **OK**.

This lesson showed you how to use Word's automatic formatting capability. In the next lesson, you'll learn how to use tables.

Tables

23

In this lesson, you'll learn how to add tables to your documents.

Uses for Tables

A *table* lets you organize information in a row and column format. Each entry in a table, called a *cell*, is independent of all other entries. You control the number of rows and columns in a table and the formatting of each cell. A table cell can contain anything except another table.

Why Tables? Use tables for columns of numbers, lists, and anything else that requires a row and column arrangement.

Inserting a Table

You can insert a new, empty table at any location within your document. Just follow these steps:

1. Move the insertion point to where you want the table.

2. Select **Table Insert Table**. The Insert Table dialog box is displayed, as shown in Figure 23.1.

3. In the Number of Columns and Number of Rows boxes, click on the arrows or enter the number of rows and columns the table should have. (You can adjust these numbers later if you need to.)

4. In the Column Width box, select the column width. Select **Auto** to have the page width evenly divided among the specified number of columns.

Figure 23.1   The Insert Table dialog box.

5. Select **OK**. A blank table is created with the insertion point in the first cell. Figure 23.2, for example, shows a blank table with four rows and three columns.

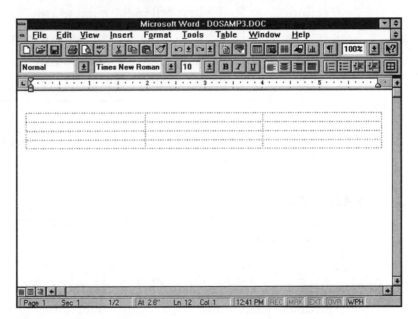

Figure 23.2   A blank table with four rows and three columns.

Tables with the Toolbar   To quickly insert a table, click on the **Table** button on the Standard toolbar, and then drag over the desired number of rows and columns.

203

Working in a Table

When the insertion point is in a table cell, you can enter and edit text as you would in the rest of the document. Text entered in a cell automatically wraps to the next line within the column width. Navigate through a table using the special key combinations described in Table 23.1.

Table 23.1   Moving Through a Table

Press	*To Move*
Tab	To the next cell in a row.
Shift+Tab	To the previous cell in a row.
Alt+Home	To the first cell in the current row.
Alt+PgUp	To the top cell in the current column.
Alt+End	To the last cell in the current row.
Alt+PgDn	To the last cell in the current column.

If the insertion point is at the edge of a cell, you can also use the arrow keys to move between cells.

Formatting a Table

Once you've created a table and entered some information, you can format it to suit your needs.

Deleting and Inserting Cells, Rows, and Columns

You can delete individual cells, erasing their contents and leaving a blank cell. You can also delete entire rows and columns. When you do so, columns to the right or rows below move to fill in for the deleted row or column.

Fast Select!   To select an entire cell, click in the left margin of the cell, between the text and the cell border. The mouse pointer changes to an arrow when it's in this area.

To delete the contents of a cell:

1. Select the cell.
2. Press **Del**.

To delete an entire row or column:

1. Move the insertion point to any cell in the row or column to be deleted.
2. Select **Table Delete Cells**. A dialog box is displayed.
3. In the dialog box, select **Delete Entire Row** or **Delete Entire Column**.
4. Select **OK**. The row or column is deleted.

To insert a row or column:

1. Move the insertion point to a cell to the right or below the location of the new column or row.
2. Select **Table Select Row** to insert a row or **Table Select Column** to insert a column. The entire row or column becomes selected.
3. Select **Table Insert Columns** to insert a new, blank column to the left of the selected column. Select **Table Insert Rows** to insert a new, blank row above the selected row.

The Commands Vary! The commands on the Table menu change according to the circumstances. For example, if you have selected a column in a table, the Insert Columns command is displayed but the Insert Rows command is not.

To insert a new row at the bottom of the table:

1. Move the insertion point to the last cell in the last row of the table.
2. Press **Tab**. A new row is added at the bottom of the table.

Changing Column Width

You can quickly change the width of a column with the mouse:

1. Point at the right border of the column you want to change. The mouse pointer changes to thin vertical lines with arrowheads pointing left and right.

2. Drag the column border to the desired width.

   You can also use a dialog box to change column widths:

1. Move the insertion point to any cell in the column you want to change.

2. Select **Table Cell Height and Width**. The Cell Height and Width dialog box is displayed.

3. In the dialog box, click on the **Column** tab, if necessary, to display the column options.

4. In the Width of Column box, enter the desired column width, or click on the up and down arrows to change the setting.

5. Change the value in the Space Between Columns box to modify spacing between columns.

6. Select **Next Column** or **Previous Column** to change the settings for other columns in the table.

7. Select **OK**. The table changes to reflect the new column settings.

Automatic Table Formatting

The AutoFormat command makes it a snap to apply attractive formatting to any table:

1. Place the insertion point anywhere in the table.

2. Select **Table Table AutoFormat**. The Table AutoFormat dialog box is displayed (see Figure 23.3)

3. The Formats box lists the available table formats. As you scroll through the list, the Preview box shows the appearance of the highlighted format.

4. In the lower section of the dialog box are a number of formatting options. Select and deselect options as necessary until the preview shows the table appearance you want.

5. Select **OK**. The selected formatting is applied to the table.

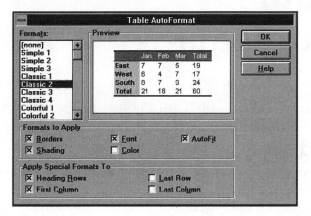

Figure 23.3   Use the Table AutoFormat dialog box to apply table formatting.

In this lesson, you learned how to add tables to your documents. In the next lesson, you'll learn how to add graphics to your documents.

Adding Graphics to Your Documents

In this lesson, you'll learn how to add graphics to your documents.

Adding a Graphic Image

A graphic image is a picture that is stored on disk in a graphic file. Word for Windows can utilize graphic files created by a wide variety of applications, including Lotus 1-2-3, Windows Metafiles, Micrografx Designer, and AutoCAD. In addition, Word comes with a small library of clip art images that you can use in your documents. Figure 24.1 shows a document that includes a graphic image.

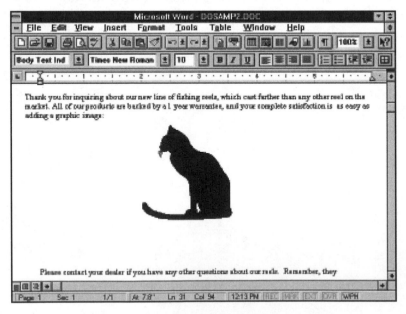

Figure 24.1   A document with a displayed graphic.

To add a graphic image to a Word for Windows document, follow these steps:

1. Move the insertion point to the location for the graphic.

2. Select **Insert Picture**. The Insert Picture dialog box is displayed, as shown in Figure 24.2.

3. If necessary, use the Directories and Drives boxes to specify the drive and directory where the graphics file is located.

4. The File Name box normally lists all graphic files in the specified directory. To have the list restricted to certain types of graphics files, open the List Files of Type drop-down box, and select the desired file type.

5. In the File Name box, type the name of the file to insert, or select the file name from the list.

6. (Optional) To preview the picture in the Preview box, select the **Preview Picture** option.

7. (Optional) Select the **Link to File** option if you want the graphic in your document updated if the graphics file on disk changes.

8. Select **OK**. The graphic image is inserted into your document.

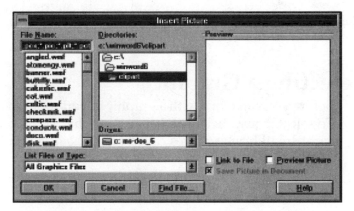

Figure 24.2   The Insert Picture dialog box.

Displaying Graphics

The display of graphic images can slow down screen scrolling. If you're working on the document text and don't need to see the images, you can speed up screen display by displaying empty rectangles called *placeholders* in place of the images. If you selected the **Link to File** option when inserting the graphic file, Word for Windows inserts a field code in the document. The screen will display this code instead of the picture when field codes are displayed. Here's how to use picture placeholders and field codes:

1. Select **Tools Options** to display the Options dialog box.

2. If necessary, click on the **View** tab to display the View options.

3. In the Show section, turn the **Picture Placeholders** and **Field Codes** options on or off as desired.

4. Select **OK**.

The screen display of placeholders or field codes does not affect printing, which will always include the actual graphics.

Fast Takes When working on a document that contains graphics, you can speed up screen display and scrolling by displaying placeholders for the graphics.

Selecting a Graphic

Before you can work with a graphic in your document, you must select it. To select it, just click on it. When a graphic is selected, it is surrounded by eight small black squares called *sizing handles*. You'll see their use in the next section.

Cropping and Resizing a Graphic

You can resize a graphic in your document, displaying the entire picture at a different size. You can also crop a graphic, hiding portions of the picture that you don't want to show. To resize or crop a graphic:

1. Select the graphic.

2. Point at one of the resizing handles. The mouse pointer will change to a double-headed arrow.

3. To resize, press the left mouse button, and drag the handle until the outline of the graphic is at the desired size. You can either enlarge or shrink the graphic.

4. To crop, press and hold **Shift**. Then hold down the left mouse button, and drag a handle toward the center of the graphic.

Deleting, Moving, and Copying Graphics

To delete a graphic, select it, and press **Del**. To move or copy a graphic:

1. Select the graphic.

2. Select **Edit Copy** (to copy the graphic), or select **Edit Cut** (to move the graphic). Alternatively, you can click on the **Copy** or **Cut** button on the Standard toolbar.

3. Move the insertion point to the new location for the graphic.

4. Select **Edit Paste**, or click on the **Paste** button on the Standard toolbar.

In this lesson, you learned how to add graphics to your documents. The next lesson shows you how to use AutoText entries.

Using AutoText Entries

25

In this lesson, you'll learn how to use the AutoText feature.

What Is AutoText?

The AutoText feature lets you define a collection of commonly used words, phrases, or sentences to be inserted into a document so you don't have to type them each time. You insert an AutoText entry in the document by typing a short abbreviation or name that you assigned to it. Typical uses for AutoText entries are your company name, the closing sentence for a business letter, and your name and title. An AutoText entry can contain just text or text along with special formatting.

Creating an AutoText Entry

To create an AutoText entry, you must first type it into your document and add any special formatting that you want included. Then follow these steps:

1. Select the text for the AutoText entry. If you want its formatting included as well, be sure to include the ending paragraph mark in the selection.

2. Select **Edit AutoText**. The AutoText dialog box is displayed (see Figure 25.1).

3. In the Name text box, enter a name or abbreviation for the AutoText entry, or accept the name suggested by Word. This should be a short name that is descriptive of the entry. You will later use this name when inserting the AutoText entry into documents.

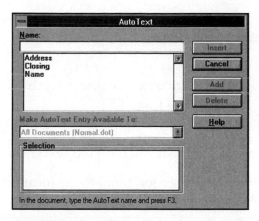

Figure 25.1   The AutoText dialog box.

4. If your document is based on any template besides NORMAL, you have two choices as to where the AutoText entry should be stored. Pull down the Make AutoText Entry Available To list, and then choose one of these options:

   - Select **All Documents** to have the AutoText entry available for all future documents.

   - Select **Documents Based On** to have the entry available only for future documents created with the current template.

5. Select **Add**.

Return Address   Save time by creating an AutoText entry that contains your name and address.

Inserting an AutoText Entry

You have two options for inserting an AutoText entry into your document. The first method is fastest if you remember the name that you assigned to the AutoText entry.

1. Move the insertion point to the location where you want the AutoText entry inserted.

2. Type the name that you assigned to the AutoText entry, but do not press Enter. Be sure the AutoText name is preceded by a space if it is not the first item on a line.

3. Press **F3**. The corresponding AutoText entry is inserted in place of its name.

TIP

    Quick Access   To insert an AutoText entry, type the entry name, and press **F3**.

If you are not sure of the AutoText entry name, follow this procedure:

1. Move the insertion point to the location where you want the AutoText entry inserted.

2. Select **Edit AutoText**. The AutoText dialog box is displayed, with a list of defined AutoText entries.

3. Type the name of the desired AutoText entry, or select it from the list.

4. Select the **Formatted Text** option to insert the AutoText entry with its formatting. Select the **Plain Text** option to insert the AutoText text without formatting.

5. Select **Insert**.

Modifying an AutoText Entry

You can modify an existing AutoText entry. Such modifications will not affect previous instances of the AutoText entry in your documents.

1. Insert the AutoText entry into a document as described earlier in this lesson.

2. Edit the text and/or formatting as desired.

3. Select the newly edited text, including the paragraph mark if you want the formatting included in the AutoText entry.

4. Select **Edit AutoText**. From the list of entries, select the name of the AutoText entry that you are modifying.

5. Select **Add**.

6. When asked whether to redefine the AutoText entry, select **Yes**.

Deleting an AutoText Entry

You can delete an unneeded AutoText entry from the AutoText list. Deleting an AutoText entry has no effect on instances of the entry that were inserted previously.

1. Select **Edit AutoText**.

2. Type the AutoText entry name, or select it from the list.

3. Select **Delete**. The entry is deleted.

In this lesson you learned how to use AutoText entries. The next lesson shows you how to open more than one document at the same time.

Opening Multiple Documents

In this lesson, you'll learn how to open multiple documents in Word for Windows.

Why Use Multiple Documents?

You may feel that working on one document at a time is quite enough. In some situations, however, the ability to work on multiple documents at the same time can be very useful. You can refer to one document while working on another, and you can copy and move text from one document to another. Word for Windows can have as many as nine documents open simultaneously.

Starting a New Document

You can start a new document while you're working on an existing document. To do so, follow these procedures:

1. With the original document displayed on-screen, select **File New**. The New dialog box is displayed (see Figure 26.1).

2. Select the **Document** option if it is not already selected.

3. In the Template list, select the template on which you want to base the new document.

4. Select **OK**. A new, blank document window is opened over the existing document. The new document is assigned a default name by Word for Windows, such as DOCUMENT1, DOCUMENT2, and so on.

5. Enter text, and edit the new document in the normal fashion. The original document remains in memory. If you close the new document, you will be returned to the original document.

Figure 26.1   The New dialog box.

   Fast Open!   To open a new document based on the NOR-
MAL template, click on the **File New** button on the Standard
toolbar.

Opening an Existing Document

While working in one document, you can also open another existing
document. Simply select **File Open**, or click on the **File Open** button on
the Standard toolbar, and then select the name of the document you want
to open, and select **OK**. A new window opens, displaying the document.
Both the newly opened document and the original document are in
memory, and can be edited, printed, and so on.

Switching Between Documents

When you have multiple documents open at one time, only one of them can
be active at a given moment. The active document is displayed onscreen
and is the only one affected by editing commands. You can have as many
as nine documents open at the same time, and you can switch between
them at will.

To switch between open documents:

1. Select **Window**. The Window menu lists all open documents, with
a check mark next to the name of the currently active document.

217

2. Select the name of the document you want to make active. You can either click on the document name with the mouse or press the key corresponding to the number listed next to the name on the menu.

3. The selected document becomes active and is displayed on-screen.

Next Please!   To cycle to the next open document, press **Ctrl+F6**.

In this lesson, you learned how to open multiple documents. The next lesson shows you how to work with multiple documents.

Working with Multiple Documents

In this lesson, you'll learn how to work with multiple documents in Word for Windows.

Moving and Copying Text Between Documents

When you have more than one document open, you can move and copy text between documents. Follow these steps:

1. Make the source document active (the document containing the text to move or copy) by selecting it from the Window menu, and select the text to be moved or copied.

2. Select **Edit Cut** (to move the text), or select **Edit Copy** (to copy the text). Or, if you prefer, click on the **Cut** or **Copy** button on the Standard toolbar.

3. Make the destination document active (the document to receive the cut or copied text) by selecting it from the Window menu. Move the insertion point to the location for the new text.

4. Select **Edit Paste**, or click on the **Paste** button on the Standard toolbar.

Seeing Multiple Windows

At times, you may want to have two or more open documents visible on the screen at the same time. To do so, select **Window Arrange All**. Word displays each open document in its own window in the work area. For example, Figure 27.1 shows three documents displayed in the work area. Note that each document window has its own title bar, displaying the document's name.

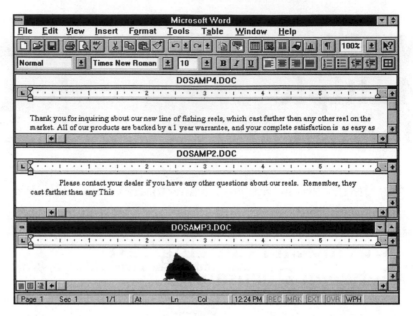

Figure 27.1   Multiple documents displayed with Window Arrange All.

Only one document can be active at any given time. The active document is indicated by a dark background in the title bar and a dark border. In Figure 27.1, the third document, called DOSAMP3.DOC, is active. To make a different document window active, select it from the Window menu, or click anywhere in the window with the mouse. Or you can press **Ctrl+F6** one or more times to cycle between windows.

With multiple document windows displayed, you can control the size and position of each window. If you don't already know how, the Windows section of this book shows you how to control document windows.

Redisplaying a Document at Full-Screen Size

To clear multiple documents from your screen and return to full-screen display of a single document, follow these steps:

1. Make current the document that you want to display full-screen.

2. Maximize the window by clicking on the **Maximize** button. (The Maximize button is the upward-pointing arrowhead immediately to the right of the window's title bar.)

Saving Multiple Documents

When you are working with multiple documents, you save documents with the **File Save** and **File Save As** commands that you learned in Lesson 5. These commands will save only the active document. You can save all open documents with a single command, **File Save All**.

Closing a Document

You can close an open document once you are finished working with it. To close a document:

1. Make the document active.

2. Select **File Close**.

3. If the document contains unsaved changes, Word for Windows prompts you to save the document.

4. The document is closed.

In this lesson, you learned how to work with multiple documents. In the next lesson, you'll learn how to use the Mail Merge feature.

Using Mail Merge

In this lesson, you'll learn how to use Word's mail merge feature to create form letters.

What Is Mail Merge?

Word's mail merge feature combines two basic components, a *main document* and a *data source file*, into one document. It is used to create form letters, envelopes, mailing labels, and so on.

Main Document   A main document is just like any other letter, except it omits the information that is unique to each individual, such as name, address, and so on.

Data Source File   The data source file contains the unique information about each recipient of your letter, such as name, address, and so on.

Merging the Main Document and the Data Source File

You can start a merge with an existing document, or Word gives you a chance to create the document during the process. If you already have a letter that you want to merge, open it. If not, open a new document window. For practice, you can use a Letter Wizard accessible through the **File New** command. To start the merge:

1. Select **Tools Mail Merge**. The Mail Merge Helper dialog box will appear, as shown in Figure 28.1.

2. Click the **Create** button. Word opens a list. Choose **Form Letters**.

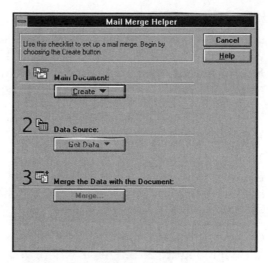

Figure 28.1   The Mail Merge Helper dialog box.

3. In the information box that Word displays, choose **Active Window** if you have already opened the letter that you want to merge; choose **New Main Document** if you are starting with a new document. You are returned to the Mail Merge Helper dialog box.

4. Click on the **Get Data** button, and select **Create Data Source** from the list. (To use an existing data source file, select **Open Data Source**.) Word displays the Create Data Source dialog box shown in Figure 28.2.

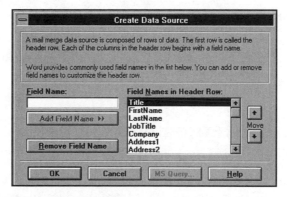

Figure 28.2   The Create Data Source dialog box.

5. Word provides the most common field names in the Field Names in Header Row list box. Remove any field names that you don't want to use by clicking on the field name, and then selecting **Remove Field Name**. To add a new field name, type it in the Field Name text box, and select **Add Field Name**.

6. When you are finished, click on the **OK** button, or press **Enter**. Word displays the Save Data Source dialog box.

7. Type a name in the File Name text box, and click on the **OK** button, or press **Enter**. Word returns to the Mail Merge dialog box and displays an information box from which you can edit the data source file or the main document.

8. Choose **Edit Data Source**. Word displays the Data Form dialog box shown in Figure 28.3. This is where you enter the information unique to the individuals on your mailing list.

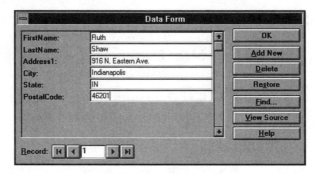

Figure 28.3   The Data Form dialog box.

9. Enter each record, choosing **Add New** after each one until you are finished, then click on the **OK** button, or press **Enter**. Word returns you to your main document window.

Adding Merge Fields to Your Main Document

You are now ready to prepare your main document for the information that will be merged with it from the data source files. You will notice that Word has displayed a new toolbar to help you. Its tools are shown in Table 28.1.

Table 28.1 The Mail Merge Toolbar Buttons

Icon	Name
Insert Merge Field	Insert merge field
Insert Word Field	Insert word field
«» ABC	View merged data
◄|	First record
◄	Previous record
1	Record number window
►	Next record
►|	Last record
	Mail Merge helper
	Check for errors
	Merge to new document
	Merge to printer
	Mail merge
	Search
	Open

In order for Word to know where to put the information from the data source files, you must enter *merge fields* into your main document. At this point, you should have either the letter you are wanting to merge open on your screen, or a blank document window. If you have a blank document window, type in the letter that you want to merge.

Merge Field A merge field is a code inserted into the body of your main document that tells Word where to put the information from the data source files when the files are merged.

To add the merge fields to your main document:

1. Place the insertion point where you want to insert the first merge field, such as in the salutation of your letter to insert the individual's name.

2. Click on the **Insert Merge Field** button on the Mail Merge toolbar.

3. Select a merge field from the list that appears.

4. Continue steps 1–3 throughout your letter until it is complete. You may need to add spaces and punctuation between fields, such as a comma and space between the city field and the state field.

5. (Optional) You can check for errors in your document by selecting the **Check for Errors** button on the Mail Merge toolbar.

6. Save your document. Your main document is now ready for the merge process.

The Merge

To finally merge the main document and the data source file, complete the following steps:

1. Make sure the main document is in the active document window, then click on the **Mail Merge** button. The Merge dialog box is displayed as shown in Figure 28.4.

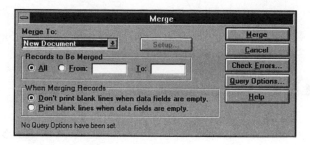

Figure 28.4 The Merge dialog box.

2. Under **Merge To**, choose whether you want to merge the main document and the data source file into a new document to be saved to disk, or whether you want to merge it directly to the printer.

3. Under **When Merging Records**, choose whether or not you want a blank line printed when a data field is left empty.

4. Choose **Merge**. The merged documents appear either on the screen or on your print-out, depending on which you specified.

In this lesson, you learned how to use Mail Merge to create form letters. In the next lesson, you will learn how to create time-saving macros.

Saving Time with Macros

In this lesson, you'll learn how to use macros to save time.

What Is a Macro?

A *macro* is a sequence of commands and keystrokes that has been recorded and saved by Word for Windows. You can easily play back a macro at any time, achieving the same result as if you had entered each command and keystroke individually. For example, you could create a macro that:

- Converts an entire document from single-spaced to double-spaced.

- Goes through a document and formats the first word of each paragraph in 18-point italics.

- Saves the document to disk and then prints it in draft mode.

Why Macros? Macros save time. By recording frequently needed command sequences as macros, you can save time and reduce errors.

Word for Windows macros are a complex and powerful feature. The basics you'll learn in this lesson will enable you to create many useful macros.

Recording a Macro

The simplest way to create a macro is to enter the keystrokes and commands yourself while Word for Windows records them. The only operations that Word for Windows cannot record are mouse editing actions. That is, a macro cannot record the mouse moving the insertion point or selecting text; you must use the keyboard for these actions while recording a macro. Other mouse actions, such as selecting menu commands or dialog box options, can be recorded in a macro.

To record a macro:

1. Plan the macro. It is often a good idea to try a procedure out before recording it in a macro to ensure that it works the way you want it to.

2. Select **Tools Macro** to display the Macro dialog box, and then select **Record** to display the Record Macro dialog box (see Figure 29.1).

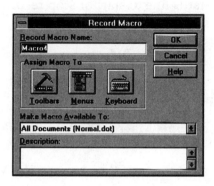

Figure 29.1 The Record Macro dialog box.

3. In the Record Macro Name box, enter a name for the macro. The name should be descriptive of the macro's function. Use any characters except spaces, commas, and periods in the macro name.

4. In the Description box, enter a short description of the macro. Entering a description is optional, but recommended.

5. If the document is based on a template other than NORMAL, you can pull down the Make Macro Available To list and select All Documents (if you want the macro available to all documents) or Documents based On (if you want the macro available only to documents based on the current template).

6. Select **OK**. Word starts recording the macro. While recording is in progress, Word displays the Macro toolbar in a corner of the document. In addition, the **REC** indicator is displayed in the status line at the bottom of the screen, and the mouse pointer changes to a recorder symbol to remind you to use the keyboard—not the mouse—to select text and move the insertion point.

7. Execute the actions and commands that you want in the macro.

8. During recording, you can click on the **Pause** button on the Macro toolbar if you want to perform actions that you don't want recorded in the macro. Click on **Pause** again to resume recording.

9. When you are finished, click on the **Stop** button to terminate macro recording and store the macro.

Quick Start   Double-click on the **REC** indicator on the status line to start or stop recording a macro.

Playing Back a Macro

You can play back any macro at any time while you're working on a document, as follows:

1. Select **Tools Macro**. The Macro dialog box appears (see Figure 29.2).

2. Type the name of the macro in the Macro Name box, or highlight the name in the list.

3. Select **Run**. The chosen macro is executed.

Figure 29.2   Choose a macro to run in the Macro dialog box.

Assigning a Shortcut Key to a Macro

If you assign a shortcut key for a macro, you can play the macro back simply by pressing its shortcut key. The shortcut keys are really key combinations; you can select from the following (where *key* is a letter, number, function, or cursor movement key):

Ctrl+*key*

Alt+*key*

Alt+Ctrl+*key*

Alt+Shift+*key*

Ctrl+Shift+*key*

Ctrl+Shift+Alt+*key*

To assign a shortcut key to a macro, follow these steps:

1. Select **Tools Customize** to display the Customize dialog box.

2. If necessary, click on the **Keyboard** tab to display the keyboard options (see Figure 29.3).

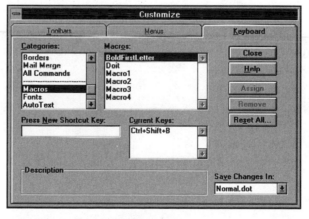

Figure 29.3   Use the Customize dialog box to assign a shortcut key to a macro.

3. Scroll through the Categories list until the **Macros** entry is highlighted.

4. In the Macros list, highlight the name of the macro to which you want to assign a shortcut key.

5. Click on the **Press New Shortcut Key** box.

6. Press the shortcut key combination that you want to assign. Its description is displayed in the Press New Shortcut Key box.

7. Under Current Keys, Word displays the name of the macro or command that the selected shortcut key is assigned to, or Word displays **(unassigned)** if the shortcut key is not assigned.

8. If the shortcut key is unassigned, select **Assign** to assign it to the macro. If it is already assigned, press **Backspace** to delete the shortcut key display and return to step 6 to try another key combination.

TIP

Shortcut Keys   Assign a shortcut key to macros that you will use frequently. To play the macro, simply press the shortcut key while editing the document.

In this lesson, you learned how to use macros to automate your work. In the next lesson, you will learn how to customize Word's toolbars and create your own.

Customizing the Toolbars

In this lesson, you'll learn how to customize Word's toolbars.

Part of the power of Word for Windows comes from its flexibility. Word gives you eight predefined toolbars to work with:

- **Standard toolbar**   Contains the tools most frequently used during document creation, file handling, and printing. (We covered the Standard toolbar in Lesson 2.)

- **Formatting toolbar**   Contains tools used for formatting fonts, setting alignment, applying numbering or bullets, applying format styles, and formatting borders. (We covered the Formatting toolbar in Lesson 2.)

- **Forms toolbar**   Contains tools to help you insert edit boxes, check boxes, lists, and tables. You can also change the properties of a form field and lock the form when you are finished.

- **Database toolbar**   Contains tools to help you sort lists, edit a database, add or delete columns from a database, start mail merge, and insert data from a database outside of Word for Windows.

- **Drawing toolbar**   Contains tools for drawing, filling, reshaping, and grouping objects in the document.

- **Borders toolbar**   Enables you to quickly apply borders and change their thicknesses.

- **Microsoft toolbar**   Contains tools that let you quickly start and activate other Microsoft Windows applications.

- **Word for Windows 2.0 toolbar**   The toolbar used in the previous version of Word for Windows.

Customizing Toolbars

If you find that none of these toolbars quite fit your needs, Word allows you to easily modify them by removing buttons you don't use and adding buttons you need. Alternatively, rather than modifying Word's predefined toolbars, you can create you own from scratch. It's not as difficult as it sounds.

To modify an existing toolbar:

1. If the toolbar you want to modify isn't on-screen, choose **View Toolbars**, and select the toolbar you want.

2. Select **View Toolbars Customize** to open the Customize dialog box with the Toolbars tab up front (see Figure 30.1).

When you select a category...

...you get a collection of buttons to choose from.

Click on a button to see a description of it here.

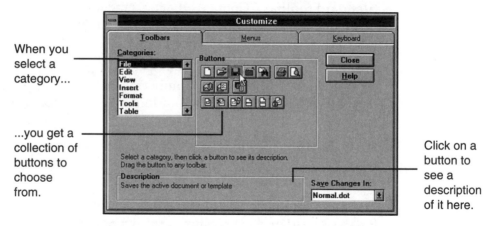

Figure 30.1 The Customize dialog box.

3. To remove a button from the toolbar, drag it off the toolbar into the document area or dialog box.

4. To add a button to the toolbar, select the type of item you want to add from the Categories list. To see what a button does, click on it, and its description will appear in the Description box. When you find the button you want to add, drag it up to where you want in on the toolbar.

5. Repeat this for as many buttons as you want to add, and then click on **Close**.

I Don't Like It   If you totally mess up a toolbar, and you decide you want it back the way it was, you can return to the factory settings by choosing **View Toolbars**, highlighting the name of the toolbar you want, and clicking on the **Reset** button. Word will ask you for confirmation. Click on **OK**.

Creating Your Own Toolbar

You may be afraid of altering Word's predefined toolbars too much. If so, just create your own:

1. Choose **View Toolbars**.

2. Click on **New**.

3. Type a name for the toolbar, and click on **OK**. Word gives you a floating toolbar and the Customize dialog box. You can drag the empty toolbar up the top of the screen, if you want, to add the new buttons.

4. Drag the desired buttons onto the toolbar.

5. When you're finished, click on **Close**.

In this lesson, you learned how to customize Word's predefined toolbars, and how to create your own.

EXCEL 5

Starting and Exiting Excel

In this lesson, you'll learn how to start and end a typical Excel work session and how to get on-line help.

Starting Excel

To use Excel, you must master some basic techniques in Microsoft Windows, including opening program group windows, running applications, dragging, and scrolling. If these terms are unfamiliar to you, refer to the appendix at the back of this book before moving on.

After you installed Excel, the installation program returned you to the Program Manager and displayed the Microsoft Office program group window as shown in Figure 1.1. This window contains the icon you use to start Excel. To start Excel, follow these steps:

- Double-click on the **Microsoft Excel** icon.

  OR

- Use the arrow keys to highlight the icon, and press **Enter**.

The Excel opening screen appears (see Figure 1.2) with a blank workbook labeled **Book1**. Excel is now ready for you to begin creating your workbook.

Workbook   Excel files are called *workbooks*. Each workbook consists of 16 worksheets. Each worksheet consists of columns and rows that intersect to form boxes called *cells* into which you enter text. The tabs at the bottom of the workbook let you flip through the worksheets.

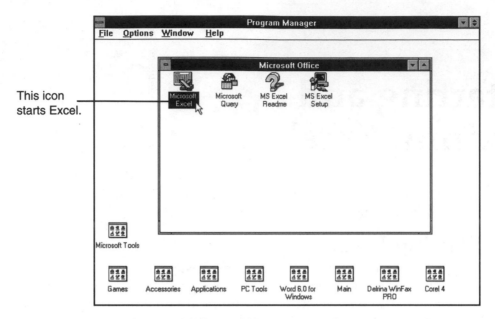

This icon
starts Excel.

Figure 1.1   Select the Microsoft Excel application icon to run the program.

Excel program window   Menu bar   Standard toolbar

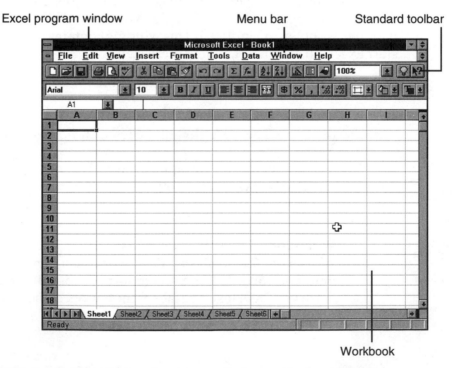

Workbook

Figure 1.2   Excel's opening screen displays a blank workbook.

You perform most operations in Excel using the menu bar at the top of the screen, and the Standard toolbar just below it. You'll learn about the various operations in later lessons.

Getting Help

You can get help in Excel for Windows in three different ways:

Pull down the Help menu.   Pull down the **Help** menu for various help options. You can then select Contents (for groups of help topics), Search for Help on (to search for a specific topic), Index (for a list of help topics from A to Z), Quick Preview (for a brief tour of Excel), Examples and Demos (to see how to perform various tasks), Lotus 1-2-3 or Multiplan (for specific details on how to make the transition from those programs), Technical Support (for information on what to do when all else fails), or About Microsoft Excel (for licensing and system information).

Press F1.   Press the **F1** key to view various groups of Help topics. Pressing **F1** is equivalent to choosing **Contents** from the **Help** menu. If you press **F1** when a menu item or dialog box is displayed, you get help for that item or box. If you press **F1** when a Help window is displayed, you get information about how to use the Help system.

Click on the Help button.   The Help button is on the Standard toolbar; it's the button that has the arrow and the question mark on it. When you click on the **Help** button, the mouse pointer turns into an arrow with a question mark. Click on any item or part of the screen with which you need help, and Excel displays help for that item or screen area. Double-click on the **Help** button to search for a Help topic.

Getting Around in a Help Window

When you select a Help option, Excel displays a Help window like the one in Figure 1.3. You can resize the window as you can resize any window. Use the scroll bar to view any information that does not fit in the window.

Most Help windows contain terms or topics that are underlined with a solid or dotted line. These are called *jumps*. If you click on a term that's dotted underlined, Excel displays a pop-up text box that provides a bit more information about the term. Click on a term or topic that is solid underlined, Excel displays help for the selected item or kicks you out to a How To Help screen.

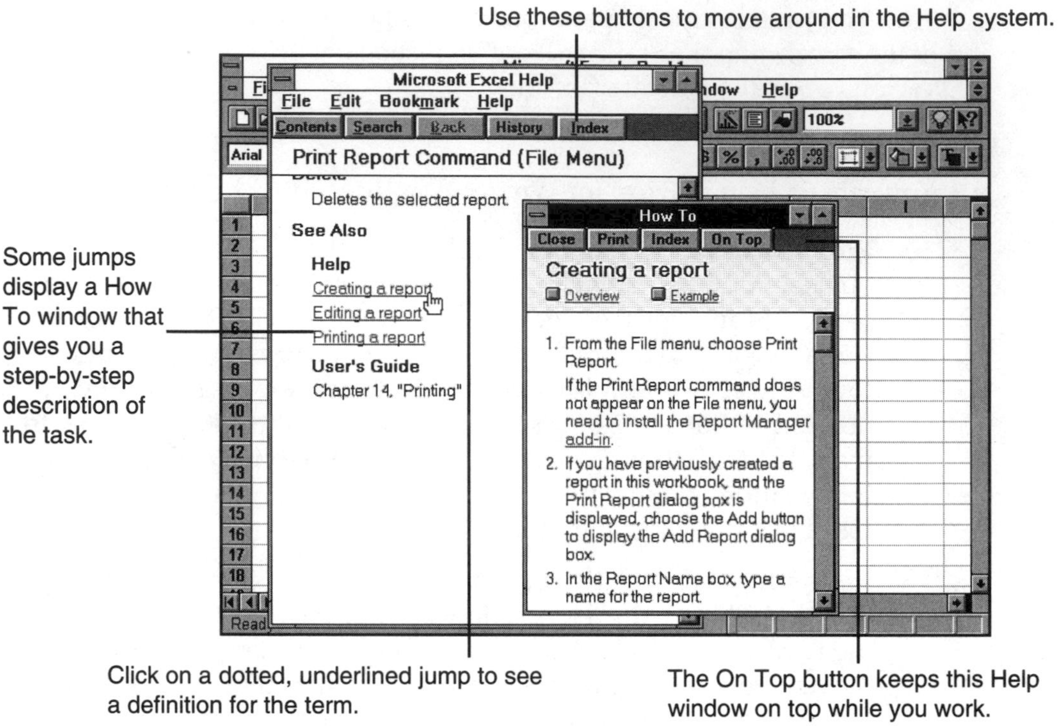

Use these buttons to move around in the Help system.

Some jumps display a How To window that gives you a step-by-step description of the task.

Click on a dotted, underlined jump to see a definition for the term.

The On Top button keeps this Help window on top while you work.

Figure 1.3 When you choose a Help option, a Help window appears, covering a portion of the screen.

To move around in the Help system, click on the following buttons at the top of the Help window, or hold down the **Alt** key and press the underlined letter in the button's name:

Contents   Displays groups of Help topics.

Search   Allows you to search for a topic by typing the name of the topic. As you type, the cursor highlights the name of the topic that matches your entry. Keep typing until the desired topic is displayed, and then press **Enter**.

Back   Displays the previous Help screen.

History   Displays a list of recently accessed Help topics. This is useful if you commonly view the same Help topic.

Index   Displays a comprehensive list of Help topics in alphabetical order.

Glossary (not always displayed)   Provides a list of terms for which you can get definitions.

To exit Help, perform any of the following steps:

- Press **Alt+F4**, or double-click on the **Control-menu** box in the upper left corner of the Help window.

- Press **Alt+F**, or click on **File** in the Help window, and select **Exit** (or press **X**).

- Click on the **Minimize** button in the upper right corner of the Help window to shrink the window down to an icon. This doesn't exit the Help system, it just moves it out of the way. To get the help window back, press **Ctrl+Esc**, and double-click on its name.

TIP

Discovering More   Excel 5.0 offers a new feature called the *TipWizard* that provides information about how to fully exploit the power of Excel. The TipWizard looks at what you are currently doing and provides tips on how to do it faster. To turn the TipWizard on or off, click on the **TipWizard** button on the Standard toolbar, as shown in Figure 1.4.

Exiting Excel

To exit Excel and return to the Program Manager, follow these steps:

1. Press **Alt+F** or click on **File** on the menu bar.

2. Press **X**, or click on **Exit**.

If you changed the workbook in any way without saving the file, Excel will display a prompt asking if you want to save the file before exiting. Select the desired option.

TIP

Quick Exit   For a quick exit, press **Alt+F4**, or double-click on the **Control-menu** box in the upper left corner of the Excel window.

Here's where the TipWizard appears.　　　　　　　　　　　　　Standard toolbar

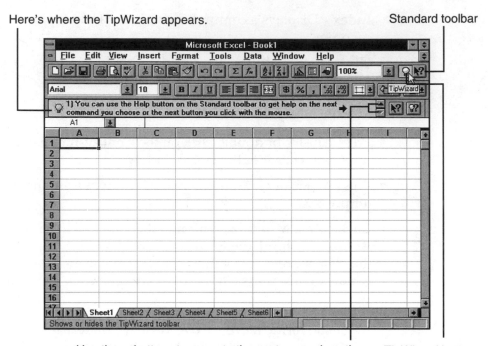

Use these buttons to move to the next or previous tip.　　　TipWizard button

Figure 1.4　The TipWizard offers timesaving advice.

In this lesson, you learned how to enter and exit Excel and get on-line help. In the next lesson, you'll learn about the Excel workbook window.

Moving Around in the Excel Window

In this lesson, you'll learn the basics of moving around in the Excel window and in the workbook window.

Navigating the Excel Window

As you can see in Figure 2.1, the Excel window contains several elements that allow you to enter commands and data:

Menu bar   Displays the names of the available pull-down menus. When you select a menu, it drops down over a portion of the screen, presenting you with a list of options.

Toolbars   Contain several icons, buttons, and drop-down lists that give you quick access to often-used commands and features.

Formula bar   To enter information in a cell, you select the cell and type the information in the formula bar. When you press **Enter**, the information is inserted in the selected cell.

Workbook window   Contains the workbook where you will enter the data and formulas that make up your workbook.

Status bar   Displays information about the current activity, including help information and keyboard and program modes.

TIP

Sizing Windows   When you run Excel, it starts in full-screen mode. You can resize the window at any time. Click on the **Restore** button in the upper right corner of the window, and then drag the window border to size the window.

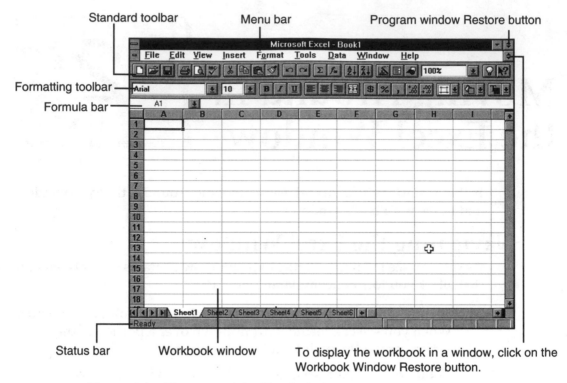

Standard toolbar   Menu bar   Program window Restore button

Formatting toolbar

Formula bar

Status bar   Workbook window

To display the workbook in a window, click on the Workbook Window Restore button.

Figure 2.1 Elements of the Excel window.

Navigating the Workbook Window

Workbook Window   Inside the Excel program window is a workbook window with the current worksheet in front. In this window, you will enter the labels, values, and formulas that make up each worksheet. Figure 2.2 illustrates the various parts of the workbook. Table 2.1 describes the parts.

Table 2.1 Workbook Window Items

Item	*Function*
Tabs	A workbook consists of 16 worksheets. You can use the tabs to flip worksheets.
Tab scrolling buttons	Allow you to scroll through the worksheets in the workbook.

Item	Function
Scroll bars	Allow you to view a section of the current worksheet that is not displayed.
Column heading	Identifies the column by letters.
Row heading	Identifies the row by numbers.
Selector	Outline that indicates the active cell.
Split bars	Let you split the workbook window into two panes to view different portions of the same worksheet.

What's a Cell? Each page in a workbook is a separate worksheet. Each worksheet contains a grid consisting of alphabetized columns and numbered rows. When a row and column intersect, they form a box called a *cell*. Each cell has an *address* that consists of the column letter and row number (A1, B3, C4, and so on). You will enter data and formulas in the cells to form your worksheets. You will learn more about cells in Lesson 5.

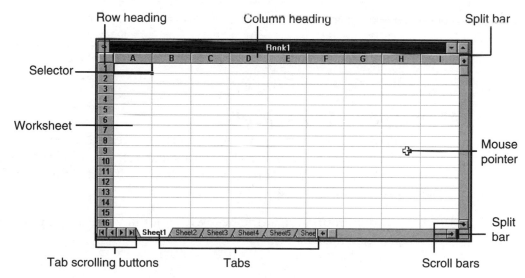

Figure 2.2 Elements of the workbook window.

Flipping Worksheets Because each workbook consists of 16 worksheets, you need a way to move from worksheet to worksheet. If you are using the keyboard, you can flip worksheets by pressing **Ctrl+PgDn** and **Ctrl+PgUp**.

If you are using the mouse, there are easier ways to flip worksheets. If a tab is shown for the worksheet you want to move to, click on the tab for that worksheet (see Figure 2.3). If the tab is not shown, use the scroll buttons to bring the tab into view, and then click on the tab.

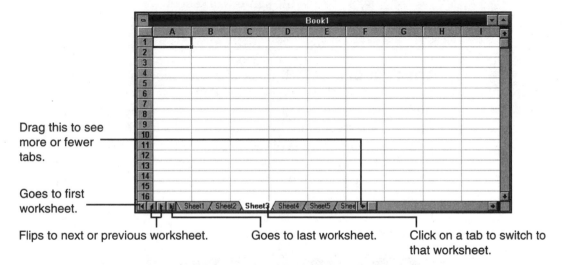

Drag this to see more or fewer tabs.

Goes to first worksheet.

Flips to next or previous worksheet.

Goes to last worksheet.

Click on a tab to switch to that worksheet.

Figure 2.3 You can move from worksheet to worksheet with tabs.

Moving on a Worksheet

Once the worksheet you want to work on is displayed, you need some way of moving to the various cells on the worksheet. Keep in mind that the part of the worksheet displayed on-screen is only a small part of the worksheet, as illustrated in Figure 2.4.

To move around the worksheet with your keyboard, use the keys as described in Table 2.2.

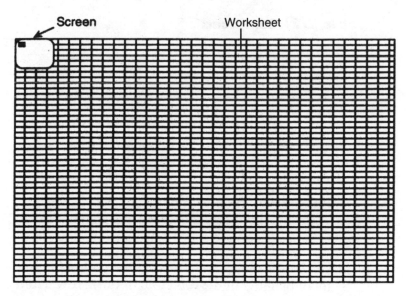

Figure 2.4 The worksheet area displayed on-screen is a small portion of the worksheet.

Table 2.2 Moving Around a Worksheet With the Keyboard

Press	To Move
←→↑↓	One cell in the direction of the arrow.
Ctrl+↑ or Ctrl+↓	To the top or bottom of a data region (an area of the worksheet that contains data).
Ctrl+← or Ctrl+→	To the leftmost or rightmost cell in a data region.
PgUp	Up one screen.
PgDn	Down one screen.
Home	Leftmost cell in a row.
Ctrl+Home	Upper left corner of a worksheet.
Ctrl+End	Lower left corner of a worksheet.
End+↑, End+↓,	If the active cell is blank, moves to

continues

Table 2.2   Continued

Press	To Move
End+←, End+→	the next blank cell in the direction of the arrow. If the active cell contains an entry, moves in the direction of the arrow to the next cell that has an entry.
End+Enter	Last column in row.

If you have a mouse, moving on a worksheet is easier. Use the scroll bars to scroll to the area of the screen that contains the cell you want to work with. Then, click on the cell. To use the scroll bars:

- Click once on a scroll arrow at the end of the scroll bar to scroll incrementally in the direction of the arrow. Hold down the mouse button to scroll continuously.

- Drag the scroll box inside the scroll bar to the area of the worksheet you want to view. For example, to move to the middle of the worksheet, drag the scroll box to the middle of the scroll bar.

- Click once inside the scroll bar, on either side of the scroll box, to move the view one screenful at a time.

F5 (Goto) for Quick Movement!   To move to a specific cell on a worksheet, pull down the **Edit** menu and select **Go To**, or press **F5**. Type the cell's address in the Reference text box; the address consists of the column letter and row number that define the location of the cell, for example **m25**. To go to a cell on a specific page, type the page name, an exclamation point, and the cell address (for example, **sheet3!m25**. Click on the **OK** button.

Splitting a Worksheet

Because a worksheet can be so large, you may want to view different parts of the worksheet at the same time. To do this, you need to split the workbook window into panes. Here's how you work with panes:

- To split a workbook window, drag one of the split bars, as shown in Figure 2.5.

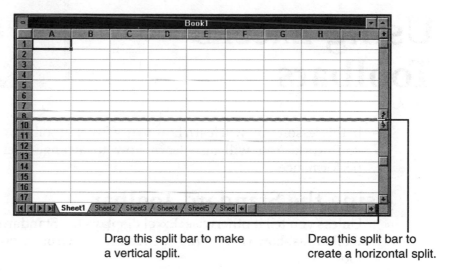

Drag this split bar to make
a vertical split.

Drag this split bar to
create a horizontal split.

Figure 2.5 Drag one of the split bars to divide the window into two panes.

- To switch from one pane to the other, click in the pane you want to work with.

- To close a pane, drag the split bar to the right side or bottom of the window, and release the mouse button.

- To keep the top or left pane from scrolling, open the **Window** menu, and choose **Freeze Panes**. With the panes frozen, as you scroll in the bottom or right pane, the view in the other pane stays put.

- To free the panes, open the **Window** menu, and choose **Unfreeze** Panes.

In this lesson, you learned how to move around in the Excel window and move around in workbooks. In the next lesson, you will learn how to use Excel's toolbars.

Using Excel's Toolbars

In this lesson, you will learn how to use Excel's toolbars to save time when you work. You will also learn how to arrange them for maximum performance.

Using the Standard Toolbar

Unless you tell it otherwise, Excel displays the Standard and Formatting toolbars as shown in Figure 3.1. To select a tool from a toolbar, click on that tool.

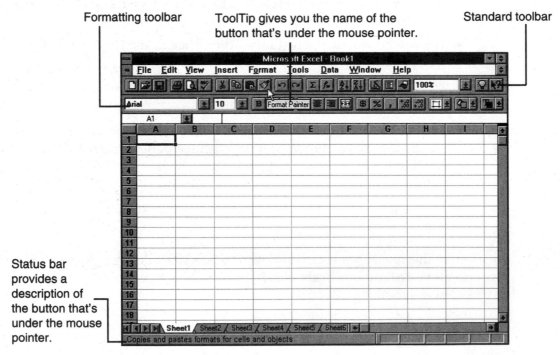

Figure 3.1 The Standard and Formatting toolbars contain buttons for the most commonly used features.

252

What Is a Toolbar?   An Excel toolbar is a collection of tools or shortcut icons displayed on a long bar that can be moved and reshaped to suit your needs.

Learning More About Toolbar Buttons

Although I could give you a list of all the tools in the Standard toolbar and in all the other toolbars (over 270 buttons in all), here are some better ways to learn about the buttons for yourself:

- To see the name of a button, move the mouse pointer over the button. Excel displays a *ToolTip* that provides the name of the button, as shown in Figure 3.1.

- To learn what a button does, move the mouse pointer over the button and look at the status bar (bottom of the screen). If the button is available for the task you are currently performing, Excel displays a description of what the button does.

- To learn more about a button, click on the **Help** button in the Standard toolbar (the button with the arrow and question mark), and then click on the button for which you want more information.

Turning Toolbars On or Off

Excel initially displays the Standard and Formatting toolbars. If you never use one of these toolbars, you can turn one or both of them off to free up some screen space. In addition, you can turn on other toolbars. You can turn a toolbar on or off by using the View Toolbars option or the shortcut menu.

To use the View Toolbars option:

1. Open the **View** menu, and choose **Toolbars**. The Toolbars dialog box appears, as shown in Figure 3.2.

2. Select the toolbar(s) you would like to hide or display. An **X** in the toolbar's check box means the bar will be displayed.

3. Click on the **OK** button.

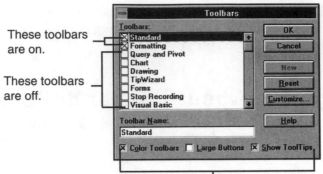

These toolbars are on.

These toolbars are off.

These options let you customize the look of the buttons.

Figure 3.2   Use the Toolbars dialog box to control the toolbars.

To use the shortcut menu to hide or display a toolbar:

1. Move the mouse pointer anywhere inside any toolbar.

2. Click on the right mouse button. The Toolbars shortcut menu appears.

3. Click on a toolbar name to turn it on if it is off or off if it is on. Excel places a check mark next to the name of a displayed toolbar.

TIP

Is It Getting Crowded in Here?   Display only the toolbars you need. Toolbars take up screen space and memory.

Moving Toolbars

After you have displayed the toolbars you need, you may position them in your work area where they are most convenient. Figure 3.3 shows an Excel screen with three toolbars in various positions on the screen.

Here's what you do to move a toolbar:

1. Move the mouse pointer over a buttonless part of the toolbar.

2. Hold down the mouse button, and drag the toolbar where you want it:

   • Drag the toolbar to a toolbar dock. There are four toolbar docks: between the formula bar and menu bar, on the left and right sides of the Excel window, and at the bottom of the Excel window. If a toolbar contains a drop-down list, you cannot drag it to a left or right toolbar dock.

- Drag the toolbar anywhere else on the screen to create a floating toolbar.

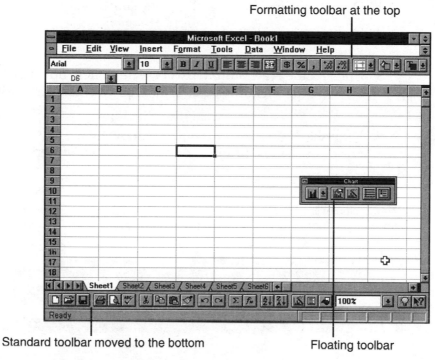

Figure 3.3 Three toolbars in various positions.

Floating Toolbar A floating toolbar acts just like a window. You can drag its title bar to move it or drag a border to size it. If you drag a floating toolbar to a toolbar dock, it turns back into a regular toolbar.

Docking a Floating Toolbar To quickly move a floating toolbar to the top of the screen, double-click on its title bar.

255

Customizing the Toolbars

If Excel's toolbars provide too few (or too many) options for you, you can create your own toolbars or customize existing toolbars. To make your own toolbar, do this:

1. Open the **View** menu, and choose **Toolbars**.

2. In the Toolbar Name text box, type the name you want to give your toolbar.

3. Click on the **New** button. Excel creates a new floating toolbar and displays the Customize dialog box, so you can start adding buttons to your bar.

4. Drag the desired buttons onto the toolbar, as shown in Figure 3.4. For more details, continue on to the next set of steps.

5. Select **Close**.

New toolbar will expand as you drag buttons onto it.

You can drag buttons off any toolbar to delete them, or drag them to a different toolbar to move them.

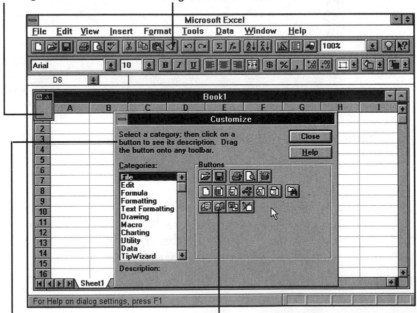

Select a category of commands or options.

Drag one of these buttons to the new toolbar.

Figure 3.4 Drag buttons from the Customize dialog box to the new toolbar.

You can add or remove buttons from any toolbar (Excel's or your own) by performing the following steps:

1. Do one of the following:

   - Right-click on the toolbar you want to customize, and choose **Customize**.

   - Open the **View** menu, and choose **Toolbars**. Highlight the name of the toolbar you want to customize, and choose **Customize**.

2. To remove a button from any toolbar, drag it off the toolbar.

3. Select the type of item you want to add from the Categories list. For example, you can add buttons for file commands, formulas, formatting, or macros. You'll see a collection of buttons. Click on a button to view its description.

4. Drag the desired button(s) onto a toolbar (any toolbar that's displayed).

5. Click on the **Close** button when you're done.

Resetting Toolbars   If you mess up one of Excel's toolbars, you can return to the factory settings at a click of the button. Choose **View Toolbars**, highlight the name of the toolbar you want to reset, and then click on the **Reset button**.

In this lesson, you learned how to use Excel's toolbars and customize toolbars for your own unique needs. In the next lesson, you will learn how to work with Excel's workbooks.

Working with Workbook Files

In this lesson, you will learn how to save, close, and open workbook files, and how to create new workbooks.

Saving a Workbook

Whatever you type into a workbook is stored only in your computer's memory. If you exit Excel, that data will be lost, so it is important to save your workbook files to disk regularly.

The first time you save a workbook to disk, you have to name it. Here's how you do it:

1. Pull down the **File** menu, and select **Save**, or click on the **Save** button in the Standard toolbar. The Save As dialog box appears as shown in Figure 4.1.

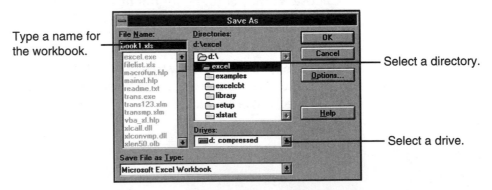

Type a name for the workbook.

Select a directory.

Select a drive.

Figure 4.1 The Save As dialog box.

2. Type a name for the workbook in the File Name text box. You may use any combination of letters or numbers up to eight characters (no spaces), such as **1994BDGT**. Excel automatically adds **.XLS** to

the file name as an extension. The full file name is then
1994BDGT.XLS.

3. To save the file on a different drive, click on the arrow to the right
   of the Drives drop-down list, and click on the desired drive.

4. To save the file to a different directory, double-click on that directory in the Directories list box. (You can move up the directory tree
   by double-clicking on the directory name or drive letter at the top
   of the tree.)

5. Click on **OK**, or press **Enter**.

Default Directory You can set up a default directory where
Excel will save all your workbook files. Open the **Tools**
menu, and select **Options**. Click on the **General** tab. Click
inside the Default File Location text box, and type a complete
path to the drive and directory you want to use (the directory
must be an existing one). Click on **OK**.

To save a file you have already saved (and named), simply click on the
Save button, or press **Ctrl+S**. Or open the **File** menu, and select **Save**. Excel
automatically saves the workbook (including any changes you entered)
without displaying the Save As dialog box.

Saving a File Under a New Name

Sometimes, you may want to change a workbook without changing the
original workbook, or you may want to create a new workbook by
modifying an existing one. You can do this by saving the workbook under
another name or in another directory. Here's how you do it:

1. Pull down the **File** menu, and select **Save As**. You get the Save As
   dialog box, just as if you were saving the workbook for the first
   time.

2. To save the workbook under a new name, type the new file name
   over the existing name in the File Name text box.

3. To save the file on a different drive or directory, select the drive
   letter from the Drives list and the directory from the Directories
   list.

4. To save the file in a different format (for example, Lotus 1-2-3 or Quattro Pro), click on the arrow to the right of the Save File as Type drop-down list, and select the desired format.

5. Click on **OK**, or press **Enter**.

Backup Files You can have Excel create a backup copy of each workbook file you save. That way, if anything happens to the original file, you can use the backup copy. Backup copies have the same file name as the original workbook but include the extension **.BAK**. To turn the backup feature on, click on the **Options** button in the Save As dialog box, select **Always Create Backup**, and click on **OK**.

Creating a New Workbook

You can create a new workbook by modifying an existing one or by opening a blank workbook and starting from scratch. Here's how you open a blank workbook:

1. Pull down the **File** menu, and select **New** or press **Ctrl+N**. The New dialog box, shown in Figure 4.2, may or may not appear, depending on whether the Slideshow feature is installed.

Figure 4.2 The New dialog box.

2. Choose **Workbook**.

3. Click on **OK**, or press **Enter**. A new workbook opens on-screen with a default name in the title bar. Excel numbers the files sequentially. For example, if you already have **Book1** open, the Workbook title bar will read **Book2**.

Instant Workbook You can bypass the New dialog box (assuming you get it when you select **File New**) by simply clicking on the **New Workbook** button (the leftmost button) in the Standard toolbar. Excel opens a new workbook window without prompting you.

Closing Workbooks

Closing a workbook removes its workbook window from the screen. To close a workbook, do this:

1. Make the window you want to close active.

2. Pull down the **File** menu, and select **Close**. If you have not yet saved the Workbook, you will be prompted to do so.

In a Hurry? To quickly close a workbook, double-click on the **Control-menu** box located in the upper left corner, or press **Ctrl+F4**. If you have more than one workbook open, you can close all of them by holding down the **Shift** key while selecting **File Close All**.

Opening an Existing Workbook

If you close a workbook and you want to use the workbook later, you must open it. Here's how you do it:

1. Pull down the **File** menu, and select **Open**, or click on the **Open** button in the Standard toolbar (it's the button that looks like a manila folder). The Open dialog box appears, as shown in Figure 4.3.

2. If the file is not on the current drive, click on the arrow to the right of the Drives list box, and select the correct drive.

3. If the file is not in the current directory, select the correct directory from the Directories list box.

4. Do one of the following:

   • Choose the file you want to open from the File Name list.

- Type the name of the file in the File Name box. As you type, Excel highlights the first file name in the list that matches your entry (this is a quick way to move through the list).

5. Click on **OK**, or press **Enter**.

Type the file
name, or select
the file from the
list.

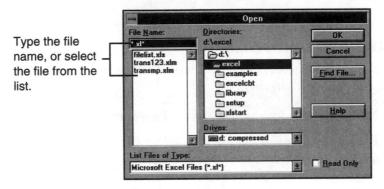

Figure 4.3 The Open dialog box.

Recently Used Workbooks   Near the bottom of the File menu is a list of the most recently opened workbooks. You can quickly open the workbook by selecting it from the **File** menu.

Searching for Misplaced Files

If you forgot where you saved a file, Excel can help you with its new Find File feature. Here's what you do to have Excel hunt for a file:

1. Open the **File** menu, and select **Find File**, or click on the **Find File** button in the Open dialog box. You'll get the Search dialog box, as shown in Figure 4.4.

Wrong Dialog Box?   If you get the Find File dialog box instead of the Search dialog box, click on the **Search** button at the bottom of the Find File dialog box.

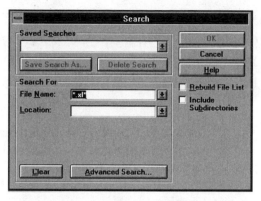

Figure 4.4 The Search dialog box asks you to specify what you want to search for.

2. In the File Name text box, type the name of the file you are looking for. You can use wild-card characters in place of characters you can't remember. Use an asterisk (*) in place of a group of characters, or use a question mark (?) in place of a single character. For example, *.xls finds all files with the extension .xls, and sales??.xls finds all files, such as SALES01.XLS, SALES02.XLS, and so on.

3. In the Location text box, type the drive and directory you want to search. For example, if you type **c:**, Excel will search the entire drive C. Type **c:\excel**, and Excel searches only the EXCEL directory on drive C.

4. To have Excel search all subdirectories of the drive you specify, place an **X** in the Include Subdirectories check box.

5. Don't worry about the Clear option. It clears out anything you may have typed in the File Name and Location text boxes.

6. Click on the **OK** button. Excel finds the files that match the search instructions you entered, and displays them in the Find File dialog box.

7. Look through the list, highlight the file you want, and click on the **Open** button.

Moving Among Open Workbooks

Sometimes, you may have more than one workbook open at a time. There are several ways to move among open workbooks:

- If part of the desired workbook window is visible, click on it.

- Open the **Window** menu, and select the name of the workbook you want to go to.

- Press **Ctrl+F6** to move from one workbook window to another.

The Active Window   If you have more than one workbook open, only one of them is considered active—the workbook where the cell selector is located. The title bar of the active workbook will be darker than the title bars of other open workbooks.

In this lesson, you learned how to save, close, and open workbooks. The next lesson teaches you how to work with the worksheets in a workbook.

Working with Worksheets

This lesson teaches you how to add worksheets to and delete worksheets from workbooks. You will also learn how to copy, move, and rename worksheets.

Add or Delete Pages By default, each workbook consists of 16 worksheet pages that are separated by tabs. You can insert new worksheet pages or delete worksheet pages as desired. You can also copy and move worksheets within a workbook or from one workbook to another.

Selecting Worksheets

Before we get into the details of inserting, deleting, and copying worksheets, you should know how to select one or more worksheets. Here's what you need to know:

- To select a single worksheet, click on its tab.

- To select several neighboring worksheets, click on the first worksheet in the group, and then hold down the **Shift** key while clicking on the last worksheet.

- To select several non-neighboring worksheets, hold down the **Ctrl** key while clicking on each worksheet.

- If you select two or more worksheets, they remain selected until you ungroup them. To ungroup worksheets, do one of the following: right-click on one of the selected worksheets, and choose **Ungroup Sheets**; hold down the **Shift** key while clicking on the active tab; or click on any tab outside the group.

Inserting Worksheets

To insert a new worksheet in a workbook, perform the following steps:

1. Select the worksheet before which you want the new worksheet inserted. For example, if you select **Sheet4**, the new worksheet (Sheet17) will be inserted before Sheet4.

2. Open the **Insert** menu.

3. Select **Worksheet**. Excel inserts the new worksheet, as shown in Figure 5.1.

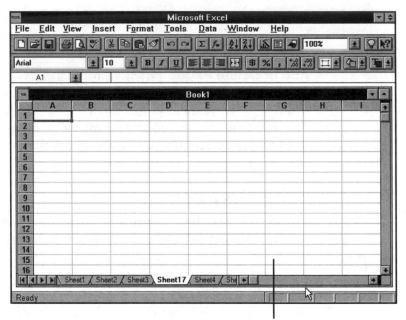

Worksheet inserted before Sheet 4.

Figure 5.1 Excel inserts the new worksheet before the current worksheet.

Shortcut Menu   A faster way to work with worksheets is to right-click on the worksheet tab. This brings up a shortcut menu that lets you insert, delete, move, copy, or rename worksheets.

Deleting Worksheets

If you plan on using only one worksheet, you can remove the 15 other worksheets to free up memory and system resources. Here's how you remove a worksheet:

1. Select the worksheet(s) you want to delete.

2. Open the **Edit** menu.

3. Click on **Delete Sheet**. A dialog box appears, asking you to confirm the deletion.

4. Click on the **OK** button. The worksheets are deleted.

Moving and Copying Worksheets

You can move or copy worksheets within a workbook or from one workbook to another. Here's how:

1. Select the worksheet(s) you want to move or copy.

2. Open the **Edit** menu, and choose **Move or Copy Sheet**. The Move or Copy dialog box appears, as shown in Figure 5.2.

To move the selected worksheet(s) to a different workbook, select the workbook.

Tell Excel where to copy or move the worksheet(s).

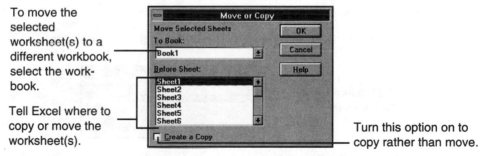

Turn this option on to copy rather than move.

Figure 5.2 The Move or Copy dialog box asks you to specify your preferences.

3. To move the worksheet(s) to a different workbook, select the workbook's name from the To Book drop-down list.

4. Choose the worksheet before which you want the selected worksheet(s) moved from the Before Sheet list box.

5. To copy the selected worksheet(s) (rather than move), select **Create a Copy** to put an **X** in the check box.

6. Click on **OK**. The selected worksheet(s) are copied or moved, as specified.

Drag and Drop An easier way to copy or move worksheets is to use the Drag & Drop feature. First, select the worksheet tab(s) you want to copy or move. Move the mouse pointer over one of the selected tabs, and drag the tab where you want it moved. To copy the worksheet, hold down the **Ctrl** key while dragging. When you release the mouse button, the worksheet is copied or moved.

Changing the Worksheet Tab Names

By default, all worksheets are named **Sheet** and are numbered starting with the number **1**. You can change the names that appear on the tabs. Here's how you do it:

1. Select the worksheet whose name you want to change.

2. Open the **Format** menu, select **Sheet** and then **Rename**. Or double-click on the worksheet's tab. Excel shows you the Rename Sheet dialog box, as shown in Figure 5.3.

3. Type a new name for the worksheet, and click on the **OK** button.

Type a new name for the worksheet.

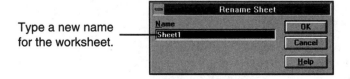

Figure 5.3 Excel lets you give your worksheets more meaningful names.

In this lesson, you learned how to insert, delete, move, copy, and rename worksheets. In the next lesson, you will learn how to enter data into the cells in a worksheet.

Entering and Editing Data

In this lesson, you will learn how to enter different types of data in an Excel worksheet.

Types of Data

To create a worksheet that does something, you must enter data into the cells that make up the worksheet. There are many types of data that you can enter, including:

- Text
- Numbers
- Dates
- Times
- Formulas and functions

Entering Text

You can enter any combination of letters and numbers as text. Text is automatically left-aligned in a cell.

To enter text into a cell:

1. Select the cell into which you want to enter text.

2. Type the text. As you type, your text appears in the cell and in the formula bar, as shown in Figure 6.1.

3. Click on the Enter button on the formula bar (the button with the check mark on it), or press Enter.

Cancel button   Enter button   Insertion point

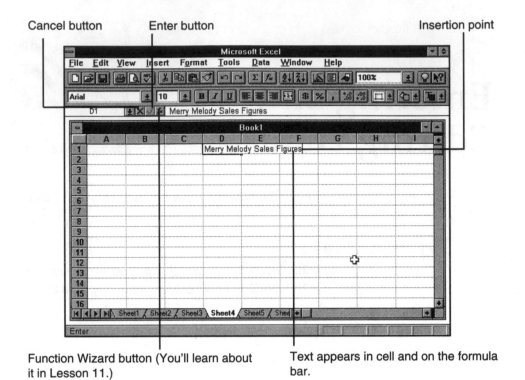

Function Wizard button (You'll learn about it in Lesson 11.)

Text appears in cell and on the formula bar.

Figure 6.1   Data that you enter also appears on the formula bar.

Bail Out!   To cancel an entry before you are done, click on the **Cancel** button (the button with the **X** on it), or press **Esc**.

Number Text   You may want to enter a number as text (for example, a ZIP code). Precede your entry with a single quotation mark ('), as in **'46220**. The single quotation mark is an alignment prefix that tells Excel to treat the following characters as text and left-align them in the cell.

Entering Numbers

Valid numbers can include the numeric characters 0–9 and any of these special characters: $+ - ( ) , \$ \% ..$ Numbers are automatically right-aligned.

You can include commas, decimal points, dollar signs, percentage signs, and parentheses in the values that you enter.

Although you can include punctuation, you may not want to. For example, rather than type a column of dollar amounts including the dollar signs and decimal points, you can type numbers such as 700 and 81.2, and then format the column with currency formatting. Excel would then change your entries to $700.00 and $81.20, respectively. Refer to Lesson 13 for more information.

To enter a number:

1. Select the cell into which you want to enter a number.

2. Type the number. To enter a negative number, precede it with a minus sign, or surround it with parentheses.

3. Click on the **Enter** button on the formula bar, or press **Enter**.

####### If you enter a number, and it appears in the cell as all number signs, don't worry—the number is okay. The cell is not wide enough to display the number. For a quick fix, select the cell, and choose **Format Column AutoFit Selection**. For more information, refer to Lesson 16.

Entering Dates and Times

You can enter dates and times in a variety of formats. When you enter a date using a format shown in Table 6.1, Excel converts the date into a number which represents the number of days since January 1, 1900. Although you won't see this number (Excel displays it as a normal date), the number is used whenever a calculation involves a date.

Table 6.1 Valid Formats for Dates and Times

Format	Example
MM/DD/YY	4/8/58 or 04/08/58
MMM–YY	Jan–92
DD–MMM–YY	28–Oct–91

continues

Table 6.1 Continued

Format	Example
DD–MMM	6–Sep
HH:MM	16:50
HH:MM:SS	8:22:59
HH:MM AM/PM	7:45 PM
HH:MM:SS AM/PM	11:45:16 AM
MM/DD/YY HH:MM	11/8/80 4:20
HH:MM MM/DD/YY	4:20 11/18/80

To enter a date or time:

1. Select the cell into which you want to enter a date or time.

2. Type the date or time in the format in which you want it displayed.

3. Click on the **Enter** button on the formula bar, or press **Enter**.

To Dash or to Slash   You can use dashes (–) or slashes (/) when typing dates. Capitalization is not important. For example, 21 FEB becomes 21–Feb. By the way, FEB 21 also becomes 21– Feb.

Day or Night?   Unless you type AM or PM, Excel assumes that you are using a 24-hour military clock. Therefore, 8:20 is assumed to be AM, not PM. If you type 8:20 PM, Excel inserts the military time equivalent: 20:20.

Entering Data Quickly

Excel offers several features for helping you copy entries into several cells.

• To copy an existing entry into several surrounding cells, you can use the Fill feature.

- To have Excel insert a sequence of entries in neighboring cells (for example Monday, Tuesday, Wednesday), you can use AutoFill.

- To have Excel calculate and insert a series of entries according to your specifications (for example 5, 10, 15, 20), you can fill with a series.

These features are explained in greater detail in the following sections.

Copying Entries with Fill

You can copy an existing entry into any surrounding cells, by performing the following steps:

1. Select the cell whose contents and formatting you want to copy.

2. Position the mouse pointer over the selected cell, and drag it over all the cells into which you want to copy the cell entry.

3. Open the **Edit** menu, and select **Fill**. The Fill submenu appears.

4. Select the direction in which you want to copy the entry. For example, if you choose Right, Excel inserts the entry into the selected cells to the right.

An easier way to fill is to drag the fill handle in the lower right corner of the selected cell to highlight the cells into which you want to copy the entry (see Figure 6.2). When you release the mouse button, the contents and formatting of the original cell are copied to the selected cells.

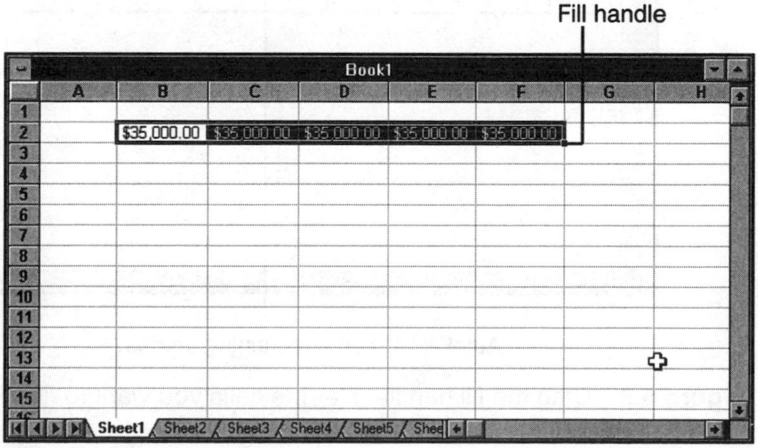

Figure 6.2 Drag the fill handle to copy the contents and formatting into neighboring cells.

273

TIP

Copying Across Worksheets You can copy the contents and/or formatting of cells from one worksheet to one or more worksheets in the workbook. To copy to worksheets, first select the worksheet you want to copy from and the worksheets you want to copy to (see Lesson 5). Then, select the cells you want to copy. Open the **Edit** menu, select **Fill**, and select **Across Worksheets**. Select **All** (to copy the cells' contents and formatting), **Contents**, or **Formats**, and select **OK**.

Smart Copying with AutoFill

Unlike Fill, which merely copies an entry to one or more cells, AutoFill copies intelligently. For example, if you want to enter the days of the week (Sunday through Saturday), you type the first entry (Sunday), and AutoFill inserts the other entries for you. Try it:

1. Type **Monday** into a cell.

2. Drag the fill handle up, down, left, or right to select six more cells.

3. Release the mouse button. Excel inserts the remaining days of the week, in order, into the selected cells (see Figure 6.3).

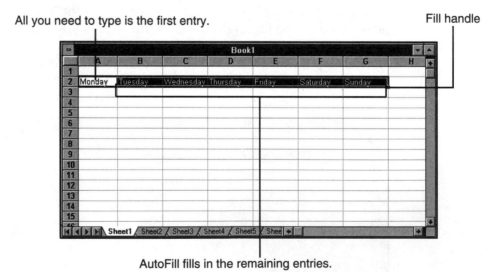

All you need to type is the first entry.

Fill handle

AutoFill fills in the remaining entries.

Figure 6.3 Drag the fill handle over the cells you want to fill.

Excel has the days of the week stored as an AutoFill entry. You can store your own series as AutoFill entries. Here's how you do it:

1. Open the **Tools** menu, and choose **Options**. The Options dialog box appears.

2. Click on the **Custom Lists** tab. The selected tab moves up front, as shown in Figure 6.4.

3. Click on the **Add** button. An insertion point appears in the List Entries text box.

4. Type the entries you want to use for your AutoFill entries (for example, Q1, Q2, Q3, Q4). Press **Enter** at the end of each entry.

5. Click on the **OK** button.

Type your entries here. Press Enter after each entry.

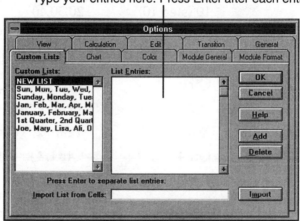

Figure 6.4   Excel lets you create your own AutoFill series.

Now that you have your own AutoFill entry, you can type any item in the list and use AutoFill to insert the remaining entries.

TIP   **Transforming Existing Entries to AutoFill**   If you have already typed the entries you want to use for your AutoFill entries, select the entries before you choose **Options** from the **Tools** menu. Click on the **Custom Lists** tab, and select the **Import** button. Excel lifts the selected entries from your worksheet and sticks them in the List Entries text box.

More Control with Series

Although AutoFill is good for a brief series of entries, you may encounter situations in which you need more control or need to fill lots of cells with incremental entries. In such situations, you should use the series feature. Excel recognizes four types of series, shown in Table 6.2.

Table 6.2   Data Series

Series	Initial Entry	Resulting Series
Linear	1,2	3,4,5
	100,99	98,97,96
	1,3	5,7,9
Growth	10 (step 5)	15,20,25
	10 (step 10)	20,30,40
Date	Mon	Tue, Wed, Thur
	Feb	Mar, Apr, May
	Qtr1	Qtr2, Qtr3, Qtr4
	1992	1993, 1994, 1995
Autofill	Team 1	Team 2, Team 3, Team 4
	Qtr 4	Qtr 1, Qtr 2, Qtr 3
	1st Quarter	2nd Quarter, 3rd Quarter, 4th Quarter

Here's what you do to create a series:

1. Enter a value in one cell. This value will be the starting or ending value in the series.

2. Select the cells into which you want to extend the series.

3. Pull down the **Edit** menu, select **Fill**, and select **Series**. The Series dialog box, shown in Figure 6.5, appears.

Figure 6.5 The Series dialog box.

4. Under Series in, select **Rows** or **Columns**. This tells Excel whether to fill down a column or across a row.

5. Under Type, choose a series type. (Look back at Table 6.2.)

6. Adjust the Step value (amount between each series value), and Stop value (last value you want Excel to enter), if necessary.

7. Click on **OK**, or press **Enter**, and the series is created.

Editing Data

After you have entered data into a cell, you may change it by editing. To replace an entry, simply select the cell and start typing.

In-Cell Editing In previous versions of Excel, you had to edit an entry in the formula bar. In Excel 5.0, you can display the insertion point in either the formula bar or in the cell itself.

To edit an entry, do this:

1. Select the cell in which you want to edit data.

2. Position the insertion point in the formula bar with the mouse, press **F2**, or double-click on the cell. This puts you in Edit mode; **Edit** appears in the status bar.

3. Press ← or → to move the insertion point. Use the **Backspace** key to delete characters to the left, or the **Delete** key to delete characters to the right. Type any additional characters.

4. Click on the **Enter** button on the formula bar, or press **Enter** to accept your changes.

Spell Checking   Excel 5.0 offers a spell checking feature. To run the spell checker, open the **Tools** menu, and select **Spelling**, or click on the **Spelling** button in the Standard toolbar. For more information, click on the **Help** button when the Spelling dialog box appears.

Undoing an Action

You can undo almost anything you do in a worksheet, including any change you enter into a cell. To undo a change, do one of the following:

- Open the **Edit** menu, and choose **Undo**.

- Press **Ctrl+Z**.

- Click on the **Undo** button in the Standard toolbar. (This is the button with the counterclockwise arrow on it.)

    To undo an Undo (reverse a change), take one of these actions:
- Open the **Edit** menu, and select **Redo**.

- Click on the **Repeat** button in the Standard toolbar. (This is the button with the clockwise arrow on it.)

Undo/Repeat One Act   The Undo and Repeat features only undo or repeat the most recent action you performed.

In this lesson, you learned how to enter different types of data, how to automate data entry, and how to make changes and undo those changes.

Working with Ranges

In this lesson, you will learn how to select and name cell ranges.

What Is a Range?

A *range* is a rectangular group of connected cells. The cells in a range may all be in a column, or a row, or any combination of columns and rows, as long as the range forms a rectangle, as shown in Figure 7.1.

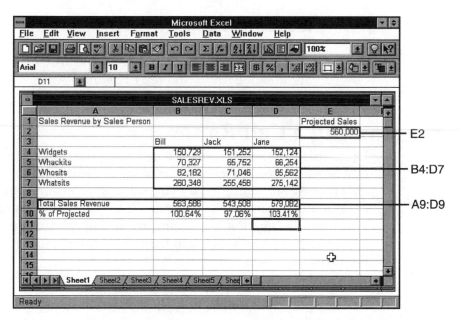

Figure 7.1 A range is any combination of cells that forms a rectangle.

Learning how to use ranges can save you time. For example, you can select a range and use it to format a group of cells with one step. You can use a range to print only a selected group of cells. You can also use ranges in formulas.

Ranges are referred to by their anchor points (the top left corner and the lower right corner). For example, the ranges shown in Figure 7.1 are B4:D7, A9:D9, and E2.

Selecting a Range

To select a range, use the mouse:

1. Move the mouse pointer to the upper left corner of a range.

2. Click and hold the left mouse button.

3. Drag the mouse to the lower right corner of the range and release the mouse button.

4. To select the same range of cells on more than one worksheet, select the worksheets (see Lesson 5).

5. Release the mouse button. The selected range will be highlighted.

A Quick Selection   To quickly select a row or a column, click on the row number or column letter at the edge of the worksheet. To select the entire worksheet, click on the rectangle above row 1 and left of column A.

Naming a Cell Range

Up to this point, you have used cell addresses to refer to cells. Although that works, it is often more convenient to name cells with more recognizable names. For example, say you want to determine your net income by subtracting expenses from income. You can name the cell that contains your total income INCOME, and name the cell that contains your total expenses EXPENSES. You can then determine your net income by using the formula:

=INCOME–EXPENSES

to make the formula more logical and easier to manage. Naming cells and ranges also makes it easier to cut, copy, and move blocks of cells, as explained in Lessons 8 and 9.

To name a cell range:

1. Select the range of cells you want to name. Make sure all the cells are on the same worksheet.

2. Click inside the name box (left side of the formula bar). See Figure 7.2.

Name box   Selected range

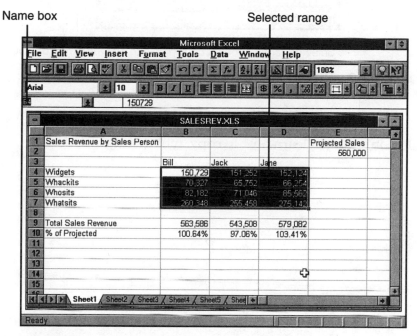

Figure 7.2   Type a name in the name box.

3. Type a range name (up to 255 characters). Valid names can include letters, numbers, periods, and underlines, but NO spaces.

4. Press **Enter**.

Another way to name a range is to select it, open the **Insert** menu, and select **Name Define**. This displays the Define Name dialog box, shown in Figure 7.3. Type a name in the Names in Workbook text box, and click on **OK**. This dialog box also lets you delete names.

Type a name here.────

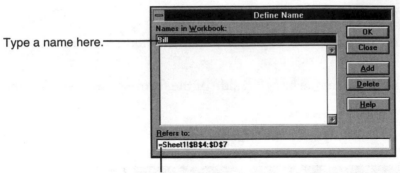

Selected range appears here. You can edit the range or type a new one.

Figure 7.3   The Define Name dialog box.

In this lesson, you learned how to select and name ranges. In the next lesson, you will learn how to copy, move, and erase data.

Copying, Moving, and Erasing Data

In this lesson, you will learn to organize your worksheet to meet your changing needs by copying, moving, and erasing data.

When you copy or move data, a copy of that data is placed in a temporary storage area called the *Clipboard*.

What Is the Clipboard?   The Clipboard is an area of memory that is accessible to all Windows programs. The Clipboard is used by all Windows programs to copy or move data from place to place within a program, or between programs. The techniques that you learn here are the same ones used in all Windows programs.

Copying Data

You make copies of data to use in other sections of your worksheet or in other worksheets or workbooks. The original data remains in place, and a copy of it is placed where you indicate.

To copy data:

1. Select the range or cell that you want to copy.

2. Pull down the **Edit** menu, and select **Copy**, or press **Ctrl+C**. The contents of the selected cell(s) are copied to the Clipboard.

3. Select the first cell in the area where you would like to place the copy. (To copy the data to another worksheet or workbook, change to that worksheet or workbook.)

4. Pull down the **Edit** menu, and choose **Paste**, or press **Ctrl+V**.

Watch Out! When copying or moving data, be careful when you indicate the range where the data should be pasted. Excel will paste the data over any existing data in the indicated range.

You can copy the same data to several places in the worksheet by repeating the **Edit Paste** command. Data copied to the Clipboard remains there until you copy or cut something else.

Cut, Copy, and Paste Buttons When copying and pasting data, don't forget the Standard toolbar. It includes buttons for cutting, copying, and pasting data, allowing you to bypass the menu system.

Quick Copying with Drag & Drop The fastest way to copy is to use the Drag & Drop feature. Select the cells you want to copy, and then hold down the **Ctrl** key while dragging the cell selector border where you want the cells copied (see Figure 8.1). When you release the mouse button, the contents are copied to the new location. If you forget to hold down the Ctrl key, Excel moves the data rather than copying it.

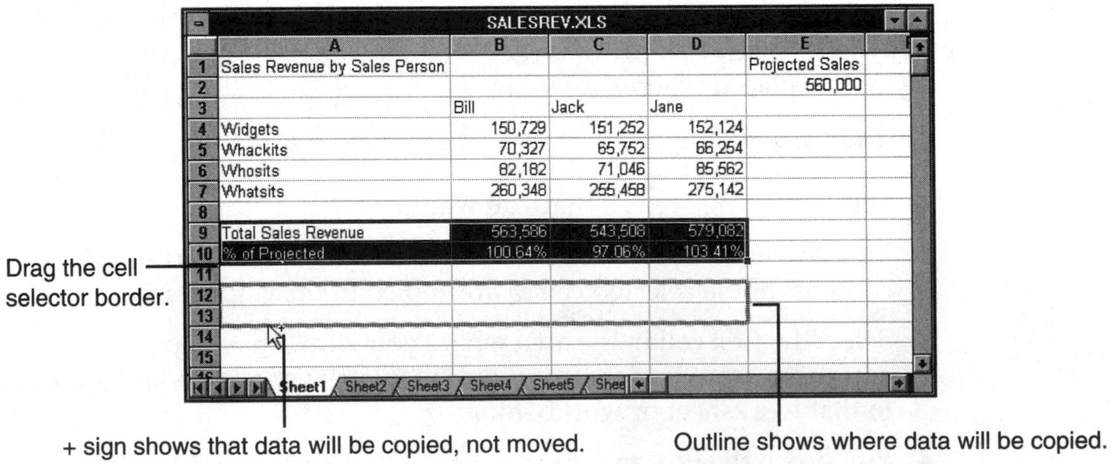

	A	B	C	D	E	
					SALESREV.XLS	
1	Sales Revenue by Sales Person				Projected Sales	
2					560,000	
3		Bill	Jack	Jane		
4	Widgets	150,729	151,252	152,124		
5	Whackits	70,327	65,752	66,254		
6	Whosits	82,182	71,046	85,562		
7	Whatsits	260,348	255,458	275,142		
8						
9	Total Sales Revenue	563,586	543,508	579,082		
10	% of Projected	100.64%	97.06%	103.41%		
11						
12						
13						
14						
15						

Drag the cell selector border.

Sheet1 / Sheet2 / Sheet3 / Sheet4 / Sheet5 / Shee

+ sign shows that data will be copied, not moved.   Outline shows where data will be copied.

Figure 8.1 Hold down the Ctrl key while dragging the cell selector border.

Moving Data

Moving data is similar to copying, except that the data is removed from its original place and moved to the new location.

To move data:

1. Select the range or cell that you want to move.

2. Pull down the **Edit** menu, and select **Cut**, or press **Ctrl+X**.

3. Select the first cell in the area where you would like to place the data. To move the data to another worksheet, change to that worksheet.

4. Pull down the **Edit** menu, and select **Paste**, or press **Ctrl+V**.

Move It Fast!   To move data quickly, use the Drag & Drop feature. Select the data to be moved, and then drag the cell selector border without holding down the **Ctrl** key.

Shortcut Menu   When cutting, copying, and pasting data, don't forget the shortcut menu. Simply select the cells you want to cut or copy, and then right-click on the selected cells.

Erasing Data

Although erasing data is fairly easy, you must decide exactly what you want to erase first. Here are your choices:

- Use the **Edit Clear** command to erase only the contents or formatting of the cells. The Edit Clear command is covered next.

- Use the **Edit Delete** command to remove the cells and everything in them. This is covered in Lesson 9.

With the Clear command, you can remove the data from a cell, or just its formula, formatting, or attached notes. Here's what you do:

1. Select the range of cells you want to clear.

2. Pull down the **Edit** menu, and choose **Clear**. The Clear submenu appears, as shown in Figure 8.2.

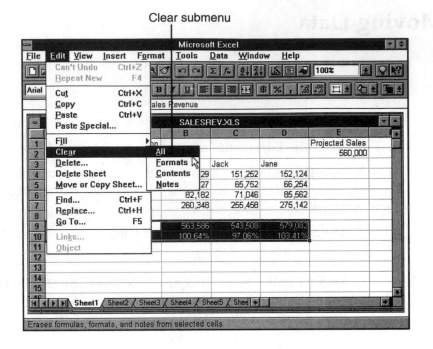

Clear submenu

Figure 8.2 The Clear submenu.

3. Select the desired clear option: All (clears formats, contents, and notes), Formats, Contents, or Notes.

TIP **A Clean Slate** To quickly clear the contents of cells, select the cells, and press the **Delete** key.

TIP **Shortcut Menu** When clearing cells, don't forget the shortcut menu. Select the cells you want to clear, right-click on one of them, and then choose **Delete**.

In this lesson, you learned how to copy and move data. You also learned how to clear data from cells. In the next lesson, you will learn how to insert and delete cells, rows, and columns.

Inserting and Deleting Cells, Rows, and Columns

In this lesson, you will learn how to rearrange your worksheet by adding and deleting cells, rows, and columns.

Inserting Cells

Sometimes, you will need to insert information into a worksheet, right in the middle of existing data. With the Insert command, you can insert one or more cells, or entire rows and columns.

Shifting Cells   Inserting cells in the middle of existing data will cause those other cells to shift down a row or over a column. If you added formulas to your worksheet that rely on the contents of the shifting cells, this could throw off the calculations.

To insert a single cell or a group of cells:

1. Select the cell(s) where you want the new cell(s) inserted. Excel will insert the same number of cells as you select.

2. Pull down the **Insert** menu, and choose **Cells**. The Insert dialog box shown in Figure 9.1 appears.

3. Select **Shift Cells Right** or **Shift Cells Down**.

4. Click on **OK**, or press **Enter**. Excel inserts the cell(s) and shifts the data in the other cells in the specified direction.

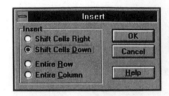

Figure 9.1   The Insert dialog box.

Drag Insert   A quick way to insert cells is to hold down the **Shift** key while dragging the fill handle (the little box in the lower right corner of the selected cell(s)). Drag the fill handle up, down, left, or right to set the position of the new cells.

Inserting Rows and Columns

Inserting entire rows and columns in your worksheet is similar to inserting a cell(s). Here's what you do:

1. Do one of the following:

- To insert a single row or column, select a cell. Columns are inserted to the left of the current cell. Rows are inserted above the current cell.

- Select the number of columns or rows you want to insert. To select columns, drag over the column letters at the top of the worksheet. To select rows, drag over the row numbers.

2. Open the **Insert** menu.

3. Select **Rows** or **Columns**. Excel inserts the row(s) or column(s) and shifts the adjacent rows down or adjacent columns right. Figure 9.2 simulates a worksheet before and after a row is inserted.

Shortcut Insert   To quickly insert rows or columns, select one or more rows or columns, and then right-click on one of them. Choose **Insert** from the shortcut menu.

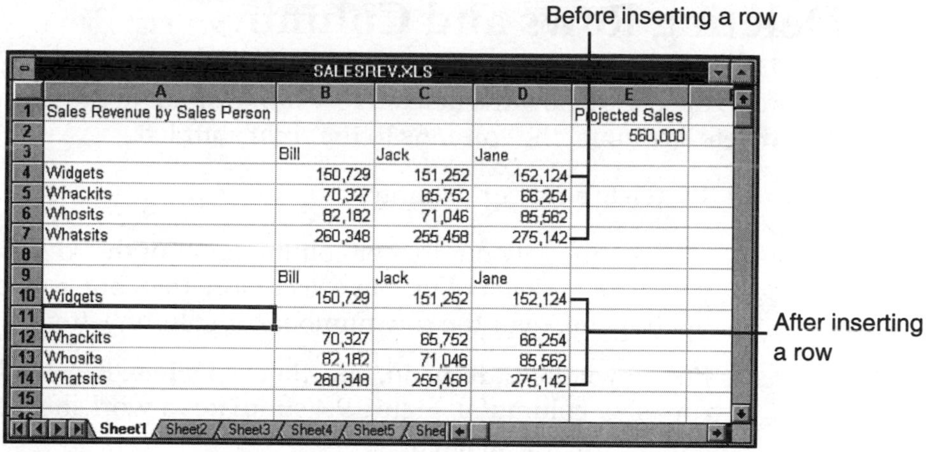

Before inserting a row

	A	B	C	D	E	
1	Sales Revenue by Sales Person				Projected Sales	
2					560,000	
3		Bill	Jack	Jane		
4	Widgets	150,729	151,252	152,124		
5	Whackits	70,327	65,752	66,254		
6	Whosits	82,182	71,046	85,562		
7	Whatsits	260,348	255,458	275,142		
8						
9		Bill	Jack	Jane		
10	Widgets	150,729	151,252	152,124		
11						
12	Whackits	70,327	65,752	66,254		
13	Whosits	82,182	71,046	85,562		
14	Whatsits	260,348	255,458	275,142		
15						

SALESREV.XLS

After inserting a row

Figure 9.2   Inserting a row in a worksheet.

Deleting Cells

In Lesson 8, you learned how to clear the contents and formatting of selected cells. This merely removed what was inside the cells. If you want to remove the cells completely, perform the following steps:

1. Select the range of cells you want to delete.

2. Pull down the **Edit** menu, and choose **Delete**. The Delete dialog box appears, as shown in Figure 9.3.

3. Select the desired Delete option: Shift Cells Left, Shift Cells Up, Entire Row, or Entire Column.

Figure 9.3   The Delete dialog box asks where you want surrounding cells shifted.

Deleting Rows and Columns

Deleting rows and columns is similar to deleting cells. When you delete a row, the rows below the deleted row move up to fill the space. When you delete a column, the columns to the right shift left.

To delete a row or column:

1. Click on the row number or column letter of the row or column you want to delete. You can select more than one row or column by dragging over the row numbers or column letters.

2. Pull down the **Edit** menu, and choose **Delete**. Excel deletes the row(s) or column(s). Figure 9.4 simulates a worksheet before and after a row was deleted.

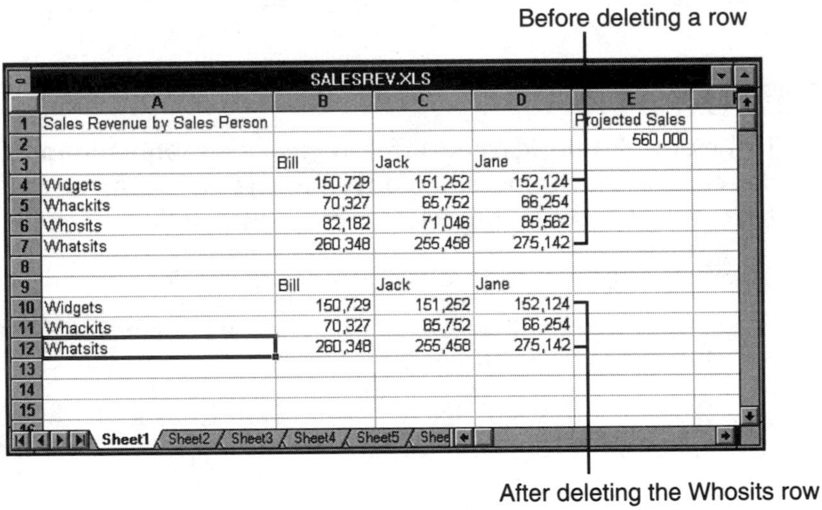

Before deleting a row

	A	B	C	D	E
1	Sales Revenue by Sales Person				Projected Sales
2					560,000
3		Bill	Jack	Jane	
4	Widgets	150,729	151,252	152,124	
5	Whackits	70,327	65,752	66,254	
6	Whosits	82,182	71,046	85,562	
7	Whatsits	260,348	255,458	275,142	
8					
9		Bill	Jack	Jane	
10	Widgets	150,729	151,252	152,124	
11	Whackits	70,327	65,752	66,254	
12	Whatsits	260,348	255,458	275,142	
13					
14					
15					

SALESREV.XLS

Sheet1 / Sheet2 / Sheet3 / Sheet4 / Sheet5 / Shee

After deleting the Whosits row

Figure 9.4   Deleting a row in a worksheet.

In this lesson, you learned how to insert and delete rows and columns. In the next lesson, you will learn how to use formulas.

Writing Formulas

In this lesson, you will learn how to use formulas to calculate results in your worksheets.

What Is a Formula?

Worksheets use *formulas* to perform calculations on the data you enter. With formulas, you can perform addition, subtraction, multiplication, and division using the values contained in various cells.

Formulas typically consist of one or more cell addresses and/or values and a mathematical operator, such as + (addition), - (subtraction), * (multiplication), or / (division). For example, if you wanted to determine the average of the three values contained in cells A1, B1, and C1, you would use the following formula:

=(A1+B1+C1)/3

CAUTION

Start Right Every formula must begin with an equal sign (=).

Figure 10.1 shows several formulas in action. Table 10.1 lists the mathematical operators you can use to create formulas.

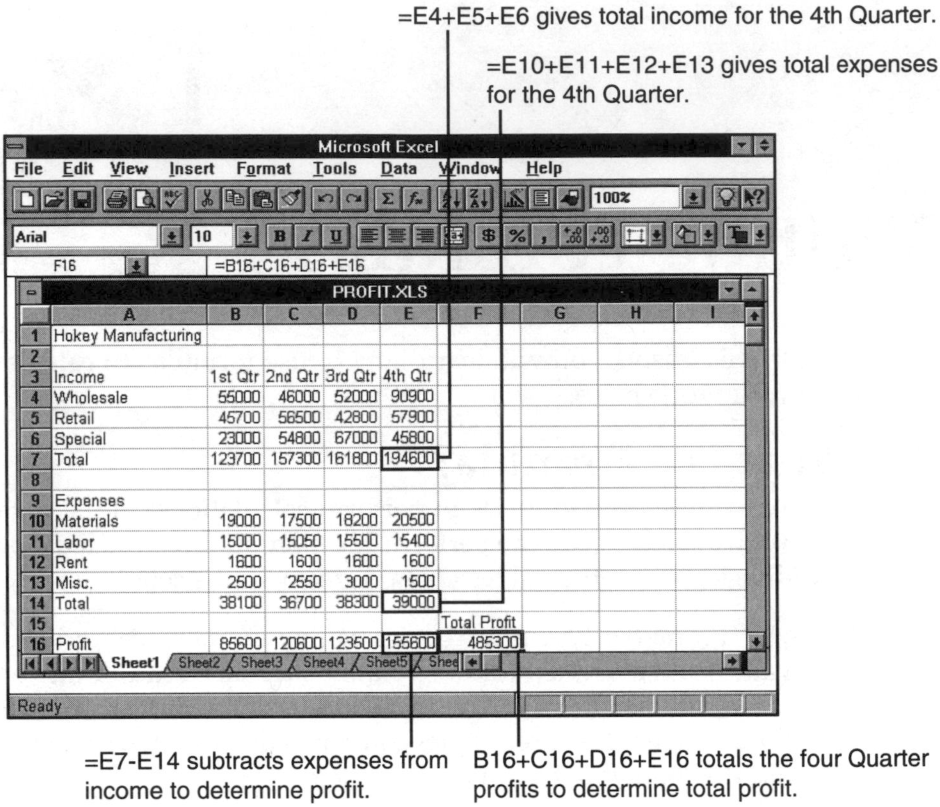

=E4+E5+E6 gives total income for the 4th Quarter.

=E10+E11+E12+E13 gives total expenses for the 4th Quarter.

=E7-E14 subtracts expenses from income to determine profit.

B16+C16+D16+E16 totals the four Quarter profits to determine total profit.

Figure 10.1 Type a formula in the cell where you want the resulting value to appear.

Table 10.1   Excel's Mathematical Operators

Operator	Performs	Example	Result
^	Exponentiation	=A1^3	Enters the result of raising the value in cell A1 to the third power.
+	Addition	=A1+A2	Enters the total of the values in cells A1 and A2.

Operator	Performs	Example	Result
–	Subtraction	=A1–A2	Subtracts the value in cell A2 from the value in cell A1.
*	Multiplication	=A2*3	Multiplies the value in cell A2 by 3.
/	Division	=A1/50	Divides the value in cell A1 by 50.
	Combination	=(A1+A2+A3)/3	Determines the average of the values in cells A1 through A3.

Order of Operations

Excel performs a series of operations from left to right in the following order, giving some operators precedence over others:

1st   Exponential equations

2nd   Multiplication and division

3rd   Addition and subtraction

This is important to keep in mind when you are creating equations, because the order of operations determines the result.

For example, if you want to determine the average of the values in cells A1, B1, and C1, and you enter =A1+B1+C1/3, you'll probably get the wrong answer. The value in C1 will be divided by 3, and that result will be added to A1+B1. To determine the total of A1 through C1 first, you must enclose that group of values in parentheses: =(A1+B1+C1)/3.

Entering Formulas

You can enter formulas in either of two ways: by typing the formula or by selecting cell references. To type a formula, perform the following steps:

1. Select the cell in which you want the formula's calculation to appear.

2. Type the equal sign (=).

3. Type the formula. The formula appears in the formula bar.

4. Press **Enter**, and the result is calculated.

To enter a formula by selecting cell references, take the following steps:

1. Select the cell in which you want the formula's result to appear.

2. Type the equal sign (=).

3. Click on the cell whose address you want to appear first in the formula. The cell address appears in the formula bar.

4. Type a mathematical operator after the value to indicate the next operation you want to perform. The operator appears in the formula bar.

5. Continue clicking on cells and typing operators until the formula is complete.

6. Press **Enter** to accept the formula or **Esc** to cancel the operation.

Error!   Make sure that you did not commit one of these common errors: trying to divide by zero or a blank cell, referring to a blank cell, deleting a cell being used in a formula, or using a range name when a single cell address is expected.

Displaying Formulas

Excel does not display the actual formula in a cell. Instead, Excel displays the result of the calculation. You can view the formula, by selecting the cell and looking in the formula bar. If you want to see the formulas in the cells, do this:

1. Open the **Tools** menu, and choose **Options**.

2. Click on the **View** tab.

3. Click on the Formulas check box. An **X** appears, indicating that the option has been turned on.

4. Click on **OK**, or press **Enter**.

Display Formulas Quickly   Use the keyboard shortcut, **Ctrl+`**, to toggle between viewing formulas or values. Hold down the **Ctrl** key, and press ` (the accent key; it's the key with the tilde (~) on it).

Editing Formulas

Editing formulas is the same as editing any entry in Excel. Here's how you do it:

1. Select the cell that contains the formula you want to edit.

2. Position the insertion point in the formula bar with the mouse, or press **F2** to enter Edit mode.

Quick In-Cell Editing   To quickly edit the contents of a cell, simply double-click on the cell. The insertion point appears inside the cell.

3. Press ← or → to move the insertion point. Use the **Backspace** key to delete characters to the left, or the **Delete** key to delete characters to the right. Type any additional characters.

4. Click on the **Enter** button on the formula bar, or press **Enter** to accept your changes.

Copying Formulas

Copying formulas is similar to copying other data in a worksheet. (For more details, refer to Lesson 8.) To copy formulas:

1. Select the cell that contains the formula you want to copy.

2. Pull down the **Edit** menu, and select **Copy**, or press **Ctrl+C**.

3. Select the cell(s) into which you want to copy the formula. To copy the formula to another worksheet or workbook, change to it.

4. Pull down the **Edit** menu, and select **Paste**, or press **Ctrl+V**.

Drag and Drop Formulas   To quickly copy a formula, use the Drag & Drop feature. Select the cell that contains the formula you want to copy, and then hold down the **Ctrl** key while dragging the cell selector border where you want the formula copied. When you release the mouse button, the formula is copied to the new location. If you need to copy one formula into two or more cells, use the AutoFill feature as explained in Lesson 6.

Get an Error?   If you get an error after copying a formula, verify the cell references in the copied formula. See the next section, "Using Relative and Absolute Cell Addresses," for more details.

Using Relative and Absolute Cell Addresses

When you copy a formula from one place in the worksheet to another, Excel adjusts the cell references in the formulas relative to their new positions in the worksheet. For example, in Figure 10.2, cell B9 contains the formula =B4+B5+B6+B7, which determines the total sales revenue for Bill. If you copy that formula to cell C9 (to determine the total sales revenue for Jack), Excel would automatically change the formula to =C4+C5+C6+C7.

Sometimes, you may not want the cell references to be adjusted when formulas are copied. That's when absolute references become important.

Absolute vs. Relative   An *absolute reference* is a cell reference in a formula that does not change when copied to a new location. A *relative reference* is a cell reference in a formula that is adjusted when the formula is copied.

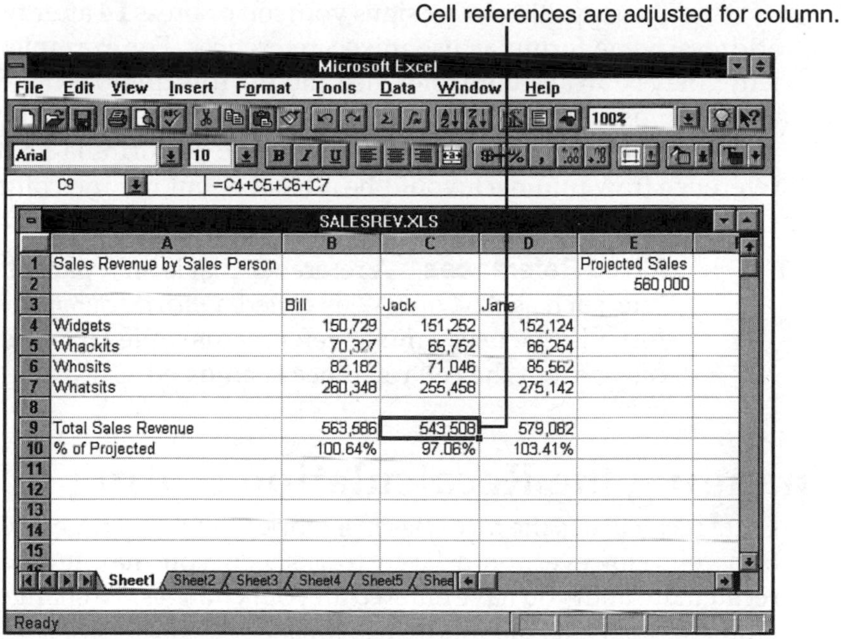

Cell references are adjusted for column.

Figure 10.2 Excel adjusts cell references when copying formulas.

The formula in cells B10, C10, and D10 uses an absolute reference to cell E2, which holds the projected sales for this year. (B10, C10, and D10 divide the sums from row 9 of each column by the contents of cell E2.) If you didn't use an absolute reference, when you copied the formula from B10 to C10, the cell reference would be incorrect, and you would get an error message.

To make a cell reference in a formula absolute, you must add a $ (dollar sign) before the letter and number that make up the cell address. For example, the formula in B10 would read as follows:

B9/E2

You can type the dollar signs yourself or press **F4** after typing the cell address. Some formulas use mixed references. For example, the column letter may be an absolute reference and the row number may be a relative reference, as in the formula **$A2/2**. If you had this formula in cell C2, and you copied it to cell D10, the result would be the formula **$A10/2**. The row reference (row number) would be adjusted, but not the column.

Mixed References A reference that is only partially absolute, such as A$2 or $A2, is called a *mixed reference*. When a formula that uses a mixed reference is copied to another cell, only part of the cell reference is adjusted.

Changing the Recalculation Setting

Excel recalculates the formulas in a worksheet every time you edit a value in a cell. However, on a large worksheet, you may not want Excel to recalculate until you have entered all your changes. To change the recalculation setting, take the following steps:

1. Open the **Tools** menu, and choose **Options**.

2. Click on the **Calculation** tab.

3. Select one of the following Calculation options:

   Automatic is the default setting. It recalculates the entire workbook each time you edit or enter a formula.

   Automatic Except Tables automatically recalculates everything except formulas in a data table. You'll learn about data tables in Lesson 21.

   Manual tells Excel to recalculate only when you say so. To recalculate, you must press **F9** or choose **Tools Options Calculation Calc Now**. If you choose **Manual**, you can turn the Recalculate before Save option off or on.

4. Click on the **OK** button.

In this lesson, you learned how to enter and edit formulas. You also learned when to use relative and absolute cell addresses. In the next lesson, you will learn how to use Excel's Function Wizard to insert more complex formulas.

Performing Complex Calculations with Functions

In this lesson, you will learn how to perform complex calculations with functions and how to use Excel's new Function Wizard to quickly insert functions in cells.

What Are Functions?

Functions are complex ready-made formulas that perform a series of operations on a specified range of values. For example, to determine the sum of a series of numbers in cells A1 through H1, you can enter the function =SUM(A1:H1), instead of entering =A1+B1+C1+ and so on. Functions can use range references (such as B1:B3), range names (such as SALES), and/or numerical values (such as 585.86).

Every function consists of the following three elements:

- The = sign indicates that what follows is a function.

- The function name (for example, SUM) indicates the operation that will be performed.

- The argument, for example (A1:H1), indicates the cell addresses of the values that the function will act on. The argument is often a range of cells, but it can be much more complex.

You can enter functions either by typing them in cells or by using the Function Wizard, as you'll see later in this lesson.

Using the AutoSum Tool

Because SUM is one of the most commonly used functions, Excel created a fast way to enter it; you simply click on the **AutoSum** button in the

Standard toolbar. AutoSum guesses what cells you want summed, based on the currently selected cell. If AutoSum selects an incorrect range of cells, you can edit the selection.

To use AutoSum:

1. Select the cell in which you want the sum inserted. Try to choose a cell at the end of a row or column of data.

2. Click on the **AutoSum** tool in the Standard toolbar. AutoSum inserts =SUM and the range of the cells to the left of or above the selected cell (see Figure 11.1).

3. You can adjust the range of cells by doing one of the following:

   • Click inside the selected cell or the formula bar, and edit the range.

   • Drag the mouse pointer over the correct range of cells.

4. Click on the **Enter** box in the formula bar, or press **Enter**. The total for the selected range is calculated.

SUM function appears in the selected cell and in the formula bar.

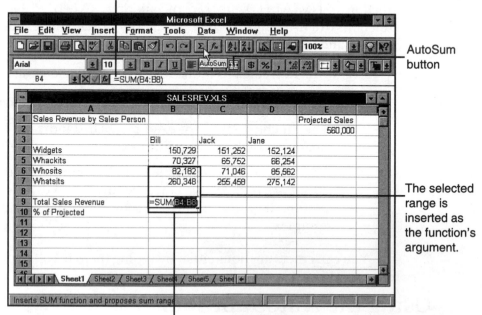

AutoSum button

The selected range is inserted as the function's argument.

AutoSum selects a range of cells above or to the left of the selected cell.

Figure 11.1   AutoSum inserts the SUM function and selects the cells it plans to total.

Using Function Wizard

Although you can type a function directly into a cell, just as you can type formulas, you may find it easier to use the Function Wizard. The Function Wizard is a new feature that leads you through the process of inserting a function. Here's how you do it:

1. Select the cell in which you want to insert the function. (You can insert a function by itself or as part of a formula.)

2. Open the **Insert** menu, and choose **Function**, or click on the **Function Wizard** button (the **fx** button) on the Standard toolbar or formula bar. The Function Wizard – Step 1 of 2 dialog box appears, as shown in Figure 11.2.

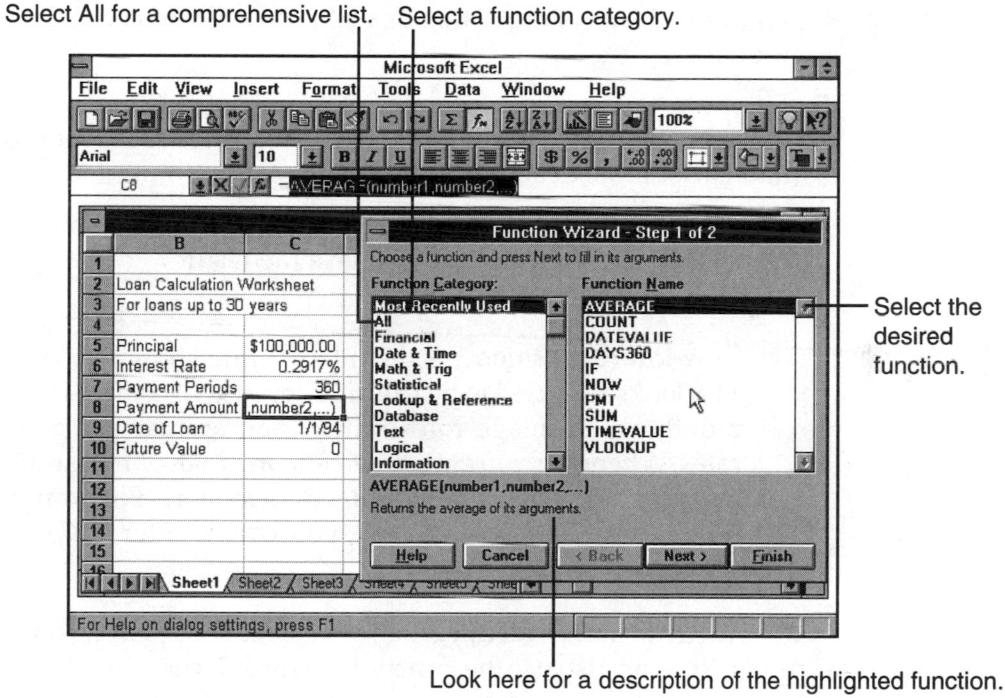

Select All for a comprehensive list. Select a function category.

Select the desired function.

Look here for a description of the highlighted function.

Figure 11.2 The first step is to select the function you want to use.

TIP

Function Names   If this is your first encounter with functions, don't expect them to be simple. However, you can learn a lot about a function and what it does by reading the descriptions in the dialog box. Whenever you highlight a function name, Excel displays a description of the function. If you need more help, click on the **Help** button, or press **F1**.

3. In the Function Category list, select the type of function you want to insert. Excel displays the names of the available functions in the Function Name list.

4. Select the function you want to insert from the Function Name list, and then click on the **Next** button. Excel displays the Step 2 of 2 dialog box. This box will differ depending on the selected function. Figure 11.3 shows the dialog box you'll see if you chose the PMT function.

5. Enter the values or cell ranges for the argument. You can type a value or argument, or drag the dialog box title bar out of the way and click on the desired cells with the mouse pointer.

6. Click on the **Finish** button. Excel inserts the function and argument in the selected cell and displays the result.

Low Interest Rates   If the interest rate shown in Figure 11.3 looks too good to be true, it's because Excel works with monthly percentage rates rather than annual percentage rates. Whenever you enter a percent on a loan or investment, enter the annual percentage rate divided by 12. For example, if your mortgage is at 7% (.07), you would enter =.07/12.

To edit a function, you can type your corrections just as you can with a formula. You can also use the Function Wizard. To use the Wizard, select the cell that contains the function you want to edit. (You want the cell selected, but you don't want to be in Edit mode; that is, the insertion point should not be displayed in the cell.) Open the **Insert** menu, and choose **Function**, or click on the **Function Wizard** button. The Editing Function 1 of 1 dialog box appears, allowing you to edit the function's argument.

In this lesson, you learned the basics of dealing with functions, and you learned how to use Excel's Function Wizard to quickly enter functions. You also learned how to quickly total a series of numbers with the AutoSum tool. In the next lesson, you will learn how to print your workbook.

Printing Your Workbook

In this lesson, you will learn how to print an entire workbook or only a portion of it.

Changing the Page Setup

Before you print a workbook, you should make sure that the page is set up correctly for printing. To do this, open the **File** menu, and choose **Page Setup**. You'll see the Page Setup dialog box, as shown in Figure 12.1.

Right-Click on the Workbook Title Bar   For quick access to commands that affect a workbook, right-click on the workbook's title bar. For example, to check the page setup, right-click on the title bar, and choose **Page Setup**.

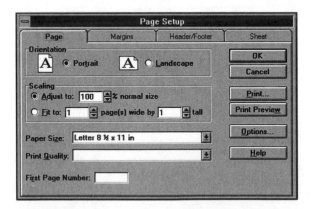

Figure 12.1   The Page Setup dialog box.

Enter your page setup settings as follows:

Page tab

Orientation   Select **Portrait** to print from left to right across a page or **Landscape** to print from top to bottom on a page. (Landscape makes the page wider than it is tall.)

Scaling   You can reduce and enlarge your workbook or force it to fit within a specific page size.

Paper Size   This is 8 1/2-by-11-inches, by default. You can choose a different size from the list.

Print Quality   You can print a draft of your spreadsheet to print quickly and save wear and tear on your printer, or you can print in high quality for a final copy. Print quality is measured in dpi (dots per inch)—the higher the number, the better the print.

First Page Number   You can set the starting page number to something other than 1.

Margins tab

Top, Bottom, Left, Right   You can adjust the size of the left, right, top, and bottom margins.

From Edge   You can specify how far you want a Header or Footer printed from the edge of the page. (You use the Header/Footer tab to add a header or footer to your workbook.)

Center on Page   You can center the printing between the left and right margins (Horizontally) and between the top and bottom margins (Vertically).

Header/Footer tab

Header/Footer   You can add a Header (such as a title, which repeats at the top of each page) or a Footer (such as page numbers, which repeat at the bottom of each page).

Custom Header/Custom Footer   You can choose the Custom Header or Custom Footer button to create headers and footers that insert the time, date, worksheet tab name, and workbook file name.

Print Area   You can print a portion of a workbook or worksheet by entering the range of cells you want to print. You can type the range, or drag the dialog box title bar out of the way and drag the mouse pointer over the desired cells. If you do not select a print area, Excel will print all the cells that contain data.

Print Titles   If you have a row or column of entries that you want repeated as titles on every page, type the range for this row or column, or drag over the cells with the mouse pointer.

Print   You can tell Excel exactly how to print some aspects of the workbook. For example, you can have the gridlines (the lines that define the cells) printed. You can also have a color spreadsheet printed in black-and-white.

Page Order   You can indicate how data in the workbook should be read and printed: in sections from top to bottom or in sections from left to right.

When you are done entering your settings, click on the **OK** button.

Adjusting Page Breaks

When you print a workbook, Excel determines the page breaks based on the paper size and margins and the selected print area. You may want to override the automatic page breaks with your own breaks. However, before you add page breaks, try these options:

- Adjust the widths of individual columns to make the best use of space (see Lesson 16).

- Consider printing the workbook sideways (using Landscape orientation).

- Change the left, right, top, and bottom margins to smaller values.

If after trying these options, you still want to insert page breaks, first determine whether you need to limit the number of columns on a page or the number of rows.

To limit the number of columns:

1. Select a cell that's in the column to the right of the last column you want on the page. For example, if you want Excel to print only columns A through G on the first page, select a cell in column H.

2. Move to row one of that column.

3. Open the **Insert** menu, and choose **Page Break**. A dashed line appears to the left of the selected column, showing the position of the page break.

To limit the number of rows:

1. Select a cell in row just below the last row you want on the page. For example, if you want Excel to print only rows 1 through 12 on the first page, select a cell in row 13.

2. Move to column A of that row.

3. Open the **Insert** menu, and choose **Page Break**. A dashed line appears above the selected row.

One Step Page Breaks You can set the lower right corner of a workbook in one step. Select the cell that is below and to the right of the last cell for the page, and then open the **Insert** menu, and select **Page Break**. For example, if you wanted cell G12 to be the last cell on that page, move to cell H13, and set the page break.

Remove a Page Break To remove a page break, move to the cell that you used to set the page break, open the **Insert** menu, and choose **Remove Page Break**.

Previewing a Print Job

After you've determined your page setup, print area, and page breaks (if any), you can preview your print job before you print. To preview a print job, open the **File** menu, and select **Print Preview**, or click on the **Print Preview** button in the Standard toolbar. Your workbook appears as it will when printed, as shown in Figure 12.2.

Page Setup Print Preview You can also preview a print job when you are setting up a page. When the Page Setup dialog box is displayed, click on the **Print Preview** button.

To return to the normal workbook window, click on Close.

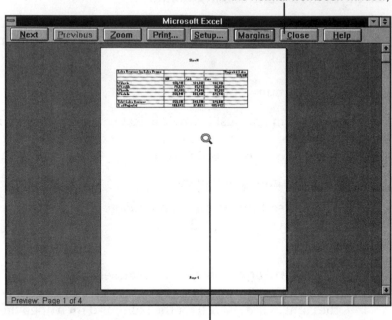

The mouse pointer allows you to zoom in on a portion of the worksheet.

Figure 12.2   You can preview your workbook before printing it.

A Close-Up View   Zoom in on any area of the preview by clicking on it with the mouse. You can also use the **Zoom** button.

Printing

After setting the page setup and previewing your data, it is time to print.

To print your workbook:

1. Open the **File** menu, and select **Print** (or press **Ctrl+P**). The Print dialog box appears, as shown in Figure 12.3.

2. Select the options you would like to use:

   Print What   Allows you to print the currently selected cells, the selected worksheets, or the entire workbook.

   Copies   Allows you to print more than one copy of the selection, worksheet, or workbook.

Page Range Lets you print one or more pages. For example, if the selected print area will take up 15 pages, and you want to print only pages 5–10, select **Page(s)**, and then type the numbers of the first and last page you want to print in the From and To spin boxes.

3. Click on **OK**, or press **Enter**.

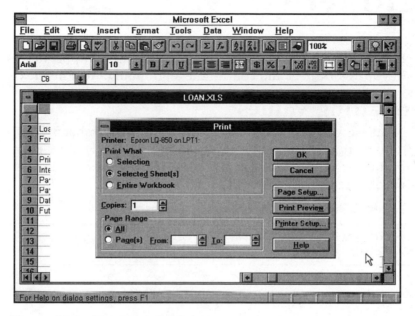

Figure 12.3 The Print dialog box.

Quick Print To print one copy of all the data in a workbook using the default page setup settings, click on the **Print** button in the Standard toolbar. Excel bypasses the Print dialog box and immediately starts printing the workbook.

In this lesson, you learned how to print your workbook. In the next lesson, you will learn how to improve the look of your text by adding character and number formatting.

Adjusting Number Formats and Text Alignment

In this lesson, you will learn how to customize the appearance of numbers in your worksheet and control the alignment of text inside cells.

Formatting Values

Numeric values are usually more than just numbers. They represent a dollar value, a date, a percent, or some other real value. To indicate what particular values stand for, you must display the value in a certain format. Excel offers a wide range of formats as listed in Table 13.1.

Table 13.1   Excel's Numeric Formats

Number Format	Display when you enter: 2000	2	–2	.2
General	2000	2	–2	0.2
0	2000	2	–2	0
0.00	2000.00	2.00	–2.00	0.20
#,##0	2,000	2	–2	0
#,##0.00	2,000.00	2.00	–2.00	0.20
$#,##0_); ($#,##0)	$2,000	$2	($2)	$0
$#,##0.00_); ($#,##0.00)	$2,000.00	$2.00	($2.00)	$0.20
0%	200000%	200%	–200%	20%
0.00%	200000.00%	200.00%	–200.00%	20.00%
0.00E+00	2.00E+03	2.00E+00	–2.00E+00	2.00E-01
#?/ ?	2000	2	–2	1/5

After deciding on a suitable numeric format, follow these steps:

1. Select the cell or range that contains the values you want to format.

2. Pull down the **Format** menu, and select **Cells**, or press **Ctrl+1**. The Format Cells dialog box appears.

3. If the Number tab is not up front, click on it. (See Figure 13.1.)

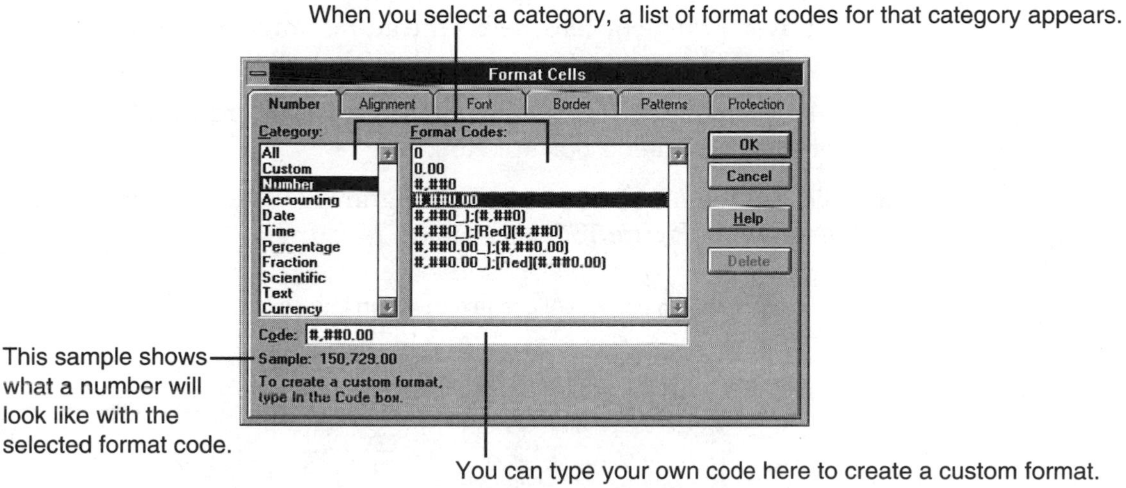

When you select a category, a list of format codes for that category appears.

This sample shows what a number will look like with the selected format code.

You can type your own code here to create a custom format.

Figure 13.1   The Format Cells dialog box with the Number tab up front.

4. In the Category list, select the numeric format category you want to use. Excel displays the formats in that category in the Format Codes list.

5. In the Format Codes list, select the format code you want to use. When you select a format code, Excel shows you what a sample number would look like formatted with that code.

6. Click on **OK**, or press **Enter**.

TIP

Quick Formatting Techniques   The Formatting toolbar (just below the Standard toolbar) contains several buttons for selecting a number format, including the following: Currency Style, Percent Style, Comma Style, Increase Decimal, and Decrease Decimal. You can also change the Number format of a cell by using the shortcut menu; click the right mouse button on a cell to display the shortcut menu, and then choose **Format Cells**.

Aligning Text in Cells

When you enter data into an Excel worksheet, that data is aligned automatically. Text is aligned on the left, and numbers are aligned on the right. Text and numbers are initially set at the bottom of the cells.

To change the alignment:

1. Select the cell or range you want to align. To center a title or other text over a range of cells, select the entire range of cells in which you want the text centered, including the cell that contains the text.

2. Pull down the **Format** menu, and select **Cells**, or press **Ctrl+1**. The Format Cells dialog box appears.

3. Click on the **Alignment** tab. The alignment options jump up front as shown in Figure 13.2.

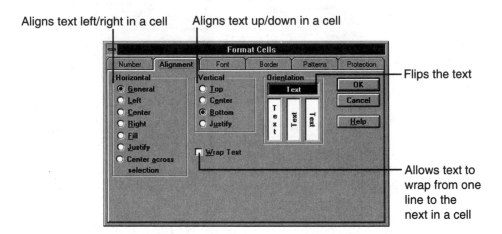

Figure 13.2 The Alignment options.

4. Choose from the following options and option groups to set the alignment:

    Horizontal   Lets you specify a left/right alignment in the cell(s). (The Center across selection option lets you center a title or other text inside a range of cells.)

Vertical   Lets you specify how you want the text aligned in relation to the top and bottom of the cell(s).

Orientation   Lets you flip the text sideways or print it from top to bottom (rather than left to right).

Wrap Text   Tells Excel to wrap long lines of text within a cell. (Normally, Excel displays all text in a cell on one line.)

5. Click on **OK**, or press **Enter**.

Alignment Buttons   A quick way to align text and numbers is to use the alignment buttons in the Formatting toolbar. These buttons allow you to align the text Left, Right, Center, or Center Across Columns.

Repeat Performance   To repeat the alignment format command in another cell, use the **Repeat Format Cells** command from the **Edit** menu, or click on the **Repeat** button in the Standard toolbar.

Changing the Default Format and Alignment

When you enter the same type of data into a large worksheet, it is sometimes convenient to change the default format. You then can change the format for only those cells that are exceptions. Note that when you change the default, it affects all the cells in the worksheet.

You can change the default settings for number format, alignment, and others. To change the defaults:

1. Open the **Format** menu, and choose **Style**. The Style dialog box appears, as shown in Figure 13.3.

2. In the Style Name list box, select **Normal**.

3. Click on the **Modify** button. Excel displays the Format Cells dialog box, as shown in Figure 13.2.

Select the Normal style.

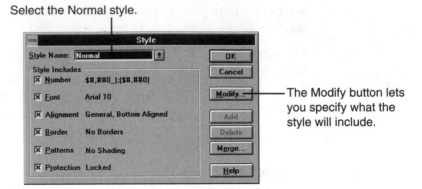

The Modify button lets you specify what the style will include.

Figure 13.3 The Style dialog box.

4. Click on the tab for the group of format settings you want to change. For example, you can click on Number to change the default numeric formatting.

5. Select the desired format settings, and then click on the **OK** button. Excel returns you to the Style dialog box.

6. Click on **OK**, or press **Enter**.

In this lesson, you learned how to format numbers and align data in cells. In the next lesson, you will learn how to format text.

Improving the
Look of Your Text

In this lesson, you will learn how to change the appearance of the text in the cells.

How Can You Make Text Look Different?

When you type text or numbers, Excel inserts plain text, which doesn't look very fancy. You can change the following text attributes to improve the appearance of your text or set it apart from other text:

Font   For example, System, Roman, and MS Sans Serif.

Font Style   For example, Bold, Italic, Underline, and Strikeout.

Size   For example, 10-point, 12-point, and 20-point. (There are approximately 72 points in an inch.)

Color   For example, Red, Magenta, and Cyan.

What's a Font?   In Excel, a font is a set of characters that have the same typeface, for example, Helvetica. When you select a font, Excel also allows you to change the font's size, add an optional *attribute* to the font, such as bold or italic; underline the text; change its color; or add special effects.

Figure 14.1 shows a worksheet after different attributes have been changed for selected text.

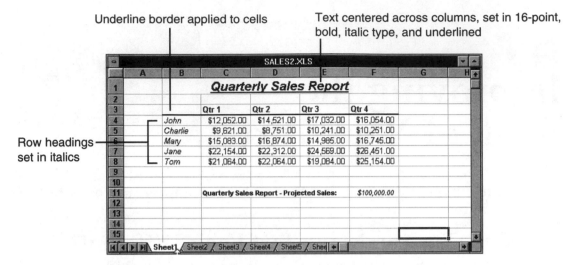

Figure 14.1 A sampling of several text attributes.

Using the Format Cells Dialog Box

You can change the look of your text by using the Format Cells dialog box or by using the Font buttons in the Formatting toolbar. To use the Format Cells dialog box, do this:

1. Select the cell or range that contains the text you want to format.

2. Open the **Format** menu, and choose **Cells**, or press **Ctrl+1**. (You can also right-click on the selected cells, and choose **Format** Cells.)

3. Click on the **Font** tab. The options jump to the front, as shown in Figure 14.2.

4. Enter your font preferences.

5. Click on **OK**, or press **Enter**.

Excel uses a default font to style your text as you type it. To change the default font, enter your font preferences in the Font tab, and then click on the **Normal Font** option. When you click on the **OK** button, Excel makes your preferences the default font.

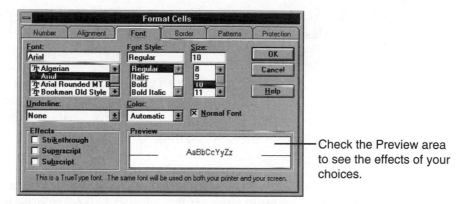

Check the Preview area to see the effects of your choices.

Figure 14.2 The Format Cells dialog box with the Font tab up front.

Font Shortcuts A faster way to change text attributes is to use the keyboard shortcuts. Press **Ctrl+B** for bold; **Ctrl+I** for Italic; **Ctrl+U** for Underline; and **Ctrl+5** for Strikethrough.

Changing Text Attributes with Toolbar Buttons

A faster way to enter font changes is to use the buttons and drop-down lists in the Formatting toolbar, as shown in Figure 14.3.

Select a font size. Italic

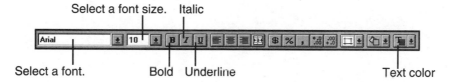

Select a font.   Bold   Underline   Text color

Figure 14.3 Use the Formatting toolbar to quickly enter font changes.

To use a tool to change text attributes:

1. Select the cell or range that contains the text whose look you want to change.

2. To change the font or font size, pull down the appropriate drop-down list, and click on the font or size you want.

317

3. To add an attribute (such as bold or underlining), click on the desired button.

Change Before You Type   You can activate the attributes you want before you type text. For example, if you want a title in Bold, 12-point MS Sans Serif, set these attributes before you start typing.

In this lesson, you learned how to customize your text to achieve the look you want. In the next lesson, you will learn how to add borders and shading to your worksheet.

Adding Cell Borders and Shading

In this lesson, you will learn how to add pizzazz to your worksheets by adding borders and shading.

Adding Borders to Cells

As you work with your worksheet on-screen, each cell is identified by a gridline that surrounds the cell. In print, these gridlines may appear washed out. To have better defined lines appear on the printout, you can add borders to selected cells or cell ranges. Figure 15.1 shows the options for adding lines to cells and cell ranges.

All	All
All	All
All	All

Outline	Outline
Outline	Outline
Outline	Outline

Inside	Inside
Inside	Inside
Inside	Inside

Single	Single
Single	Single
Single	Single

Double	Double
Double	Double
Double	Double

Thick	Thick
Thick	Thick
Thick	Thick

Top	Top
Top	Top
Top	Top

Bottom	Bottom
Bottom	Bottom
Bottom	Bottom

Left	Right
Left	Right
Left	Right

Figure 15.1   A sampling of borders.

To add borders to a cell or range, perform the following steps:

1. Select the cell(s) around which you want a border to appear.

2. Open the **Format** menu, and choose **Cells**. The Format Cells dialog box appears.

3. Click on the **Border** tab. The Border options jump up front, as shown in Figure 15.2.

319

4. Select the desired border position, style (thickness), and color for the border.

5. Click on **OK**, or press **Enter**.

Select a border position.   Select a border style.

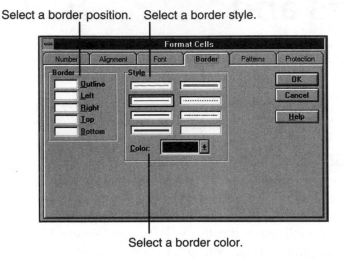

Select a border color.

Figure 15.2   The Format Cells dialog box with the Border tab up front.

TIP

Hiding Gridlines   When adding borders to a worksheet, hide the gridlines to get a better idea of how the borders will print. Open the **Tools** menu, select **Options**, click on the **View** tab, and select **Gridlines** to remove the **X** from the check box. To prevent gridlines from printing, open the **File** menu, select **Page Setup**, click on the **Sheet** tab, and clear the **X** from the Gridlines check box.

TIP

Borders Button   To add borders quickly, select the cells around which you want the border to appear, and then click on the arrow to the right of the Borders button in the Formatting toolbar. Click on the desired border. If you click on the **Borders** button itself (rather than on the arrow), Excel automatically adds a bottom borderline or the borderline you last selected to the selected cells.

Adding Shading to Cells

For a simple but dramatic effect, add shading to your worksheets. Figure 15.3 illustrates the effects that you can create with shading.

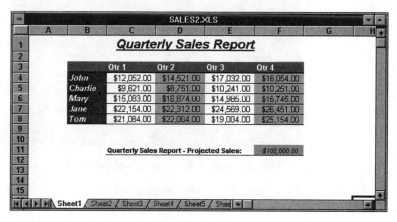

Figure 15.3 A worksheet with added shading.

To add shading to cell or range:

1. Select the cell(s) you want to shade.

2. Pull down the **Format** menu, and choose **Cells**.

3. Click on the **Patterns** tab. The shading options jump to the front, as shown in Figure 15.4.

4. Select the shading color and pattern you want to use. The Color options let you choose a color for the overall shading. The Pattern options let you select a black-and-white or colored pattern that lies on top of the overall shading. A preview of the result is displayed in the Sample box.

5. Click on **OK**, or press **Enter**.

Color Button A quick way to add shading (without a pattern) is to select the cells you want to shade and then click on the arrow to the right of the Color button (the button that has the bucket on it). Click on the color you want to use. If the shading is dark, consider using the **Font Color** button (just to the right of the Color button) to select a light color for the text.

Select an overall color.

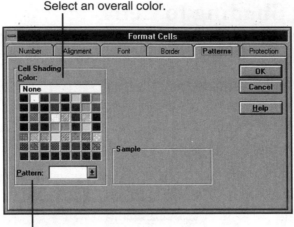

Select a pattern to lay on top of the color.

Figure 15.4   Selecting a shading pattern.

More Formatting Tricks

Excel offers a couple of features that take some of the pain out of formatting: AutoFormat and the Format Painter. AutoFormat provides you with several predesigned table formats that you can apply to a worksheet. The Format Painter lets you quickly copy and paste formats that you have already used in a workbook.

To use AutoFormat, perform the following steps:

1. Select the worksheet(s) and cell(s) that contain the data you want to format.

2. Open the **Format** menu, and choose **AutoFormat**. The AutoFormat dialog box appears, as shown in Figure 15.5.

3. In the Table Format list, choose the predesigned format you want to use. When you select a format, Excel shows you what it will look like in the Sample area.

4. To exclude certain elements from the AutoFormat, click on the **Options** button, and choose the formats you want to turn off.

5. Click on the **OK** button. Excel formats your table to make it look like the one in the preview area.

Select a predesigned table format.   Sample area shows effects of the table format.

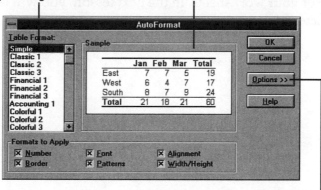

Click on the Options button to view the formats
that make up the selected table format.

Figure 15.5   Use the AutoFormat dialog box to select a prefab format.

Deformatting an AutoFormat   If you don't like what AutoFormat did to your worksheet, click on the **Undo** button, or press **Ctrl+Z**. Or open the **Edit** menu, and choose **Undo AutoFormat**.

Excel gives you two ways to copy and paste formatting. You can use the **Edit Copy** command and then the **Edit Paste Special** command, or the **Format Painter** button in the Standard toolbar. Because the Format Painter button is faster, I'll give you the steps you need to paint formats:

1. Select the cell(s) that contain the formatting you want to copy and paste.

2. Click on the **Format Painter** button (the one with the paintbrush on it) in the Standard toolbar. Excel copies the formatting. The mouse pointer changes into a paintbrush with a plus sign next to it.

3. Drag over the cells to which you want to apply the copied formatting.

4. Release the mouse button. The copied formatting is applied to the selected cells.

In this lesson, you learned some additional ways to enhance the appearance of your worksheets. In the next lesson, you will learn how to change the sizes of rows and columns.

Changing Column Width and Row Height

In this lesson, you will learn how to adjust the column width and row height to make the best use of the worksheet space. You can set these manually or let Excel make the adjustments for you.

Adjusting Column Width and Row Height with a Mouse

You can adjust the width of a column or the height of a row by using a dialog box or by using the mouse. Here's how you adjust the row height or column width with the mouse:

1. Move the mouse pointer inside the heading for the row or column. To change the row height or column width for two or more rows or columns, drag over the headings with the mouse pointer.

2. Move the mouse pointer to one of the borders, as shown in Figure 16.1. (Use the right border to adjust column width or the bottom border to adjust the row height.)

3. Hold down the mouse button, and drag the border.

4. Release the mouse button, and the row height or column width is adjusted.

Custom-Fit Cells   To quickly make a column as wide as its widest entry, double-click on the right border of the column heading. To make a row as tall as its tallest entry, double-click on the bottom border of the row heading. To change more than one column or row at a time, drag over the desired row or column headings and then double-click on the bottommost or rightmost heading border.

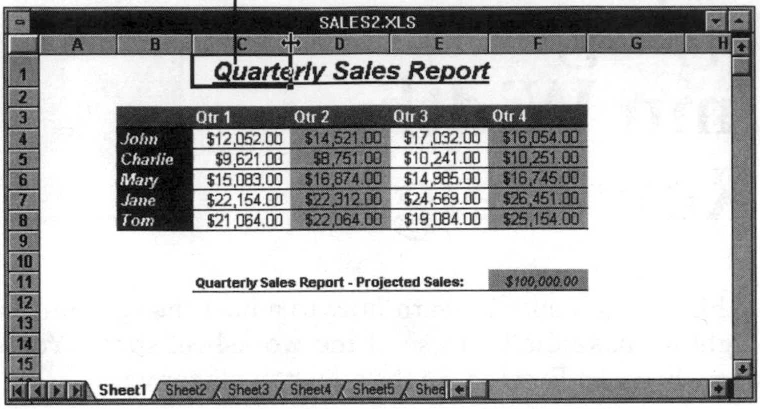

Dragging the right border of column C changes its width.

	A	B	C	D	E	F	G	H
			SALES2.XLS					
1			*Quarterly Sales Report*					
2								
3			Qtr 1	Qtr 2	Qtr 3	Qtr 4		
4		*John*	$12,052.00	$14,521.00	$17,032.00	$16,054.00		
5		*Charlie*	$9,621.00	$8,751.00	$10,241.00	$10,251.00		
6		*Mary*	$15,083.00	$16,874.00	$14,985.00	$16,745.00		
7		*Jane*	$22,154.00	$22,312.00	$24,569.00	$26,451.00		
8		*Tom*	$21,064.00	$22,064.00	$19,084.00	$25,154.00		
9								
10								
11			Quarterly Sales Report - Projected Sales:			$100,000.00		
12								
13								
14								
15								

Sheet1 / Sheet2 / Sheet3 / Sheet4 / Sheet5 / Shee

Figure 16.1   The mouse pointer changes when you move it over a border in the row or column heading.

Using the Format Menu

The Format menu contains the commands you need to change the column width and row height of selected rows and columns. Here's how you use the Format menu to change the column width:

1. Select the column(s) whose width you want to change. To change the width of a single column, select any cell in that column.

2. Pull down the **Format** menu, select **Column**, and select **Width**. The Column Width dialog box appears, as shown in Figure 16.2.

3. Type the number of characters you would like as the width. The standard width shown is based on the current default font.

   Click on **OK**, or press **Enter**.

Figure 16.2   Changing the column width.

AutoFit Column Width To make selected columns as wide as their widest entries, select the columns, open the **Format** menu, select Column, and select **AutoFit Selection**.

By default, Excel makes a row a bit taller than the tallest text in the row. For example, if the tallest text is 10 points tall, Excel makes the row 12.75 points tall. To use the Format menu to change the row height:

1. Select the row(s) whose height you want to change. To change the height of a single row, select any cell in that row.

2. Pull down the **Format** menu, select **Row** and then **Height**. The Row Height dialog box appears, as shown in Figure 16.3.

3. Type the desired height in points.

4. Click on **OK**, or press **Enter**.

Figure 16.3 Changing the row height.

Auto Height To make selected rows as tall as their tallest entries, select the rows, open the **Format** menu, select **Row**, and select **AutoFit**.

In this lesson, you learned how to change the row height and column width. In the next lesson, you will learn how to use styles (collections of format settings).

Formatting with Styles

In this lesson, you'll learn how to apply several formatting effects by applying a single style to selected cells.

What Is a Style?

In Lessons 13 through 15, you enhanced a spreadsheet by applying various formats to cells. *Styles* allow you to apply several formats to a selected cell or cell block by assigning a named style.

What's a Style?   A style is a group of cell formatting options that you can apply to a cell or cell block. If you change the style's definition later, that change affects the formatting of all cells formatted with that style.

Each style contains specifications for one or more of the following options:

- **Number Format**   Controls the appearance of values, such as dollar values and dates.

- **Font**   Specifies the type style, type size, and any attributes for text contained in the cell.

- **Alignment**   Specifies general, left, right, or center alignment.

- **Border**   Specifies the border placement and line style options for the cell.

- **Patterns**   Adds specified shading to the cell.

- **Protection**   Allows you to protect or unprotect a cell. However, if you protect a cell or range of cells, the cells are not locked until you protect a worksheet as well by selecting **Tools Protection Protect Sheet**.

Excel has six precreated styles:

Normal   The default style. Number is set to 0, Font to Arial, Size to 10-point, Alignment of numbers is right, and Alignment of text is left, No Border, No Pattern, and Protection is set to locked.

Comma Number is set to #,##0.00.

Comma (0) Number is set to #,##0.

Currency Number is set to $#,##0.00_); (Red) ($#,##0.00).

Currency (0) Number is set to $#,##0); (Red) ($#,##0).

Percent Number is set to 0%.

Style Buttons   You can apply most of Excel's existing styles by selecting the cell or cell range and then clicking on the appropriate button in the Formatting toolbar. For example, to set the currency format, select the cells, and then click on the **Currency Style** button (the button with the dollar sign on it).

Applying Existing Styles

To apply an existing style to a cell or range, perform the following steps:

1. Select the cell or range.

2. Open the **Format** menu, and select **Style**. The Style dialog box appears, as shown in Figure 17.1.

3. Click on the down arrow to the right of the Style Name list box, and select the style you want to use.

4. Click on **OK**, or press **Enter**. The style is applied to the selected cell or range.

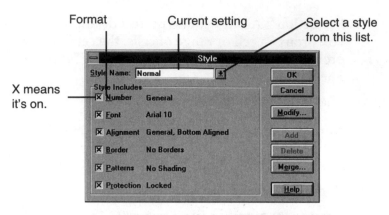

Figure 17.1 Use the Style dialog box to apply styles to cells.

Toolbar Style List Instead of separate Style buttons for each of its existing styles, Excel 4.0 had a style drop-down list in the toolbar. If you miss that list, you can add it back to the toolbar. Choose **View Toolbars Customize**. Click on the **Formatting** category, and then drag the Style box up into one of the toolbars. While the Customize dialog box is displayed, you can drag the Style buttons off the toolbar to make room for the Style list.

Creating Styles

To save time, save your favorite formatting combinations as styles. You can create your own styles in various ways:

- Define the style: Create a style, and then assign one or more formatting attributes to it.

- Define by example: Select a cell that contains the formatting you want to use, and then create a style.

- Copy a format: Select a cell in another workbook that contains the formatting you want to use, and then merge it with the styles used in the current workbook.

To define a style, perform the following steps:

1. Open the **Format** menu, and choose **Style**. The Style dialog box appears.

2. Type a name for the style in the Style Name list box, and click on the **Add** button. The style is added to the list, and you can now modify it.

3. Remove the **X** from any check box whose attribute you do not want to include in the style. (See Figure 17.2.)

Type a name for the
new style.

Turn a format
attribute on or
off.

Click on Modify to
change the format
settings.

Figure 17.2 Defining a new style.

4. To change any of the format settings for the attributes in the list, click on the **Modify** button. Excel displays the Format Cells dialog box.

5. Click on the tab for the format attribute whose settings you want to change, and enter your preferences.

6. Repeat step 5 for each attribute whose settings you want to change.

7. Click on **OK**, or press **Enter**. You are returned to the Style dialog box.

8. Click on **OK**, or press **Enter**. The Style is created and saved.

TIP

Modifying a Style Later   If you apply a style to one or more cells and then modify the style later, any changes you enter will immediately be applied to all cells you formatted with that style.

To create a new style by example:

1. Select a cell whose formatting you want to use.

2. Open the **Format** menu, and choose **Style**.

3. Type a name for the style in the Style Name box.

4. Click on the **Add** button. The named style is added to the Style Name list box.

5. Click on **OK**, or press **Enter**.

To copy existing styles from another workbook:

1. Open both workbooks.

2. Switch to the workbook you want to copy the styles to.

3. Open the **Format** menu, and choose **Style**.

4. Click on the **Merge** button.

5. Select the name of the worksheet to copy from.

6. Click on **OK**, or press **Enter** to close the Merge dialog box. Click on **Yes** if the dialog box asks, **Merge styles that have the same names?**.

7. Click on **OK**, or press **Enter**.

In this lesson, you learned how to create and apply styles. In the next lesson, you will learn how to create charts.

Creating Charts

In this lesson, you will learn to create charts (graphs) to represent your workbook data as a picture.

Charting with Excel

With Excel, you can create various types of charts. Some common chart types are shown in Figure 18.1. The chart type you choose depends on your data and on how you want to present that data. These are the major chart types and their purposes:

Pie   Use this chart to show the relationship between parts of a whole.

Bar   Use this chart to compare values at a given point in time.

Column   Similar to the Bar chart; use this chart to emphasize the difference between items.

Line   Use this chart to emphasize trends and the change of values over time.

Area   Similar to the Line chart; use this chart to emphasize the amount of change in values.

Most of these basic chart types also come in 3-dimensional varieties. In addition to looking more professional than the standard flat charts, 3-D charts can often help your audience distinguish between different sets of data.

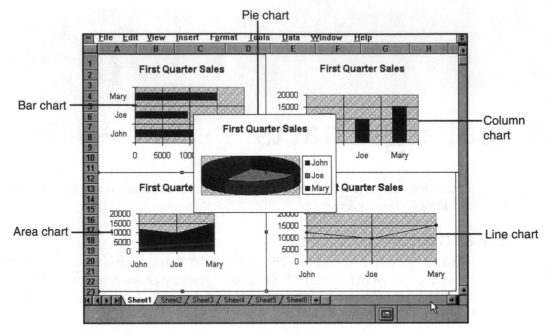

Figure 18.1   Commonly used Excel chart types.

Embedded Charts   A chart that is placed on the same worksheet that contains the data used to create the chart. Embedded charts are useful for showing the actual data and its graphic representation side-by-side.

Charting Terminology

Before you start creating charts, familiarize yourself with the following terminology:

Data Series   A collection of related data, such as the monthly sales for a single division. A data series is usually a single row or column on the worksheet.

Axis   One side of a chart. In a two-dimensional chart, there is an X-axis (horizontal) and a Y-axis (vertical). In a three-dimensional chart, the Z-axis represents the vertical plane; the X-axis (distance) and Y-axis (width) represent the two sides on the floor of the chart.

Legend   Defines the separate elements of a chart. For example, the legend for a pie chart will show what each piece of the pie represents.

Creating a Chart

You can create charts as part of a worksheet (an embedded chart) or as a separate chart worksheet. If you create an embedded chart, it will print side-by-side with your worksheet data. If you create a chart on a chart worksheet, you can print it separately. Both types of charts are linked to the worksheet data that they represent, so when you change the data, the chart is automatically updated.

Creating an Embedded Chart

The ChartWizard button in the Standard toolbar allows you to create a graph frame on a worksheet. To use the ChartWizard, take the following steps:

1. Select the data you want to chart. If you typed names or other labels (for example, Qtr 1, Qtr 2, and so on) and you want them included in the chart, make sure you select them.

2. Click on the **ChartWizard** button in the Standard toolbar (see Figure 18.2).

3. Move the mouse pointer where you want the upper left corner of the chart to appear.

4. Hold down the mouse button, and drag to define the size and dimensions of the chart. To create a square graph, hold down the **Shift** key as you drag. If you want your chart to exactly fit the borders of the cells it occupies, hold down the **Alt** key as you drag.

5. Release the mouse button. The ChartWizard Step 1 of 5 dialog box appears, asking if the selected range is correct. You can correct the range by typing a new range or by dragging the dialog box title bar out of the way, and dragging over the cells you want to chart.

6. Click on the **Next** button. The ChartWizard Step 2 of 5 dialog box appears, as shown in Figure 18.2, asking you to select a chart type.

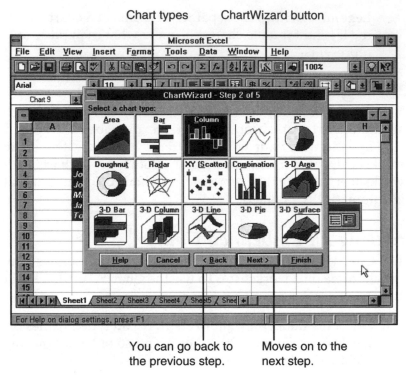

Figure 18.2   ChartWizard asks you to choose the chart type you want.

7. Select a chart type, and click on the **Next** button. The ChartWizard Step 3 of 5 dialog box appears, asking you to select a chart format (a variation on the selected chart type).

8. Select a format for the chosen chart type, and click on the **Next** button. The ChartWizard Step 4 of 5 dialog box appears, as shown in Figure 18.3. (Your dialog box may look different, depending on the chart type you chose.)

9. Choose whether the data series is based on rows or columns, and choose the starting row and column. Click on the **Next** button. The ChartWizard Step 5 of 5 dialog box appears.

10. If desired, add a legend, title, or axis labels. Click on the **Finish** button. Your completed chart appears on the current worksheet.

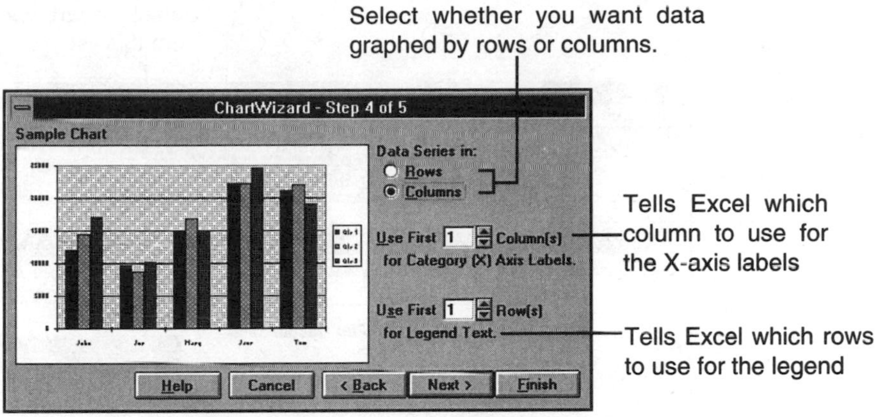

Select whether you want data
graphed by rows or columns.

ChartWizard - Step 4 of 5

Sample Chart

Data Series in:
○ **R**ows
◉ **C**olumns

U**s**e First 1 ⬍ Column(s)
for Category (X) Axis Labels.

U**s**e First 1 ⬍ Row(s)
for Legend Text.

Help   Cancel   < **B**ack   Next >   **F**inish

Tells Excel which
column to use for
the X-axis labels

Tells Excel which rows
to use for the legend

Figure 18.3 The ChartWizard prompts you to specify exactly how you want
the data charted.

Moving and Resizing a Chart   To move an embedded
chart, click anywhere in the chart area and drag it to the new
location. To change the size of a chart, select the chart, and
then drag one of its handles (the black squares that border
the chart). Drag a corner handle to change the height and
width, or drag a side handle to change only the width.

Creating a Chart on a Separate Worksheet

If you don't want your chart to appear on the same page as your worksheet
data, you can create the chart on a separate worksheet. To create a chart in
this way, select the data you want to chart, and then open the **Insert** menu,
choose **Chart**, and choose **As New Sheet**. Excel inserts a separate chart
worksheet (named Chart 1) to the left of the current worksheet and starts
the ChartWizard. Perform the same steps given in the previous section for
creating a chart with the ChartWizard.

Using the Chart Toolbar

You can use the Chart toolbar to create a chart, or to change an existing
chart, as shown in Figure 18.4. If the Chart toolbar is not displayed, you can
turn it on by choosing **View Toolbars**, placing an **X** in the Chart check box,
and clicking on **OK**.

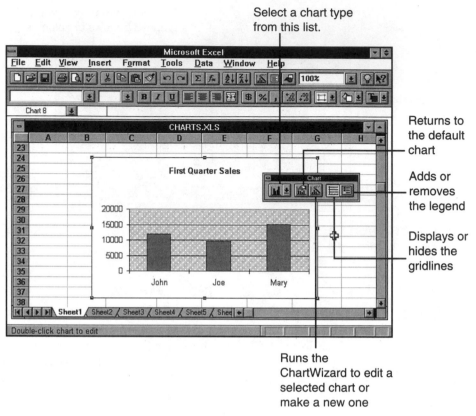

Figure 18.4 The Chart toolbar.

Still Not Satisfied? If you need to make changes to your chart, select the chart, and then click on the **ChartWizard** tool to redefine the data area and make other changes.

Saving Charts

The charts you create are part of the current workbook. To save a chart, simply save the workbook that contains the chart. For more details, refer to Lesson 4, "Working with Workbook Files."

Printing a Chart

If a chart is an embedded chart, it will print when you print the worksheet that contains the chart. If you created a chart on a separate worksheet, you can print the chart separately by printing only the chart worksheet. For more information about printing, refer to Lesson 12, "Printing Your Workbook."

In this lesson, you learned about the different chart types and how to create them. You also learned how to save and print charts. In the next lesson, you will learn how to enhance your charts.

Enhancing Charts

In this lesson, you will learn how to enhance your charts to display data more clearly and more attractively.

What Can You Add to a Chart?

You can format existing elements and add elements to a chart to enhance it. Following is a list of some of the more common enhancements:

Fonts Specify a type style, size, and attributes for the text used in the chart.

Colors Change the color of text or of the lines, bars, and pie slices that are used to represent data.

Titles and Labels Add a title to the chart or add labels for any of the axes.

Axes Display or hide the lines used for the X- and Y-axes.

Text Boxes Add explanatory text or other text in a separate box.

Borders and Shading Add a border around a chart or add background shading.

Text Boxes and Lines Text boxes and lines are available both in charts and in worksheets. Refer to Lesson 20 for details about adding lines and other shapes to charts and worksheets.

Opening a Chart Window

Before you can add enhancements to a chart, you have to open the chart in its own window. To open a chart window for an embedded chart, double-click on the chart to display it in a frame. If the chart is on a separate worksheet, click on its tab to display it in a window. See Figure 19.1. The frame and window serve the same purpose; they just look different.

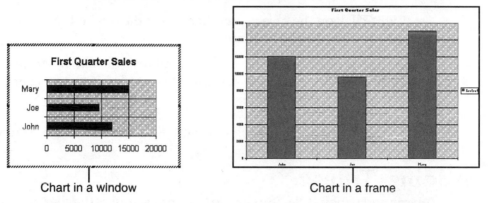

Chart in a window   Chart in a frame

Figure 19.1 Before you add enhancements, you must display the chart in a window.

Before you start adding enhancements to a chart, you should understand that a chart is made up of several objects. By clicking on an object, you make it active, and handles appear around it, as shown in Figure 19.2.

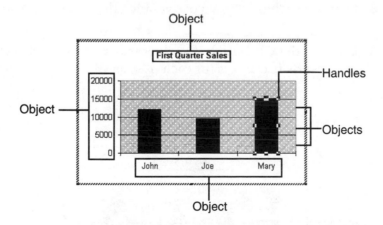

Figure 19.2 Each chart consists of several individual objects.

You can then move or resize the object or change its appearance, by doing any of the following:

341

- Double-click on an object to display a dialog box that lets you change the object's appearance. For example, if you double-click on a column in a column chart, you can change its color.

- Right-click on the object, and then select the desired formatting option from the shortcut menu.

- Select the object, and then select an option from the **Insert** or **Format** menu. The Insert menu lets you add objects to a chart, including a legend, data labels, and a chart title.

The following sections tell you how to add some more commonly used enhancements to a chart.

Adding Titles

You can add various titles to a chart to help indicate what the chart is all about. You can add a chart title that appears at the top of the chart, and you can add axis titles that appear along the X- and Y-axes. Here's how you do it:

1. Make sure the chart is displayed in a chart window.

2. Right-click on the chart, and choose **Insert Titles**, or open the **Insert** menu, and **choose** Titles.

3. Click on each title type you want to add, to put an **X** in their check boxes.

4. Click on the **OK** button. Excel returns you to the chart window and inserts text boxes for each title, as shown in Figure 19.3.

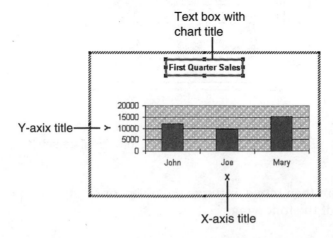

Figure 19.3   Excel inserts text boxes for each specified title.

5. Click on a text box to select it, click inside the text box, and then edit the text as desired.

More Text If you want to add text that is not a chart title or axis title, use the **Text Box** button in the Standard toolbar (just to the right of the ChartWizard button). Click on the button, and then drag the mouse pointer to create the text box. When you release the mouse button, an insertion point appears inside the text box. Type your text. You can use this same technique to add text to your worksheets as well.

Formatting Text on a Chart

Any text you add to a chart is added inside a text box. (You'll learn how to format text that was lifted from the worksheet data in the next section.) To format text you added, do this:

1. Right-click on the text that you want to format. A text box appears around the text, and a shortcut menu appears.

2. Select the **Format** option. The Format option differs depending on the object. If you right-click on the chart title, the option reads **Format Chart Title**.

3. Enter your preferences in the Format dialog box. This dialog box typically contains tabs for changing the font, adding borders and shading to the text box, and changing the alignment of text in the box, but you may get only the Font tab.

4. Click on **OK** when you are done.

Formatting Text You Did Not Add Charts may contain some text that was obtained from the worksheet data. A quick way to format this text is to right-click on the chart (not on any specific object), and choose **Format Chart Area**. Click on the **Font** tab, enter your preferences, and click on **OK**.

Formatting the Axes

You can enhance the X- and Y-axes in a number of ways, including changing the font of the text, scaling the axes, and changing the number format. Here's how you do it:

1. Right-click on the axis you want to format, and choose **Format Axis**, or click on the axis, open the **Format** menu, and choose **Selected Axis**. The Format Axis dialog box appears, as shown in Figure 19.4.

2. Enter your preferences in the dialog box.

3. Click on **OK**, or press **Enter**.

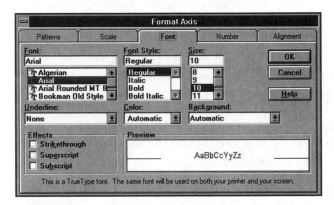

Figure 19.4 The Format Axis dialog box lets you change the look of the axis and its text.

Enhancing the Chart Frame

You can change the overall look of a chart by adding a border or shading. You can do this when the chart is displayed in a window, or when it appears in a worksheet. Here's what you do if the chart is displayed in its own window:

1. Click on the chart anywhere outside a specific chart object. Handles appear around the entire chart.

2. Open the **Format** menu and choose **Selected Chart Area**, or right-click on the chart and choose **Format Chart Area**. The Format Chart Area dialog box appears.

3. Click on the **Patterns** tab, enter your preferences, and then click on the **OK** button.

If the chart is not in a separate window, click on the chart, open the **Format** menu, and choose **Object**, or right-click on the chart and choose **Format Object**. The Format Object dialog box appears. Enter your preferences, and then click on **OK**.

Selecting a Chart Design with AutoFormat

Excel 5 comes with several predesigned chart formats that you can apply to your chart. You simply select the design, and Excel reformats your chart, giving it a professional look. Here's how to use AutoFormat to select a chart design:

1. Make sure the chart is displayed in a separate chart window.
2. Open the **Format** menu, and choose **AutoFormat**. The AutoFormat dialog box appears, as shown in Figure 19.5.
3. From the Galleries list, choose a chart type. In the Formats list, Excel shows the available formats for the selected chart type.
4. Select the desired chart type from the Formats list.
5. Click on the **OK** button. Excel reformats the chart, using the selected format.

Select a design.

Select a chart type.

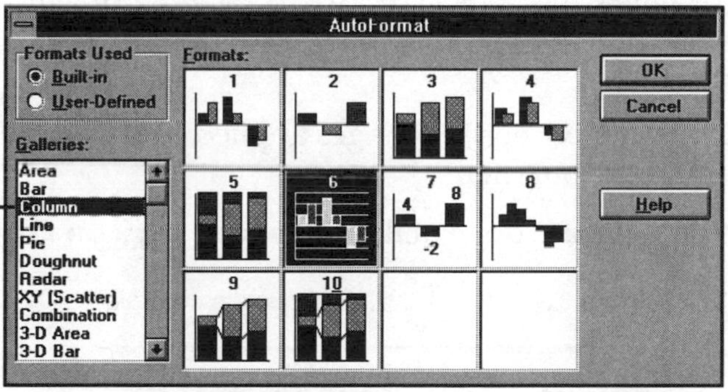

Figure 19.5 Select a chart design from the AutoFormat dialog box.

TIP

Make Your Own Formats You can create your own chart designs for AutoFormat. Display the chart you want to use in a separate window. Open the **Format** menu, and choose **AutoFormat**. Click on **User-Defined** and then click on the **Customize** button. Excel displays the current graph and lets you add it to AutoFormat. Click on the **Add** button, type a name and description of your chart format, click on **OK**, and then click on the **Close** button.

Changing the Look of 3-D Charts

3-D charts are commonly used to illustrate volume. In order to make the various 3-dimensional elements stand out, you may want to tilt the chart or rotate it. Here's how you do it:

1. Make sure the 3-D chart you want to change is displayed in its own window.

2. Open the **Format** menu and choose **3-D View**, or right-click on the chart and choose **3-D View**. The Format 3-D View dialog box appears, as shown in Figure 19.6. As you make changes, they are reflected in the wire-frame picture in the middle of the 3-D View dialog box.

3. To change the elevation (height from which the chart is seen), click on the up or down elevation controls, or type a number in the Elevation box.

4. To change the rotation (rotation around the Z-axis), click on the left or right rotation controls, or type a number in the Rotation box.

5. To change the perspective (perceived depth), click on the up or down perspective controls, or type a number in the Perspective box.

6. To see the proposed changes applied to the actual chart, click on the **Apply** button.

7. When you are done making changes, click on **OK**, or press **Enter**.

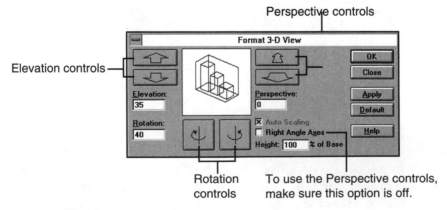

Figure 19.6   Changing the 3-D view.

In this lesson, you learned how to improve the appearance of your chart. In the next lesson, you will learn how to use Excel's drawing tools to enhance the appearance of worksheets and charts.

Adding Graphics to Charts and Workbooks

In this lesson, you will learn how to add graphic objects to your charts and worksheets.

Working with Graphic Objects

Excel comes with several tools that allow you to add pictures to your workbooks and charts. You can add a picture created in another program, you can add clip art, or you can draw your own pictures using the Drawing toolbar.

Graphic Object   A graphic object is anything in your worksheet that isn't data. Graphic objects include things you can draw (such as ovals and rectangles), text boxes, charts, and clip art.

Inserting Pictures

If you have a collection of clip art or pictures that you created and saved using a graphics program or scanner, you can insert those pictures on a worksheet or in a chart. To insert a picture, do this:

1. Select the cell where you want the upper left corner of the picture placed. (To insert the picture in a chart, double-click on the chart to display it in a separate window.)

2. Open the **Insert** menu, and choose **Picture**. The Picture dialog box appears, as shown in Figure 20.1.

3. Change to the drive and directory that contains your clip art or graphics files. A list of graphics files appears in the File Name list.

4. Select the name of the graphics file you want to insert, and click on the **OK** button. Excel imports the picture.

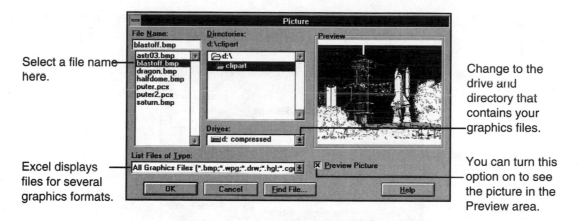

Select a file name here.

Change to the drive and directory that contains your graphics files.

Excel displays files for several graphics formats.

You can turn this option on to see the picture in the Preview area.

Figure 20.1 You can insert a picture or a clip art file.

You can move the picture by dragging it. To resize the picture, drag one of its handles. Drag a corner handle to change both the width and height. Drag a side handle to change only the width, or drag a top or bottom handle to change only the height.

Copy and Paste Pictures Another way to insert a picture is to copy it from one program and then paste it in Excel. First, display the picture in the program you used to create it, and use the **Edit Copy** command in that program to copy it to the Windows Clipboard. Change back to Excel, and use the **Edit Paste** command to paste the picture from the Clipboard into your workbook or graph.

Inserting Other Objects

In addition to pictures, you can insert objects created in other programs. For example, you can insert a sound recording (if you have a sound board that has a microphone attached) or WordArt objects (if you have Microsoft Publisher or Word for Windows). When you choose to insert an object, Excel runs the required program and lets you create the object. When you quit the other program, the object is inserted on the current chart or worksheet. Here's what you do:

1. Select the cell where you want the upper left corner of the picture placed. (To insert the picture in a chart, double-click on the chart to display it in a separate window.)

2. Open the **Insert** menu, and choose **Object**. The Object dialog box appears, as shown in Figure 20.2.

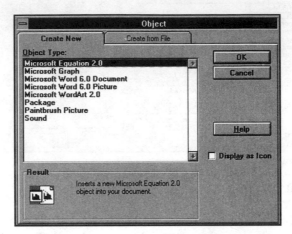

Figure 20.2 Select the program you need to create the object.

3. Make sure the **Create New** tab is up front. The Create New tab lets you run another program and create the object. Create from File allows you to insert an object that you have already created and saved.

4. Select the program you need to run to create the object from the Object Type list.

5. Click on the **OK** button. Excel runs the selected program.

6. Use the program as you normally would to create the object. When you are done, save the object, and exit the program as you usually do. When you exit, a dialog box appears asking if you want to update the link before exiting.

7. Choose **Yes**.

Create from File The Create from File tab is like using Insert Picture; both commands insert an object without running a program.

Drawing Your Own Pictures

If you don't have a drawing program, or you don't want to use it to create a separate file, you can use Excel's Drawing toolbar to create a picture or add simple lines and shapes to a chart or workbook. To turn on the Drawing toolbar, choose **View Toolbars**, click on **Drawing**, and click on **OK**. The Drawing toolbar appears on-screen, as shown in Figure 20.3.

Drawing tools   Tools for working with drawn objects

Figure 20.3   The Drawing toolbar lets you add shapes and lines to your workbook.

Drawing Objects

To draw an object, you select the tool for the line or shape you want to use and then drag the shape on the screen. Here's the step-by-step procedure:

1. Click on the desired tool on the Drawing toolbar. Your mouse will change to a cross-hair pointer.

2. Move the cross-hair pointer to the upper left corner of where you would like to draw the object.

3. Hold down the mouse button, and drag the pointer until the object is the size and shape you want. See Figure 20.4.

4. Release the mouse button.

Tips for Working with Objects

Following is a list of additional drawing tips that can save you some time and reduce frustration:

- To draw several objects of the same shape, double-click on the tool, and then use the mouse to create as many of those shapes as you like.

- To draw a uniform object (a perfect circle or square), hold down the **Shift** key while dragging.

- To select an object, click on it.

- To delete an object, select it, and press **Del**.

- To move an object, select it, and drag one of its lines.

- To resize or reshape an object, select it, and drag one of its handles. If you used one of the Freeform tools or the Freehand tool to draw an irregularly shaped object, you must click on the **Reshape** button to reshape the object.

- To copy an object, hold down the **Ctrl** key while dragging it.

- To quickly change the look of an object, right-click on it, and select the desired option from the shortcut menu.

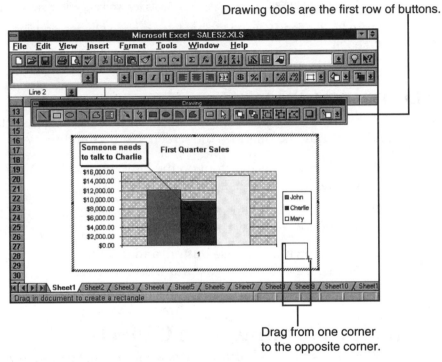

Figure 20.4   Drawing an object on a chart.

Working with Layers of Objects

As you place objects on-screen, they may start to overlap, making it difficult or impossible to select the objects in the lower layer. To reveal or work with items in the lower layers, you may have to use the Bring To Front and Send To Back buttons shown in Figure 20.5.

Bring To Front button ——— 🔲🔳 ——— Send To Back button

Figure 20.5   Use these buttons to relayer overlapping objects.

Grouping and Ungrouping Objects

Each object you draw acts as an individual object. However, sometimes, you'll want two or more objects to act as a group. For example, you may want to make the lines of several objects the same thickness, or move the objects together. To select more than one object, you have two options:

Option 1: Hold down the **Shift** key while clicking on each object you want to include in the group.

Option 2: Click on the **Drawing Selection** button (the button with the mouse pointer on it) in the Drawing toolbar, and then use the mouse to drag a selection box around the items you want included in the group.

However you do it, handles appear around each object, showing you that it is selected. If you want two or more objects to always be treated as a group, select the objects, and then click on the **Group Objects** button. To ungroup the objects later, click on the **Ungroup Objects** button. See Figure 20.6.

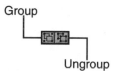

Group

Ungroup

Figure 20.6 Excel lets you group or ungroup objects.

Changing the Appearance of an Object

Objects typically are made up of a thin, black line with white or gray shading inside it. If you want to add color to an object, or change its line thickness or color, you must format the object. There are three ways to format an object:

- Right-click on the object, and choose **Format Object**.
- Click on the object, open the **Format** menu, and choose **Selected Object**, or press **Ctrl+1**.
- Double-click on the object.

Any way you do it, the Format Object dialog box appears. Enter your preferences, and then click on the **OK** button.

In this lesson, you learned how to add graphic objects and other objects to your worksheets and charts. In the next lesson, you will learn how to turn your worksheet data into a database.

Creating a
Database

In this lesson, you will learn how to create your own database.

Database Basics

A database is a tool used for storing, organizing, and retrieving information. For example, if you want to save the names and addresses of all the people on your holiday card list, you can create a database for storing the following information for each person: first name, last name, street number, and so on. Each piece of information is entered into a separate field. All of the fields for one person on the list make a record. In Excel, a cell is a field, and a row of field entries makes a record. Figure 21.1 shows a database and its component parts.

Database or Data List?   Excel has simplified the database operations by treating the database as a simple *list* of data. This data acts as any other worksheet data, until you select a command from the Data menu. Then, Excel recognizes the list as a database.

You must observe the following rules when you enter information into your database:

- **Field Names**   You must enter field names in the first row of the database; for example, type **First Name** for first name, and **Last Name** for the last name. Do NOT skip a row between the field names row and the first record.

355

- **Records** Each record must be in a separate row, with no empty rows between records. The cells in a given column must contain information of the same type. For example, if you have a ZIP CODE column, all cells in that column must contain a ZIP code. You can create a calculated field; one that uses information from another field of the same record and produces a result. (To do so, enter a formula, as explained in Lesson 10.)

Field names are used as column headings.

	A	B	C	D	E	F	G
1	Record #	First Name	Last Name	Address	City	State	ZIP Code
2	1	William	Kennedy	5567 Bluehill Circle	Indianapolis	IN	46224
3	2	Marion	Kraft	1313 Mockingbird Lane	Los Angeles	CA	77856
4	3	Mary	Abolt	8517 Grandview Avenue	San Diego	CA	77987
5	4	Joseph	Fugal	2764 W. 56th Place	Chicago	IL	60678
6	5	Gregg	Lawrence	5689 N. Bringshire Blvd.	Boston	MA	56784
7	6	Lisa	Kasdan	8976 Westhaven Drive	Orlando	FL	88329
8	7	Nicholas	Capetti	1345 W. Bilford Ave.	New Orleans	LA	12936
9	8	Allison	Milton	32718 S. Visionary Drive	Phoenix	AZ	97612
10	9	Barry	Strong	908 N. 9th Street	Chicago	IL	60643
11	10	Chuck	Burger	6754 W. Lakeview Drive	Boston	MA	56784
12	11	Carey	Bistro	987 N. Cumbersome Lane	Detroit	MI	88687
13	12	Marie	Gabel	8764 N. Demetrius Blvd.	Miami	FL	88330
14	13	Adrienne	Bullow	5643 N. Gaylord Ave.	Philadelphia	PA	27639
15	14	John	Kramden	5401 N. Bandy	Pittsburgh	PA	27546
16	15	Mitch	Kroll	674 E. Cooperton Drive	Seattle	WA	14238

ADDRESS2.XLS

Sheet1 / Sheet2 / Sheet3 / Sheet4 / Sheet5 / Shee

Each row is a record.

Each cell contains a single field entry.

Figure 21.1 The parts of a database.

Record Numbering It is a good idea to add a column that numbers the records. If the records are sorted incorrectly, you can use the numbered column to restore the records to their original order.

Planning a Database

Before you create a database, you should ask yourself a few questions:

- What fields make up an individual record? If you are creating the database to take the place of an existing form (a Rolodex card, information sheet, or address list), use that form to determine which fields you need.

- What is the most often referenced field in the database? (This field should be placed in the first column.)

- What is the longest entry in each column? (Use this information to set the column widths. Otherwise, you can make your entries and then use Format Column AutoFit Selection to have Excel adjust the column widths.)

Creating a Database

To create a database, enter data into the cells as you would enter data on any worksheet. As you enter data, follow these guidelines:

- You must enter field names in the top row of the database.

- Type field entries into each cell in a single row to create a record. (You can leave a field blank, but you may run into problems later when you sort the database.)

- Do NOT leave an empty row between the field names and the records or between any records.

- If you want to enter street numbers with the street names, start the entry with an apostrophe so that Excel interprets the entry as text instead of as a value.

- Keep the records on one worksheet. You cannot have a database that spans several worksheets.

Forget Someone?   To add records to a defined database, either add the rows above the last row in the database, or use the Data Form dialog box.

5.0   In the previous version of Excel (Excel 4.0 and earlier), you had to enter a command to transform the data you type into a database. In Excel 5, this step is unnecessary. Excel 5 treats the data you typed as a *list*. Whenever you select a database command from the Data menu, Excel automatically treats the list as a database.

Using Data Forms to Add, Edit, or Delete Records

Data forms are like index cards; there is one data form for each record in the database, as shown in Figure 21.2. You may find it easier to flip through these data form "cards" and edit entries rather than editing them as worksheet data. To display a data form, open the **Data** menu, and select **Form**.

To flip from one form to the next or previous form, use the scroll bar, or the ⬆ or ⬇ key. To edit an entry in a record, tab to the text box that contains the entry, and type your correction. Press **Enter** when you're done.

Come Back! To restore data changed in a field, before you press **Enter**, select the **Restore** button.

Information for
one record

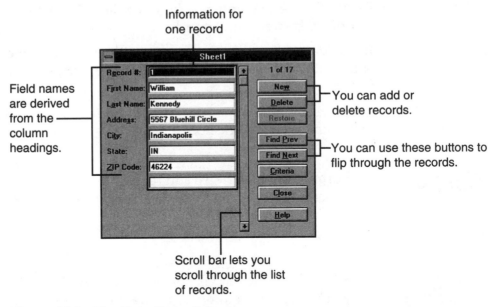

Field names
are derived
from the
column
headings.

You can add or
delete records.

You can use these buttons to
flip through the records.

Scroll bar lets you
scroll through the list
of records.

Figure 21.2 The Data Form dialog box.

You can also use the Data Form dialog box to add records to the database:

1. Select the **New** button.

2. Type an entry into each of the text boxes.

3. Click on **OK**, or press **Enter**.

To delete a record:

1. Select the record you want to change by selecting the **Find Prev** or **Find Next** buttons, or by using the scroll bars or up and down arrow keys to move through the database.

2. Select **Delete**.

3. Click on **OK**, or press **Enter**.

When you are done with the Data Form dialog box, click on the **Close** button.

In this lesson, you learned how to create a database. In the next lesson, you will learn how to sort the database and find individual records.

Finding and Sorting Data in a Database

In this lesson, you will learn how to sort a database and how to find individual records.

Finding Data with a Data Form

To find records in a database, you must specify the individual criteria (the specific information or range of information you want to find). You could type something specific like **Red** under the Color field of the form, or something that must be evaluated, like **<1000** (less than 1000) in the Sales field. Table 22.1 shows the operators that you can use for comparison:

Table 22.1   Excel's Comparison Operators

Operator	Meaning
=	Equal to
>	Greater than
<	Less than
>=	Greater than or equal to
<=	Less than or equal to
<>	Not equal to

You can also use the following wild cards when specifying criteria:

?   Represents a single character

*   Represents multiple characters

For example, in the Name field, type **M*** to find everyone whose name begins with an M. To find everyone whose three-digit department code has 10 as the last two digits, type **?10**.

To find individual records in a database:

1. Pull down the **Data** menu, and select **Form**. The Data Form dialog box appears.

2. Click on the **Criteria** button; the dialog box shown in Figure 22.1 appears.

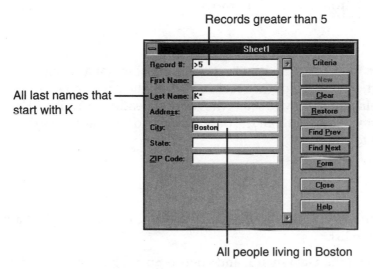

Figure 22.1   Selecting search criteria.

3. Type the criteria you would like to use in the appropriate fields. Use only the fields you want to search. For example, if you want to find all Bostonians whose last name starts with K, type **Boston** in the City field and **K*** in the Last Name field.

4. Click on **Form**, or press **Enter**.

5. Select **Find Next** or **Find Prev** to locate certain matching records.

6. When you are done reviewing records, select **Close**.

Sorting Data in a Database

To sort a database, first decide which field to sort on. For example, an address database can be sorted by Name or by City (or it can be sorted by Name within City within State). Each of these sort fields is considered a key.

You can use up to three keys when sorting your database. The first key in the above example would be Name, then City, and then State. You can sort your database in ascending or descending order.

Sort Orders Ascending order is from beginning to end, for example from A to Z or 1 to 10. Descending order is backward, from Z to A or 10 to 1.

For the Record When you select the database range to sort, include all of the records but not the column headings (field names). If you select the column heading row, it will be sorted along with all the other rows and may not remain at the top.

To sort your database:

1. Select the area to be sorted. To sort the entire data list, select any cell in the list.

2. Pull down the **Data** menu, and choose **Sort**. The Sort dialog box appears, as shown in Figure 22.2.

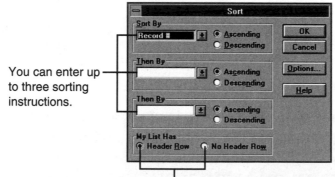

You can enter up to three sorting instructions.

If you selected a header row by mistake, you can choose Header Row to omit it from the sort.

Figure 22.2 Selecting the sort criteria.

3. Use the Sort By drop-down list to select the first field you want to sort on, and click on **Ascending** or **Descending** to specify a sort order.

4. To sort on another field, repeat step 3 for the first and second Then By drop-down lists.

5. Click on **OK**, or press **Enter**.

Undoing a Sort   If the sorting operation does not turn out as planned, you can undo the sort by selecting the **Undo Sort** command on the **Edit** menu (or pressing **Ctrl+Z**). To sort even more safely, you might also consider saving your database file before sorting. That way, if anything goes wrong, you can open your original database file.

Quick Sort   To quickly sort by the first column entries, use the **Sort Ascending** or **Sort Descending** buttons on the Standard toolbar.

Narrowing Your List with AutoFilter

Excel 5 offers a new feature called AutoFilter that allows you to easily display only a select group of records in your database. For example, you can display the records for only those people who live in Boston. Here's how you use AutoFilter:

1. Select the entire database, including the row you used for headings.

2. Open the **Data** menu, select **Filter**, and select **AutoFilter**. Excel displays drop-down list arrow buttons inside each cell at the top of your database.

3. Click on the drop-down list button for the field you want to use to filter the list. For example, if you want to display records for those people living in Boston, click on the button in the City cell. A drop-down list appears, as shown in Figure 22.3. This list contains all the entries in the column.

4. Select the entry you want to use to narrow your list. You can use the arrow keys to scroll through the list, or type the first character in the entry's name to quickly move to it. Press **Enter**, or click on the entry with your mouse. Excel filters the list.

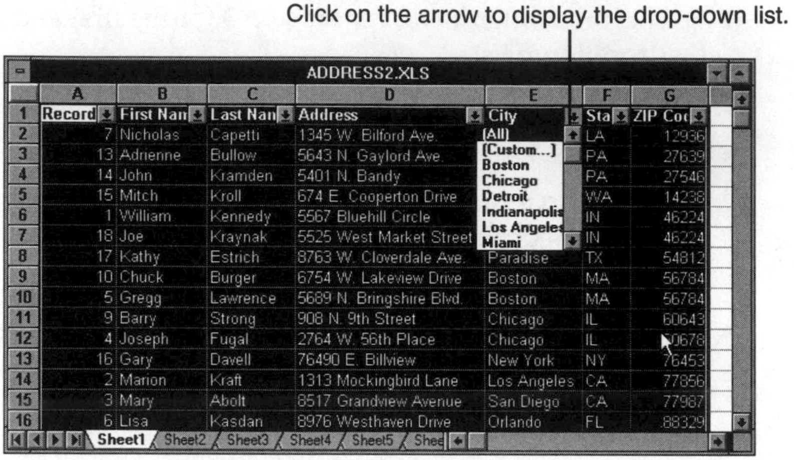

Click on the arrow to display the drop-down list.

	A	B	C	D	E	F	G	
				ADDRESS2.XLS				
1	Record	First Nan	Last Nan	Address	City	Sta	ZIP Co	
2	7	Nicholas	Capetti	1345 W. Bilford Ave.	(All)	LA	12936	
3	13	Adrienne	Bullow	5643 N. Gaylord Ave.	[Custom...]	PA	27639	
4	14	John	Kramden	5401 N. Bandy	Boston	PA	27546	
5	15	Mitch	Kroll	674 E. Cooperton Drive	Chicago	WA	14238	
6	1	William	Kennedy	5567 Bluehill Circle	Detroit	IN	46224	
7	18	Joe	Kraynak	5525 West Market Street	Indianapolis	IN	46224	
8	17	Kathy	Estrich	8763 W. Cloverdale Ave.	Los Angeles	TX	54812	
					Miami			
					Paradise			
9	10	Chuck	Burger	6754 W. Lakeview Drive	Boston	MA	56784	
10	5	Gregg	Lawrence	5689 N. Bringshire Blvd.	Boston	MA	56784	
11	9	Barry	Strong	908 N. 9th Street	Chicago	IL	60643	
12	4	Joseph	Fugal	2764 W. 56th Place	Chicago	IL	60678	
13	16	Gary	Davell	76490 E. Billview	New York	NY	76453	
14	2	Marion	Kraft	1313 Mockingbird Lane	Los Angeles	CA	77856	
15	3	Mary	Abolt	8517 Grandview Avenue	San Diego	CA	77987	
16	6	Lisa	Kasdan	8976 Westhaven Drive	Orlando	FL	88329	

Sheet1 / Sheet2 / Sheet3 / Sheet4 / Sheet5 / Shee

Figure 22.3 AutoFilter lets you narrow your list.

Unfiltering a List   To return to the full list, open the drop-down list again, and choose **(All)**. You can turn AutoFilter off by selecting **Data Filter AutoFilter**.

In this lesson, you learned how to find individual records and how to sort and filter your database. In the next lesson, you will learn how to use the data in your database to create a report.

Summarizing and Comparing Data in a Database

In this lesson, you will learn how to summarize data in complex databases to create reports.

Using the PivotTable Wizard

Excel 5.0 has improved its Crosstab ReportWizard, and has renamed it the PivotTable Wizard. This feature allows you to create reports that summarize worksheet data and lay it out in a more meaningful format. For example, suppose you had a database that kept track of your monthly sales, by product and salesperson. You can create a report that summarizes the amount of each product sold each month by each salesperson. You can then quickly rearrange the table to analyze the data in various ways. Figure 23.1 illustrates how a pivot table works.

First Encounters   If this is your first encounter with pivot tables, expect to spend some time working with them. Once you get the hang of the data buttons, it will seem easy to you, but getting the hang of the data buttons takes patience.

Worksheet data list

You can quickly rearrange data by dragging the field buttons.

Month	Salesperson	Pianos	Violins	Guitars	Drums
January	Arial	$5,783.98	$667.43	$453.98	$785.93
February	Arial	$4,783.98	$838.49	$323.87	$875.83
March	Arial	$2,783.98	$874.98	$674.92	$574.36
January	Goya	$6,098.00	$765.00	$645.00	$820.00
February	Goya	$2,348.76	$0.00	$874.38	$834.67
March	Goya	$3,298.82	$765.00	$824.00	$764.83
January	Kribble	$8,765.37	$6,488.00	$764.98	$56.00
February	Kribble	$1,500.00	$904.00	$674.45	$846.43
March	Kribble	$0.00	$873.39	$645.38	$345.00
January	Tasha	$7,645.89	$887.00	$784.30	$873.98
February	Tasha	$1,567.32	$894.57	$846.82	$743.67
March	Tasha	$3,489.89	$764.98	$674.82	$457.83

Pivot table

Month	(All)	
Data	Salesperson	Total
Sum of Pianos	Arial	13351.94
	Goya	11745.58
	Kribble	10265.37
	Tasha	12703.1
Sum of Violins	Arial	2380.9
	Goya	1530
	Kribble	8265.39
	Tasha	2546.55
Sum of Guitars	Arial	1452.77
	Goya	2343.38
	Kribble	2084.81
	Tasha	2305.94
Sum of Drums	Arial	2236.12
	Goya	2419.5
	Kribble	1247.43
	Tasha	2075.48
Total Sum of Pianos		48065.99
Total Sum of Violins		14722.84
Total Sum of Guitars		8186.9
Total Sum of Drums		7978.53

Totals are for all months January-March.

Figure 23.1 A pivot table summarizes and organizes your data.

When you create a pivot table, you must specify four elements:

Pages   Pages allow you to create a drop-down list for one of the rows or columns in your worksheet. For example, you can use the Salesperson column to create a drop-down list that contains the names of all your salespeople. Select a salesperson from the list to see how much of each item that person is selling per month.

Rows   Cells that form the rows for the report. You can have up to eight rows. For example, these could be months.

Columns   Cells that form the column headings for the report. You can have up to eight columns. For example, this could be salespeople.

Sum of Value   These are the values you want added for each intersection of a column or row. For example, displaying months in rows and salespeople in columns indicates how much each salesperson sold each month.

Creating a Pivot Table

You create a pivot table by running Excel's PivotTable Wizard, which leads you through the process with a series of dialog boxes. Here's how you use the PivotTable Wizard:

1. Open the **Data** menu, and select **PivotTable**. Excel displays the PivotTable Wizard Step 1 of 4 dialog box.

2. Click on the **Next** button. The PivotTable Wizard Step 2 of 4 dialog box appears, asking you to select the range of cells you want to transform into a pivot table. Excel shows a blinking dotted box that indicates what data it thinks you want to use.

3. Type the cell addresses that define the range, or drag over the desired cells with the mouse pointer.

4. Click on the **Next** button. The PivotTable Wizard Step 3 of 4 dialog box appears.

5. Drag the buttons on the right where you want the row headings, column headings, or data to appear, as shown in Figure 23.2.

6. Click on the **Next** button. The PivotTable Wizard Step 4 of 4 dialog box appears, asking if you want to specify additional preferences and location for the pivot table.

7. Enter your preferences, and then click on the **Finish** button. The PivotTable Wizard creates the table according to your specifications.

If you did not specify a location for the pivot table in step 7, the Wizard inserts a worksheet before the current worksheet and sets the pivot table on the new worksheet. To see your original data, click on its worksheet tab.

Not Quite What You Expected?   When the PivotTable Wizard is done, it creates a table that may or may not be exactly what you wanted. Don't worry. You can rearrange the data simply by dragging field buttons around on-screen.

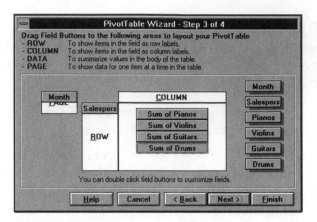

Figure 23.2 Drag the field buttons to specify how you want the table arranged.

In this lesson, you learned to create a pivot table. In the next lesson, you'll learn how to use macros to automate the tasks you frequently perform.

Automating Your Work with Macros

In this lesson, you'll learn the value of macros, and how to create and use them.

What Are Macros?

A *macro* is actually a small program that contains a list of instructions for Excel to execute. It is written in a programming language call Visual BASIC, but you don't need any special programming skills to create one. The purpose of a macro is to make repetitive tasks go more quickly and easily, and to reduce the risk of error.

You can create a macro to do anything that you can normally do yourself in Excel, such as performing commands, selecting data, entering data, and so on. When you create a macro, you can decide whether you want it to run only with specific worksheets, or whether you want it available to all of your worksheets. Once you create a macro, you can run it as many times as you want.

Creating A Macro

The easiest way to create a macro is to turn the recording feature on, then perform the steps you want to record. Follow these instructions:

1. Open the workbook in which you want to create the macro.

2. Choose **Tools Record Macro**, then select the **Record New Macro** command. (See Figure 24.1)

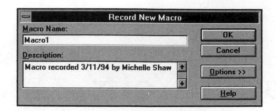

Figure 24.1   The Record New Macro dialog box.

3. (Optional) Enter a descriptive name to replace the default name, Macro1.

4. (Optional) Select **Options>>** to designate a shortcut key. The shortcut key can be one character which should remind you of the macro it stands for. You will press it in combination with the **Ctrl** key to play back your macro.

5. Click on the workbook you want your macro stored in. If you want to use it only with the current workbook, choose **This Workbook**. If you want it to be available to all of your workbooks, choose **Personal Macro Workbook**.

6. Select **OK**. You're returned to your open workbook and Excel is ready to record your actions in a macro. (You'll notice the **recording** indicator in the status bar.)

7. Perform the procedures you want to record in a macro. When you are finished, click on the **Macro Stop Recording** icon.

Enter the information you want in your macro.   The Visual Basic toolbar

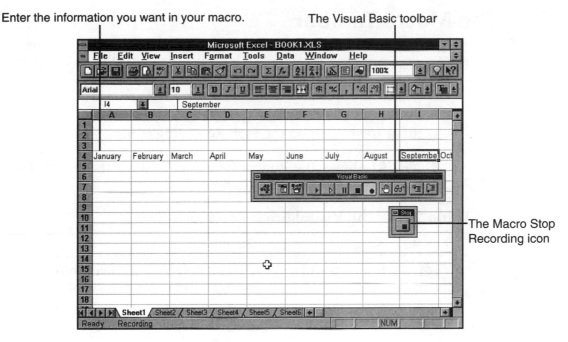

The Macro Stop
Recording icon

Figure 24.2   Recording a macro.

Macro Names   Be sure to choose a name and shortcut key that will remind you of your macro, otherwise, once you've created several macros, it will be hard to remember which is which.

Shortcut Keys   Excel distinguishes between upper-and lowercase characters in shortcut keys, so you can have one macro activated by **Ctrl+R** and another by **Ctrl+r**. Be careful not to confuse them. It's best to use lowercase, so you don't waste time pressing the Shift key.

The Macro Toolbar

The Macro toolbar makes it easier to work with macros by providing the most common commands as toolbar buttons. To display the macro toolbar:

1. Choose **View Toolbars**.

2. Select **Visual Basic Toolbar**. If you want to display the Stop Recording Toolbox, select the **Stop Recording** option.

Table 24.1 shows the buttons you will find on the Visual Basic Toolbar, and a description of their actions.

Table 24.1 The Visual Basic Toolbar Buttons

Button	Name	Function
	Insert Module	Adds a new Visual Basic module or dialog sheet to the workbook.
	Menu Editor	Creates or customizes menus and menu bars.
	Object Browser	Lists all procedures, properties, methods, and objects currently available.
	Run Macro	Runs a selected macro, or deletes or modifies it.
	Step Macro	Opens the Debug window and activates debug tools.
	Resume Macro	Resumes playing a paused macro.
	Stop Macro	Stops either a running macro or a recording macro.
	Record Macro	Opens the submenu Record Macro.
	Toggle Breakpoint	Either removes or inserts a breakpoint in a line of code.

Button	Name	Function
	Instant Watch	Shows the value of the Visual Basic expression selected.
	Step Into	Runs next line of code, stepping into any Visual Basic procedures.
	Step Over	Continues running Visual Basic procedures without stepping into them.

Opening the Macro Worksheet

As mentioned earlier, Excel stores your macro commands in a special worksheet. Depending on whether you selected **This Workbook** or **Personal Macro Workbook** when you were setting up your macro, there are a couple of ways to open the macro worksheet:

- If you selected **This Workbook**, select the macro's name past sheet16.

- If you selected **Personal Macro Workbook**, choose **Window Unhide**, and double-click on **PERSONAL.XLS**.

You will notice that the macro looks like a computer program (see Figure 24.3). Excel has converted your macro commands into Visual Basic commands, but, as noted earlier, you don't have to know Visual Basic to create a macro. You can edit the macro using Excel's normal editing commands, which were covered in Lesson 6.

To do much editing of the macro, however, you will need to learn some Visual Basic programming skills. To do this, you should refer to the Visual Basic manual that comes with Excel 5.0.

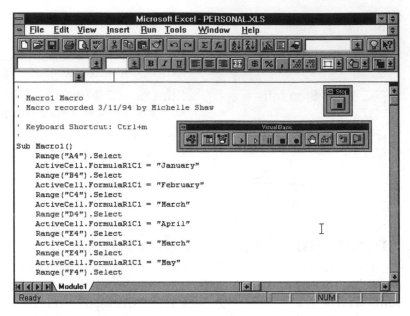

Figure 24.3 A sample macro in the macro worksheet.

Running the Macro

Once you have created a macro, you can run it at any time.

Watch Your Cells! Be careful that the same conditions exist within the worksheet where you run a macro as existed within the worksheet where you created it. If there is information in the cells that the macro is supposed to run in, it will overwrite that information.

To run a macro, simply press **Ctrl** plus the shortcut key you assigned to it. You will notice that the macro enters the information into the same cells that you entered it into when you created the macro. If you were in Row 7 when you started recording the macro, the macro will play back in

Row 7 of your new worksheet. That is because the macro recorded your keystrokes exactly. If you want a macro to play back in any row, depending on where you have your cell cursor when you run it, you have to use *relative referencing*.

Relative Referencing All movement commands in a macro are recorded relative to the pointer's position at the time you begin recording.

Creating A Relative Macro

As you learned above, relative referencing means the commands are relative to the pointer's position. To create a macro using relative referencing:

1. Choose **Tools Record Macro**.

2. Choose **Use Relative References**. The Tools menu will disappear. When you select it again you will notice that there is a check mark in front of **Use Relative References**.

3. Choose **Record New Macro**, and then continue as you did when creating a macro in the steps above.

When you're finished creating this macro, open the macro worksheet as described earlier in this lesson (see Figure 24.4). You will notice that the cell references here look very different from the ones in your first macro. That is because they were recorded as relative to your cell pointer. When you run this macro, it will run starting with the position your cell pointer is in when you activate it.

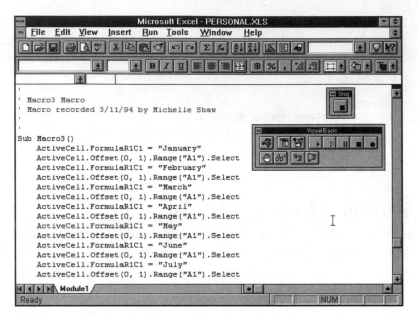

Figure 24.4 A macro recorded with relative referencing.

In this lesson, you learned how to create and run macros.

Starting and Exiting PowerPoint

In this lesson, you will learn how to start and exit Microsoft PowerPoint, and how to get help.

PowerPoint is a presentation graphics software. With it, you can create impressive graphics to use as slides, transparencies, report enclosures, and so on.

Starting PowerPoint

If you have not yet installed PowerPoint on your computer, refer to the Appendix at the back of this book for instructions, or follow the instructions that came with PowerPoint. Installing PowerPoint adds its program icons to the Microsoft Office program group in Windows Program Manager.

From Program Manager, perform the following steps to start PowerPoint.

1. If the Microsoft Office program group is not displayed, select **Microsoft Office** from the **Window** menu to display it.

No Microsoft Office Window?   The PowerPoint application icon may be in a different program group window, depending on how you installed it. Likely places to look might include program groups called Applications or PowerPoint.

2. Double-click on the **Microsoft PowerPoint** icon, as shown in Figure 1.1. PowerPoint starts, and the Tip of the Day dialog box appears.

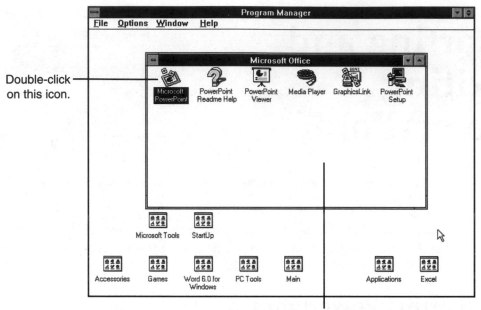

Double-click on this icon.

Microsoft Office program group window

Figure 1.1 Double-click on the Microsoft PowerPoint application icon.

3. (Optional) To prevent the Tip of the Day from appearing when you start PowerPoint in the future, click on the **Show Tips at Startup** check box. The **X** in the check box disappears.

4. Click on the **OK** button. The Tip of the Day dialog box disappears, and the PowerPoint dialog box appears, prompting you to create a new presentation. (See Figure 1.2.)

> **TIP**
>
> **Creating a New Presentation** The PowerPoint dialog box is designed to lead you through the process of creating a new presentation. For details on how to use this dialog box, see Lesson 2.

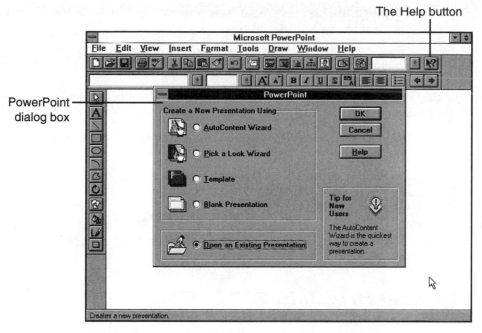

Figure 1.2 PowerPoint can lead you through the process of creating a new presentation.

Getting Help

PowerPoint offers several help features that can teach you how to perform a simple task or use an advanced feature:

Help Menu

The Help menu for PowerPoint is very similar to that of other Microsoft Office products, such as Word. The choices are:

Contents Shows a table of contents for Help.

Search for Help on Activates a Search dialog box that enables you to search for certain words in the Help system.

Index Lists all topics from A to Z.

Quick Preview Provides an on-screen demonstration of some common features. Select the feature you want PowerPoint to demonstrate, and then sit back and watch.

Tip of the Day Shows a time-saving tip. Click on the **Next Tip** button to see additional tips.

Cue Cards Displays step-by-step instructions for a task. Click on the button for the task you want to perform.

Technical Support Provides information on what to do when all else fails.

About Microsoft PowerPoint Shows licensing and system information.

F1 Key

Press the **F1** key anytime to see the Help Table of Contents. If you press **F1** when a dialog box is displayed, PowerPoint displays help that relates to that dialog box.

Toolbar Help Button

At the right end of the Standard toolbar is the Help button. It has an arrow and a question mark on it. Click on this button, and then click on the object or command about which you want more information.

Navigating the Help System

Most Help windows contain *jumps* that let you get more information about related topics. If you select a topic that is solid-underlined, PowerPoint will open a Help window for that topic. If you select a term that is dotted-underlined, PowerPoint displays a definition for that term. To select a topic or term, click on it.

Jumps A jump is a term or phrase that appears underlined and in another color and that links one help window to another. There are two types of jumps: solid and dotted underlined. Solid underlined jumps display a new help screen. Dotted underlined jumps display the definition for a term.

To exit the Help system, double-click on the **Control-menu** box in the upper left corner of the Help window, or select **File Exit**.

Exiting PowerPoint

To leave PowerPoint, perform the following steps:

1. If the PowerPoint dialog box is on-screen, click on the **Cancel** button to close it.

2. Do one of the following:

   - Open the **File** menu, and select **Exit**.

   - Press **Alt+F4**.

   - Double-click on PowerPoint's **Control-menu** box.

In this lesson, you learned how to start and exit PowerPoint and how to get on-line help. In the next lesson, you will learn how to create a presentation using the PowerPoint dialog box.

Creating a New Presentation

In this lesson, you will learn several ways to create a presentation.

Starting a New Presentation

If you just started PowerPoint, and the PowerPoint dialog box is displayed, you are ready to start a new presentation. If the PowerPoint dialog box is not displayed, perform the following steps:

1. Open the **File** menu.

2. Select **New**. The New Presentation dialog box appears as shown in Figure 2.1.

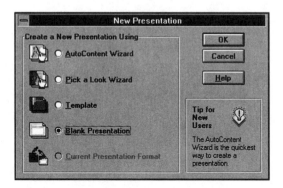

Figure 2.1 The New Presentation dialog box provides five simple ways to create a new presentation.

Quick New File To bypass the File menu, click on the **New** button in the Standard toolbar. The New button is the leftmost button just under the menu bar.

The PowerPoint dialog box gives you the following five ways to create a new presentation. Several of these methods are explained further in this lesson.

AutoContent Wizard   Creates outlines for any of six presentations, including strategy, sales, and training presentations. The presentation acts as a rough draft, which you can edit and enhance.

Pick a Look Wizard   Creates a collection of slides; all have a consistent, professional look. You can add the content for the presentation later.

Template   Lets you build a slide show from a predesigned slide. You provide the content, and PowerPoint takes care of the appearance.

Blank Presentation   Allows you to start from scratch. You build the presentation by supplying both the content and design.

Current Presentation Format   Is available if you have a previously created presentation displayed. This option lets you create a new presentation that is based on the design of the existing presentation.

Wizards   Wizards are a unique feature in most Microsoft products. A Wizard displays a series of dialog boxes that ask you design and content questions. You select options and type text. When you are done, the Wizard creates something (in this case, a presentation) according to your instructions.

Using the AutoContent Wizard

With the AutoContent Wizard, you select the type of presentation you want to create (strategy, sales, training, reporting, conveying bad news, or general), and PowerPoint creates an outline for the presentation. Here's how you use the Auto-Content Wizard:

1. In the PowerPoint dialog box, click on the **AutoContent Wizard** option button, and then click on the **OK** button. The AutoContent Wizard Step 1 of 4 dialog box appears.

2. Read the dialog box, and then click on the **Next** button, or press **Enter**. The AutoContent Wizard Step 2 of 4 dialog box appears.

Going Back Each Wizard dialog box contains a Back button that lets you trace back through previous dialog boxes to change your selections or edit your text. Simply click on the **Back** button, or press **Alt+B**.

3. Type a title for the presentation. (For example, Marketing Strategy.)

4. Press **Tab**, and type your name or the name of the person who is going to give the presentation.

5. Press **Tab**, and type any other information that you want to appear on the first slide in the presentation.

6. Choose **Next**. The AutoContent Wizard Step 3 of 4 dialog box appears. (See Figure 2.2.)

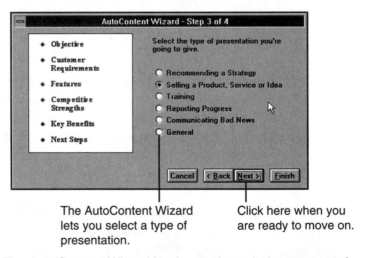

The AutoContent Wizard lets you select a type of presentation.

Click here when you are ready to move on.

Figure 2.2 The AutoContent Wizard leads you through the process of preparing a presentation.

7. Select the type of presentation you want to create, and then click on the **Next** button. The AutoContent Wizard Step 4 of 4 dialog box appears.

8. Click on the **Finish** button. The Wizard creates the presentation and displays the presentation in Outline view.

Outline View   PowerPoint can display a presentation in any of four views: Outline, Slide, Note, and Slide Sorter. To learn more about the different views and how to change views, see Lesson 4.

Using the Pick a Look Wizard

The Pick a Look Wizard lets you create black-and-white or color overheads, an on-screen presentation, or 35mm slides that have a consistent and professional look. Here's what you do to run the Pick a Look Wizard:

1. In the PowerPoint dialog box, click on the **Pick a Look Wizard** option button, and then click on the **OK** button. The Pick a Look Wizard Step 1 of 9 dialog box appears.

2. Read the dialog box, and then click on the **Next** button. The Pick a Look Wizard Step 2 of 9 dialog box appears, providing a list of output options.

3. Select the desired output for your presentation, and click on the **Next** button. The Step 3 of 9 dialog box appears, asking you to select an overall design.

Can't Decide on an Output?   If you cannot decide on an output, don't worry; you can select a different output option at any time.

Limited Choice?   If you do not like any of the designs listed, click on the **More** button. This opens a dialog box that lets you select from a list of templates. Click on a name in the File Name list, and then click on **Apply** to use the template.

4. Click on a design for your presentation, and then click on the **Next** button. The Step 4 of 9 dialog box appears.

5. By default, PowerPoint will create all the presentation items (slides, speaker's notes, audience handouts, and an outline). Select any items you want to exclude, and then click on the **Next** button. The Slide Options dialog box appears.

6. If you want PowerPoint to print the date, slide number, or other text on each slide, select any information you want included, and click on the **Next** button.

7. If you chose to include speaker's notes, audience handouts, and outline pages, repeat step 6 for each item in the presentation. The Step 9 of 9 dialog box appears.

8. Click on the **Finish** button. PowerPoint creates one slide that matches your design choices and displays it on-screen. (In Lesson 8, you will learn how to add slides to your presentation.)

Using a Template

The Template option lets you select a predesigned look for your presentation. PowerPoint creates the first slide. Here's how you use a template:

1. In the PowerPoint or New Presentation dialog box, click on **Template**, and then click on the **OK** button. The Presentation Template dialog box appears, as shown in Figure 2.3.

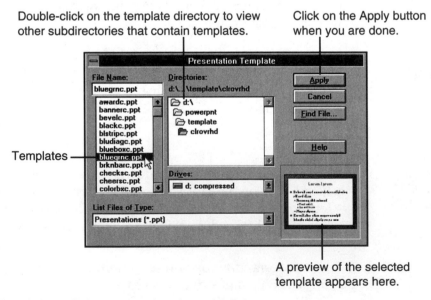

Double-click on the template directory to view other subdirectories that contain templates.

Click on the Apply button when you are done.

Templates

A preview of the selected template appears here.

Figure 2.3   Select a template from the list.

2. In the File Name list, click on a template name to see what the template looks like. The preview area shows a thumbnail view of the template.

More Templates PowerPoint has three groups of templates: black-and-white overheads, color overheads, and slides. To see a list of templates in a particular group, double-click on **template** in the Directories list, and then double-click on the desired subdirectory (bwovrhd, clrovrhd, or sldshow).

3. When you have selected a template you like, click on the **Apply** button. The New Slide dialog box appears, as shown in Figure 2.4.

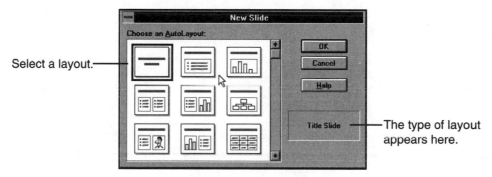

Figure 2.4 The New Slide dialog box lets you select a structure for your slides.

4. Click on the desired layout for your slides.

5. Click on the **OK** button. PowerPoint creates a slide that has the look and structure you specified.

Starting a Blank Presentation

If you are experienced in creating presentations, you may want to start a presentation from scratch and develop your own design and content. If so, take the following steps to create a blank presentation:

1. In the PowerPoint dialog box, click on **Blank Presentation**, and then click on the **OK** button. The New Slide dialog box appears, as shown in Figure 2.4.

2. Click on the desired layout for your slides, or use the arrow keys to select a layout.

3. Click on the **OK** button. PowerPoint creates a slide that has the structure you specified.

Now that you have a presentation, you can edit its text, add pictures and graphs, change the presentation's overall look, and enhance it in many other ways. The procedures you need to follow are covered in later lessons. The next lesson provides a brief tour of the PowerPoint screen and explains how to enter commands.

Getting Around in PowerPoint

In this lesson, you will learn how to get around in PowerPoint and enter commands.

A Look at PowerPoint's Application Window

If you created a new presentation using the AutoContent Wizard, your screen looks something like the screen shown in Figure 3.1. This screen contains many of the same elements you will find in any Windows programs: a Control-menu box, a title bar, Minimize and Restore buttons, a menu bar, and a status bar, which we covered in the Windows section of this book.

In addition, you will see three toolbars and a presentation window that are unique to PowerPoint. The following sections explain how to work with these unique items.

Toolbar   A toolbar is a collection of buttons that allow you to bypass the menu system. For example, instead of opening the **File** menu and selecting **New**, you can click on the **New** button to create a new presentation.

The Presentation Window

In the center of the PowerPoint window is a *presentation window*. You will use this window to create your slides and arrange the slides in a presentation. At the bottom of the presentation window are several buttons that allow you to change views. For example, Figure 3.1 shows a presentation in Outline view, whereas Figure 3.2 shows the same presentation in Slide view. For details about changing views, see Lesson 4.

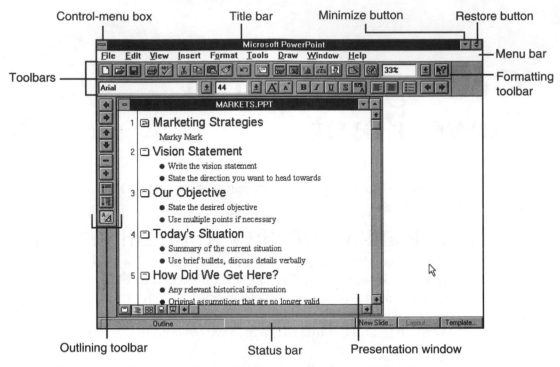

Figure 3.1 PowerPoint provides many tools for quickly entering commands.

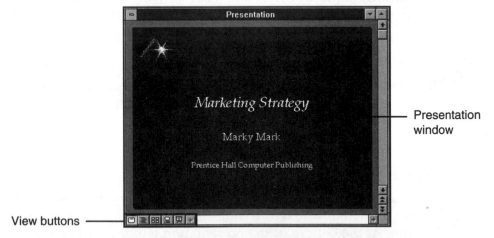

Figure 3.2 You can change views simply by clicking on a button.

Using Shortcut Menus

Although you can enter all commands in PowerPoint by pulling down a menu and selecting the command, PowerPoint 4 offers a quicker way with context-sensitive shortcut menus. To use a shortcut menu, move the mouse pointer over the object you want the command to act on, and then click on the right mouse button. A shortcut menu pops up, as shown in Figure 3.3, offering the commands that pertain to the selected object. Click on the desired command.

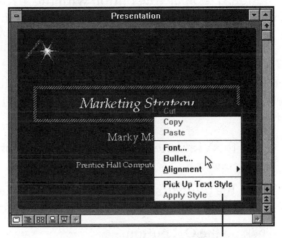

Right-click on an object to display a
context-sensitive shortcut menu.

Figure 3.3   Display a shortcut menu by right-clicking on an object.

Working with Toolbars

PowerPoint displays three toolbars: the Standard and Formatting toolbars below the menu bar (see Figure 3.1), and the Outline or Drawing toolbar to the left of the presentation window. (The toolbar on the left varies, depending on which view is displayed.) To select a button from the toolbar, click on the button.

Learning More About Toolbar Buttons

Although we could list and explain all the tools in the Standard toolbar and in all the other toolbars, here are some better ways to learn about the buttons for yourself:

- To see the name of a button, move the mouse pointer over the button. PowerPoint displays a ToolTip that provides the name of the button.

- To learn what a button does, move the mouse pointer over the button, and look at the status bar (bottom of the screen). If the button is available for the task you are currently performing, PowerPoint displays a description of what the button does.

- To learn more about a button, click on the **Help** button in the Standard toolbar (the button with the arrow and question mark), and then click on the button for which you want more information.

Turning Toolbars On or Off

If you never use a particular toolbar, you can turn it off to free up some screen space. In addition, you can turn on other toolbars. To turn a toolbar on or off:

1. Open the **View** menu, and choose **Toolbars**. The Toolbars dialog box appears.

2. Select the toolbar(s) you would like to hide or display. An **X** in the toolbar's check box means the bar will be displayed.

3. Click on the **OK** button.

Use the Shortcut Menu   A quick way to display or hide a toolbar is to use the toolbar shortcut menu. Right-click on any toolbar, and then click on the name of the toolbar you want to hide or display.

Moving Toolbars

After you have displayed the toolbars you need, you may position them in your work area where they are most convenient. Here's what you do to move a toolbar:

1. Move the mouse pointer over a buttonless part of the toolbar.

2. Hold down the left mouse button, and drag the toolbar where you want it:

- Drag the toolbar to a toolbar dock. There are four toolbar docks: just below the menu bar, on the left and right sides of the PowerPoint application window, and just above the status bar. If a toolbar contains a drop-down list, you cannot drag it to the left or right toolbar dock.

- Drag the toolbar anywhere inside the application window to create a floating toolbar.

3. Release the mouse button.

Floating Toolbar A floating toolbar acts just like a window. You can drag its title bar to move it or drag a border to size it. If you drag a floating toolbar to a toolbar dock, the toolbar turns back into a normal (nonfloating) toolbar.

Customizing Toolbars To customize a toolbar, right-click on it, and choose **Customize**. You can then drag a toolbar button from one toolbar to another or drag a button off a toolbar (to remove it). To add a button from the Customize Toolbars dialog box, select a feature category from the Categories list, and then drag the desired button to any of the toolbars.

In this lesson, you learned about the PowerPoint application and presentation windows, and you learned how to enter commands with shortcut menus and toolbars. In the next lesson, you will learn how to edit the presentation you created in Lesson 2.

Working with Slides in Different Views

In this lesson, you will learn how to display a presentation in different views, and edit slides in Outline and Slide view.

Changing Views

PowerPoint can display your presentation in different views that make it easier to perform certain tasks. For example, Outline view makes it easier to see the overall organization of the presentation, whereas Slide Sorter view lets you quickly rearrange the slides. Figure 4.1 shows the available views.

Figure 4.1 a Slide view

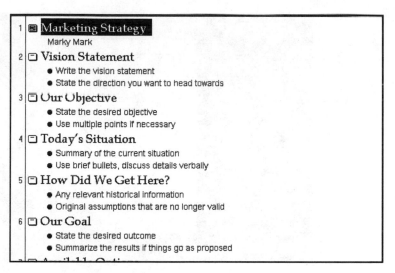

Figure 4.1 b Outline view

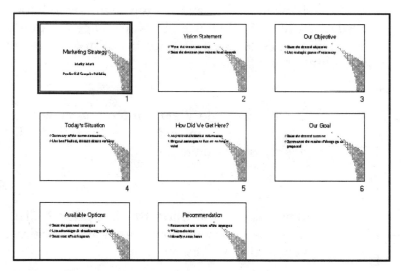

Figure 4.1 c Slide Sorter view

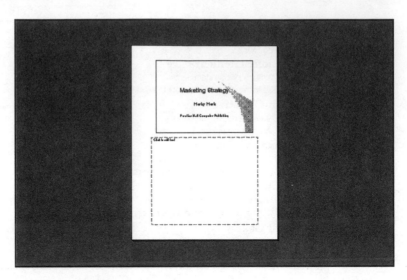

Figure 4.1   Notes Pages View.

To change views, open the **View** menu, and choose the desired view: **Slides**, **Outline**, **Slide Sorter**, or **Notes Pages**. A quicker way to change views is to click on the button for the desired view at the bottom of the presentation window.

Outline to Slide View   In Outline view, you can quickly display a slide in Slide view by double-clicking on the desired slide icon in the outline.

What About the Slide Show Option?   The Slide Show option lets you view your presentation as a timed slide show. For details, see Lesson 21.

Moving from Slide to Slide

When you have more than one slide in your presentation, you will need to move from one slide to the next in order to work with a specific slide. The procedure for moving to a slide depends on which view you are currently using:

- In **Outline view**, use the scroll bar to display the slide you want to work with. Click on the **Slide** icon (the icon to the left of the slide's title) to select the slide, or click anywhere inside the text to edit it.

- In **Slide view**, click on the **Previous Slide** or **Next Slide** button just below the vertical scroll bar, as shown in Figure 4.2, or drag the box inside the scroll bar until the desired slide number is displayed, and then release the mouse button.

- In **Slide Sorter view**, click on the desired slide. A thick border appears around the selected slide.

- In **Notes Pages view**, click on the **Previous Slide** or **Next Slide** button, or drag the box inside the scroll bar until the desired slide number is displayed, and then release the mouse button.

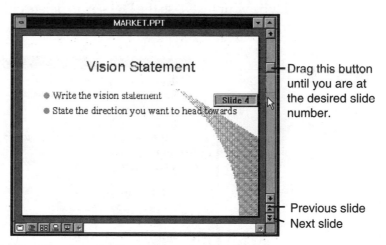

Figure 4.2   Use the Previous Slide and Next Slide buttons.

Editing Slides

If you created a presentation in Lesson 2 using the AutoContent Wizard, you already have several slides, but they may not contain the text you want to use. If you used the Pick a Look Wizard or a template, or you created a blank presentation, you have one slide on-screen that you can edit.

In the following sections, you will learn the basics of how to edit text in Outline view and Slide view. In later lessons, you will learn how to add and edit text objects, pictures, graphs, organizational charts, and other items.

Objects   An object is any item on a slide, including lines and boxes for text, graphics, and charts.

Editing in Outline View

Outline view provides the easiest way to edit text. You simply click to move the insertion point where you want it, as shown in Figure 4.3, and then type your text. Use the **Del** key to delete characters to the right of the insertion point, or the **Backspace** key to delete characters to the left.

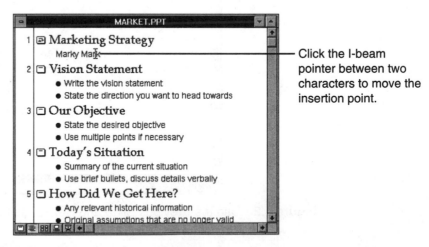

Click the I-beam pointer between two characters to move the insertion point.

Figure 4.3   Switch to Outline view to edit text.

To select text, hold down the left mouse button, and drag the mouse pointer over the desired text. You can then press the **Del** or **Backspace** key to delete the text, or drag the text where you want it.

Auto Word Select   When you select text, PowerPoint selects whole words. If you want to select individual characters, open the **Tools** menu, select **Options**, and select **Automatic Word Selection** to turn it off. Click on the **OK** button.

Editing in Slide View

Slide view provides an easy way to edit all objects on a slide, including text and graphic objects. As shown in Figure 4.4, you can edit an object by clicking or double-clicking on it. For a text object, click on the object to select it, and then click where you want the insertion point moved.

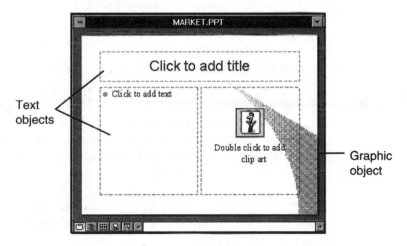

Figure 4.4   Slide view allows you to edit both text and graphic objects.

Working with a Bulleted List

The bulleted list is a powerful tool for helping you to organize and present ideas and supporting data for your presentation. As you type entries, keep in mind that you can change an entry's level and position in the list. To change the position or level of an entry (in Outline view), use the arrow keys or mouse to move the insertion point anywhere inside the entry, and then perform one of the following actions:

 Click on this button to move the entry up in the list.

 Click on this button to move the entry down in the list.

 Click on this button to indent the entry to the next lower level in the list. The item will be indented, the bullet will change, and the text will usually appear smaller.

 Click on this button to remove the indent and move the entry to the next higher level in the list. The item will be moved to the left, the bullet will change, and the text will appear larger.

Dragging Paragraphs   You can quickly change the position or level of a paragraph by dragging it up, down, left, or right. To drag a paragraph, move the mouse pointer to the left side of the paragraph until it turns into a four-headed arrow. Then, hold down the mouse button, and drag the paragraph to the desired position.

In Lesson 10, you will learn how to change the appearance of the bullet, the style and size of text for each entry, and the amount the text is indented for each level.

In this lesson, you learned how to change views for a presentation, move from slide to slide, and edit text. In the next lesson, you will learn how to save, close, and open a presentation.

Saving, Closing, and Opening Presentations

In this lesson, you will learn how to save a presentation to disk, close a presentation, and open an existing presentation.

Saving a Presentation

Soon after creating a presentation, you should save it in a file on disk to protect the work you have already done. To save a presentation for the first time, perform the following steps:

1. Open the **File** menu and select **Save**, or press **Ctrl+S**. The Save As dialog box appears, as shown in Figure 5.1.

The No-Menu Save To bypass the File menu, click on the **Save** button (the button with the disk icon on it) in the Standard toolbar.

2. In the File Name text box, type the name you want to assign to the presentation (up to eight characters). (Do not type a file name extension; PowerPoint will automatically add the extension **.PPT**.)

3. To save the file to a different disk drive, pull down the Drives drop-down list, and select the letter of the drive.

4. To save the file in a different directory, select the directory from the Directories list.

5. Click on the **OK** button. The Summary Info dialog box appears.

6. (Optional) Type a presentation title, subject description, author name, keywords, and comments for the presentation. (This information might help you find the presentation later.)

7. Click on the **OK** button. The file is saved to disk.

Save button   Type a file name here.

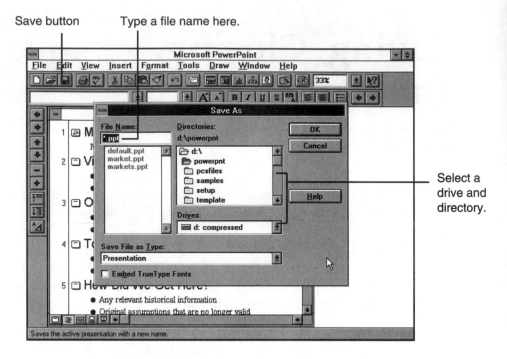

Figure 5.1   The Save As dialog box.

Quick Resaves   Now that you have named the file and saved it to disk, you can save any changes you make to the presentation simply by pressing **Ctrl+S** or clicking on the **Save** button in the Standard toolbar. Your data will be saved under the file name you assigned.

To create a copy of a presentation under a different name, open the **File** menu, and select the **Save As** command. Use the Save As dialog box to enter a different name for the copy. You can then modify the copy without affecting the original.

Closing a Presentation

You can close a presentation at any time. This closes the Presentation window (it does not exit PowerPoint), and allows you to use the space on-screen for a different presentation. To close a presentation, perform the following steps:

1. If more than one Presentation window is displayed, click on any portion of the window you want to close. This activates the window.

2. Open the **File** menu and select **Close**, or press **Ctrl+F4**. If you have not saved the presentation, or if you haven't saved your most recent changes, a dialog box appears, asking if you want to save your changes.

3. To save your changes, click on the **Yes** button. If this is a new presentation, the Save As dialog box appears, as in Figure 5.1. If you have saved the file previously, your changes are saved in the file, and the Presentation window closes.

4. If the Save As dialog box appears, enter a name for the file and any other information as explained earlier. Then, click on the **OK** button.

Opening a Presentation

Once you have saved a presentation to disk, you can open the presentation and continue working on it at any time. To open an existing presentation, perform the following steps:

1. Open the **File** menu and select **Open**, or press **Ctrl+O**. The Open dialog box appears.

TIP
Quick Open To quickly open a file, click on the **Open** button (the button with the manila folder on it) in the Standard toolbar.

2. Pull down the Drives drop-down list, and select the letter of the drive on which the file is stored.

3. In the Directories list, select the directory in which the presentation file is stored. The list below the File Name text box displays the names of all the presentation files (files that end in .PPT) in the selected directory.

4. In the list below the File Name text box, click on the file you think you want to open. The first slide in the presentation appears in the preview area (see Figure 5.2).

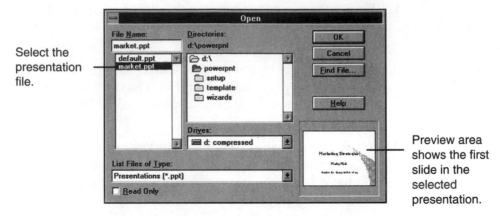

Select the presentation file.

Preview area shows the first slide in the selected presentation.

Figure 5.2 The Open dialog box lets you select and preview the presentation.

5. Double-click on the file name of the presentation you want to open, or highlight the file name and click on the **OK** button. PowerPoint opens the presentation.

Recently Opened Files PowerPoint keeps a list of the four most recently opened files at the bottom of the File menu. To open a file, simply select it from the **File** menu. You can increase the number of files listed. Open the **Tools** menu, and select **Options**. Select **Entries**, and type the number of files (up to nine) that you want listed.

Finding a Presentation File

If you forgot where you saved a file, PowerPoint can help you with its new Find File feature. To have PowerPoint hunt for a file, perform the following steps:

1. Open the **File** menu and select **Find File**, or click on the **Find File** button in the Open dialog box. You'll get the Search dialog box, as shown in Figure 5.3.

Type the name of the
file you are looking for.

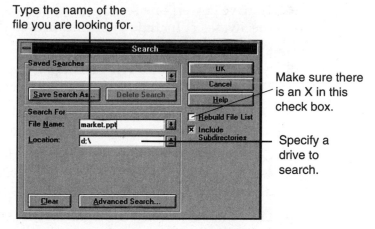

Make sure there
is an X in this
check box.

Specify a
drive to
search.

Figure 5.3 The Search dialog box asks you to specify what you want to
search for.

Find File Dialog Box? If you get the Find File dialog box
(instead of the Search dialog box), click on the **Search** button
at the bottom of the Find File dialog box.

2. In the File Name text box, type the name of the file you are looking
   for. You can use wild-card characters in place of characters you
   can't remember. Use an asterisk ***** in place of a group of characters,
   or use a question mark **?** in place of a single character. For example, ***.ppt** finds all files with the extension .PPT, and **sales??.ppt**
   finds all files such as SALES01.PPT, SALES02.PPT, and so on.

3. In the Location text box, type the drive and directory you want to
   search. For example, if you type **c:**, PowerPoint will search the
   entire C drive. Type **c:\powerpnt**, and PowerPoint searches only
   the POWERPNT directory on drive C.

4. To have PowerPoint search all subdirectories of the directory you specify, select **Include Subdirectories** to place an **X** in the check box.

5. Click on the **Rebuild File List** option to place an **X** in its check box. This ensures that PowerPoint will perform a fresh search.

6. Don't worry about the **Clear** option. It clears out anything you may have typed in the File Name and Location text boxes.

7. Click on the **OK** button. PowerPoint finds the files that match the search instructions you entered and displays them in the Find File dialog box as shown in Figure 5.4.

8. Look through the list, highlight the file you want, and click on the **Open** button.

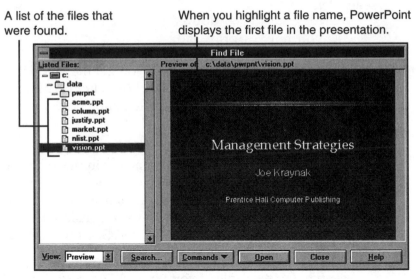

Figure 5.4 The Find File dialog box shows a list of found files.

In this lesson, you learned how to save, close, and open presentations. In the next lesson, you will learn how to print a presentation.

Printing Your Presentation

In this lesson, you will learn how to select a size and orientation for the slides in your presentation and how to print the slides, notes, and handouts you created.

Notes and Handouts The instructions in this lesson tell you how to print slides, notes, and handouts. To create audience handouts and speaker's notes pages, see Lessons 22 and 23.

Setting Up for Printing

Before you print your presentation, you should check the slide setup to determine if the selected output, size, and orientation are suitable for your needs. Perform the following steps:

1. Open the **File** menu, and select **Slide Setup**. The Slide Setup dialog box appears, as shown in Figure 6.1.

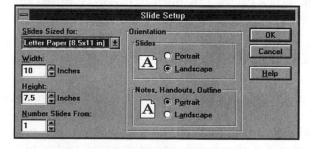

Figure 6.1 The Slide Setup dialog box lets you set the position and size of the slides.

2. Click on the arrow to the right of the Slides Sized for list, and select the desired output for your slides. (For example, you can have the slides sized for 8.5-by-11-inch paper, 35mm slides, or an on-screen slide show.)

3. (Optional) To create a custom size, enter the desired dimensions in the Width and Height text boxes. If you change a setting in either of these boxes, Custom is automatically selected in the Slides Sized for list.

Spin Boxes   To the right of the Width and Height text boxes are arrows that allow you to adjust the settings in those boxes. Click on the up arrow to increase the setting by .1-inch, or click on the down arrow to decrease the setting by .1-inch.

4. In the Number Slides From text box, type the number at which you want to start slide numbering. (This is usually 1, but may differ if this presentation is a continuation of another presentation.)

5. In the Orientation group, select an option to specify how you want the slides, notes, and handouts positioned on the page.

Orientation   The Orientation settings tell PowerPoint whether to print the slides sideways (in landscape orientation) or in normal (portrait) orientation.

6. Click on the **OK** button. If you changed the orientation setting, you may have to wait while PowerPoint repositions the slides.

Selecting a Printer

If you have only one printer, and you already use it for all your Windows applications, you do not have to select a printer (just use the printer you set up in Windows). However, if you use two printers, you should specify which printer you want to use (for example, you may want to use a color printer for overhead transparencies and a black-and-white printer for speaker's notes).

To select a printer, perform the following steps:

1. Open the **File** menu, and select **Print**. The Print dialog box appears. The name of the currently selected printer appears at the top of the dialog box.

2. To use a different printer, click on the **Printer** button. The Print Setup dialog box appears, as shown in Figure 6.2.

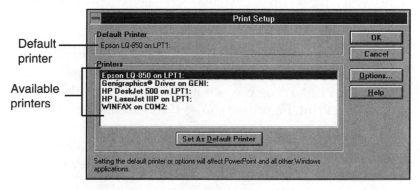

Figure 6.2 The Print Setup dialog box shows a list of installed printers.

3. In the **Printers** list, click on the name of the printer you want to use.

> **TIP**
>
> **Genigraphics** The Genigraphics option in the Printers list allows you to print your presentation to a file that you can later send (on disk or via modem) to the Genigraphics service. This service converts your presentation into slides or overhead transparencies.

4. (Optional) To make the printer you selected the default printer for all Windows applications, click on the **Set As Default Printer** button.

5. Click on the **OK** button. PowerPoint returns you to the Print dialog box and shows the name of the currently selected printer.

> **TIP**
>
> **Options** The Options button in the Print Setup dialog box opens a dialog box that gives you more control over your printer. For example, you can set the print quality, select a

font cartridge (if your printer uses font cartridges), and select a paper source. If you are using the Genigraphics service, the options allow you to specify the type of film or transparencies you want made.

Printing Your Presentation

Once you have set up your slides and selected a printer, you can print your presentation. Perform the following steps:

1. Make sure the presentation file you want to print is displayed on-screen.

2. If the Print dialog box is not displayed, open the **File** menu, and select **Print**. Figure 6.3 shows the Print dialog box.

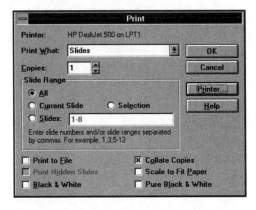

Figure 6.3 The Print dialog box

3. Click on the arrow to the right of the Print What text box, and select the item you want to print (for example, your slides, hand-outs, or speaker notes).

4. In the Copies text box, type the number of copies you want printed.

5. In the Slide Range group, select one of the following options to specify which slides you want to print:

All   Prints every slide in the presentation.

Current Slide   Prints only the slide that is selected or displayed.

Slides   Prints one or more slides as instructed. To print a single slide, type its number. To print a range, type the first page number, a dash, and then the last page number (for example, **4–8**). To print more than one range, separate the ranges with commas (for example, **2,4–8,10**).

6. (Optional) Select any of the following options at the bottom of the Print dialog box:

Print to File   Prints the presentation to a file on disk so you can print it later or print it using a different computer that does not have PowerPoint installed.

Print Hidden Slides   Prints slides that you may have marked as hidden. For more details about hidden slides, see Lesson 20.

Black & White   Prints color slides in black and white. This is useful for printing drafts of slides.

Collate Copies   Useful if you are printing two or more copies of your slides. With this option on, PowerPoint prints one full copy of the presentation before printing the next copy. With this option off, PowerPoint prints all copies of slide 1, then all copies of slide 2, and so on.

Scale to Fit Paper   Instructs PowerPoint to resize the slides automatically to fit the paper size you selected in the Slide Setup dialog box.

Pure Black & White   Prints the text and lines in black and white, without color or shading.

7. Click on the **OK** button. PowerPoint prints the specified slides.

In this lesson, you learned how to specify the dimensions and orientation of your slides, and how to print slides, audience handouts, and speaker notes. In the next lesson, you will learn how to change the overall appearance of the slides in a presentation.

Changing a Presentation's Look

In this lesson, you will learn various ways to give you presentations a professional and consistent look.

Giving Your Slides a Professional Look

PowerPoint comes with 150 professionally designed slides you can use as *templates* for your own presentations. That is, you can apply one of these predesigned slides to your own presentation, to give the slides in your presentation the same look as the professional slides.

What Is a Template? A template is a predesigned slide that comes with PowerPoint. It contains a color scheme and a general layout for each slide in the presentation. The template makes it easy for you to create a presentation; you simply fill in the blanks on each slide.

Each template has a Slide Master that works in the background to control the background color, layout, and style of each slide in the presentation. This provides all the slides in your presentation with a consistent look. In the following sections, you will learn various ways to apply templates and modify the look of your presentation.

Using the Pick a Look Wizard

The Pick a Look Wizard leads you through the process of selecting a template, customizing slides, and adding headers and footers to slides, speaker's notes, audience handouts, and outlines. You can use the Pick a Look Wizard to create a new presentation, as explained in Lesson 2, or to modify an existing presentation. To modify a presentation, do the following:

1. Open the **Format** menu and select **Pick a Look Wizard,** or click on the **Pick a Look Wizard** button in the Standard toolbar. The Pick a Look Wizard Step 1 of 9 dialog box appears.

2. Enter any preferences you have, and then click on the **Next** button.

3. Repeat step 2 for each dialog box that appears. (Refer to Lesson 2 for details.)

4. When the Step 9 of 9 dialog box appears, click on the **Finish** button.

More Color and Shading Control Each template has preset color and background settings. For details on how to modify the color or background of your presentation, refer to Lesson 19.

Using a Presentation Template

You do not have to run the Pick a Look Wizard to apply a template to a presentation. You can simply select a template by doing the following:

1. Open the **Format** menu, and select **Presentation Template.** The Presentation Template dialog box appears.

The Template Button To bypass the Format menu, click on the **Template** button on the right end of the status bar.

2. In the Directories list, change to the **\POWERPNT\TEMPLATE** directory. The template subdirectories appear. Each subdirectory contains a set of templates for a particular type of presentation: black-and-white overheads, color overheads, and slide shows.

3. Double-click on the template subdirectory for the type of presentation you want to create. A list of templates appears in the File Name list.

4. Click on a file name in the list. When you highlight the name of a template, a slide appears in the preview area, showing what the template looks like. (See Figure 7.1.)

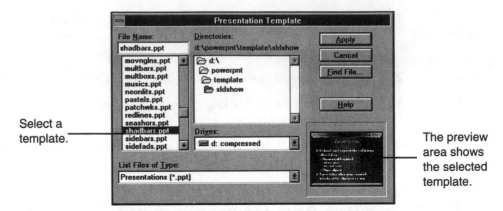

Select a template.

The preview area shows the selected template.

Figure 7.1 The Presentation Template dialog box lets you preview a template before you apply it.

5. When the desired template is highlighted, click on the **Apply** button, or press **Enter**. You are returned to your presentation, and the template is now in control of your presentation.

Apply Templates at Any Time You do not have to apply a template before you begin creating your presentation. You can change the template at any time, and your entire presentation will take on the look of the new template.

Using AutoLayouts

While templates allow you to change the color and design of a presentation, AutoLayouts allow you to set the structure of a single slide in a presentation. For example, if you want a graph and a picture on a slide, you can choose an AutoLayout that positions the two items for you. To use an AutoLayout, do the following:

1. In Slide view, display the slide whose layout you want to change.

2. Open the **Format** menu, and select **Slide Layout**. The Slide Layout dialog box appears.

Right Click A quick way to display the Slide Layout dialog box is to right-click on the slide in Slide view, and then select **Slide Layout**.

3. Click on the desired layout, or use the arrow keys to move the selection border to it.

4. Click on the **Apply** button. PowerPoint applies the selected layout to the current slide.

Editing the Slide Master

Every presentation has a Slide Master that controls the overall appearance and layout of each slide. A sample Slide Master is shown in Figure 7.2.

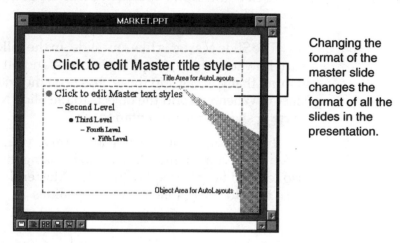

Changing the format of the master slide changes the format of all the slides in the presentation.

Figure 7.2 The Slide Master ensures that all slides in a presentation have a consistent look.

The two most important elements on the Slide Master are the *Title Area* and *Object Area* for the AutoLayout objects. The Title Area contains the formatting specifications for each slide's title; that is, it tells PowerPoint the type size, style, and color to use for the text in the title of each slide. The Object Area contains the formatting specifications for all remaining text on the slide. For most of PowerPoint's templates, the Object Area sets up specifications for a bulleted list: these include the type of bullet, as well as the type styles, sizes, and indents for each item in the list.

In addition to the Title and Object Areas, the Slide Master can contain the background color, a border, a code that inserts page numbers, your company logo, a clip art object, and any other elements you want to appear on *every* slide in the presentation.

To view the Slide Master for a presentation, perform the following steps:

1. Open the **View** menu, and select **Master**. The Master submenu appears.

2. Select **Slide Master**. The Slide Master appears, as shown in Figure 7.2.

3. To return to slide view, open the **View** menu and select **Slides**, or click on the **Slide View** button at the bottom of the presentation window.

The Slide Master is like any slide. In the following lessons, when you learn how to add text, graphics, borders, and other objects to a slide, keep in mind that you can add these objects on individual slides or on the Slide Master. When you add the objects to the Slide Master, the objects appear on *every* slide in the presentation.

In this lesson, you learned how to give your presentation a consistent look by applying a template to it and by using the Pick a Look Wizard. You also learned how to display the Slide Master. In the next lesson, you will learn how to insert, delete, and copy slides.

Inserting, Deleting, and Copying Slides

In this lesson, you will learn how to insert new slides, delete slides, and copy slides in a presentation.

Inserting a Slide

You can insert a slide into a presentation at any time and at any position in the presentation. Perform the following steps:

1. Select the slide after which you want the new slide inserted. (You can select the slide in any view: Outline, Slides, Slide Sorter, or Notes Pages.)

2. Open the **Insert** menu, and select **New Slide**. In Outline view, PowerPoint inserts a blank slide, allowing you to type a title and bulleted list. In all other views, the New Slide dialog box appears.

New Slide Button To quickly insert a new slide, click on the **New Slide** button on the right end of the status bar or the **Insert New Slide** button on the Standard toolbar.

3. In the Choose an AutoLayout list, click on the desired slide layout, or use the arrow keys to highlight it.

4. Click on the **OK** button. PowerPoint inserts a slide that has the specified layout (see Figure 8.1).

5. Follow the directions on the slide to add text or other objects. In most cases, you must click on an object to select it and then type your entry.

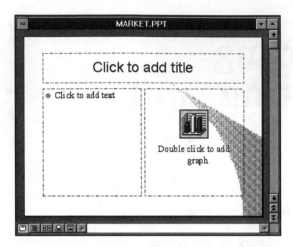

Figure 8.1 The new slide contains the structure; you must supply the content.

Cloning a Slide To create an exact replica of a slide, select the slide you want to duplicate. Open the **Edit** menu and select **Duplicate**, or press **Ctrl+D**. The new slide is inserted after the original slide.

Adding Slides from Another Presentation

If you want to add all the slides from another presentation to the current presentation, perform the following steps:

1. Open the presentation in which you want the slides added.

2. Select the slide after which you want the slides added.

3. Open the **Insert** menu, and select **Slides from File**. The Insert File dialog box appears.

4. Pull down the Drives drop-down list, and select the letter of the drive on which the presentation file is stored.

5. In the Directories list, select the directory in which the presentation file is stored.

6. In the list below the File Name text box, click on the file you think you want to open. The first slide in the presentation appears in the preview area.

7. Double-click on the file name of the presentation whose slides you want to insert, or highlight the file name and click on the **OK** button. PowerPoint inserts the slides after the currently selected slide. The new slides take on the look of the current presentation.

Taking an Outline from a Document If you created a document using a word processing program and included headings in it, PowerPoint can pull the headings from the document and use them to create slides with bulleted lists. To create slides from a document, open the **Insert** menu, and choose **Slides from Outline**. Use the Insert Outline dialog box to select the document file you want to use, and then click on the **OK** button.

Selecting Slides

In the following sections, you will be deleting, copying, and moving slides. However, before you can move one or more slides, you have to select the slide(s), as follows:

- To select a single slide, click on it. (In Slide or Notes Pages view, the currently displayed slide is selected; you don't have to click on it.)

- To select two or more neighboring slides (in Outline view only), click on the first slide, and then hold down the **Ctrl** and **Shift** keys while clicking on the last slide in the group.

- To select two or more non-neighboring slides (in Slide Sorter or Outline view), hold down the **Shift** key while clicking on each slide.

Deleting Slides

You can delete a slide from any view. Perform the following steps:

1. Display the slide you want to delete (in Slide or Notes Pages view), or select the slide(s) (in Outline or Slide Sorter view).

2. Open the **Edit** menu, and select **Delete Slide**. The selected slide(s) is removed.

Oops! If you deleted a slide by mistake, you can get it back by opening the **Edit** menu and selecting **Undo**, or by clicking on the **Undo** button (the button with the counterclockwise arrow on it) on the Standard toolbar.

Cutting, Copying, and Pasting Slides

In Lesson 20, you will learn how to rearrange slides in Slide Sorter and Outline views. However, you can also use the cut, copy, and paste features to help you create duplicate slides and move slides. To cut (or copy) a slide and paste it in a presentation, perform the following steps:

1. Change to Slide Sorter or Outline view.

2. Select the slide(s) you want to copy or cut.

3. Open the **Edit** menu, and select **Cut** or **Copy**. If you chose **Cut**, the selected slide(s) are removed from the presentation and placed on the Windows Clipboard. If you chose **Copy**, the original slides remain in the presentation.

Windows Clipboard The Windows Clipboard is a temporary holding area for cut or copied items. You can cut or copy items to the Clipboard and then paste them on a slide.

Quick Cut or Copy To bypass the Edit menu, press **Ctrl+C** to copy or **Ctrl+X** to cut, or click on the **Cut** or **Copy** button on the Standard toolbar.

4. Perform one of the following steps:

- In Slide Sorter view, select the slide after which you want the cut or copied slide(s) placed.

- In Outline view, move the insertion point to the end of the text for the slide after which you want the cut or copied slide(s) placed.

5. Open the **Edit** menu, and choose **Paste**, or press **Ctrl+V**. (You can also click on the **Paste** button in the Standard toolbar.) The cut or copied slides are inserted.

Dragging and Dropping Slides

A quick way to copy or move a slide is to use the Drag and Drop feature, as follows:

1. Change to the Slide Sorter or Outline view.

Dragging and Dropping Between Presentations You can drag and drop slides from one presentation to another. Use the **File Open** command to open both presentations (see Lesson 5). Each presentation is displayed in a separate window. Open the **Window** menu, and select **Arrange All**. The two windows appear side-by-side. Change to Slide Sorter view in each window. You can now drag and drop slides from one window to the other.

2. Click on the slide you want to move or copy.

3. Move the mouse pointer over the slide you want to move or copy.

4. Hold down the mouse button (and the **Ctrl** key if you want to copy), and drag the slide to the desired position, as shown in Figure 8.2. (If you don't hold the Ctrl key, PowerPoint moves the slide rather than copying it.)

5. Release the mouse button (and the **Ctrl** key, if you were holding it down).

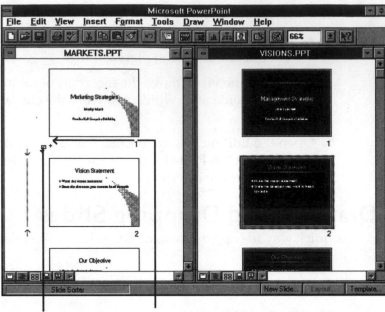

Plus sign indicates the slide will be copied.   Drag the slide before or after another slide.

Figure 8.2   You can drag a slide in a presentation or from one presentation to another.

In this lesson, you learned how to insert, delete, cut, copy, and paste slides. In the next lesson, you will learn how to add text objects to slides.

Adding a Text Object to a Slide

In this lesson, you will learn how to add text to a slide, change the text alignment and line spacing, and transform text into a bulleted list.

Creating a Text Box

If the only text you need in your presentation is the title and a bulleted list, you can add text simply by typing it in Outline or Slide view. However, if you want to type additional text on the slide, you must first create a text box. The text box acts as a receptacle for the text. Text boxes are commonly used for bulleted lists, notes, and labels (used to point to important parts of illustrations). To create a text box, perform the following steps:

1. Click on the **Text** tool as shown here:

2. Move the mouse pointer to where you want the upper left corner of the box to appear.

3. Hold down the mouse button, and drag the mouse pointer to the right until the box is the desired width.

4. Release the mouse button. A one-line text box appears. (See Figure 9.1.)

Insertion point ————

Figure 9.1   The text box appears with a blinking insertion point inside.

5. Type the text that you want to appear in the text box. When you reach the right side of the box, PowerPoint wraps the text to the next line and makes the box one line deeper. To start a new paragraph, press **Enter**.

6. Click anywhere outside the text box.

Framing a Text Box The border that appears around a text box when you create or select it does not appear on the printed slide. To add a border that does print, see Lesson 18.

Selecting, Deleting, and Moving a Text Box

If you go back and click anywhere inside the text box, a *selection box* appears around it. If you click on the selection box border, handles appear around the text box, as shown in Figure 9.2. You can drag the box's border to move the box, or drag a handle (as shown) to resize it. PowerPoint will wrap the text automatically, as needed to fit inside the box. To delete a text box, select it (so handles appear around it), and then press the **Del** key.

Handles —————— Drag the border to move the box.

Figure 9.2   Click on the selection box border to display handles.

Editing Text in a Text Box

To edit text in a text box, first click anywhere inside the text box to select it. Then, perform any of the following steps:

- To select text, drag the **I-beam pointer** over the text you want to select. (To select a single word, double-click on it. To select an entire sentence, triple-click.)

Auto Word Select When you drag over text, PowerPoint selects whole words. If you want to select individual characters, open the **Tools** menu, select **Options**, and select **Automatic Word Selection** to turn it off. Click on the **OK** button.

- **To delete text**   Select the text, and press the **Del** key. You can also use the **Del** or **Backspace** keys to delete single characters.

- **To insert text**   Click the I-beam pointer where you want the text inserted, and then type the text.

- **To replace text**   Select the text you want to replace, and then type the new text. When you start typing, the selected text is deleted.

- **To copy and paste text**   Select the text you want to copy, and choose the **Copy** command from the **Edit** menu, or press **Ctrl+C**. Move the insertion point to where you want the text pasted (it can be in a different text box), and choose **Paste** from the **Edit** menu, or press **Ctrl+V**.

- **To cut and paste (move) text**   Select the text you want to cut and choose the **Cut** command from the **Edit** menu, or press **Ctrl+X**. Move the insertion point to where you want the text pasted (it can be in a different text box), and choose **Paste** from the **Edit** menu, or press **Ctrl+V**.

Changing the Text Alignment and Line Spacing

When you first type text, it is set against the left edge of the text box and is single-spaced. To change the paragraph alignment, perform the following steps:

1. Click anywhere inside the paragraph whose alignment you want to change.

2. Open the **Format** menu, and select **Alignment**. The Alignment submenu appears.

3. Select **Left**, **Center**, **Right**, or **Justify** to align the paragraph as desired. (See Figure 9.3 for examples.)

> **TIP**
>
> **Quick Alignment**   To quickly set the alignment for a paragraph, click inside the paragraph, and press one of the following key combinations: **Ctrl+L** for left alignment or **Ctrl+R** for right alignment. You can center text by clicking on the **Center Alignment** button in the Formatting toolbar. You can left-justify text by clicking on the **Left Alignment** button.

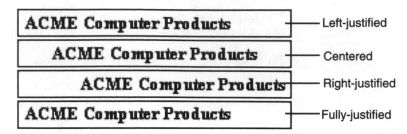

Figure 9.3 You can align each paragraph in a text box.

To change the line spacing in a paragraph, perform these steps:

1. Click inside the paragraph whose line spacing you want to change, or select all the paragraphs whose line spacing you want to change.

2. Open the **Format** menu, and select **Line Spacing**. The Line Spacing dialog box appears, as shown in Figure 9.4.

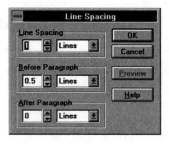

Figure 9.4 The Line Spacing dialog box.

3. Click on the arrow buttons to the right of any of the following text boxes to change the line spacing:

   Line Spacing   This setting controls the space between the lines in a paragraph.

   Before Paragraph   This setting controls the space between this paragraph and the paragraph that comes before it.

   After Paragraph   This setting controls the space between this paragraph and the paragraph that comes after it.

Lines or Points? The drop-down list box that appears to the right of each setting allows you to set the line spacing in *lines* or *points*. A line is the current line height (based on text size). A point is a unit commonly used to measure text. A point is approximately 1/72 of an inch.

4. Click on the **OK** button. Your line spacing changes are put into effect.

Making a Bulleted List

In the next lesson, you will learn the ins and outs of bulleted lists. However, here's a quick lesson on how to turn your text into a bulleted list:

1. Click inside the paragraph you want to transform into a bulleted list, or select one or more paragraphs.

2. Open the **Format** menu, and select **Bullet**. The Bullet dialog box appears.

3. Click on **Use a Bullet**, and then click on the **OK** button. PowerPoint transforms the selected text into a bulleted list. (If you press **Enter** at the end of a bulleted paragraph, the next paragraph has a bullet.)

Quick Bullets To bypass the Format menu and Bullet dialog box, simply click on the **Bullet** button in the Formatting toolbar. You can click on the **Bullet** button again to remove the bullet.

Adding a WordArt Object

PowerPoint 4 comes with an *applet* (tiny application) called WordArt that can help you create graphic text effects. To insert a WordArt object into a slide, perform the following steps:

1. Display the slide on which you want the WordArt object placed.

2. Open the **Insert** menu, and select **Object**. The Insert Object dialog box appears.

3. In the Object Type list, click on **Microsoft WordArt 2.0**, and click on the **OK** button. The Microsoft WordArt toolbar and text entry box appear, as shown in Figure 9.5.

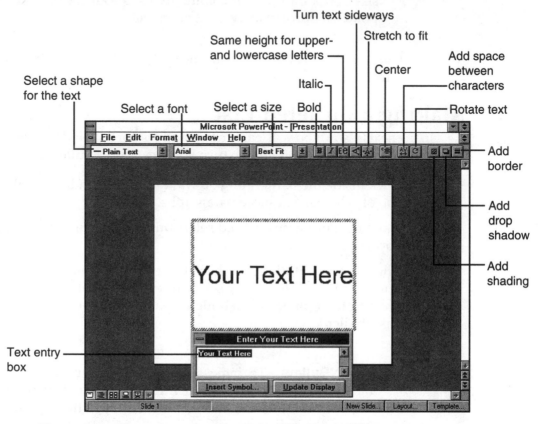

Figure 9.5 Type your text and use the WordArt toolbar to style it.

4. Type the text you want to use. Whatever you type replaces the **Your Text Here** message. (As you type, press **Enter** if you need to start a new line.)

5. Select a WordArt font from the font list.

6. Select a text size from the size list. If you do not specify a size, Word adjusts the text automatically to fit the size of the WordArt box.

7. Select a shape from the shape list. Shapes act as cookie cutters, forming the text.

8. Use the formatting buttons, as show in Figure 9.5, to create additional effects. (For more formatting options, open the **Format** menu.)

9. Click anywhere inside the presentation window to return to your slide. The WordArt appears on your slide.

To edit the WordArt object at any time, double-click on it to display the WordArt toolbar and text entry box. Enter your changes, and then click outside the WordArt object. You can move the object by dragging its border, or resize it by dragging a handle.

In this lesson, you learned how to add text to a slide, change the text alignment and spacing, transform text into a bulleted list, and add WordArt objects. In the next lesson, you will learn how to use tables, tabs, and indents to create columns and lists.

Creating Columns and Lists

In this lesson, you will learn how to use tabs to create columns of text and use indents to create bulleted lists, numbered lists, and other types of lists.

Using Tabs to Create Columns

A presentation often uses tabbed columns to display information. For example, you may use tabs to create a three-column list like the one shown in Figure 10.1.

In addition to hardware products, we carry a varied line of software:		
Business	**Home**	**Education**
WordPerfect	Quicken	Reader Rabbit 2
Microsoft Word	The New Print Shop	Oregon Trail
PowerPoint	Microsoft Works	BodyWorks
Excel	TurboTax	Where in the World is Carmen Sandiego?

Figure 10.1   You can use tabs to create a multi-column list.

To set the tabs for such a list, perform the following steps:

1. Click anywhere inside the text box for which you want to set the tabs.

2. If you already typed text inside the text box, select the text.

3. Open the **View** menu, and select **Ruler**. The ruler appears at the top of the presentation window.

4. Click on the tab icon in the upper left corner of the presentation window until it represents the type of tab you want to set:

Aligns the left end of the line against the tab stop.

Centers the text on the tab stop.

Aligns the right end of the line against the tab stop.

Aligns the tab stop on a period. This is useful for aligning a column of numbers that use decimal points.

5. Click on each place in the ruler where you want to set the selected type of tab stop, as shown in Figure 10.2.

6. Repeat steps 4 and 5 if you want to set different types of tab stops at different positions.

7. To change the position of an existing tab stop setting, drag it on the ruler to the desired position. To delete an existing tab stop setting, drag it off the ruler.

8. To turn off the ruler, open the **View** menu, and select **Ruler**.

TIP

Don't Forget the Slide Master Throughout this lesson, keep in mind that you can enter your changes on the slide master or on individual slides. If you change the slide master, the change affects all slides in the presentation. For details on displaying the slide master, see Lesson 7.

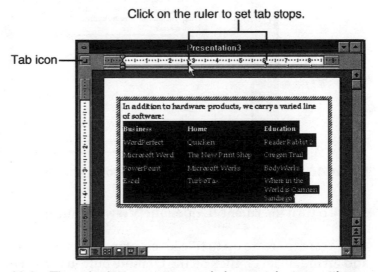

Figure 10.2 The ruler lets you enter and change tab stop settings.

Using Indents to Create Lists

Indents allow you to move one or more lines of a paragraph in from the left margin. PowerPoint uses indents to create the bulleted lists you encountered in Lesson 4. You can use indents in any text object to create a similar list, or your own custom list. To indent text, perform the following steps:

1. Select the text box that contains the text you want to indent.

2. If you already typed text, select the text you want to indent.

3. Open the **View** menu, and select **Ruler**. The ruler appears above the text box.

4. Drag one of the indent markers (as shown in Figure 10.3) to set the indents for the paragraph:

   Drag the **top marker** to indent the first line.

   Drag the **bottom marker** to indent all subsequent lines.

   Drag the **box** below the bottom marker to indent all the text.

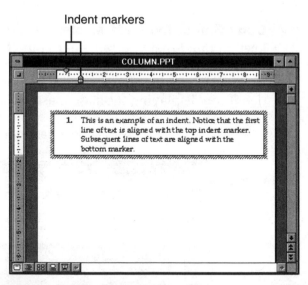

Figure 10.3 Drag the indent markers to indent your text.

5. To turn the ruler off, open the **View** menu, and select **Ruler**.

You can create up to five levels of indents within a single text box. To add an indent level, click on the **Demote** button in the Formatting toolbar, or press **Alt+Shift+→**. A new set of indent markers appears, showing the next level of indents. You can change these new indent settings as explained above.

Once you have set your indents, you can create a numbered or bulleted list by performing the following steps:

1. Type a number and a period, or type the character you want to use for the bullet.

2. Press the **Tab** key to move to the second indent mark.

3. Type the text you want to use for this item. As you type, the text is wrapped to the second indent mark.

Changing the Bullet Character

By default, whenever you click on the **Bullet** button in the Formatting toolbar to insert a bullet, PowerPoint inserts a large dot for the bullet. However, you can change the appearance of the bullet at any time by performing the following steps:

1. Select the paragraph(s) in which you want to change the bullet character.

2. Open the **Format** menu, and select **Bullet**. The Bullet dialog box appears.

3. Pull down the **Bullets From** list, and select the character set from which you want to choose a bullet. The dialog box displays the characters in the selected set.

4. Click on the character you want to use for the bullet.

5. To set the size of the bullet, use the up and down arrows to the right of the Size text box.

6. To select a color for the bullet, pull down the **Special Color** drop-down list, and select the desired color.

7. Select the **OK** button. The bullet character is changed for all selected paragraphs.

Numbered Lists PowerPoint offers little help for creating numbered lists. You must type the number for each item yourself.

Moving a Bulleted Item   You can move an item in a bulleted list by clicking on the item's bullet and then dragging the bullet up or down in the list.

In this lesson, you learned how to create columns with tabs, create lists with indents, and change the bullet character for bulleted lists. In the next lesson, you will learn how to change the style, size, and color of text.

Changing the Look of Your Text

In this lesson, you will learn how to change the appearance of text by changing its font, style, size, and color.

Enhancing Your Text with the Font Dialog Box

You can enhance your text by using the Font dialog box or by using various tools on the Formatting toolbar. Use the Font dialog box if you want to add several enhancements to your text at one time. Use the Formatting toolbar to add one enhancement at a time.

Fonts, Styles, and Effects   In PowerPoint, a *font* is a family of text that has the same design or *typeface* (for example, Arial or Courier). A *style* is a standard enhancement, such as bold or italic. An *effect* is a special enhancement, such as shadow or underline.

You can change the fonts for existing text or for text you are about to type by performing the following steps:

1. To change the look of existing text, drag the I-beam pointer over the text.

2. Open the **Format** menu, and select **Font**. The Font dialog box appears, as shown in Figure 11.1.

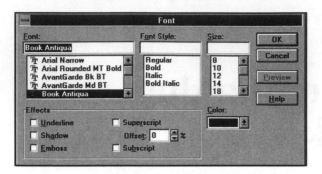

Figure 11.1   The Font dialog box allows you to select a font.

3. From the Font list, select the font you want to use.

TrueType Fonts   The **TT** next to a font name marks the font as a TrueType font. TrueType fonts are *scalable*, meaning that you can set them at any point size. When you save a presentation, you can choose to embed TrueType fonts so you can display or print the font on any computer whether or not it has that font installed.

4. From the Font Style list, select any style you want to apply to the type. (**Regular** removes any styles you may have applied.)

5. In the Size text box, type a desired type size, or select a size from the list. (With TrueType fonts, you can type any point size, even sizes that do not appear on the list.)

6. In the Effects group, select any special effects you want to add to the text, such as Underline, Shadow, or Emboss.

7. To change the color of your text, click on the arrow button to the right of the Color list, and click on the desired color. (For more colors, click on the **Other Color** option at the bottom of the list, and use the dialog box that appears to select a color.)

8. Click on the **OK** button to apply the new look to your text. (If you selected text before styling it, the text appears in the new style. If you did not select text, any text you type will appear in the new style.)

Title and Object Area Text If you change a font on an individual slide, the font is changed only on that slide. To change the font for all the slides in the presentation, change the font on the slide master. To change the Slide Master, open the **View** menu, select **Master**, and select **Slide Master**. Then, perform the steps above to change the look of the text.

Styling Text with the Formatting Toolbar

As shown in Figure 11.2, the Formatting toolbar contains many tools for changing the font, size, style, and color of text.

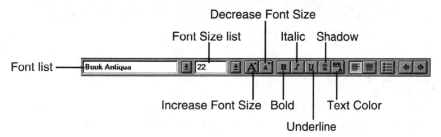

Figure 11.2 The Formatting toolbar contains several tools for styling text.

To use the tools, perform the following steps:

1. To change the look of existing text, select the text.

2. To change fonts, click on the arrow to the right of the Font list, and then click on the desired font.

3. To specify a different type size, click inside the Font Size text box and type a size (in points), or click on the arrow to the right of the text box and select a size.

Incrementing the Type Size To increase or decrease the text size to the next size up or down, click on the **Increase Font Size** or **Decrease Font Size** button in the Formatting toolbar.

4. To add a style or effect to the text (bold, italic, underline, and/or shadow), click on the appropriate button: **B** for Bold, **I** for Italic, **U** for Underline, or **S** for Shadow.

5. To change the color of the text, click on the **Text Color** button, and then click on the desired color. (For more colors, click on the **Other Color** option at the bottom of the list, and use the dialog box that appears to select a color.)

Watch Those Color Schemes   The colors listed on the Color menu complement the background colors in the template. If you choose an "other" color, you risk using one that will clash with the background colors and make your slides look inconsistent.

Copying Text Formats

If your presentation contains text that has the styling you want to use, you can pick up the style from the existing text and apply it to other text. Perform the following steps:

1. Highlight the text whose style you want to use.

2. Open the **Format** menu, and select **Pick Up Text Style**. PowerPoint copies the style.

3. Select the text to which you want to apply the style.

4. Open the **Format** menu, and select **Apply Text Style**. The selected text takes on the look of the source text.

The text style you picked up remains in a temporary holding area until you pick up another style, so you can continue to apply it to other text.

Painting Styles   You can bypass the Format menu by using the Format Painter button in the Standard toolbar. Drag over the text whose style you want to copy, and click on the **Format Painter** button. Drag over the text to which you want to copy the style. When you release the mouse button, the copied format is applied to the selected text.

In this lesson, you learned how to change the appearance of text by changing its font, size, style, and color. In the next lesson, you will learn how to draw objects on a slide.

Drawing Objects on a Slide

In this lesson, you will learn how to use PowerPoint's drawing tools to draw graphic objects on a slide.

PowerPoint's Drawing Tools

You may find it necessary to include basic graphic objects on a slide. For example, you may want to draw a simple logo, or accent your slide with horizontal or vertical lines. PowerPoint comes with several drawing tools that you can use to draw objects on a slide. PowerPoint's drawing tools are displayed along the left side of the presentation window in Slide view and Notes Pages view. (See Figure 12.1).

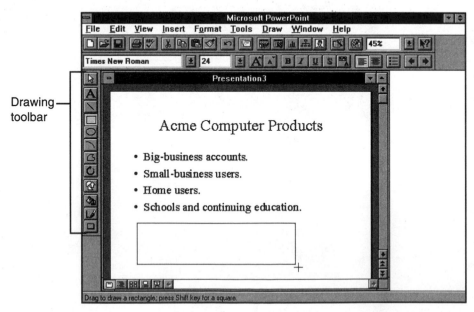

Figure 12.1 The Drawing toolbar contains tools for drawing lines and basic shapes.

Drawing a Line or Shape

The general procedure for drawing an object is the same, no matter which object you draw:

1. Click on the button in the Drawing toolbar for the line or shape you want to draw.

2. Move the mouse pointer to where you want one end of the line or one corner of the object to be anchored.

3. Hold down the mouse button, and drag to where you want the opposite end of the line or corner of the object to appear (see Figure 12.1).

4. Release the mouse button.

Drawing Irregular Objects   The previous steps work well for lines, rectangles, and ovals, but if you choose the **Freeform** tool, you must use some different techniques. To draw freehand, hold down the mouse button, and drag the pointer around on-screen. To create a polygon (an object made up of several straight line segments), click where you want the end point of each line (this works like connect-the-dots). To create a closed shape, click on the original point. To create an open shape, press **Esc**.

Tips for Working with Objects

Following is a list of additional drawing tips that can save you some time and reduce frustration:

- To draw several objects of the same shape, double-click on the tool, and then use the mouse to create as many of those shapes as you like.

- To draw a uniform object (a perfect circle or square), hold down the **Shift** key while dragging.

- To draw an object out from the center rather than from a corner, hold down the **Ctrl** key while dragging.

- To select an object, click on it.

- To delete an object, select it, and press **Del**.

- To move an object, select it, and drag one of its lines.

- To resize or reshape an object, select it, and drag one of its handles.

- To copy an object, hold down the **Ctrl** key while dragging it.

- To quickly change the look of an object, right-click on it, and select the desired option from the shortcut menu.

Line Thickness, Color, and Shading   Lesson 18 provides details about how to enhance drawings and other graphic objects by changing the line thickness, color, and shading. However, you can add the enhancements now by opening the **Format** menu and selecting **Colors and Lines**. The Colors and Lines dialog box lets you add arrow heads to lines, too.

Drawing a PowerPoint AutoShape

PowerPoint comes with several predrawn objects, called AutoShapes, that you can add to your slides. To add one of these objects, perform the following steps:

1. Click on the **AutoShapes** tool in the Drawing toolbar. The AutoShapes palette appears, as shown in Figure 12.2.

2. Click on the shape you want to draw.

3. Move the mouse pointer where you want a corner or the center of the shape to be.

4. (Optional) While drawing the object, hold down one or both of the following keys:

   Ctrl   To draw the shape out from a center point.

   Shift   To draw a shape that retains the dimensions shown on the AutoShapes palette.

5. Hold down the mouse button, and drag the mouse to draw the object.

6. Release the mouse button.

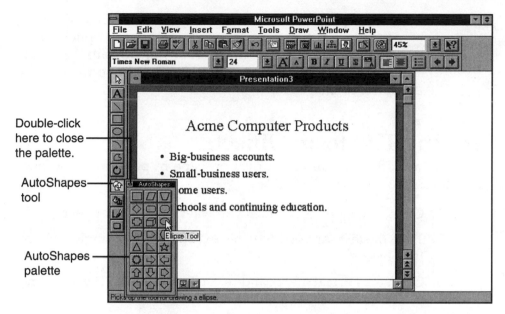

Double-click here to close the palette.

AutoShapes tool

AutoShapes palette

Figure 12.2   Select the desired shape from the AutoShapes palette.

Changing an Existing Shape   You can change an existing shape into a different shape. Select the shape you want to change, open the **Draw** menu, select **Change AutoShape**, and click on the shape you want to use.

Rotating an Object

New to PowerPoint is the Free Rotate tool that allows you to spin an object around its center point. To rotate an object, do the following:

1. Click on the object you want to spin.

2. Click on the **Free Rotate** tool in the **Drawing** toolbar (this is the button with the clockwise arrow on it).

3. Move the mouse pointer over any of the object's handles.

4. Hold down the mouse button, and drag the handle until the object is in the desired position.

5. Release the mouse button.

445

Other Spin Options   The Draw menu contains a Rotate/
Flip submenu that provides additional rotation options. You
can flip an object 90 degrees left or right, or flip the object
over an imaginary vertical or horizontal line to create a
mirrored image of it.

Adding Text to an Object

You can add text to a rectangle, oval, or shape, by performing the following
steps:

1. Click on the object in which you want the text to appear.

2. Type the text. As you type, the text appears in a single line across
   the object.

3. Open the **Format** menu, and select **Text Anchor**. The Text Anchor
   dialog box appears, as shown in Figure 12.3.

4. Select one of the following options to have the text included in the
   object:

   Adjust Object Size to Fit Text   Changes the size of the object to
   fit around the existing text.

   Word-wrap Text in Object   Wraps the text so it fits inside the
   object.

Viewing the Effects of Your Changes   You can drag the
title bar of the dialog box to move the dialog box away from
the object. That way, you will be able to view the effects of
your changes as you work.

5. Click on the arrow to the right of the Anchor Point drop-down list,
   and select an anchor point for the text. For example, if you select
   Bottom, text will sit on the bottom of the object.

6. If desired, use the Box Margins boxes to set the left, right, top, and
   bottom margins for your text. By increasing the margins, you force
   the text in toward the center of the object. By decreasing the margins, you allow the text to reach out toward the edges.

7. Click on the **OK** button to save your changes.

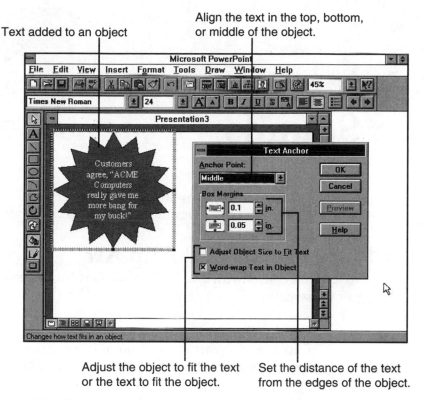

Text added to an object

Align the text in the top, bottom, or middle of the object.

Adjust the object to fit the text or the text to fit the object.

Set the distance of the text from the edges of the object.

Figure 12.3 Use the Text Anchor dialog box to position your text inside the object.

You can change the style and alignment of the text in an object in the same way you can change style and alignment in any text box. Refer to Lessons 9, 10, and 11 for details.

In this lesson, you learned how to use PowerPoint's drawing tools to add basic shapes and line drawings to your slides. In the next lesson, you will learn how to add PowerPoint clip art objects and recorded sounds to your slides.

Adding Pictures and Sounds

In this lesson, you will learn how to add PowerPoint clip art, drawings created in other graphic programs, and recorded sounds to a slide.

Adding PowerPoint Clip Art

PowerPoint comes with hundreds of clip art images that you can use in your presentations.

Clip Art   Clip art is a collection of previously created images or pictures that you can place on a slide.

To insert a clip art image onto a slide, perform the following steps:

1. In Slide view, display the slide on which you want to insert the clip art image.

2. Open the **Insert** menu, and select **Clip Art**, or click on the **Insert Clip Art** button in the Standard toolbar. The Microsoft ClipArt Gallery appears (see Figure 13.1).

First Time?   If this is the first time you have selected to insert a clip art image, PowerPoint displays a dialog box asking for your confirmation and warning that it will take some time. PowerPoint uses this time to organize the clip art library and prepare the images for your use.

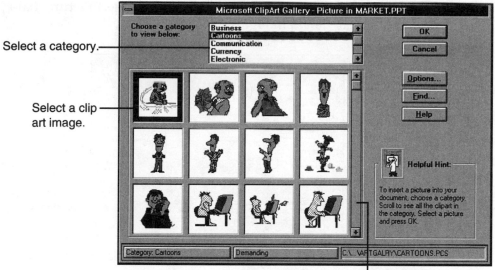

Select a category.

Select a clip art image.

Use the scroll bar to view more images.

Figure 13.1 Select a category and then a clip art image.

3. In the Choose a category list, select the desired group of clip art images. PowerPoint displays the clip art images that are in the selected category.

4. Click on the desired image. A selection border appears around it.

5. Click on the **OK** button. PowerPoint places the selected image on your slide.

6. Move the mouse pointer over the clip art object, hold down the mouse button, and drag the object to the desired position.

Picture Too Big? If the picture is too big or too small, refer to Lesson 17 to learn how to resize and crop (trim) the picture.

Inserting Pictures Created in Other Applications

In addition to inserting clip art images, PowerPoint allows you to insert pictures created in other graphics programs. To insert a picture, perform the following steps:

1. Open the **Insert** menu, and select **Picture**. The Insert Picture dialog box appears, as shown in Figure 13.2.

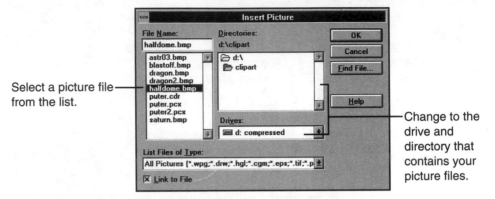

Select a picture file from the list.

Change to the drive and directory that contains your picture files.

Figure 13.2 Use the Insert Picture dialog box to insert a picture created in another program.

2. From the Drives drop-down list, select the drive that contains the desired picture file.

3. From the Directories list, change to the directory that contains the file. A list of graphics files appears in the File Name list.

4. Click on a file name in the list.

5. To link the graphics file to this slide, select **Link to File**. If you make this selection, then whenever you change the graphics file using the program you used to create it, the same changes will appear on your PowerPoint slide.

6. Click on the **OK** button. The picture is inserted on the slide.

7. Move the mouse pointer over the picture, hold down the mouse button, and drag the picture to the desired position.

TIP

Inserting a New Picture   If you have a Windows Paint or Draw program, you can insert a picture you have not yet created by opening the **Insert** menu and selecting **Object**. Make sure the **Create New** option is selected. In the Object Type list, click on the application you need to use to create the picture, and then click on **OK**. PowerPoint runs the application. After you create your picture and exit the application, PowerPoint inserts the picture on the current slide.

Changing the Colors of a Picture

When you paste a clip art image or insert a picture on a slide, the picture appears in its original colors. These colors may clash with the colors in your presentation. To change the colors in a picture, perform the following steps:

1. Click on the picture whose colors you want to change. A selection box appears around the picture.

2. Open the **Tools** menu, and select **Recolor**. The Recolor Picture dialog box appears, as shown in Figure 13.3.

Select the color you want to change.   Select the color you want to change it to.

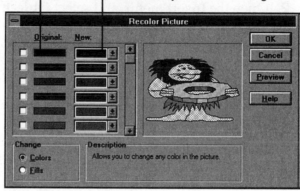

Figure 13.3   Use the Recolor Picture dialog box to change the colors in a picture.

3. In the Change group, select **Colors** to change line colors, or **Fills** to change colors between the lines.

4. Select a color you want to change in the Original list. An **X** appears in the check box next to the color.

5. Use the **New** drop-down menu to the right of the selected color to choose the color you want to change to.

TIP

Using the Other Option   At the bottom of each color's drop-down menu is the Other option. Select this option if you want to use a color that is not listed on the menu.

6. To view the effects of your changes, click on the **Preview** button.

7. Repeat steps 3 through 6 for each color you want to change.

8. Click on the **OK** button to put your changes into effect.

Adding Sounds

If you have sound files (.WAV files) that you recorded on your computer or another computer, or if you have a sound board (such as SoundBlaster Pro) installed on your computer, you can add sounds and music to your presentation. To insert a sound file (.WAV) on a slide, do the following:

1. Display the slide to which you want to apply the sound.

2. Open the **Insert** menu, and select **Object**. The Insert Object dialog box appears.

3. In the Object Type list, click on **Sound** (it's near the bottom of the list).

4. Select **Create from File**.

Recording Sounds   If you have a sound board installed in your computer, you can choose **Create New** to record sounds (if you have a microphone, music keyboard, or other input device connected), or you can plug a tape or CD player into the sound board and record music.

5. Click on the **OK** button. The dialog box changes, prompting you to type the path and file name of the sound file you want to use.

6. Click on the **Browse** button, and use the dialog box that appears to select a sound file, and then click on the **OK** button. This returns you to the Insert Object dialog box. (There are a few .WAV files in the \WINDOWS directory that you can use.)

7. Click on the **OK** button to insert the sound. A small icon appears on the slide to represent the sound.

8. Open the **Tools** menu, and select **Play Settings**. The Play Settings dialog box appears, as shown in Figure 13.4.

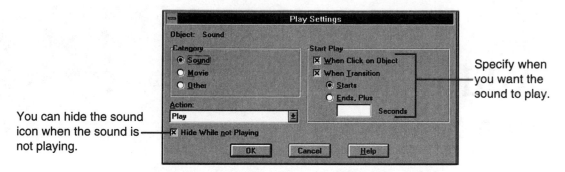

You can hide the sound icon when the sound is not playing.

Specify when you want the sound to play.

Figure 13.4 Use the Play Settings dialog box to tell PowerPoint when to play the sound.

9. In the Start Play group, specify when you want the sound to play:

   When Click on Object Tells PowerPoint to play the sound when you click on the object.

   When Transition Tells PowerPoint to play the sound when the presentation changes from the previous slide to this slide. Starts plays the sound immediately after the previous slide ends.

   Ends, Plus _____ Seconds Plays the sound the specified number of seconds after the transition between slides ends.

10. To hide the sound icon when the presentation is not playing the sound, make sure there is an **X** in the **Hide While not Playing** check box.

11. Click on the **OK** button.

In this lesson, you learned how to add clip art images, pictures, and sounds to your slides. In the next lesson, you will learn how to add a graph to a slide.

Adding a Graph to a Slide

In this lesson, you will learn how to create a graph (chart) and place it on a presentation slide.

Inserting a Graph

PowerPoint comes with a program called Microsoft Graph that can transform raw data into a professional looking graphs. To create a graph, perform the following steps:

1. Display the slide to which you want to add the graph.

2. Click on the **Insert Graph** button (shown below) in the Standard toolbar, or open the **Insert** menu, and choose **Microsoft Graph**. The Microsoft Graph window appears, as shown in Figure 14.1, with the Datasheet window up front.

 Datasheet The *Datasheet* is set up like a spreadsheet with rows, columns, and cells. Each rectangle in the Datasheet is a *cell* which can hold text or numbers. Microsoft Graph converts the data you enter into a graph which is displayed in the Graph window.

3. Click inside the cell that contains a label or value you want to change, and type your entry.

4. Click on the next cell you want to change, or use the arrow keys to move from cell to cell.

5. Repeat steps 3 and 4 until all your data is entered.

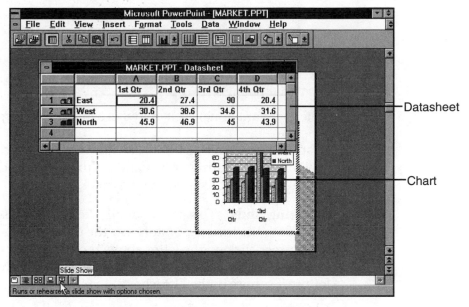

Figure 14.1   The Microsoft Graph window.

6. Click anywhere inside the graph window. The Datasheet window disappears, and the graph appears.

7. To leave Microsoft Graph and return to your slide in PowerPoint, click anywhere outside the graph.

Moving and Resizing the Graph   If the graph is too big or is poorly positioned on the slide, you can resize and move it. Refer to Lesson 17 for details.

Editing the Datasheet

If you returned to your slide and later decide that you want to edit the data that your graph is based on, perform the following steps to return to Microsoft Graph and display the Datasheet:

1. Display the slide that contains the graph you want to edit.

2. Double-click anywhere inside the graph. PowerPoint starts Microsoft Graph and displays the graph.

3. If the Datasheet window is not displayed, open the **View** menu, and select **Datasheet**, or click on the **View Datasheet** button. The Datasheet window appears.

4. Tab to the cell that contains the value you want to change, and type your change.

5. When you are done, click anywhere inside the graph window.

In addition to editing individual data entries, you can cut, copy, and paste cells; delete or insert rows and columns; and adjust the column widths. The following list gives you a quick overview:

Selecting Cells To select one cell, click on it. To select several cells, drag the mouse pointer over the desired cells. To select a row or column, click on the letter above the column or the number to the left of the row. To select all the cells, click on the upper-leftmost square in the Datasheet.

Clearing Cells To erase the contents of cells, select the cells, and then open the **Edit** menu, and select **Clear**. Select **All** (to clear contents and formatting), **Contents** (to remove only the contents), or **Formats** (to remove only the formatting).

Cutting or Copying Cells To cut cells, select the cells you want to cut, and then open the **Edit** menu, and select **Cut**. Or click on the **Cut** button in the toolbar. To copy cells, select the cells you want to copy, and then open the **Edit** menu and select **Copy**, or click on the **Copy** button in the toolbar.

Pasting Cells To paste copied or cut cells into a datasheet, select the cell in the upper left corner of the area in which you want to paste the cut or copied cells. Open the **Edit** menu, and select **Paste**, or click on the **Paste** button in the toolbar.

Inserting Blank Cells To insert blank cells, select the row, column, or number of cells you want to insert. (Rows will be inserted above the current row. Columns will be inserted to the left of the current column.) Open the **Insert** menu, and select **Cells**. If you selected a row or column, the row or column is inserted. If you selected one or more cells, the Insert Cells dialog box appears, asking if you want to shift surrounding cells down or to the right. Select your preference, and then click on the **OK** button.

Changing the Column Width   If you typed entries that are too wide for a particular column, you may want to adjust the column width. Move the mouse pointer over the column letter at the top of the column whose width you want to change. Move the mouse pointer to the right until it turns into a double-headed arrow. Hold down the mouse button, and drag the mouse until the column is the desired width.

Changing the Data Series

Say you create a graph that shows the sales figures over four quarters for several sales persons . You wanted each column in the graph to represent a salesperson, but instead, the columns represented quarters. To fix the graph, you can swap the data series by performing the following steps:

1. Open the **Data** menu.

2. Select **Series in Rows** or **Series in Columns**.

Quick Data Series Swap   To quickly swap data series, click on the **By Row** or **By Column** button in the Standard toolbar.

Changing the Graph Type

By default, Microsoft Graph creates a 3-dimensional column graph. If you want your data displayed in a different type of graph, perform the following steps:

1. Open the **Format** menu, and select **Chart Type**. The Chart Type dialog box appears, as shown in Figure 14.2.

2. In the Apply to group, make sure **Entire Chart** is selected.

3. In the Chart Dimension group, select **2-D** or **3-D**. The available graphs for the selected group appear.

4. Click on the desired chart type.

5. Click on the **OK** button.

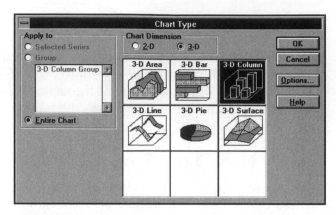

Figure 14.2   Pick the desired chart.

Selecting a Chart Design with AutoFormat

Microsoft Graph comes with several predesigned chart formats that you can apply to your chart. You simply select the design, and Microsoft Graph reformats your chart, giving it a professional look. Here's how you use AutoFormat to select a chart design:

1. Open the **Format** menu, and choose **AutoFormat**. The AutoFormat dialog box appears, as shown in Figure 14.3.

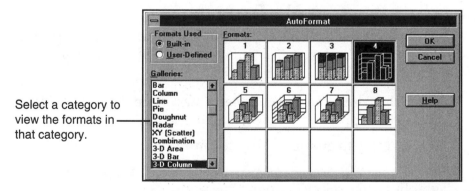

Select a category to view the formats in that category.

Figure 14.3   Select a chart design from the AutoFormat dialog box.

2. From the Galleries list, choose a chart type. In the Formats list, PowerPoint shows the available formats for the selected chart type.

3. Select the desired chart type from the Formats list.

4. Click on the **OK** button. Excel reformats the chart, using the selected format.

In this lesson, you learned how to create a graph, enter and edit data, and add the graph to a slide. In the next lesson, you will learn how to enhance the graph.

Enhancing Charts

15

In this lesson, you will learn how to enhance your charts to display data more clearly and more attractively.

What Can You Add to a Chart?

You can format existing elements and add elements to a chart to enhance it. Following is a list of some of the more common enhancements:

Fonts   You can specify a type style, size, and attributes for the text used in the chart.

Colors   You can change the color of text or of the lines, bars, and pie slices that are used to represent data.

Titles and Labels   You can add a title to the chart or add labels for any of the axes.

Axes   You can display or hide the lines used for the X and Y axes.

Text Boxes   You can add explanatory text or other text in a separate box.

Borders and Shading   You can add a border around a chart or add background shading.

Displaying the Chart in Microsoft Graph

Before you can enhance an existing chart, you must display it in Microsoft Graph. Perform the following steps:

1. In Slide view, display the slide that contains the graph you want to enhance.

2. Click on the graph to select it. A selection box appears around the graph.

3. Open the **Edit** menu, and select **Chart Object**. The Chart Object submenu appears.

4. Select **Edit**. PowerPoint starts Microsoft Graph and displays the graph.

Double-Click on the Graph A quick way to display a graph in Microsoft Graph is to double-click on the graph.

You can add text boxes, lines, arrows, and basic shapes to graphs in much the same way you can add them to slides. To display the Drawing toolbar for graphs, click on the **Drawing** button in the Standard toolbar, or right-click on the Standard toolbar and select **Drawing**. Refer to Lessons 9 and 13 for details on how to use the toolbar buttons to add text boxes, lines, and other shapes.

Parts of a Chart

Before you start adding enhancements to a chart, you should understand that a chart is made up of several objects. By clicking on an object, you make it active, and handles appear around it, as shown in Figure 15.1. You can then move or resize the object or change its appearance, by doing any of the following:

- Double-click on an object to display a dialog box that lets you change the object's appearance. For example, if you double-click on a column in a column chart, you can change its color.

- Right-click on the object, and then select the desired formatting option from the shortcut menu.

- Select the object, and then select an option from the **Insert** or **Format** menu. The Insert menu lets you add objects to a chart, including a legend, data labels, and a chart title.

The following sections tell you how to add some more commonly used enhancements to a chart.

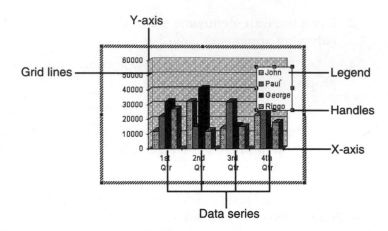

Figure 15.1 Each chart consists of several individual objects.

Adding a Title

You can add various titles to a chart to help indicate what the chart is all about. You can add a chart title that appears at the top of the chart, and you can add axis titles that appear along the X-and Y-axes. Here's how you do it:

1. Right-click on the chart, and choose **Insert Titles**, or open the **Insert** menu and choose **Titles**.

2. Click on each title type you want to add, to put an **X** in their check boxes.

3. Click on the **OK** button. Microsoft Graph returns you to the chart window and inserts text boxes for each title.

4. Click on a text box to select it, click inside the text box, and then edit the text as desired.

Formatting Text on a Chart

Any text you add to a chart is added inside a text box. To format text you added, do this:

1. Right-click on the text that you want to format. A text box appears around the text, and a shortcut menu appears.

2. Select the **Format** option. The Format option differs depending on the object. If you right-click on the chart title, the option reads **Format Chart Title**.

3. Enter your preferences in the Format dialog box. This dialog box typically contains tabs for changing the font, adding borders and shading to the text box, and changing the alignment of text in the box, but you may get only the Font tab.

4. Click on **OK** when you are done.

Formatting the Axes

You can enhance the X- and Y-axes in a number of ways, including changing the font of the text, scaling the axes, and changing the number format. Here's how you do it:

1. Right-click on the axis you want to format, and choose **Format Axis**, or click on the axis, open the **Format** menu, and choose **Selected Axis**. The Format Axis dialog box appears, as shown in Figure 15.2.

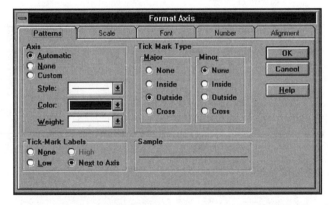

Figure 15.2   The Format Axis dialog box lets you change the look of the axis and its text.

2. Enter your preferences in the dialog box.

3. Click on **OK**, or press **Enter**.

Enhancing the Chart Frame

You can change the overall look of a chart by adding a border or shading. Perform the following steps:

1. Click on the chart anywhere outside a specific chart object. Handles appear around the entire chart.

2. Open the **Format** menu, and choose **Selected Chart Area**, or right-click on the chart and choose **Format Chart Area**. The Format Chart Area dialog box appears.

3. Enter your border and color preferences, and then click on the **OK** button.

Changing the Look of 3-D Charts

3-D charts are commonly used to illustrate volume. In order to make the various 3-dimensional elements stand out, you may want to tilt the chart or rotate it. Here's how you do it:

1. Open the **Format** menu and choose **3-D View**, or right-click on the chart and choose **3-D View**. The Format 3-D View dialog box appears, as shown in Figure 15.3. As you make changes, they are reflected in the wire-frame picture in the middle of the 3-D View dialog box.

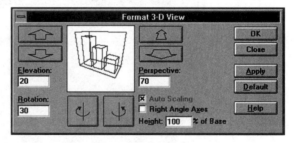

Figure 15.3   Changing the 3-D view.

2. To change the elevation (height from which the chart is seen), click on the up or down elevation controls, or type a number in the Elevation box.

3. To change the rotation (rotation around the Z-axis), click on the left or right rotation controls, or type a number in the Rotation box.

4. If there is a perspective option, you can change the perspective (perceived depth) by clicking on the up or down perspective controls, or typing a number in the Perspective box.

5. To see the proposed changes applied to the actual chart, click on the **Apply** button.

6. When you are done making changes, click on **OK**, or press **Enter**.

In this lesson, you learned how to improve the appearance of your chart. In the next lesson, you will learn how to add an organizational chart to a slide.

Adding an Organizational Chart

In this lesson, you will learn how to add an organizational chart to a slide and how to edit the chart.

Inserting an Organizational Chart

PowerPoint comes with a program called Microsoft Organization Chart that can create organizational charts to show the management structure in a company. To create and place an organizational chart on a slide, perform the following steps:

1. Display the slide on which you want the organizational chart placed.

2. Open the **Insert** menu, and select **Object**. The Insert Object dialog box appears.

3. In the Object Type list, click on **Microsoft Organization Chart 1.0**, and click on the **OK** button. The Microsoft Organization Chart window appears, as shown in Figure 16.1.

> **TIP** **The Insert Org Chart Button** To bypass the Insert menu, click on the **Insert Org Chart** button in the Standard toolbar.

4. If the Organization Chart window is small, click on the **Maximize** button in the upper right corner of the window to make it full-screen size.

5. Type the name, title, and up to two optional comments about the person in the organization. Press **Enter** after typing each item.

6. Press **Esc** when you are done.

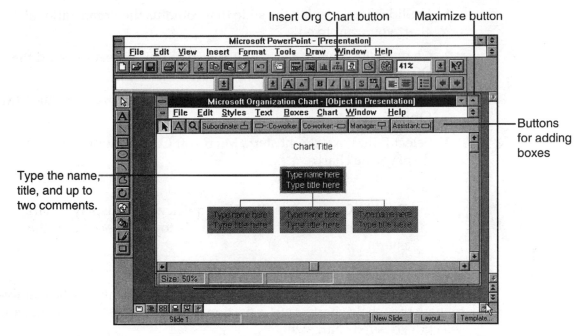

Figure 16.1 Type your entries into the basic structure to form a chart.

7. Click on the next box, or use the arrow keys to move to the next box. (The up and down arrow keys move up or down a level in the chart. The left and right arrow keys move to the left or right box on the same level.)

8. Repeat steps 5–7 for each person you want to include in the organizational chart.

9. To add boxes to the chart, click on the appropriate button at the top of the screen, and then click on the box to which you want the new box connected.

10. To return to your slide and insert the organizational chart on it, open the **File** menu, select **Exit and Return to**, and then click on the **Yes** button.

Editing an Organizational Chart

Before you can edit an existing organizational chart, you must display it in Microsoft Organization Chart. Perform the following steps:

1. In Slide view, display the slide that contains the organizational chart you want to edit.

2. Click on the chart to select it. A selection box appears around the chart.

3. Open the **Edit** menu, and select **Microsoft Organization Chart 1.0 Object**.

4. Select **Edit**. PowerPoint starts Microsoft Organization Chart and displays the chart.

Double-Click on the Chart A quick way to display a chart in Microsoft Organization Chart is to double-click on the chart.

As you work on the chart, you can enlarge it or shrink it in the window to view the whole chart or just a portion of it. Open the **Chart** menu, and select the desired chart size.

Selecting One or More Levels

As you are editing, adding to, or enhancing an organizational chart, you will need to select the boxes you want to work with. The following list explains how to select one or more boxes or levels:

- To select a single box, click on it. To move from one box to another, use the arrow keys.

- To select more than one box, hold down the **Shift** key while clicking on each box.

- To select a specific group of boxes (for example, all manager boxes), open the **Edit** menu, choose **Select**, and click on the desired group.

- To select a specific level in the organization, open the **Edit** menu, choose **Select Levels**, and type the range of levels you would like to select (for example, 2 through 5).

Cutting, Copying, and Pasting Boxes

To rearrange your organizational chart, you can cut, copy, and paste boxes. Perform the following steps:

1. Select the box(es) you want to copy or move.

2. Open the **Edit** menu, and select **Cut** (to remove the boxes) or **Copy** (to copy them).

3. Select the box to which you want the copied or cut boxes attached.

4. Open the **Edit** menu, and select **Paste Boxes**. The boxes are pasted to the right of or below the selected box.

Undoing Cut or Paste   You can undo any operation immediately after performing it by opening the **Edit** menu and selecting **Undo**. If you performed two actions, however, you can undo only the most recent one.

Selecting a Chart Style

The chart you create resembles a family tree. If that structure does not suit your needs (for all or part of the chart), you can change the structure. Perform the following steps:

1. Select the boxes to which you want to apply the new style. To apply your changes to the entire chart, select all the boxes.

2. Open the **Styles** menu, and click on the desired style (see Figure 16.2). Organization Chart applies the specified style to the selected boxes.

Select a structure for part or all of the chart.

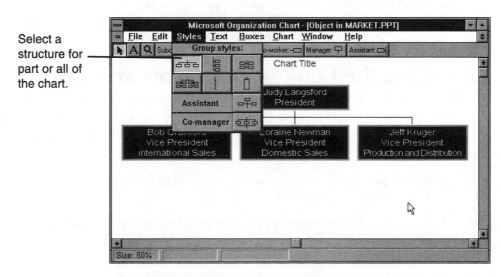

Figure 16.2   Use the Styles menu to restructure your chart.

469

Styling the Text

You may want to use a different font, type style, type size, or color for a person's name and position, or for different levels in the chart. Or you may want to change the text alignment in the box from center to left or right. To style the text in a box, do the following:

1. Select the text you want to format:

    -   Click on a box to format all the text in the box.

    -   To format part of the text in a box, drag over the desired text.

    -   Hold down the **Shift** key, and click on two or more boxes to format the text in every selected box.

2. Open the **Text** menu, and select **Font**. The Font dialog box appears.

3. Change one or more of the following options:

    Font   Select a typeface from the Font list.

    Font Style   Select a style (for example, bold or italic) from the Font Style list.

    Size   Select a type size (in points) from the Size list.

4. Click on the **OK** button.

5. To change the color of the text, open the **Text** menu, select **Color**, and click on the desired color.

6. To change the alignment of the text in the box (from centered to left or right), open the **Text** menu, and select the desired alignment.

Changing the Look of the Boxes and Lines

The boxes and lines that make up an organizational chart are formatted for you. However, if you want to change the line or box color or line thickness, or if you want to add a drop shadow to the boxes, perform the following steps:

1. Select the boxes or lines you want to format. (You can select lines by clicking on them.)

2. Open the **Boxes** menu, and select the desired option. A submenu opens, providing you with a list of available settings.

3. Click on the color, style, or shading you want to use for the selected lines or boxes. Organization Chart applies the selected
setting to your organizational chart.

Returning to Your Slide When you are done editing and
enhancing your organizational chart, you can return to your
slide by opening the **File** menu and selecting **Exit and
Return to**. Click on the **Yes** button to save your changes.

In this lesson, you learned how to create, edit, and enhance an
organizational chart. In the next lesson, you will learn how to work with
the objects (graphs, organizational charts, text boxes, and drawn objects),
which you have placed on a slide.

Positioning and Sizing Objects

In this lesson, you will learn how to cut, copy, paste, move, and resize objects on a slide.

As you may have already discovered, *objects* are the building blocks you use to create slides in PowerPoint. Objects are the shapes you draw, the graphs you create, the pictures you import, and the text you type. In this and the next lesson, you will learn how to manipulate objects on your slides to create impressive presentations.

Selecting Objects

Before you can copy, move, or resize an object, you must first select the object. Change to Slide view, and perform one of the following steps to choose one or more objects:

- To select a single object, click on it. (If you clicked on text, a frame appears around the text. Click on the frame to select the object.)

- To select more than one object, hold down the **Shift** key while clicking on each object. Handles appear around the selected objects, as shown in Figure 17.1.

- To deselect selected objects, click anywhere outside the selected objects.

Using the Selection Tool   The Selection Tool in the Drawing toolbar (the button with the mouse pointer on it), allows you to quickly select a group of objects. Click on the **Selection** tool, and then use the mouse pointer to drag a selection box around the objects you want to select. When you release the mouse button, the objects inside the box are selected.

Figure 17.1 Handles indicate which objects are selected.

Working with Layers of Objects

As you place objects on-screen, they may start to overlap, making it difficult or impossible to select the objects in the lower layers. To relayer objects, perform the following steps:

1. Click on the object you want to move up or down in the stack.

2. Open the **Draw** menu.

3. Select one of the following options:

   Bring to Front   Brings the object to the top of the stack.

   Send to Back   Sends the object to the bottom of the stack.

   Bring Forward   Brings the object up one layer.

   Send Backward   Sends the object back one layer.

Grouping and Ungrouping Objects

Each object you draw acts as an individual object. However, sometimes, you'll want two or more objects to act as a group. For example, you may want to make the lines of several objects the same thickness, or move the objects together. If you want two or more objects to always be treated as a group, perform the following steps:

1. Select the objects you want to group.

2. Open the **Draw** menu, and select **Group**.

3. To ungroup the objects later, select any object in the group, open the **Draw** menu, and select **Ungroup**.

Drawing + Toolbar For quick access to the Group, Ungroup, and layering commands, turn on the Drawing + toolbar. Right-click on any toolbar, and then click on **Drawing +**.

Cutting, Copying, and Pasting Objects

You can cut, copy, and paste objects on a slide to rearrange the objects or to use the objects to create a picture. It works just the same as in any other Windows program; you use the Clipboard.

Whenever you cut an object, the object is removed from the slide and placed in a temporary holding area called the Windows Clipboard. When you copy an object, the original object remains on the slide, and a copy of it is placed on the Clipboard. In either case, you can then paste the object from the Clipboard onto the current slide or another slide. Perform the following steps:

1. Select the object(s) you want to cut, copy, or move.

2. Open the **Edit** menu, and select **Cut** or **Copy**.

Quick Cut and Copy To quickly cut or copy a selected object, click on the **Cut** or **Copy** button in the Standard toolbar, or press **Ctrl+X** to cut or **Ctrl+C** to copy.

3. Display the slide on which you want the cut or copied object(s) placed.

4. Open the **Edit** menu and select **Paste**, or click on the **Paste** button in the Standard toolbar. The object(s) is pasted on the slide.

5. Move the mouse pointer over any of the pasted objects, hold down the mouse button, and drag the objects to where you want them.

6. Release the mouse button.

Deleting an Object   To remove an object without placing it on the Clipboard, select the object and then press **Del**, or open the **Edit** menu and select **Clear**.

The quickest way to copy or move objects is to drag and drop them. Select the objects you want to move, position the mouse pointer over any of the selected objects, hold down the mouse button, and drag the objects where you want them. To copy the objects, hold down the **Ctrl** key while dragging.

Resizing Objects

There may be times when an object you have created or imported is not the right size for your slide presentation. Resize the object by performing these steps:

1. Select the object to resize.

2. Drag one of the *handles* (the black squares that surround the object) until the object is the desired size:

   • Drag a corner handle to change both the height and width. PowerPoint retains the object's relative dimensions.

   • Drag a side, top, or bottom handle to change the height or width alone.

   • Hold down the **Ctrl** key while dragging to resize from the center of the picture.

3. Release the mouse button, and the object will be resized (see Figure 17.2).

Cropping a Picture

In addition to resizing a picture, you can crop it. That is, you can trim a side or corner of the picture to remove an element from the picture or cut off some white space. To crop a picture, perform the following steps:

Drag a handle to resize the object.

Figure 17.2 Before and after resizing an object.

1. Click on the picture you want to crop.

2. Open the **Tools** menu, and select **Crop Picture**. The mouse pointer turns into a cropping tool. (See Figure 17.3.)

Cropping tool

Figure 17.3 Use the cropping tool to chop off a section of the picture.

3. Move the mouse pointer over one of the handles. (Use a corner handle to crop two sides at once. Use a side, top, or bottom handle to crop only one side.)

4. Hold down the mouse button, and drag the pointer until the crop lines are where you want them.

5. Release the mouse button. The cropped section disappears.

Uncropping You can uncrop a picture immediately after cropping it by opening the **Edit** menu and selecting **Undo,** or clicking on the **Undo** button on the Standard toolbar. You can uncrop at any time, by performing the steps above and dragging the selected handle in the opposite direction you dragged it for cropping.

In this lesson, you learned how to select, edit, move, and resize an object in a slide. In the next lesson, you will learn how to change the look of an object.

Changing the Look of Objects

In this lesson, you will learn how to add borders, colors, patterns, and shadows to objects.

Framing an Object

You can frame an object by adding a line around the object. To add a line, perform the following steps:

1. Select the object you want to frame.

2. Open the **Format** menu, and select **Colors and Lines**. The Colors and Lines dialog box appears, as shown in Figure 18.1.

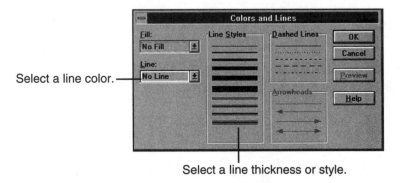

Select a line color.

Select a line thickness or style.

Figure 18.1   The Colors and Lines dialog box.

3. Click on the arrow to the right of the Line option, and then click on the desired color for the line.

4. In the Line Styles list, click on the thickness of the line you want to use.

5. Click on the **OK** button.

Instant Thin Line   To quickly add a thin border around an object, click on the object, and then click on the **Apply Line Defaults** button in the Drawing toolbar. It's the button with the paintbrush on it.

Adding a Fill

A fill is a background color and shading combination that you can add to an object to make the object stand out. To add a fill or change an existing fill, perform these steps:

1. Select the object(s) you want to fill.

2. Open the **Tools** menu, and choose **Recolor**. The Recolor Picture dialog box appears, as shown in Figure 18.2.

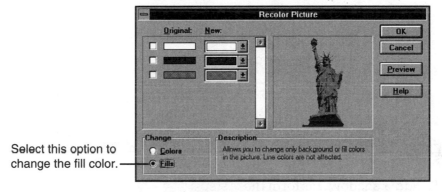

Select this option to change the fill color.

Figure 18.2   You can change each fill color.

3. Click on the **Fills** option. The displayed colors change to show the fill colors.

4. Select a color you want to change in the Original list. An **X** appears in the check box next to the color.

5. Use the New drop-down menu to the right of the selected color to choose the color you want to change to.

Using the Other Option   At the bottom of each color's drop-down menu is the Other option. Select this option if you want to use a color that is not listed on the menu.

6. To view the effects of your changes, click on the **Preview** button.

7. Repeat steps 3 through 5 for each color you want to change.

8. Click on the **OK** button to put your changes into effect.

Quick Fills To quickly apply the default fill colors, select the object, and then click on the **Apply Fill Defaults** button (the button with the paint can on it) in the Drawing toolbar. To remove a fill, select the object, and click on the **Apply Fill Defaults** button again.

Adding a Shadow

Adding a shadow gives a 3-D effect to an object, as shown in Figure 18.3.

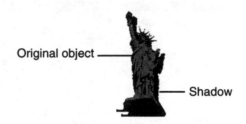

Original object ————

———— Shadow

Figure 18.3 The Statue of Liberty with a shadow added.

To add a shadow, perform these steps:

1. Select the object to add a shadow to.

2. Open the **Format** menu, and select **Shadow**. The Shadow dialog box appears.

3. Click on the arrow to the right of the Color option, and click on the desired color for the shadow.

4. To change the position and thickness of the shadow, enter your settings in the Offset group.

Offset To understand the offset options, think of the shadow as a silhouette of the original object that sits behind the object. You can move the silhouette behind the object in any direction, and move it out more from the object to make the shadow appear thicker.

5. Click on the **OK** button. PowerPoint applies the shadow to the object.

To remove the shadow, repeat the steps above, but select **No Shadow** from the Color drop-down list. You can also remove a shadow by selecting the object and then clicking on the **Apply Shadow Defaults** button in the Drawing toolbar.

Copying the Look of Another Object

If your presentation contains an object that has the frame, fill, and shadow you want to use for another object, you can pick up those design elements and apply them to another object. Perform the following steps:

1. Click on the object whose style you want to copy.

2. Open the **Format** menu, and select **Pick Up Object Style**. PowerPoint copies the style.

3. Click on the object to which you want to apply the style.

4. Open the **Format** menu, and select **Apply Object Style**. The selected object takes on the look of the source object.

The style you picked up remains in a temporary holding area until you pick up another style, so you can continue to apply it to other objects.

TIP

Painting Styles You can bypass the Format menu by using the **Format Painter** button in the Standard toolbar. Select the object whose style you want to copy, and click on the **Format Painter** button. Select the object to which you want to copy the style.

In this lesson, you learned how to change the look of individual objects on a slide. In the next lesson, you will learn how to change the background colors and designs that appear on every slide in the presentation.

Working with Colors and Backgrounds

In this lesson, you will learn how to change the color scheme and background design for a presentation.

Understanding Color Schemes and Backgrounds

Color schemes are sets of professionally selected complementary colors designed to be used as the primary colors in a presentation. Each color scheme controls the color of the background, lines, text, shadows, fills, and other items on a slide. Using one of these color schemes ensures that your presentation will look appealing and professional.

Backgrounds are designs that control the way the color is used on a slide. For example, you can select a background that spreads the color out from the upper left corner to the edges.

You can select a color scheme and background for the master slide (which controls all the slides in the presentation), for the current slide, or for all slides in the presentation (thus overriding the master slide). The following sections explain how to select and manipulate color schemes and backgrounds.

Selecting a Color Scheme

You can select a color scheme for one slide or for all the slides in your presentation. Perform the following steps:

1. Display or select the slide whose color scheme you want to change.

Stay Consistent   Be careful when selecting a color scheme for a single slide in the presentation. You don't want one slide to clash with the rest of your slides. As you will see later, you can apply the new color scheme to one or all of the slides in your presentation.

2. Open the **Format** menu, and select **Slide Color Scheme**. The Slide Color Scheme dialog box appears.

3. Click on the **Choose Scheme** button. The Choose Scheme dialog box appears.

4. From the Background Color list, select the color you want to use for the slide background. A list of complementary colors appears in the Text & Line Color list.

5. From the Text & Line Color list, select a color you want to use for the text and lines on a slide. A selection of samples appears in the Other Scheme Colors group, as shown in Figure 19.1.

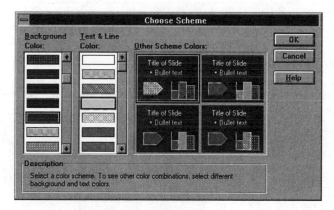

Figure 19.1   Select a background color, text color, and other colors option.

6. From the Other Scheme Colors group, click on the desired look you want for your slides.

7. Click on **OK** when finished selecting colors. You are returned to the Slide Color Scheme dialog box.

8. Click on the **Apply** button to apply the new color scheme only to this slide, or click on **Apply to All** to apply the color scheme to all the slides in the presentation.

Changing a Color in the Color Scheme

You can modify any color in a color scheme to create your own custom combinations. For example, you can create a color scheme that matches your company colors or logo. To change a color in a color scheme, perform the following steps:

1. Display or select the slide whose color scheme you want to change.

2. Open the **Format** menu, and select **Slide Color Scheme**. The Slide Color Scheme dialog box appears.

3. Click on a color you want to change. (Colors are labeled to show the corresponding items they control.)

4. Click on the **Change Color** button. The Color dialog box for the selected item appears, as shown in Figure 19.2.

Select the item whose color you want to change.

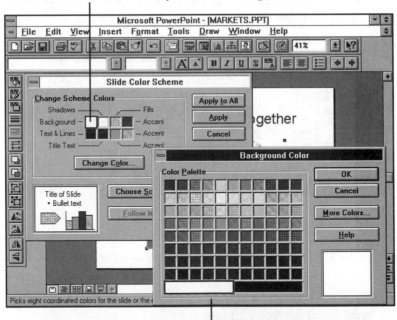

The Change Color button brings up this dialog box.

Figure 19.2 You can change colors for various items in your presentation.

5. Click on the color you want to use.

Custom Colors To create a custom color, click on the **More Colors** button, and adjust the Hue, Saturation, and Luminance to create the desired color.

6. Click on the **OK** button to change the color and return to the Color Scheme dialog box.

7. Repeat steps 3 through 6 to change any other colors.

8. When finished changing colors, click on the **Apply** or **Apply To All** button.

Copying and Applying a Color Scheme to Other Presentations

You can reuse a color scheme you have created in a presentation by copying it and applying it to another presentation. This is particularly useful if you have created a custom color scheme. To copy a color scheme from one presentation to another, do the following:

1. Open the presentation that contains the color scheme you want to copy. (See Lesson 5.)

2. Open the **View** menu, and select **Slide Sorter**, or click on the **Slide Sorter** button at the bottom of the presentation window.

3. Click on the slide which contains the color scheme you want to copy.

4. Open the **Format** menu, and select **Pick up Color Scheme**.

5. Open the presentation to which you want to apply the copied color scheme.

6. Open the **View** menu, and select **Slide Sorter**, or click on the **Slide Sorter** button at the bottom of the presentation window.

7. Select the slide(s) to which you want to apply the copied color scheme. (To select more than one slide, hold down the **Shift** key while clicking on the slides.)

8. Open the **Format** menu, and select **Apply Color Scheme**.

Changing the Background Design

An effective background can add a professional look to any presentation. To change the background for your presentation or modify the existing background, perform the following steps:

1. Display or select the slide whose background you want to change. (You will be able to apply the background changes to all the slides in the presentation.)

2. Open the **Format** menu, and select **Slide Background**. The Slide Background dialog box appears, as shown in Figure 19.3.

3. In the Shade Styles group, select the way you want the background color to fade across the slide. (For example, if you choose **From Corner**, the color appears pale in one corner and then intensifies as it reaches the edges of the slide.)

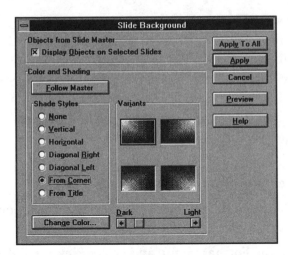

Figure 19.3 The Slide Background dialog box lets you control the background color and shading.

4. To change the background color, click on the **Change Color** button, click on the color you want to use, and then click on **OK**. (You can change the background color here or in the Color Scheme, as explained earlier.)

5. To change the intensity of the color, use the Dark/Light slide control.

6. In the Variants group, select the desired variation you want to use for the shade style.

7. Click on the **Apply** button to apply the background only to this slide, or click on **Apply To All** to apply the background to all the slides in the presentation.

In this lesson, you learned how to select and modify a color scheme, and how to copy a color scheme from one presentation to other presentations. You also learned how to change the background color and design for a slide or presentation. In the next lesson, you will learn how to rearrange the slides in a presentation.

Rearranging Slides

In this lesson, you will learn how to rearrange your slides in the presentation.

There may be times when you will need to change the sequence of slides you have created in the presentation. In PowerPoint, you are given the ability to reorder the slides in either Slide Sorter view or Outline view.

Rearranging in Slide Sorter View

Slide Sorter view shows miniature versions of the slides in your presentation. This allows you to view many of your slides at one time. To rearrange the slides in Slide Sorter view, perform the following steps:

1. Open the **View** menu, and select **Slide Sorter**. Or click on the **Slide Sorter** view button, as shown here:

2. Move the mouse pointer over the slide you want to move to a new location.

3. Hold down the mouse button, and drag the mouse pointer over the slide before or after which you want the slide moved. As you drag the mouse pointer, a line appears (as shown in Figure 20.1), showing where the slide will be moved.

4. Release the mouse button. The slide is moved to its new position, and the surrounding slides are shifted to make room for it.

Line shows new position of slide.

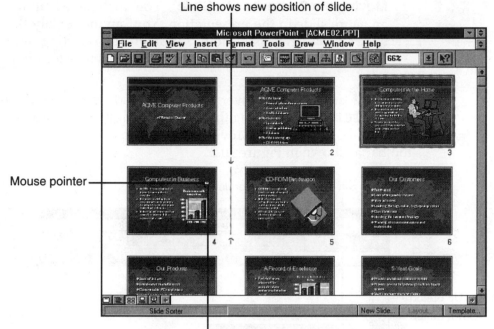

Mouse pointer

Drag to the right side of the slide to insert after the
slide, or to the left side to insert before the slide.

Figure 20.1 Drag the slide to its new position.

Copying a Slide You can copy a slide in Slide Sorter view
as easily as you can move a slide. Simply hold down the **Ctrl**
key while dragging.

Rearranging in Outline View

In Outline view, you can see the titles and text on each slide, giving you a
clear picture of the content and organization of your presentation. Because
of this, you may prefer to rearrange your slides in Outline view. Here's
how you do it:

1. Open the **View** menu, and select **Outline**, or click on the Outline
   view button.

2. Click on the slide number or slide icon to the left of the slide you
   want to move. The entire slide contents are highlighted.

Moving the Contents of a Slide   You don't have to move an entire slide in the presentation. You can move only the slide's data—from one slide to another—by selecting only what you want to move and dragging it to its new location.

3. Move the mouse pointer over the selected slide icon, hold down the mouse button, and drag the slide up or down in the outline. Or click on the **Move Up** or **Move Down** buttons in the Outlining toolbar as shown in Figure 20.2.

You can drag the icon up or down.

Move Up button ——
Move Down button ——

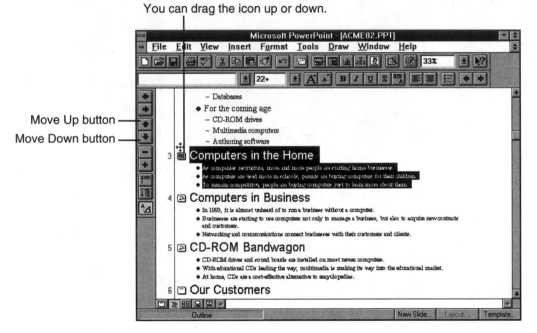

Figure 20.2   Drag the selected icon, or click on the Move Up or Move Down button.

Collapsing the Outline   You can *collapse* the outline to show only the slide titles. This allows you to see more slides at one time and rearrange the slides more easily. To collapse the outline, click on the **Show Titles** button in the Outlining toolbar. To restore the outline, click on the **Show All** button.

Hiding Slides

Before you give a presentation, you should try to anticipate any questions from your audience and be prepared to answer those questions. You may even want to create slides to support your answers and then keep the slides hidden until you need them. To hide one or more slides, perform the following steps:

1. Display or select the slide(s) you want to hide. (You can hide slides in Slide, Outline, or Slide Sorter view.)

2. Open the **Tools** menu, and select **Hide Slide**. If you are in Slide Sorter view, the hidden slide's number appears in a box with a line through it.

3. To unhide the slide(s), display or select the hidden slide(s), pull down the **Tools** menu, and select **Unhide Slide**.

In this lesson, you learned how to rearrange the slides in a presentation in either the Slide Sorter or Outline view, and how to hide slides. In the next lesson, you will learn how view a slide show on-screen and fine-tune it.

Viewing and Enhancing a Slide Show

In this lesson, you will learn how to view a slide show on-screen, add timing between slides, and add transitions and builds to animate your slide show.

An on-screen slide show is a lot like the slide show you can put on by using a slide projector. However, with an on-screen slide show, you can add impressive and professional visual effects (transitions and builds) that provide smooth and attention-getting movements from one slide to the next.

Transitions and Builds   A *transition* is a way of moving from one slide to the next. For example, with a vertical blinds transition, the slide takes on the look of window blinds that turn to reveal the next slide. A *build* displays the bulleted items on a slide, one item at a time, until all the bulleted items are added to the list.

Viewing an On-Screen Slide Show

You can view a slide show at any time to see how the show will look in real life. To view a slide show, perform the following steps:

1. Open the presentation you want to view.

2. Or open the **View** menu, select **Slide Show**, and click on the **Show** button. Or click on the **Slide Show** button at the bottom of the presentation window. The first slide in the presentation appears full-screen, as shown in Figure 21.1.

Figure 21.1   The Slide Show view provides a full-featured slide show.

3. To display the next or previous slide, do one of the following:

- To display the next slide, click the left mouse button, or press the → or ↓ key.

- To display the previous slide, click the right mouse button, or click on the ← or ↑ key.

- To quit the slide show, press the **Esc** key.

TIP

The Slide Show Dialog Box   If you select **Slide Show** from the **View** menu (rather than clicking on the Slide Show button), you get a dialog box that offers slide show options. You can use these options to specify the range of slides you want to view and to tell PowerPoint how to advance the slides.

Adding a Slide Transition

In the previous section, you had to click or press an arrow key to move from one slide to another. If you add timed transitions to slides, you don't have to click to move from one slide to the next. The slide show proceeds automatically.

Transition Effect and Timing   You can specify two settings for a transition: the effect and the timing. The transition effect will apply to the transition from the previous slide to this slide. The transition timing will apply to the transition from this slide to the next slide.

To apply a slide transition to a slide, perform the following steps:

1. Open the presentation to which you want to add transitions.

2. Open the **View** menu, and select **Slide Sorter**. Or click on the **Slide Sorter** button at the bottom of the presentation window.

3. Select the slide to which you want to add a transition.

More Than One   To select more than one slide, hold down the **Shift** key while clicking on slides. To select all the slides, open the **Edit** menu and choose **Select All**, or press **Ctrl+A**.

4. Open the **Tools** menu, and select **Transition**. Or click on the **Transition** button in the Slide Sorter toolbar. The Transition dialog box appears, as shown in Figure 21.2.

No Slide Sorter Toolbar?   If the Slide Sorter toolbar is not displayed, right-click on any toolbar, and then click on **Slide Sorter**.

5. Click on the arrow to the right of the Effect list, and click on a transition effect. (Keep an eye on the preview area to see a demonstration of the effect.)

6. In the Speed group, select the desired speed for the transition to take effect: Slow, Medium, or Fast.

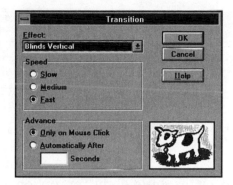

Figure 21.2   You can add transition effects and timing to selected slides.

7. To set a time for automatic slide advance, select one of the options in the Advance group:

Only on Mouse Click   Moves from this slide to the next slide only when you click the mouse button or press an arrow key.

Automatically After ____ Seconds   Moves automatically from slide to slide after the specified number of seconds.

8. Click on the **OK** button.

Quick Effects   To quickly apply a transition effect (without timing), pull down the Transition Effects drop-down list in the Slide Sorter toolbar, and select the desired transition.

Adding Builds to Slides

A build displays the bulleted points from a slide's Body Area one item at a time on the slide. The build effects are similar to transition effects. To add a build, perform the following steps:

1. In Slide Sorter view, select the slide to which you want to add a build.

2. Open the **Tools** menu and select **Build**, or click on the **Build** tool in the Slide Sorter toolbar. The Build dialog box appears, as shown in Figure 21.3.

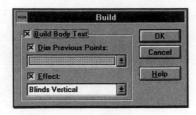

Figure 21.3   You can have PowerPoint build your slide as your audience looks on.

3. Click on the **Build Body Text** option to turn the Build feature on. An **X** appears in the check box.

4. To have bulleted items appear faded as the next bulleted item appears on the slide, select **Dim Previous Points**, and select the desired dim color from the list.

5. To add a special build effect, click on the **Effect** option, and select the desired effect from the drop-down list. (If you do not select an effect, the items will pop up on the slide.)

6. Click on the **OK** button.

In this lesson, you learned how to run an on-screen slide show presentation, add timed transitions between slides, and add builds to animate your bulleted lists. In the next lesson, you will learn how to create speaker's notes pages.

Creating Speaker's Notes Pages

In this lesson, you will learn how to create speaker's notes to help you during the delivery of your presentation.

The problem with most presentations is that the presenter merely flips from one slide to the next, without telling the audience his point or providing any overview that adds meaning to the slides. To make your slide show a success, you can put together a set of speaker's notes pages that can help you deliver an effective, coherent presentation making sure you do not miss any crucial points you want to highlight.

Each notes page is divided into two parts. A small version of the slide appears at the top of the page, and your notes appear below the slide.

Creating Speaker's Notes Pages

You already have the slide part of the speaker's notes pages. All you have to do is type the notes. You type notes in Notes Pages view, as follows:

1. Open the presentation for which you want to create speaker's notes pages.

2. Open the **View** menu, and select **Notes Pages**, or click on the **Notes Pages View** button at the bottom of the presentation window. The currently selected slide appears in Notes Pages view, as shown in Figure 22.1.

3. Click on the notes text box in the lower half of the notes page to select it.

4. To see what you are typing, open the **View** menu, select **Zoom**, select a Zoom to percent (**100%** works well), and click on the **OK** button.

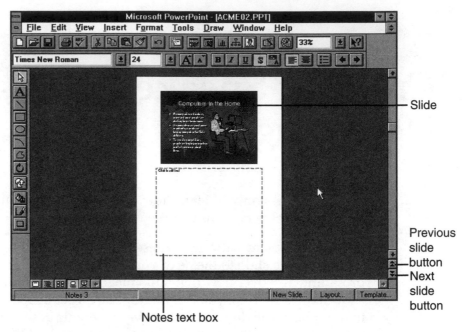

Figure 22.1 Example of a speaker's notes page.

  Quick Zoom A quicker way to zoom in or out is to open the Zoom Control drop-down list in the Standard toolbar and click on a zoom percent.

5. Type the text that you want to use as note material for this slide. (You can include gentle reminders, jokes, supporting data, or explanations as to how this slide fits in the big picture.)

6. Click on the **Next Slide** or **Previous Slide** button to move to another notes page, and then repeat step 5.

7. Format your text as desired. (For details on how to format text, refer to Lessons 10 and 11.)

When you are done, you can print your speaker's notes pages with or without your slides, as explained in Lesson 6.

Save Your Notes   When typing your notes, don't forget to save your work on a regular basis. Once you've saved and named your presentation file, saving again is as simple as pressing **Ctrl+S**.

Changing the Size of the Slide and Text Box

As explained earlier, each notes page contains two objects: a slide and a text box. You can change the size of either object just as you can change the size of any object in PowerPoint:

1. Click on the picture or text box to select it. (If you clicked on the text box, a frame appears around it. Click on the frame to display handles.)

2. Move the mouse pointer over one of the object's handles. (Use a corner handle to change both the width and height of the object. Use a side, top, or bottom handle to change only one dimension at a time.)

3. Hold down the mouse button, and drag the handle until the object is the desired size and dimensions.

4. Release the mouse button.

Consistent Notes Pages   To keep the size of the slides and note text boxes consistent on all the notes pages, change the size on the Notes Master. The following section explains how to display and work with the Notes Master.

Working with the Notes Master

Just as a slide show has a slide master that contains the background and layout for all the slides in the presentation, the Notes Master contains the background and layout for all your notes pages. You can use the Notes Master to do the following:

- Add background information (such as the date, time, or page numbers) and have that information appear on all the notes pages.

- Add a picture, such as a company logo, that will appear on each notes page.

- Move or resize the notes page objects.

- Choose a color scheme or background for the slide (this affects the look of the slide only on the notes pages, not in the presentation itself).

- Set up the Body Area to control the general layout and formatting of the text in the notes area of each notes page.

To change the Notes Master, perform the following steps:

1. Open the **View** menu, and select **Master**. The Master submenu appears.

2. Select **Notes Master**. The Notes Master appears.

3. Change any of the elements of the Notes Master as you would a Slide Master.

In this lesson, you learned how to create speaker's notes pages to help in the delivery of a presentation. In the next lesson, you will learn how to create audience handouts.

Creating Audience Handouts

In this lesson, you will learn how to create handouts to pass out to your audience.

Most presentations move fairly quickly, giving the audience little time to filter through all the data on the slides. Because of this, it is often useful to give the audience handouts or copies of the presentation slides. You can do this by printing an exact replica of your slide show on paper, or by printing several slides per page using audience handouts.

Creating handouts is fairly easy; you simply tell PowerPoint to print audience handouts, placing X number of slides on each page. For example, if you open the **File** menu and select **Print**, and then pull down the Print What drop-down list, you see the audience Handouts options shown in Figure 23.1. (For details on how to print, refer to Lesson 6.)

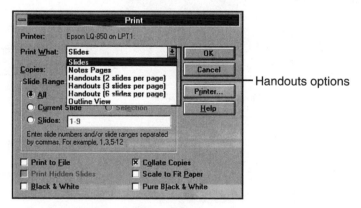

Figure 23.1   PowerPoint can print 2, 3, or 6 slides per page.

Displaying the Handout Master

A handout master controls the placement and look of the slides on the audience handouts. The handout master has *slide image placeholders* so you can see where a slide will be placed on a handout. To display the handout master, perform the following steps:

1. Open the **View** menu, and select **Master**. The Master submenu appears.

2. Select **Handout Master**. The handout master appears, as shown in Figure 23.2.

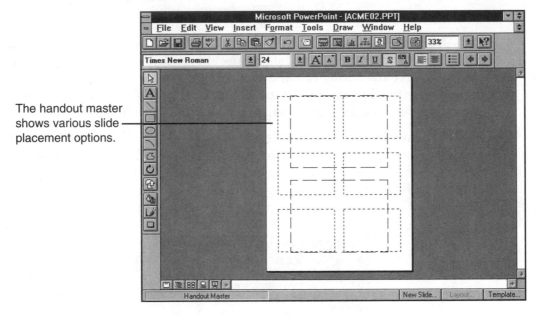

The handout master shows various slide placement options.

Figure 23.2   The handout master.

In this lesson, you learned how to create audience handouts to accompany your slide presentation. In the next lesson, you will learn how to use advanced editing tools to check the spelling and ensure consistency in your presentation.

Using Advanced Editing Tools

In this lesson, you will learn how to spell check text in your slide presentation, and find and replace text.

Checking for Misspellings and Typos

PowerPoint uses a built-in dictionary to spell check your entire presentation, including all slides, outlines, note and handout pages, and all four master views. To check the spelling in your presentation, perform the following steps:

1. Open the **Tools** menu, and select **Spelling**. The Spelling dialog box appears. (If the spelling dialog box does not appear with a Start button displayed, skip step 2.)

Menu Bypass   To bypass the Tools menu, click on the **Spelling** button (the button with **ABC** and a check mark on it) in the Standard toolbar, or press **F7**.

2. Click on the **Start** button to start spell checking. The spell checker starts and then stops on the first word that does not match an entry in the dictionary (see Figure 24.1).

3. If the Spelling dialog box appears displaying a questionable word, select one of these options:

   Ignore   To skip only this occurrence of the word.

   Ignore All   To ignore every occurrence of the word.

Change To replace only this occurrence of the word with the word in the Change To box. (You can type a correction in the Change To box or select a correct spelling from the Suggestions list.)

Change All To replace every occurrence of the word with the word in the Change To box. (To insert an entry in the Change To box, type it, or select an entry from the Suggestions list.)

Add To add the word to the dictionary, so the spell checker will not question it again.

Suggest To display a list of suggested words. You can select a word from the list to insert it in the Change To box.

Close To close the Spelling dialog box.

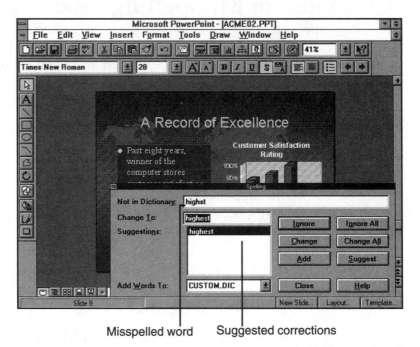

Misspelled word   Suggested corrections

Figure 24.1 The Spelling dialog box displays the questionable word and suggested corrections.

4. Repeat step 3 until the spell checker reaches the end of the presentation. A dialog box will appear, telling you that spell checking has been completed.

5. Click on the **OK** button.

Finding and Replacing Text

If you used a particular word or phrase, but you can't remember which slide you used it on, you can have PowerPoint find the word or phrase for you. You can also have PowerPoint search for a word or phrase and replace one or all instances of the word or phrase.

To search for specific text, perform the following steps:

1. Open the **Edit** menu, and select **Find**. The Find dialog box appears.

2. In the **Find What** text box, type the word or phrase you want to search for.

3. (Optional) Select either or both of the following options:

   Match Case   Finds text that matches the capitalization in the Find What text box. For example, if you typed **Widget**, the search will skip **widget**.

   Find Whole Words Only   Skips any occurrences of the text that are a part of another word. For example, if you typed **book**, the search will skip **bookkeeper**.

4. Click on the **Find Next** button. PowerPoint finds the word and highlights it.

> **TIP**   **Editing and Formatting Text**   To edit or format text, simply perform the operation as you normally would. The Find dialog box remains on-screen as you work.

5. You can find the next occurrence of the text by clicking on the **Find Next** button again.

6. To close the Find dialog box, click on the **Close** button.

To replace a word or phrase with another word or phrase, perform the following steps:

1. Open the **Edit** menu, and select **Replace**. The Replace dialog box appears, as shown in Figure 24.2.

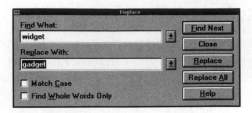

Figure 24.2 The Replace dialog box.

2. In the Find What text box, type the word or phrase you want to search for.

3. In the Replace With text box, type the word or phrase you want to use as the replacement.

4. (Optional) Select either or both of the following options:

Match Case Finds text that matches the capitalization in the Find What text box.

Find Whole Words Only Skips any occurrences of the text that are a part of another word.

5. Click on one of the following buttons:

Replace Replaces one occurrence of the Find What text with the Replace With text.

Replace All Replaces all occurrences of the Find What text (throughout your presentation) with the Replace With text.

Find Next Skips the current occurrence of the Find What text and moves to the next occurrence.

6. When you are finished replacing text, click on the **Close** button.

In this lesson, you learned how to check your presentation for misspelled words and typos, and how to find and replace words and phrases.

MAIL 3

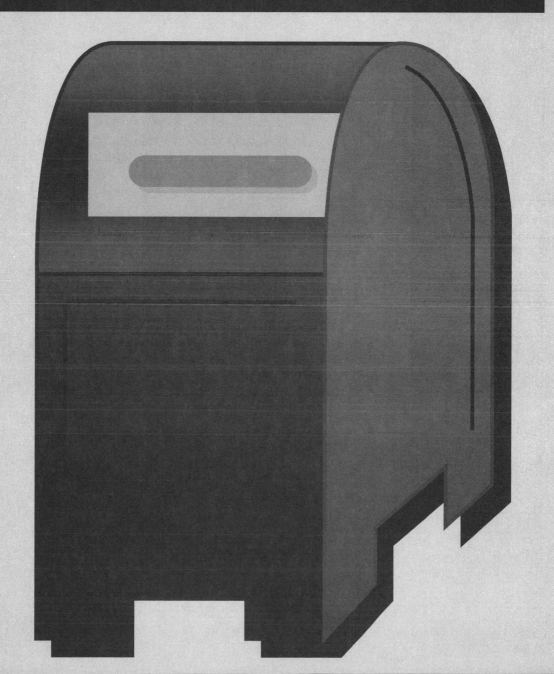

Starting and Quitting Microsoft Mail

In this lesson, you will learn how to start and exit Microsoft Mail.

Starting Mail and Logging In

To use Microsoft Mail, you must first start the application. Another term for starting the application is *logging in*. To start Microsoft Mail:

1. Open the program group window that contains the Microsoft Mail icon. Most users find it in the **Applications** or **Microsoft Office** group. Windows for Workgroups users find Microsoft Mail in the **Main** group.

2. Double-click on the **Microsoft Mail** icon.

 **First Time Only** The very first time you use Microsoft Mail, you need to connect to the postoffice. (In later sessions, the postoffice you belong to is remembered, and you are automatically connected to it by Mail.) Choose **Connect to an existing postoffice**.

3. To log in, type your mailbox name, press **Tab**, and type your password. The password is displayed. (See Figure 1.1.)

Figure 1.1 Logging in to Microsoft Mail.

Forgot Your Password? See your system administrator, the person who is in charge of the network or the Mail system.

After you log in, you see the screen displayed in Figure 1.2.

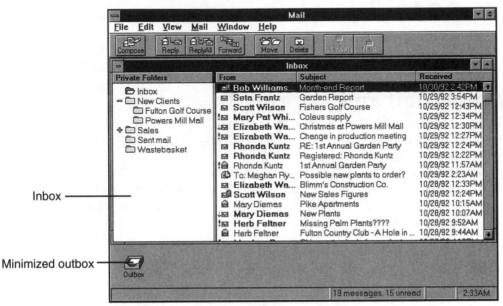

Inbox

Minimized outbox

Figure 1.2 The Microsoft Mail for Windows screen.

Quitting Microsoft Mail

Microsoft Mail offers two ways to quit. If you choose **Exit**, you quit Mail, but you still are able to access the postoffice with other applications such as Schedule+. If you choose **Exit and Sign Out**, you are disconnected from the postoffice and need to log back in to use Mail.

Not the Final Exit Even if you choose **Exit and Sign Out**, you still are able to receive mail as long as you are connected to the network.

Wait a Minute, Mr. Postman!   If you sign out of Mail, you will not be notified when you receive mail. Mail must be active before you will be notified. Therefore, I recommend that you don't exit Mail until the end of the day.

To exit Mail:

1. Open the **File** menu.

2. Select either **Exit** or **Exit and Sign Out**.

Quick Exit   You can double-click on the **Control-menu** button to exit and sign out of Mail quickly.

In this lesson, you learned how to start and quit Microsoft Mail. In the next lesson, you will learn about the Microsoft Mail screen.

What Is Microsoft Mail?

In this lesson, you will learn how Microsoft Mail works. You will also be introduced to the Microsoft Mail screen and its parts.

A Look at the Microsoft Mail System

A *network* is a system that connects different computers so that programs, data files, and printers can be shared. Through this system of interconnecting cables, Microsoft Mail can send and receive messages.

Working Offline If your network is *down* (not functional), you can still work in Microsoft Mail. Working when you are not connected to a network is called working offline. Simply create your messages and send them later when you are connected to the network, as described in Lesson 10.

Your network has a *system administrator*, a person who is in charge of setting up new users and maintaining the system. Microsoft Mail requires an administrator to maintain the *postoffice*, a central directory where messages are stored. Your network may have several postoffices if your company is large.

Each user has a *mailbox* at the postoffice where individual messages are stored. Users are added to or deleted from the system by the system administrator.

Your network may be connected to other networks through a *gateway*. A gateway is a program that provides a path to another mail system. Through a gateway, you can send messages to users on a mail system different from Microsoft Mail. The gateway program translates the message for the other mail system. Your system administrator can provide you with additional information about gateways that are connected to your network.

Gateway A program that provides a link through the network to another mail system.

Windows for Workgroups Users Windows for Workgroups Mail does not offer the ability to connect to gateways.

The Process of Sending a Message

To send a message with Microsoft Mail, you select users from an address list that was created by the system administrator. Alternatively, you can select users from a personal address book that you establish.

Personal Address Book A personal address book contains the names of users to whom you frequently send messages. You copy users from the central address list to create a personal address book.

After selecting a user (or users) to send a message to, you can select the name or names of users to receive a cc (courtesy copy) of the message.

Groupies You can connect several users in a *personal group* for faster message addressing. For example, you could create a group called **Sales** that contains all of the sales people.

After the message is addressed, you enter the message text and send the message. You can also attach files to be sent with the message. Now that you understand a little about the Mail system, let's take a closer look.

The Microsoft Mail Screen

After starting Microsoft Mail and logging in, you see the screen shown in Figure 2.1.

The Mail screen contains several components:

Menu bar   Use the menu bar to select commands.

Tool bar   With a mouse, you can use the tool bar instead of the menu to work with messages.

Inbox   This window contains all of your incoming messages.

Outbox   This window (shown in Figure 2.1, reduced to an icon) contains all of your outgoing messages.

Status bar   Shows the current time. If the Inbox is open, you also see the number of messages and the total unread messages displayed. You also see mailbox icons from time to time as messages are sent or received.

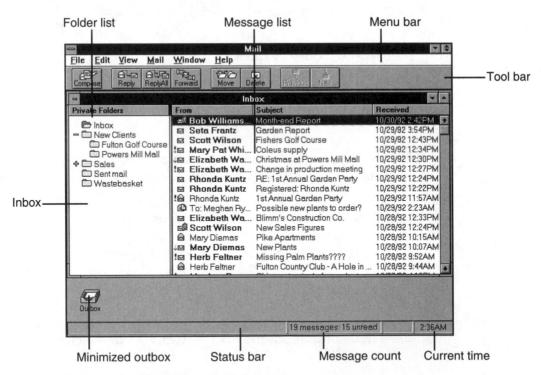

Figure 2.1   The Microsoft Mail screen.

Using the Tool Bar

Mail provides a tool bar for issuing common commands with the mouse. The tool bar is located under the menu bar, as shown in Figure 2.1.

The tool bar includes the Compose, Reply, ReplyAll, Forward, Move, Delete, Previous, and Next commands. You will learn how to use each of these commands in upcoming lessons.

To issue a command from the tool bar, simply click on the appropriate command button. For example, to delete a message, select the message you want to delete, and click on the **Delete** button.

Looking at the Inbox

When you log in to Mail, it displays the contents of the Inbox. The Inbox contains all of the messages that have been sent to you that have not yet been deleted or moved.

You can place your Inbox messages in folders (and subfolders) for better organization, as shown in Figure 2.2. For example, the folder **New Clients** contains two subfolders, **Fulton Golf Course** and **Powers Mill Mall**. A plus sign (+) next to a folder (such as Sales) indicates subfolders that are not displayed. A minus sign (-) indicates that all subfolders are displayed. You will learn to create folders in Lesson 19.

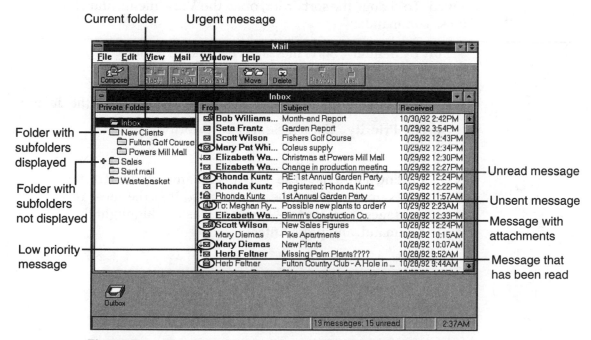

Figure 2.2 The Inbox displays important information about your messages.

Could You Throw This Away for Me?   When Mail is first installed, three folders are set up in the Inbox: **Inbox** (incoming messages), **Sent Mail** (copies of outgoing messages), and **Wastebasket** (messages to delete).

Message headers are displayed on the right side of the Inbox window. The *message list* displays the sender's name, the subject, and the date and time the message was received. One of the following icons appears next to each message:

Closed envelope   An unread message. Unread messages also appear in bold, with larger letters so that they are easily identified.

Open envelope   A message that has been read.

Exclamation point   A message with an urgent priority.

Paperclip   A message with attachments.

Down arrow   A message with a low priority.

Open envelope with letter   A message that has not yet been sent.

Messages are initially displayed in the order in which they are received. To change the sort order, open the **View** menu, and choose one of these commands:

Sort by Sender   Sorts messages by who sent them.

Sort by Subject   Sorts messages by subject matter.

Sort by Date   Sorts messages by time received. This is the default.

Sort by Priority   Sorts messages by priority.

Putting It into Reverse   To reverse any of the sort orders—for example, to sort the messages so that the most recent messages are at the top—press **Ctrl** as you highlight the sort command, and press **Enter**.

Sort It Out! Quickly change the sort order of messages by clicking on the appropriate button in the Message window. For example, to sort by subject, click on the **Subject** button at the top of the window.

In this lesson, you learned about the Mail system and how it works. You also learned about the Microsoft Mail screen. In the next lesson, you will learn how to use the Mail help system.

Help and Demos

In this lesson, you will learn how to use Mail's Help system, which includes demonstrations you can run as many times as you want.

Accessing Help

Microsoft Mail has an extensive Help system with a complete index and animated demonstrations. Mail's Help system is context-sensitive, so that when you access help, you are automatically provided with information that's pertinent to whatever you're working on.

Context-Sensitive Help   Help that is pertinent to the context in which you are working.

To access Mail help, as with any Windows program, you can either:

- Press **F1**.

OR

- Open the **Help** menu, and select a command: **Contents**, **Index**, or **Demos**.

Using the Help System

The Mail Help system is nearly the same as the Help system in all other Windows programs. The Contents, Search, Back, History, and Index buttons all work the same. For more information, refer to the Windows section of this book.

Pluses and Minuses

One small difference in the Mail Help system is the buttons that appear next to the entries when you select Contents. The Contents screen lists the major topics contained in the Help system. Some topics contain several subtopics, indicated by a plus sign (see Figure 3.1). To expand the Table of Contents so each topic is displayed, select the **Expand** button. To collapse the Table of Contents to major headings, select the **Collapse** button.

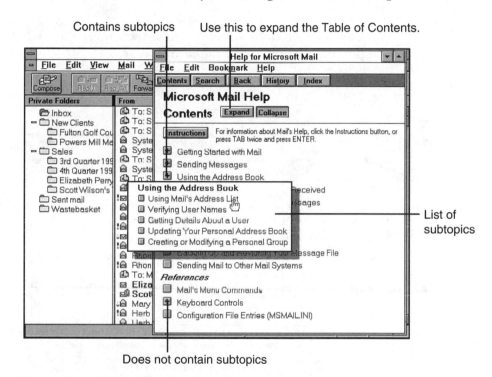

Figure 3.1   Mail's Help Table of Contents.

To activate a topic, click on it. (When the mouse pointer is over a topic, definition, or pop-up screen, it changes into a hand pointer.) When you activate a heading that contains subtopics, a second listing is displayed.

Topic Information

When you select a topic that does not have a plus sign next to it from one of the listings in the Table of Contents, you jump to a screen containing information on that topic, as shown in Figure 3.2. This information is much like the Help information in any other Windows program, but the screen contains two buttons: Overview and Demo. Click on the **Overview** button for an overview of the topic. (We'll look at the Demo button later in this lesson.)

Just as in other Help screens, you can click on a dotted-underlined term to pop up a definition of the term.

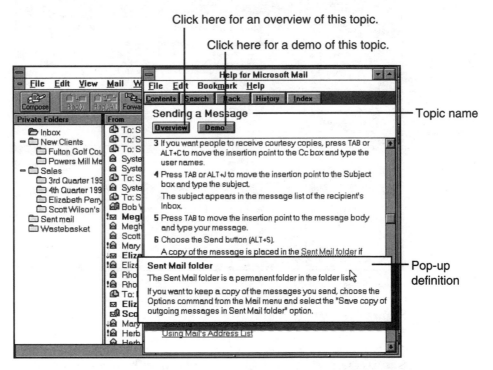

Figure 3.2 Selecting a topic from the Table of Contents provides detailed information.

Searching for a Specific Topic

Searching is the same in Mail Help as in other Windows programs. Click on the **Search** button to display the Search dialog box, enter a subject in the text box, select a topic from those listed, and select **Show Topics**. A list of available topics is displayed. Select a topic, then select **Go To**. To close the search window at any time, press **Esc**.

Using the Help Index

Selecting the **Help Index** command will display the Index dialog box. To find a word, click on the first letter of the word. When you select the first letter of a word, you are taken to that part of the index. From there, use the scroll bars or **Page Up** and **Page Down** to find a topic. Select a topic by clicking on it or highlighting it and pressing **Enter**. If you want to return to the Table of Contents screen, select the **Contents** button.

Playing a Demo

Microsoft Mail comes with several animated demos that visually explain how to use specific features. There are several ways to access a demo:

- Select the **Help Demos** command.

- Select the **Demo** button displayed at the top of some topic windows.

- Select a topic in the index that indicates that a demo is available.

If you use the **Help Demos** command, a list of available topics appears, as shown in Figure 3.3. Mail keeps track of the number of demos you have completed, as shown by the figure. Review the navigational instructions first by pressing **T**.

Mail tracks the demos you've seen.

Demo categories —

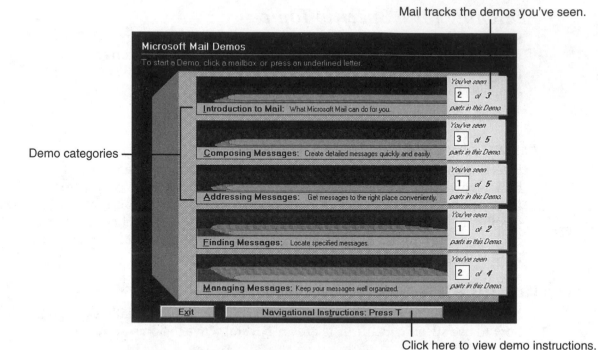

Click here to view demo instructions.

Figure 3.3   You can select from several different demo topics.

Select a topic (by pressing the underlined letter or by clicking on it), and a list of demos appears (see Figure 3.4). Completed demos are indicated by a postmark on the envelope. Each demo takes only a few minutes to complete. During the demo, you can use the **Back** and **Next** buttons to move back and forth between screens.

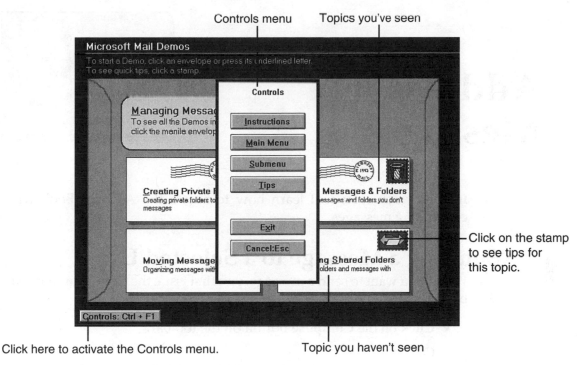

Figure 3.4 Select a specific demo to play.

To activate the Controls menu (shown in the middle of Figure 3.4), click on the **Controls** menu button, or press **Ctrl+F1**. From the Controls menu, you can navigate back to the Main menu, to a submenu, or to an Instructions screen.

In this lesson, you learned how to use Mail's Help system. In the next lesson, you will learn how to use Mail's address lists.

Addressing Messages

In this lesson, you will learn how to access the Address Book when composing messages.

Sending a Message to a Selected User

When you want to send a message, you first issue the Compose command by one of two methods:

- Click on the **Compose** button on the toolbar.

  OR

- Open the **Mail** menu, and select the **Compose Note** command.

  A window opens, such as the one shown in Figure 4.1.

Keep Your Composure   You can quickly compose a new message by pressing **Ctrl+N**.

With the Compose Note window open, follow these steps to select an addressee:

1. Click on the **Address** button. The Address window appears (see Figure 4.2).

Selecting a User from a Different Postoffice   To access the global list of users, click on the **Directory** button, or press **Ctrl+L**. Select **Global Address List,** and press **Enter**.

2. Use the scroll bars to scroll through the list.

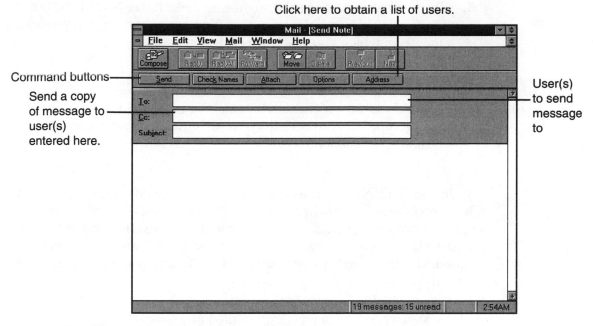

Figure 4.1 The Send Note window.

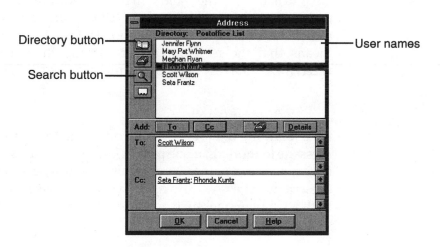

Figure 4.2 The Address window.

3. Press **Enter** to send a message to the selected user, or click on the **To** button.

4. If you want, select another user, and click on the **Cc** button to send a courtesy copy.

5. When you are finished selecting users, press **Enter** or click on **OK** to return to the Send Note window. You are now ready to compose a message, which you will learn to do in Lesson 5.

Lost and Found   Find a user quickly by pressing the first few characters of the user's name. For example, to find Jane Doe, type **J** or **Ja**, and Mail scrolls to the first user whose name matches those letters.

In the Send Note window, you can enter a user's name instead of selecting it from the Address list, but it must match exactly. Prior to sending any message, Mail verifies each name against the Address list. If the name is correctly entered, it is underlined to indicate that it has been verified. Use the **Check names** button to verify any name that you enter manually.

Now I Cc!   There is no difference between using the To and Cc fields of the Send Note window, in terms of results; anyone listed in either field will receive your message. Treat the Cc field in the same manner as the cc notation often used at the end of a typewritten memo. The use of cc generally means that the recipient is not directly involved but is receiving a courtesy copy of the message as an FYI.

He's Making a List . . .   If you want to address your message to more than one person, simply insert a semicolon (;) between user names. You can also create a personal group (described in Lesson 13) to collectively address several people with a single name, such as Sales.

Finding a Name in the Address Book

Finding one person in a long list can be difficult, especially if you are not sure how to spell the person's name. These steps show you how to use Name Finder to locate users in the Address Book:

1. From the Address window, click on the **Search** button (a small magnifying glass), or press **Ctrl+F**. The Name Finder dialog box appears.

2. Type a few letters from the person's name. If you want to search for a specific last name, type a space and a few characters from the last name. Here are some examples (assuming that the address list is sorted by first name):

   Ja   Finds users with first names Jane and Janet, but not Joe.

   P Ja   Finds Peggy James, Paul Jansen, and Peter Jantz, but not Paulina Jenkins.

   Pe Ja   Finds Peggy James and Peter Jantz, but not Paul Jansen.

   (space)Jo   Finds the last names Jones and Johnson.

Getting Details About a User

When your system administrator adds a new user, she can include additional information, such as the person's phone number, department, office location, mail stop number, and so on. To view any of this information, select a user in the Address window, and click on the **Details** button. The Details window, shown in Figure 4.3, appears. To return to the Address window, press **Esc** when you are done.

Mail Stop   A mail stop number is often used in large corporations to sort mail. The mail stop number acts like a ZIP code, indicating the location (mail drop) nearest to an individual where internal mail is delivered. By adding a mail stop number to a letter or other internal document, mail can be quickly sorted and delivered to an individual within the corporation.

In this lesson, you learned how to access the Address Book while composing a message. In the next lesson, you will learn how to enter the message text and send a message.

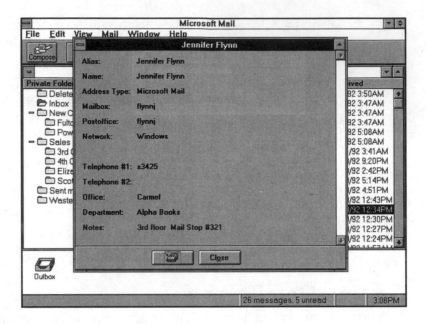

Figure 4.3   The Details window provides additional information about a user.

Sending Messages

In this lesson, you will learn how to enter and send messages.

Entering the Message Subject

Enter a message subject so your users can easily identify what your message is about. To do so, follow these steps:

1. In the Send Note window, click on the Subject text box, shown in Figure 5.1.

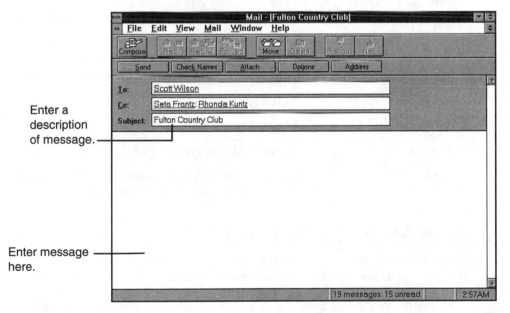

Enter a description of message.

Enter message here.

Figure 5.1 Enter a description of your message in the Subject text box.

2. Enter a brief description of the message. This description is displayed (along with your name and the time that the message was received) in the user's Inbox.

Entering Your Message

After entering the description of your message, you are ready to enter the message itself:

1. Click in the message area.

2. Enter the message. If you make a mistake, press **Backspace**, and retype. You can use the keys listed in Table 5.1 to edit your message.

Wrap It Up! You should not press Enter at the end of each line; Mail automatically *wraps* words to the next line when they bump into the right-hand margin.

Table 5.1 Quick Keys for Editing Messages

Press this . . .	*. . . to do this.*
Backspace	Delete the previous character.
Enter	Start a new paragraph.
Page Up	Move up one screen.
Page Down	Move down one screen.
Home	Move to the beginning of the line.
End	Move to the end of the line.

Setting Message Options

Prior to sending your message, you may want to change the default message options. To change a message option:

1. From within the Send Note window, click on the **Options** button. The dialog box shown in Figure 5.2 appears.

Check here to receive notification when your message is read.

Change the priority of your message.

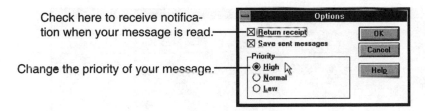

Figure 5.2   The Options dialog box.

2. Select from these options:

   Return receipt   Notifies you when messages you've sent have been read. Messages sent with this option are displayed on the recipient's screen with an exclamation point, like high priority messages.

   Save sent messages   Saves a copy of messages you send in the Sent Mail folder.

   Priority   Makes an exclamation point (High priority messages) or a down arrow (Low priority messages) appear on the recipient's screen in front of your message.

3. When you are done, press **Enter** or click **OK** to return to the Send Note window.

Return to Sender   After the recipient reads a message that you've marked with the **Return** receipt option, you will receive a message with the word **Registered** shown in the Subject column of the message list. You can read your receipt to learn when the message was read (see Figure 5.3).

Sending Your Message

Once your message is addressed and composed, you are ready to send it. To send your message, click on the **Send** button.

Unless you have changed the default options, a copy of the message you sent will be saved in the Sent Mail folder. You will learn more about reading messages (including those you've sent) in Lesson 6.

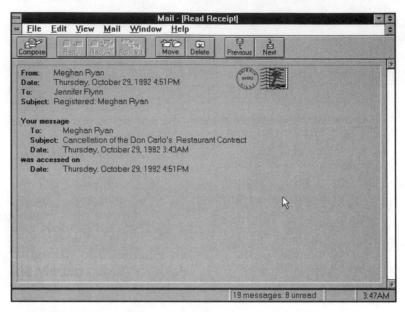

Figure 5.3 When a registered message is sent, you get a receipt.

Deliver da Letter. . .   If for some reason your message could not be delivered, you will be notified. Open the notification, and you will see your original message, along with the reason for the nondelivery. Use the **Send Again** button to resend the message after the problem has been resolved.

In this lesson you learned how to enter a message and send it. In the next lesson, you will learn how to read messages you receive.

Reading Messages

In this lesson, you will learn how to read messages that have been sent to you or that you have sent and saved in your Sent Mail folder.

Selecting a Message to Read

Messages that have been sent to you are stored in the Inbox folder. If you have not yet read a message, it is displayed with a closed envelope, as shown in Figure 6.1. When a message has been read, it is displayed with an open envelope.

To read a message:

1. If the Inbox folder is not open, double-click on the **Inbox** folder.

2. Double-click on a message to open it.

To review messages you've sent, follow these same instructions, but open the **Sent Mail** folder instead.

Next, Please After you've opened a message, you can easily read the next message in the list by clicking on the **Next** button. To view the previous message, click on **Previous**. Press **Esc** when you are done viewing messages.

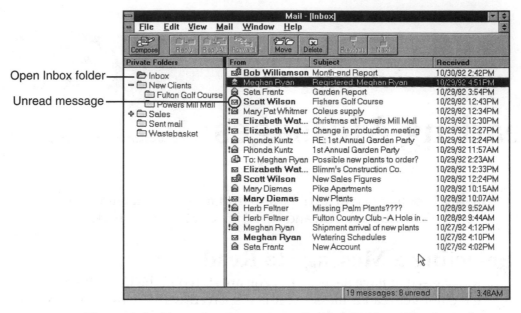

Figure 6.1 Unread messages are displayed with a closed envelope.

Locating a Specific Message to Read

If you want to find a message from a specific person, or about something in particular, follow these steps:

1. Open the **File** menu.

2. Select the **Message Finder**. The Message Finder dialog box appears, as shown in Figure 6.2.

3. Enter the information to search for by filling in as many of the text boxes as needed:

   From   Searches for messages from a specific person.

   Subject   Searches for a particular message based on its description.

   Recipients   Searches the courtesy copy field for a match.

   Message Text   Searches the text of a message for a match.

   Where to look   Opens an additional dialog box that can be used to identify the folders to search. You may select a single folder or all folders.

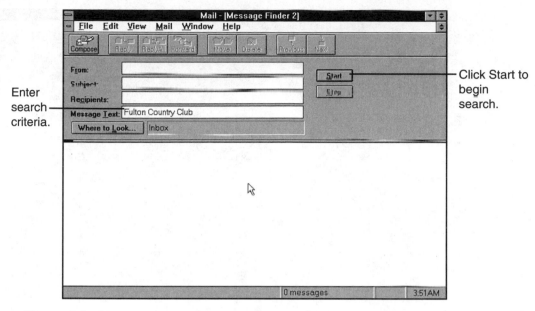

Enter search criteria.

Click Start to begin search.

Figure 6.2   You can find messages easily with message Finder.

4. When you have entered the information to search for, click on **Start**.

Hide and Seek?   If the search seems to be taking too long and you wish to quit, click **Stop**.

When the search is complete, the messages are listed below the search box, as shown in Figure 6.3. You can open, delete, move, or perform any other task on the listed messages.

Multiple Personalities   To search for messages sent to you by more than one person, enter both names separated by a semi-colon (;). Use this same technique in any of the Message Finder boxes. For example, enter **sales; success** to find messages that discuss successful sales months.

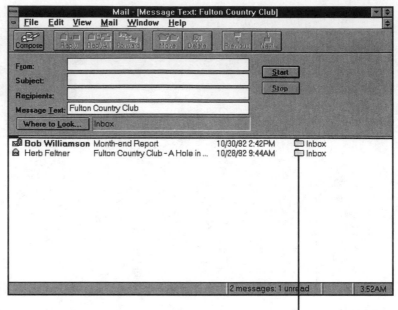

Figure 6.3   The search is on!

In this lesson, you learned how to find a message and read it. In the next lesson, you will learn how to reply to a message.

Sending Replies and Forwarding Messages

In this lesson, you will learn how to reply to messages that have been sent to you. You will also learn how to forward messages with your comments.

Entering the Reply

After reading a message, you may want to send a reply. Sending a reply is easy:

1. Select the message you want to reply to.

2. Click on the **Reply** button, or press **Ctrl+R**. To send a reply to everyone listed in the To and Cc boxes, click on **Reply All**, or press **Ctrl+A**. The reply window appears, as shown in Figure 7.1.

3. Enter your message. The original message appears below the line. You can perform any normal message task (such as include attachments or change the priority) and delete all or part of the original message if you want.

4. When you are ready to send the message, click on the **Send** button.

Replies to messages are displayed on the recipient's computer with an **RE:** in front of the subject, as shown in Figure 7.2.

Forwarding a Message

Forward a copy of a message along with your comments to a colleague. To forward a message:

1. Select the message you want to forward.

2. Click on the **Forward** button, or press **Ctrl+F**. The forward window appears, as shown in Figure 7.3.

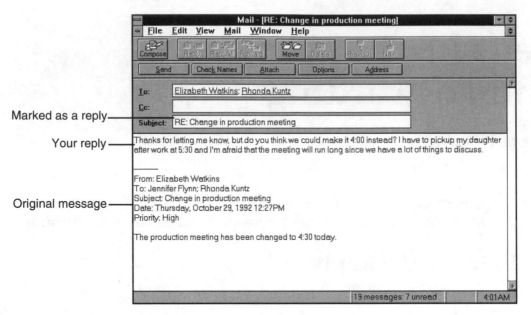

Marked as a reply —

Your reply —

Original message —

Figure 7.1 You can address your reply to the sender or to everyone involved.

3. Enter the name of the person to whom you would like to forward the message in the **To** box, and that of any courtesy copy recipients in the **Cc** box.

4. Enter your comments. The original message appears below the line. You can perform any normal message task (such as include attachments or change the priority) and delete all or part of the original message if you want.

5. When you are ready to send the message, click the **Send** button.

Forwarded messages are displayed on the recipient's computer with an **FW:** in front of the subject, as shown in Figure 7.3.

Fast Forward   You can also drag a message to the Outbox to forward it.

Forwarded
message

Reply to your
message

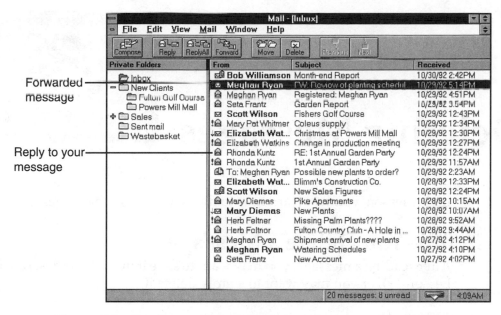

Figure 7.2 Replies and forwarded messages are easy to identify.

Message
marked as
forwarded

Your comments

Original message

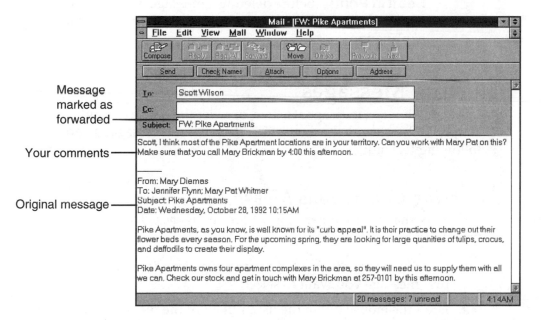

Figure 7.3 You can forward a message along with your comments.

Deleting Messages

In this lesson, you will learn how to delete unwanted messages.

Before You Delete a Message

After reading a message, you may want to save it in a folder (described in Lesson 19), or you may want to simply delete it.

See It in Print!   Before deleting a message, you can print it out and file the hard copy. See Lesson 22 for a detailed explanation.

Selecting Messages

You can delete one message at a time, or several. To select a single message, simply click on it with the mouse. To select several messages, use one of the following techniques.

Selecting Contiguous Messages

Messages that are together in a list are *contiguous*. To select contiguous messages:

1. Click in the area in front of the message icon (see Figure 8.1) on the first message you want to select.

2. Drag the mouse down the list until all of the messages you want are selected. The contiguous messages are now highlighted, as shown in Figure 8.1.

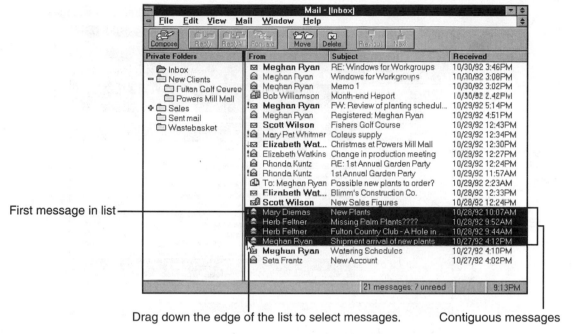

First message in list —————

Drag down the edge of the list to select messages.   Contiguous messages

Figure 8.1   Selecting contiguous messages.

Selecting Noncontiguous Messages

Messages that are not together in a list are *noncontiguous*.

To select noncontiguous messages:

1. Click on the first message you want to select.

2. Press and hold the **Ctrl** key.

3. Click on the additional messages you want to select. The noncontiguous messages are now highlighted, as shown in Figure 8.2.

Noncontiguous messages

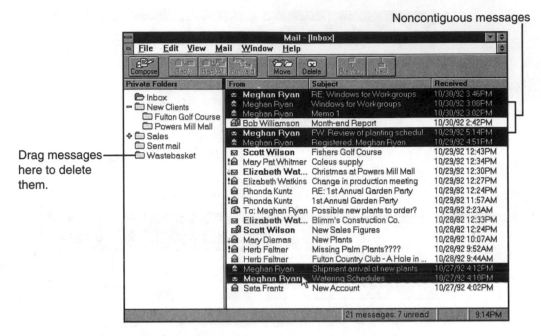

Drag messages here to delete them.

Figure 8.2   Selecting noncontiguous messages.

Deleting Unwanted Messages

After you have selected the message(s) you want to delete, follow these steps to delete the unwanted message(s) with the mouse:

1. Select the message(s) you want to delete.

2. Drag the selected messages to the Wastebasket folder.

Fast Delete   You can quickly delete selected messages by pressing the **Del** key.

The messages you delete are placed in the Wastebasket folder. Those messages will not be deleted permanently until you log out of Mail.

Windows for Workgroups Users The folder that holds your deleted mail is called Deleted Mail instead of Wastebasket.

Reading Messages? You can delete a single message after you read it by clicking on the **Delete** key or pressing **Ctrl+D** from the Read window. The next message in the message list will automatically be displayed.

In this lesson, you learned how to delete unwanted messages. In the next lesson, you will learn how to retrieve messages that you've deleted by mistake.

Retrieving Deleted Messages

In this lesson, you will learn how to retrieve messages that are currently marked for deletion.

Retrieving a Deleted Message

Because messages are not deleted until you log out of Mail, you can retrieve them if you change your mind. When you retrieve a message, it is moved from the Wastebasket folder to a folder that you select. Because the retrieved message will not be in the Wastebasket folder when you log out of Mail, it will not be deleted.

Act Now for Extra Savings   You must retrieve a deleted message *before* you log out of Mail, or it will be permanently deleted.

Windows for Workgroups Users   The folder that holds your deleted mail is called Deleted Mail instead of Wastebasket.

To retrieve a deleted message:

1. Open the **Wastebasket** folder by double-clicking on it.

2. Select the message(s) you want to retrieve.

3. Drag the selected message(s) to any folder you want (see Figure 9.1).

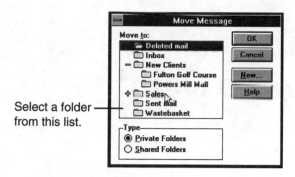

Select a folder — from this list.

Figure 9.1 Move the deleted message to a folder you select.

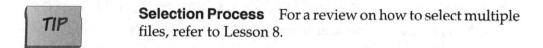

Selection Process For a review on how to select multiple files, refer to Lesson 8.

Fast Moves You can move selected messages in one step by pressing **Ctrl+M**.

In this lesson, you learned how to retrieve messages that were marked for deletion. In the next lesson, you will learn how to create a message that you will send at a later time.

Preparing a Message to Send Later

In this lesson, you will learn how to prepare messages in advance to send at a later time.

Saving a Message So You Can Send It Later

You can create a message to send at a later time. Create the message in the regular way following the instructions in Lessons 4 and 5, *but don't send the message*.

To save your message to send at a later time:

1. After entering your message (as described in Lesson 5), double-click on the **Control-menu** box, or press **Ctrl+F4**.

2. The dialog box shown in Figure 10.1 appears. Answer yes by clicking on the **Yes** button.

Your message is saved in the Inbox. You can open it and make additional changes later if you want. Unsent messages are displayed with an open envelope and letters icon, as shown in Figure 10.2.

Figure 10.1 Answer yes to save your unsent message.

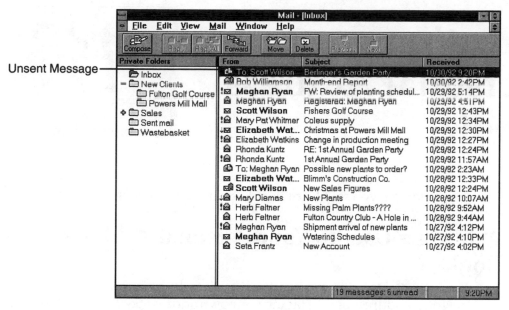

Unsent Message

Figure 10.2 It's easy to identify an unsent message.

Do You Send the Same Type of Message Often? Create a message template with the instructions found in Lesson 24.

Sending Your Unsent Message

Later, when you're finished composing your message, you can send it. To send a previously unsent message:

1. Open the unsent message by selecting it and pressing **Enter**.

2. Click on the **Send** button.

In this lesson, you learned how to prepare a message to send later. You also learned what to do when you are ready to send your unsent message. In the next lesson, you will learn how to create a personal address book.

Creating a Personal Address Book

In this lesson, you will learn how to create your own address book.

Adding a User to Your Personal Address Book

You can create your own address book with names selected from the postoffice address book. Having your own address book makes it easier to send messages to those people with whom you converse frequently.

To create a personal address book, you simply select the users you want to add. To add a user to your personal address book:

1. Open the **Mail** menu.

2. Select **Address book**. The Address Book dialog box opens, as shown in Figure 11.1.

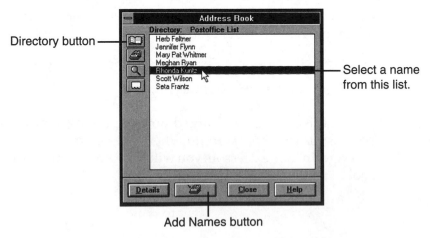

Figure 11.1   The Address Book window.

548

3. Select a name to add to your personal address book.

Different Postoffice?   If you need to add a user from a different postoffice, click on the **Directory** button, or press **Ctrl+L**. Select the postoffice you want to access, and press **Enter**.

Lots of Friends?   Add multiple names to your Address book by selecting several names before issuing the **Add names** command.

4. Add the name to your personal address book by clicking on the **Add Names** button.

5. Repeat steps 3 and 4 for additional names.

6. When you are done, press **Esc** to close the Address Book window.

Forgot Someone?   You can add names to your personal address book as you're composing a message. Simply click on the **Add Names** button, or press **Ctrl+A** in the Address dialog box.

Deleting a User from Your Personal Address Book

If you need to delete a user from your personal address book, follow these instructions:

1. Open the **Mail** menu.

2. Select **Address Book**.

3. Click on the **Personal Address Book** button, or press **Ctrl+P**. This displays your personal address book.

4. Select the name you want to remove.

5. Click on the **Remove** button (see Figure 11.2). A dialog box appears asking you to confirm the deletion. Press **Enter**, or click **Yes**, and the user is removed from your personal address book as well as any personal groups you may have created. (Personal groups are described in Lesson 13.)

TIP

Make Your Selection You can delete more than one user at a time by selecting multiple users before issuing the **Remove** command. Use the same techniques described in Lesson 8 for selecting multiple users.

Personal Address
Book button

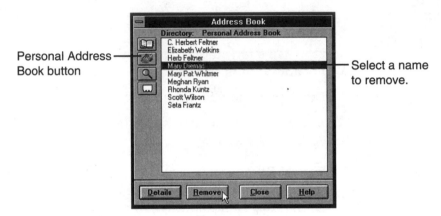

Select a name
to remove.

Figure 11.2 Keep your personal address book updated by deleting users you no longer need.

In this lesson, you learned how to create a personal address book. In the next lesson, you will learn how to use this personal address book when addressing messages.

Using a Personal Address Book

In this lesson, you will learn how to use your personal address book when sending messages.

Addressing Messages with Your Personal Address Book

When you use the **Address** button from the Send Note window (for example, when you are addressing a message to send to someone), it displays the postoffice address list. To display your personal address book, click on the **Personal Address Book** button in the Address window, as shown in Figure 12.1, or press **Ctrl+P**.

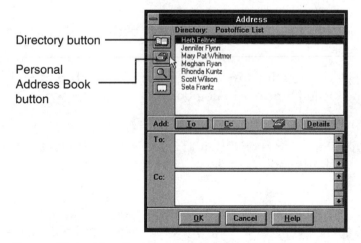

Figure 12.1 Use the Personal Address Book button to access your personal address book.

551

Once your personal address book is displayed, you can select users (or personal groups, which are explained in Lesson 13) to place in the To and Cc fields of your message. Simply follow the same techniques described in Lesson 4:

1. Use the scroll bars to scroll through the list.

2. Press **Enter** to send a message to the selected user, or click on the **To** button.

3. If you want, select another user, and click the **Cc** button to send a courtesy copy to a user.

Lost Someone? By pressing the first few characters of the user's name, you can locate him or her quickly in the user list. For example, to find Jane Doe, type **J** or **Ja**, and Mail scrolls to the first user whose name matches those letters.

Switching Back to the Postoffice Address Book

After you've opened your personal address book, you may need to return to the postoffice address list. To switch between address books, follow these steps:

1. Click on the **Directory** button, or press **Ctrl+L**, and press **Enter**. The Open Directory dialog box appears, as shown in Figure 12.2.

2. Select the address book.

3. Press **Enter**, or click **OK**, and the selected address book appears in the Address Book window.

Where's My List? Make your personal address book appear every time you open the Address Book window by selecting **Personal Address Book** in the Open Directory dialog box and clicking on the **Set Default** button.

Directory button ————

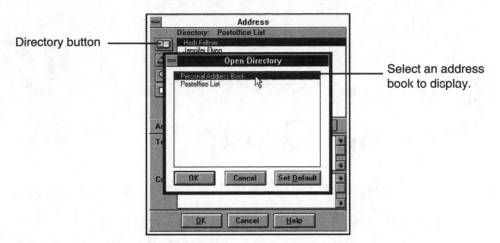

Select an address book to display.

Figure 12.2   Switch between address books with the Directory button.

In this lesson, you learned how to access your personal address book and use it to address your messages. In the next lesson, you will learn how to create personal groups.

Creating a
Personal Group

In this lesson, you will learn how to create personal groups.

Creating Your Personal Groups

If you often send messages to whole departments or other groups of people, create your own personal groups. For example, you can create a group called Sales for all of the sales staff in your organization. When addressing a message to all salespeople, you can select the **Sales** group from your personal address book, as shown in Figure 13.1, and your message will be sent to all of the salespeople in the group.

You can create as many personal groups as needed. The same users can be included in multiple groups. For example, as the head of Marketing, Meghan Ryan could be included in the Marketing group and also in the Sales group.

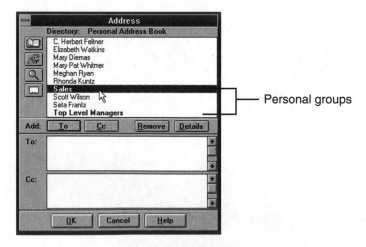

Figure 13.1 Addressing a message to a group is as easy as addressing a message to a single user.

554

To create a personal group:

1. Open the **Mail** menu.

2. Select the **Personal Groups** command. The dialog box shown in Figure 13.2 appears.

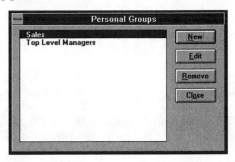

Figure 13.2 Add new groups with the Personal Groups dialog box.

3. Click on **New**.

4. Enter the new group name. The name can be up to 19 characters long, including spaces.

5. Click on **Create**, or press **Enter**. A list of user names appears (see Figure 13.3).

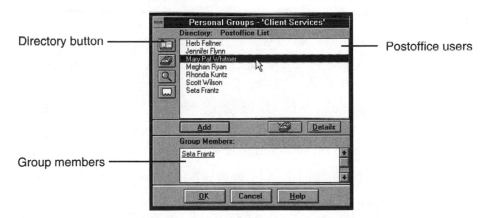

Directory button

Postoffice users

Group members

Figure 13.3 Select the users for your new group with this dialog box.

TIP

Need to Switch to a Different Postoffice? If you need to add a user from a different postoffice, click on the **Directory** button, or press **Ctrl+L**. Select the postoffice you want to access, and press **Enter**.

6. Select users for your group by double-clicking on them. Selected users appear in the Group Members section of the dialog box, as shown in Figure 13.3.

7. After selecting the last user for the group, press **Enter**, or click **OK**, and you return to the Personal Groups dialog box.

8. Repeat steps 3 through 7 to create additional groups. Press **Esc**, or click on the **Control-menu** button when you are done.

Adding and Deleting Users from a Personal Group

From time to time, you may need to add or delete members from your personal groups. Follow these steps to add a new member to a personal group:

1. Open the **Mail** menu.

2. Select the **Personal Groups** command. The Personal Groups dialog box shown in Figure 13.2 appears.

3. Select a group to edit.

4. Click on **Edit**. The selected address book appears, as shown in Figure 13.3.

5. Select a user by clicking on the user's name or highlighting it with the arrow keys.

6. To add the selected user, press **Enter**.

7. Repeat steps 5 and 6 to add additional users to the group.

8. When you are done, press **Ctrl+O**, or click **OK**, and you return to the Personal Groups dialog box.

9. Repeat steps 3 through 8 to edit a different personal group. Press **Esc** when you are done.

Follow these steps to delete users from a personal group:

1. Open the **Mail** menu.

2. Select the **Personal Groups** command. The Personal Groups dialog box shown in Figure 13.2 appears.

3. Select a group to edit.

4. Click on **Edit**. The selected address book appears, as shown in Figure 13.3.

5. Press **Tab** to move to the Group Members area.

6. Select a user by clicking on the user's name.

7. To delete the selected user, press **Delete**. If necessary, delete any leftover semicolons.

8. Repeat steps 5 and 6 to delete additional users from the group.

9. When you are done, press **Ctrl+O**, or click **OK**, and you return to the Personal Groups dialog box.

10. Repeat steps 3 through 9 to edit a different personal group. Press **Esc** when you are done.

In this lesson, you learned how to create a personal group and how to add and delete group members. In the next lesson, you will learn how to use a personal group to address a message.

Using a Personal Group

In this lesson, you will learn how to use your personal groups when addressing messages.

Sending Messages to a Personal Group

Sending messages to a personal group is as easy as sending messages to a single user:

1. Click on the **Compose** button on the tool bar, or press **Ctrl+N**. Or open the **Mail** menu, and select the **Compose Note** command.

2. Click on the **Address** button. The Address window appears.

3. If necessary, click on the **Personal Address Book** button, or press **Ctrl+P** to change to your personal address book as shown in Figure 14.1.

Personal Address Book button

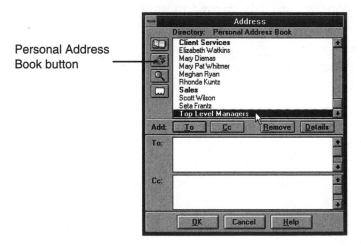

Figure 14.1   The Address window.

4. Select a personal group.

5. Press **Enter**, or click on the **To** button to send a message to the selected group.

6. If you want, select another group or a single user, and click on the **Cc** button to courtesy copy the message to them.

7. When you are done addressing your message, press **Enter**, or click on **OK** to return to the Send Note window. Complete the message, and send it in the normal manner, as described in Lesson 5.

The message is sent to all members in the group, plus any additional users you may have selected.

Direct Mail   You can simply type in a group's name in the To or Cc boxes of the Send Note window, instead of selecting it from the Address dialog box. Make sure, however, that you spell the name correctly so it matches the group name found in your personal address book.

Sending Mail to Selected Members of a Group

Having personal groups set up makes it easy to send messages to large numbers of people. However, there may be times when you need to exclude some members of a group from receiving a single message. Follow these steps to send a message to only certain members of a group:

1. Click on the **Compose** button on the tool bar, or press **Ctrl+N**. Or open the **Mail** menu, and select the **Compose Note** command.

2. Click on the **Address** button. The Address window appears.

3. If necessary, click on the **Personal Address Book** button, or press **Ctrl+P** to change to your personal address book.

4. Select a personal group.

5. Click on **Details**. The Group Detail window opens, as shown in Figure 14.2.

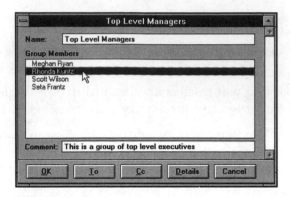

Figure 14.2 You can view the members of a group from the Group Detail window.

6. To send a message to only certain members of a group, select them from the list:

   Press and hold the **Ctrl** key as you click on the names of the users you want to select. To select a contiguous range of users, click on the first user in the range, press and hold the **Shift** key, and click on the last user in the range.

7. When you have selected the users to whom you want to send a message, click on the **To** button.

8. Repeat steps 3 through 5 to send courtesy copies to another group or to selected users. Select the users you want, and click on the **Cc** button to send a courtesy copy of the message to them.

9. When you are finished addressing your message, send it in the normal manner, as described in Lesson 5. The message is sent to only those group members listed in the To or Cc boxes of the Send Note window.

   In this lesson, you learned how to send messages to all the members of a group or to only selected members. In the next lesson, you will learn how to include files with your messages.

Copying Information from a File

In this lesson, you will learn how to copy information from a file into a message.

Copying Information into a Message

With Mail, you can copy information from a file into a message, instead of retyping it. For example, you can copy text into a Mail message from a report that was originally created in Word for Windows. Or you can copy spreadsheet data instead of re-entering it. (Beware: there are some special problems that occur when copying data that has to retain some type of format, such as data that appears in columns. You'll learn how to cope with this problem later in this lesson.) Follow these instructions to copy information:

1. Start **Mail**, and create a new message or open an existing one.

2. Start the original application, and open the file that contains the information you want to include in your message.

Original Application   The program (such as Word for Windows) that was used to create the file whose information you now want to include in your Mail message.

3. Select the information you want to copy.

4. Open the **Edit** menu.

5. Select the **Copy** command by clicking on it or pressing **C**. This copies the selected information to the Clipboard.

Clipboard   A special area in memory that Windows uses to hold information as it is copied or moved from one document to another.

6. Move to the place in the Mail message where you want the information copied.

7. In the **Send Note** window, open the **Edit** menu.

8. Select the **Paste** command. The information on the Clipboard is copied to your current location in the open message, as shown in Figure 15.1.

 **Didn't Copy?**   Most DOS applications do not access the Clipboard correctly, so you may not be able to copy information from their files. You can insert an entire file by following the instructions for inserting text files later in this lesson.

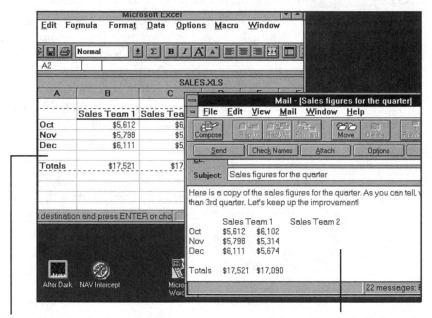

Original information in spreadsheet   Information copied into mail message

Figure 15.1   You can copy information from a pre-existing file into a message.

 **Line Up, Please!**   Information copied in this manner loses the formatting created in the host application. For example, the spreadsheet information shown in Figure 15.1 has lost its column alignment and the bold formatting that had been

applied to the headings. Follow the instructions in Lesson 18 to learn how to copy information from a file and retain its formatting.

Copying an Entire Text File into a Message

If you have a file created in a DOS application, chances are you will not be able to simply copy text from that file into a Mail message. Because most DOS applications cannot access the Windows Clipboard, the copy instructions given in the previous section will not work. You can, however, copy the entire contents of a text file into a message by following these instructions:

1. Save your file as a text file. (Follow the instructions in your application's manual.)

2. Open a message in Mail.

3. Move to the location in the message where you want to insert the text file.

4. Open the **Edit** menu.

5. Select the **Insert from File** command. The dialog box shown in Figure 15.2 appears.

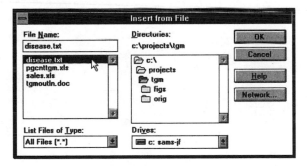

Figure 15.2 You can insert a complete text file into a message using this dialog box.

6. Select the text file you want to insert into your message, and press **Enter**. The entire contents of the text file is inserted at your current location in the message. You can delete any part of the text file once it is inserted.

Lost Your Formatting?   Information copied from a file loses the formatting created in the host application. For example, the text shown in Figure 15.1 has lost the bold formatting of the headings and its column alignment. If your original application has access to the Windows Clipboard, you have some options. See Lesson 18.

In this lesson, you learned how to include all or part of a file with a message. In the next lesson, you will learn how to attach files.

Including Files and Messages

In this lesson, you will learn how to include files with messages.

Attaching a File to a Message

You can send a complete file with a message if you want. Using this method, you can send any file with your message, such as a document file (even one created with a DOS application), a program, or a batch file. A copy of the file or files is attached to the message and sent as a big package to the recipient.

If the recipient has the same application that the file was created in, she can open the file from the Read Message window and edit it. For example, if you create a document using Microsoft Word or even Lotus 1-2-3, you can send that file with a message to one of your co-workers. If your co-worker has the Microsoft Word or Lotus 1-2-3 program, she can open your file and make changes, print it, or do anything else that's necessary.

Give Me a Hint Help your recipient identify the original application (the source of the attached file) by mentioning it in your Mail message. Mail takes its best guess and assigns an icon to the attached file, but if the proper file associations are not set up, the assigned icon may not be clear.

Follow these instructions to attach a file to a message:

1. Open a new message by clicking on the **Compose** button.

2. Enter any message. When you are at the point in the message where you want to attach a file, click on the **Attach** button. The Attach dialog box appears, as shown in Figure 16.1.

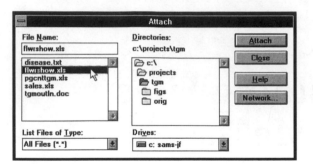

Figure 16.1   You can attach any file you want to a message.

3. Select the file you want to attach, and press **Enter**. An icon that represents the file is inserted at the current location within the message, as shown in Figure 16.2.

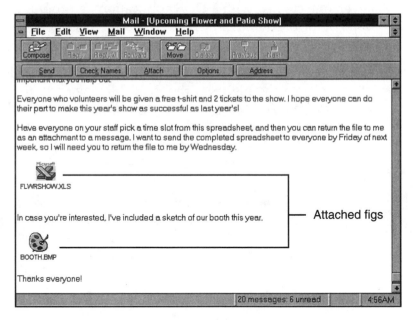

Figure 16.2   A file attached to a message is represented by an icon.

4. Repeat step 3 for any additional file(s) you want to attach. When you are done, click on the **Close** button.

5. Click on the **Send** button to send the message with the attached file(s).

Better Yet   With Windows 3.1, you can attach a file to a message by dragging that file from the File Manager window onto the message. You can also drag a file onto the Outbox, and a message will be created with the file attached.

In this lesson, you learned how to send a file with a message. In the next lesson, you will learn how to work with messages you receive that have files attached.

Working with Attachments to Messages

In this lesson, you will learn how to work with files that are attached to messages.

Opening an Attachment

Messages with files attached are displayed with a paper clip icon in the Message window. You must have your own copy of the program that was used to create the file in order to open that file in Mail. The icon used to represent the file gives you an idea of the program you need to open that file.

To open an attached file:

1. Open the message that contains the attached file.

2. Double-click on the icon that represents the file. The program that created the file is started, with the file open and ready to edit, as shown in Figure 17.1.

CAUTION

No Program   If you do not have the program that created the file installed on your computer, you'll get an error message when you double-click on the file. You may be able to open the file by importing it into Word or Excel, which accept many file formats.

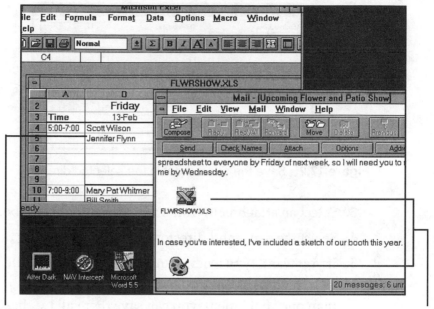

Attached file is ready to edit.

Attached files

Figure 17.1 You can edit attached files.

Saving an Attached File

When a file is attached to a message and sent, it arrives on your system incorporated into the message. If the message is deleted, so are the attached files. While a file is attached, you can work on it and even save changes, but those changes are still part of the original message package; if the message is deleted, you lose the file and your changes. It's best to separate the attached file from the original message by using the **Save Attachment** command. You can save an attached file in whatever directory you want:

1. Open the **File** menu.

2. Select the **Save Attachment**. The Save Attachment dialog box appears (see Figure 17.2).

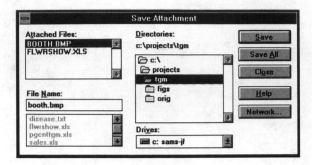

Figure 17.2 Save the attachment in the selected directory.

3. Select an attachment from the **Attached Files** list box.

4. Select the drive and directory to use when saving the file.

5. If you want, type a new name for the file in the **File Name** text box.

6. Click on the **Save** button to save the attached file. If there is more than one attachment, you can save them all by clicking on the **Save All** button.

7. When you are done saving attachments, click on the **Close** button.

In this lesson, you learned how to open and save attachments. In the next lesson, you will learn how to embed an object in a message.

Embedding an Object in a Message

In this lesson, you will learn how to embed an object in a message.

What Is an Object?

Objects can be created by most Windows applications. *Objects* are parts of files that retain a relationship with the application that created them. For example, a part of an Ami Pro file that is copied into a message remembers that it is an Ami Pro document. Because of this, objects can be edited by the recipient of your message. Therefore, the recipient of a message with an Ami Pro object embedded in it can open Ami Pro from Mail and edit the object, providing that they have Ami Pro on their system.

Making a Change   You can still embed objects in messages, even if the recipient does not have a copy of the originating program. However, without the program, the recipient is not able to change the embedded object.

Unlike information that is simply copied from a file, embedded objects retain their formatting. For example, in Figure 18.1, the information copied from an Excel spreadsheet has retained its columnar format. (For a comparison, turn back to Figure 15.1, and look at the same data that was simply copied into a message.) An object embedded into a message from a Word for Windows or other word processing document likewise retains its text formatting (bold, underline, italic, and so on).

So why would you want to simply copy information from a file (as explained in Lesson 15)? Embedding an object (as explained in this lesson) has obvious advantages:

- The data retains its formatting (so it looks better).
- The recipient can work with the data in the original application and make changes.

571

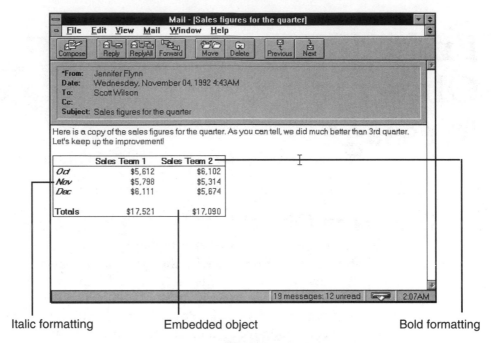

Italic formatting   Embedded object   Bold formatting

Figure 18.1 An object retains its original formatting.

So when would you copy information, and not embed it? When you have no other choice (the application does not support OLE—object linking and embedding), or the information you're copying does not contain any special formatting, so it doesn't deserve the special treatment.

Embedding an Object in a Message

Follow these steps to embed an object in a message:

1. Start **Mail**, and create a new message or open an existing one.

2. Start the original application, and open the file that contains the information you want to embed in your message.

3. Select the information you want to copy.

4. Open the **Edit** menu.

5. Select the **Copy** command. This copies the selected information to the Clipboard.

6. Move to the place in the Mail message where you want the object embedded.

7. In the Send Note window, open the **Edit** menu.

8. Select the **Paste Special** command. The Paste Special dialog box appears asking you to identify the data type.

9. Select the appropriate data type, and click on the **Paste** button. The object on the Clipboard is embedded into your open message in the current location, as shown in Figure 18.2.

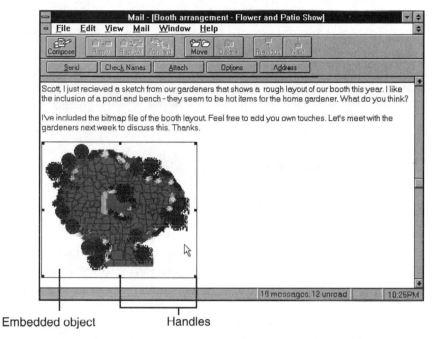

Embedded object   Handles

Figure 18.2   You can copy information from a pre-existing file and embed it into a message.

Editing an Embedded Object

You can edit an embedded object in a message you receive or that you're composing. Follow these steps:

1. Open the message that contains the embedded object.

2. Click on the object. The object is surrounded by a box with *handles*.

Handles   Small boxes that surround an object. You can use these boxes to move and resize the object by dragging them with the mouse.

573

3. Open the **Edit** menu.

4. Select the **Object** command. The application that was used to create the object opens, with the object ready to edit.

 **Protecting Your Sources** In order to edit an object, you must have a copy of the source application on your system.

5. Make any changes to the object that you want. To save your changes, open the application's **File** menu.

6. Select the **Update** command. The object is updated.

7. Close the application in the usual manner, and you are returned to Microsoft Mail.

 Double the Fun! To edit an embedded object quickly, double-click on it. The application that created the object opens immediately.

In this lesson, you learned how to create and edit embedded objects in a Mail message. In the next lesson, you will learn how to use folders to organize your Mail system.

Using Folders to Organize Mail

In this lesson, you will learn how to use folders to organize your messages.

Creating a Folder

Folders are used to organize the messages you receive. For example, if you are in charge of the Sales department, you might want a folder called Sales.

You can create subfolders if you want. For example, you can create a subfolder under Sales for each of your salespeople. The Sales folder could hold general sales information and messages, and each subfolder could hold messages sent or received from each salesperson.

Microsoft Mail comes with three folders already set up: Inbox, Sent Mail, and Wastebasket (called Deleted Mail in Workgroups for Windows). These folders each serve a specific purpose; you cannot delete or rename them. To create a folder of your own:

1. Open the **File** menu.

2. Select the **New Folder** command. The New Folder dialog box opens.

3. Enter the name of the folder in the **Name** text box.

4. If you would like other users to have access to this folder, select **Shared**.

5. To determine where the new folder should be placed, click on the **Options** button. The dialog box expands, as shown in Figure 19.1.

6. Under **Level**, select either **Top Level Folder**, or **Subfolder Of:**. If you select **Subfolder Of:**, select the parent folder from the list box.

7. If this is a shared folder, select the rights you want other users to have: Read, Write, and Delete.

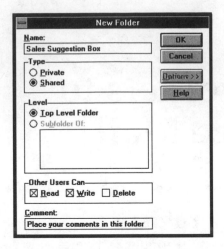

Figure 19.1 The expanded version of the New Folder dialog box.

8. When you are done making selections, click the **OK** button, or press **Enter**. The folder is added to the Folder List.

Deleting Folders

When you delete a folder, all of the messages in that folder are also deleted. To delete a folder:

1. Select the folder from the Folder List by clicking on it or using the arrow keys to highlight it.

2. Press **Delete**. A message box appears, asking for confirmation.

3. Click on the **Yes** button, or press **Y** to delete the folder.

Expanding and Collapsing Folders

In the Folder List, folders that contain subfolders *that are currently displayed* (expanded) are marked with a minus sign, as shown in Figure 19.2. Folders that contain subfolders *that are not currently displayed* (collapsed) are marked with a plus sign. You can expand and collapse the Folder List to customize the display.

Collapsed and Expanded Folders   Collapsed folders are those that do not currently display their subfolders (marked with a plus). Expanded folders are those that currently display their subfolders (marked with a minus).

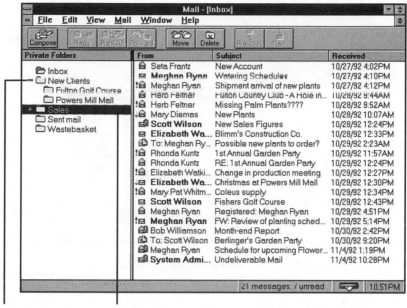

Expanded folder   Collapsed folder

Figure 19.2   Folders that contain subfolders are marked with a plus or a minus.

To collapse a folder, select the folder, and press the - key.

To expand a folder, select the folder, and press the + key.

Which Key to Press?   It's easy to remember which key to press when customizing your Folder List. A collapsed folder is displayed with a + sign. To expand it, use the + key! The same holds true with expanded folders, which are displayed with a - sign, and can be collapsed by pressing -.

Moving Messages Between Folders

To stay organized, move your messages into the appropriate folder after reading them. This way, you'll never have a problem finding a specific message.

To move messages:

1. Select the messages you want to move. (For a review on selecting messages, see Lesson 8.) See Figure 19.3.

Figure 19.3   The Move Messages dialog box.

2. Drag the messages to the folder you want them to reside in.

Copy Cat!   To copy files instead of moving them, hold down the **Ctrl** key as you drag the files.

In this lesson, you learned how to create folders and move messages into them. In the next lesson, you will learn how to find a misplaced message.

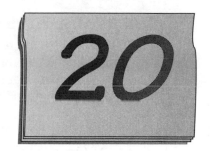

Editing Messages

In this lesson, you will learn how to make changes to your messages.

Selecting Text in a Message

Before you can copy, move, or delete text, you must first select it. To select text, follow these steps:

1. Click on the first character you want to select. Hold the mouse button down.

2. Drag the mouse pointer to the last character you want to select, and release the mouse button. The selected text is highlighted, as shown in Figure 20.1.

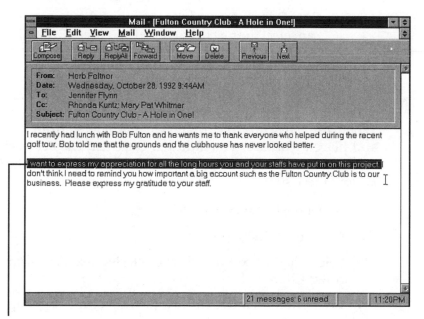

Selected text

Figure 20.1   Text you select is highlighted.

Copying Message Text

When you copy text, the original text is left in its current location, and a copy is placed wherever you want. Once text has been selected, it can be copied to another message or to an additional place in the same message. Follow these steps:

1. Select the text you want to copy.

2. Open the **Edit** menu.

3. Select the **Copy** command. The selected text is copied to the Windows Clipboard.

4. If you want to copy the text to another message, open that message now.

5. Move the cursor to the location in the message where you want to place the selected text.

6. Open the **Edit** menu.

7. Select the **Paste** command. The selected text is copied to the current location.

Fast Copy   Instead of using the Edit Copy command, you can select the text to be copied and press **Ctrl+C**. To paste the text into its new location, press **Ctrl+V**.

Moving Message Text

When you move text, the original text is deleted from its current location and placed wherever you indicate. Once text has been selected, it can be moved to another message, or to an additional place in the same message. Follow these steps:

1. Select the text you want to move.

2. Open the **Edit** menu.

3. Select the **Cut** command. The selected text is moved to the Windows Clipboard.

4. If you want to move the text to another message, open that message now.

5. Move the cursor to the location in the message where you would like to place the selected text.

6. Open the **Edit** menu.

7. Select the **Paste** command. The selected text is moved to the current location.

Fast Moves   Instead of using the Edit Cut command, you can select the text to be moved and press **Ctrl+X**. To paste the text into its new location, press **Ctrl+V**.

Deleting Message Text

You can easily delete selected text. Follow these steps:

1. Select the text you want to delete.

2. Press the **Delete** key.

In this lesson, you learned how to copy, move, and delete text within a message. In the next lesson, you will learn how to spell check your messages.

Using the Spelling Checker

21

In this lesson, you will learn how to use the spelling checker to proofread your messages.

Spell Checking a Message

Nothing is more embarrassing than a misspelled word—especially if the message was sent to your boss. You can save yourself potential embarrassment by checking your messages before you send them.

Windows for Workgroups Users   The Spelling option is not included with your Mail program. If you need to spell check a message, copy the text into your word processor, and spell check it there.

Horrible Speller?   You can have every message automatically spell checked before it is sent. See Lesson 23 for more details.

You can use the spelling checker to check the spelling of a single word, a paragraph, or an entire message. Follow these instructions to spell check a message:

1. If you want to spell check only part of a message, select the text you want to check. Do not select any text at all if you want to spell check the entire message.

2. Open the **Edit** menu.

3. Select the **Spelling** command by clicking on it or pressing **L**.

4. When the spelling checker encounters a misspelled word, the Spelling dialog box appears, as shown in Figure 21.1.

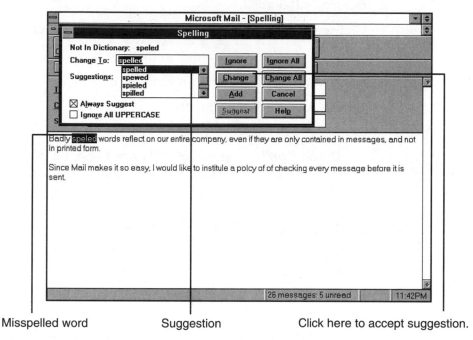

Misspelled word   Suggestion   Click here to accept suggestion.

Figure 21.1   Select an option to correct your misspelled word.

5. To correct the misspelled word, either:

- Enter the correct spelling in the **Change To** text box.

OR

- Ask the spelling checker to provide suggestions by clicking on the **Suggest** button. Select a suggested word from the **Suggestions** list box.

May I Make a Suggestion?   The spelling checker provides suggestions automatically if you select the **Always Suggest** check box.

The spelling checker provides additional options for dealing with misspelled words, just click on the appropriate button:

Ignore the word and continue spell checking the message.

Ignore All occurrences of this word in the message and do not flag them as misspelled.

Change All occurrences of the misspelled word automatically.

Add this word to your personal dictionary.

Suggest a correct spelling for the word.

Ignore All UPPERCASE words.

Quick Spell   You can quickly spell check a document by pressing **F7**.

Correcting Duplicate Words

If you type the same word twice in a row, as in the sentence below:

This sentence contains a duplicate word word.

the spelling checker displays a Spelling dialog box with two additional buttons, as shown in Figure 21.2.

Click here to delete duplicate.

Duplicate word

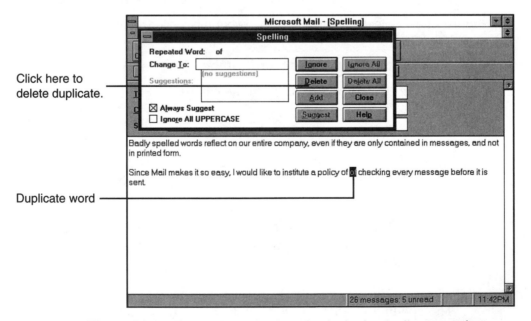

Figure 21.2   The spelling checker also looks for duplicate words.

To correct the sentence, select one of these options:

- Select **Delete** to delete the first occurrence of the word.

- Select **Delete All** to delete all duplicate occurrences of the same word. If the repetition is intentional, just click on **Ignore**.

In this lesson, you learned how to spell check your messages. In the next lesson, you will learn how to print a message.

Printing a Copy of Your Messages

In this lesson, you will learn how to print your messages.

Printing a Message

Before you delete a message, you can print a copy of it for your files. To print a message, follow these steps:

1. Select the message you want to print from the message list. (See Lesson 8 for instructions on selecting more than one message.)

2. Open the **File** menu.

3. Select the **Print** command. The Print dialog box appears, as shown in Figure 22.1.

4. You can choose to have each message printed on a separate page by deselecting the Print Multiple Notes on a Page check box.

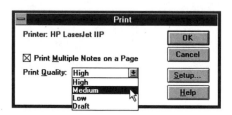

Figure 22.1   The Print dialog box.

5. You can lower the level of print quality (and reduce the amount of time it takes to print the messages) by using the **Print Quality** drop-down list box.

6. You can change your print setup (described in the next section) by clicking on the **Setup** button.

586

7. When you are ready to print, press **Enter**, or click **OK**.

Singles You can print a single message after reading it by using these same instructions. Simply access the **File** menu from the Read Note window.

Quick Print To print selected messages quickly, simply press **Ctrl+P**.

Printing Attached Files When you print a message, embedded objects also print, but not attached files. To print attached files, print from the application that created the file.

Changing Your Print Setup

You can change the printer you use to print your messages by using the Print Setup dialog box. You can access the Print Setup dialog box in one of two ways:

- Open the **File** menu, and select the **Print Setup** command.

  OR

- Click on the **Setup** button in the Print dialog box.

  The Print Setup dialog box is shown in Figure 22.2.

  To change to a different printer, use one of the following methods:

- Select a different printer connected to your computer by using the **Specific Printer** drop-down list box.

  OR

- Select a network printer with the **Network** button. Connecting to a network printer is covered in more detail in a later section of this lesson.

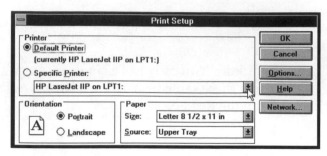

Figure 22.2   The Print Setup dialog box.

You can change the orientation of the printed message between **Portrait** (the default) and **Landscape**. Simply click on the appropriate option button.

Portrait vs. Landscape   Landscape orientation means that the message is printed along the paper's widest edge, as in 11-x-8 1/2-inch. Portrait orientation for the same size paper prints the message as 8 1/2-x-11-inch.

You can change the paper size or source by using the appropriate drop-down list box. Press **Alt+Z** to change the paper size and **Alt+S** to change the source.

Changing Printer Options

You can adjust the quality of your printed messages through the Options dialog box. To access the Options dialog box, click on the **Options** button in the Print dialog box. The Options dialog box is shown in Figure 22.3.

If you have a laser printer, you can choose from these dithering options: None, Course, Fine, Line Art. Additional time may be required to print messages of different dithering. Use this option to improve the quality of graphics included in your messages. If you have a dot-matrix printer, use the **Gray scale** option to improve the quality of your graphic images.

Dithering   Adjusts the quality (detail) of printed graphics.

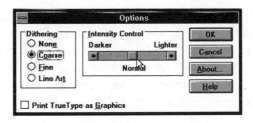

Figure 22.3   The Options dialog box.

You can darken the text of your messages (like a copier) by changing the intensity. With a laser printer, drag the scroll box to the left or right. With a dot-matrix printer, use the **Duplex** option to darken the text.

If you use Windows' Truetype fonts, you can have them printed as graphics by selecting the **Print Truetype as Graphics** option. Using this option requires less printer memory and less time. This option works best when you have a lot of graphics in a message and only one or two Truetype fonts.

Keep Your Options Open   Additional options may appear in the Options dialog box, depending on the type of printer you have.

Printing Your Messages on a Network Printer

Often the printer that is connected to your network server is of a better quality than the printer connected to your computer. To use a network printer to print your messages, use the Connect Network Printer dialog box, shown in Figure 22.4. To access the Connect Network Printer dialog box, use the **Network** button from the Print Setup dialog box.

Use the **Device Name** drop-down list box to select the device to connect to from among the available printer ports on your computer. LPT1 is typically assigned to your local printer, so you may want to select a different printer port to retain access to both the network printer and your local printer.

To display a list of available network printers, either select the network path to the printer in the **Path** drop-down list box, or select a computer from those listed under the **Show Shared Printers on** area. For example, by selecting the computer marked HERB, any shared printer that is connected to HERB will be displayed in the Shared Printers area. Once a path has been identified, a list of available printers appear in the Shared Printers area. Select one of the listed printers, and press **Enter**, or click **OK**. Your messages print on the selected network printer. Check the **Reconnect at Startup** option if you would like to automatically connect to the network printer each time you start Windows.

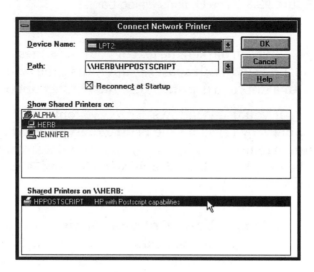

Figure 22.4 The Connect Network Printer dialog box.

In this lesson, you learned how to print your messages. In the next lesson, you will learn how to set various Mail options.

Setting Mail Options

In this lesson, you will learn how to set various Mail options.

Selecting Various Mail Options

You can change various Mail options through the Options dialog box. To access the Options dialog box:

1. Open the **Mail** menu.

2. Select the **Options** command. The Options dialog box appears, as shown in Figure 23.1.

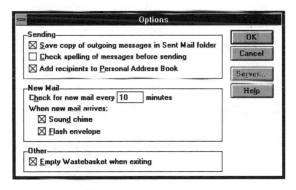

Figure 23.1 The Options dialog box.

Through this dialog box, you can change what happens when Mail sends, receives, or discards messages.

Changing the Options for Mail You Send

There are three options you can change that affect mail that you send:

- **Save copy of outgoing messages in Sent Mail folder**. This option is on by default. If you turn this option off, Mail will not save copies of the messages you send.

- **Check spelling of messages before sending**. When this option is on, Mail checks the spelling of all messages before they are sent. This option increases the amount of time it takes to send a message. To spell check an individual message, see Lesson 21.

- **Add recipients to Personal Address Book**. This option is on by default. When this option is on, your message recipients is added to your personal address book.

Changing Options for Mail You Receive

There are three options you can change that affect mail that you receive:

- **Check for new mail every XXXX minutes**   Change how often Mail checks the network for messages. You can enter any number of minutes from 1 to 9999.

- **Sound chime**   This option is on by default. If this option is on, a chime sounds whenever you receive a message.

- **Flash envelope**   This option is on by default. If this option is on, an envelope flashes on the cursor whenever a message is received.

Changing Other Mail Options

There are a few additional Mail options you can select:

- **Empty Wastebasket when exiting**. This option is on by default. As you learned in Lesson 8, when you delete a message, it is not actually deleted, but moved to the Wastebasket folder. If this option is on, the messages that you've indicated for deletion will be permanently deleted when you log out of Mail. If this option is not on, messages marked for deletion accumulate in the Waste basket folder until you delete them yourself.

Windows for Workgroups Users   Your delete folder is called Deleted Mail, not Wastebasket.

- **Server**   Use this command button to access additional server related options, such as the location of your message file. Options vary by system.

In this lesson, you learned how to change various Mail options. In the next lesson, you will learn how to create a message template for messages you send often.

Creating a
Message Template

In this lesson, you will learn how to create a message template for messages that you send often.

Saving the Message Template

You can create a message template (a message that contains information that can be reused) for messages that you send often. A sample template is shown in Figure 24.1.

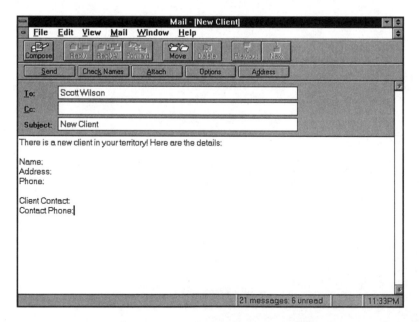

Figure 24.1 Create a message template for basic messages that you send often.

Creating a message template is similar to saving an unsent message. To create the template, follow these steps:

1. Compose a new message. Enter only the information (such as recipient names, and so on) that doesn't change.

2. After entering your template information, double-click on the **Close** box, or press **Ctrl+F4**.

3. A dialog box appears. Answer yes by clicking on the **Yes** button, or pressing **Y**.

Organize Your Templates   Store your template in a special folder called Templates so you can locate them easily. See Lesson 19 for details on creating folders.

Using Your Message Template

When you are ready to use your message template, follow these steps:

1. Select the message from the message list, and click on the **Forward** button (or press **Ctrl+F**). Your message template appears.

2. Add or change any information you need. Click on the **Send** button to send your message. Your original template remains in your message file.

Drag and Drop   You can drag the message template to the **Outbox** instead of clicking on the **Forward** button.

In this lesson, you learned how to create and use message templates. In the next lesson, you will learn how to back up your messages.

Maintaining Your Mail System

In this lesson, you will learn how to archive (back up) your messages.

Archiving Your Messages

You should perform regular backups of your system, including your message file.

Message File   The file MSMAIL.MMF is where all of your messages are stored. This file can be kept either on your computer or on the server.

Even if you perform regular backups on your own system, if your message file is on the server of your network, it may not be backed up. If your message file is damaged or deleted, you will lose all of your messages if you don't have a backup of your message file. For this reason, you should back up your message file often.

To perform a backup of your message file:

1. Open the **Mail** menu.

2. Select the **Backup** command. The Backup dialog box appears.

3. Enter the name of your backup file. You can call it anything you like using up to eight characters. The file name extension should be .MMF, as in BACKUP.MMF.

4. If you want, you can change the drive and directory that will be used to store the file.

5. When you are ready to backup your message file, press **Enter**, or click on **OK**. A copy of your message file is saved under the name you indicated.

Back Up What You Say You should perform a backup of your message file at least once a week, or more often if you receive many important messages. As added protection, you can copy your message file onto a diskette (in case something happens to your hard drive).

What to Do If Your Message File Is Damaged

If your message file is damaged or deleted, you receive a warning when you log into Mail. Press **Enter**, and the Open Message File dialog box appears, as shown in Figure 25.2.

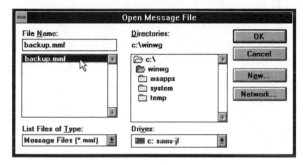

Figure 25.2 The Open Message File dialog box.

Follow these steps to restore your message file:

1. Select your backup file from the file list. If necessary, change drives and directories until you locate your backup file.

2. If you want to create a new message file (because you don't have a backup), click on **New**.

3. After you've selected your backup file, press **Enter**, or click on **OK**.

4. You will see the message: **This message file is a backup file. Would you like to make it your primary message file?** Click on **Yes**. Your backup file will be converted for use as your regular message file.

If You Don't Convert Your Backup File If you answer **No** to the message in step 4, your backup file will not be converted, but it will be opened. You will then be able to move, copy, and delete the messages in the file. New messages you receive will not be saved in this file. When you log back into Mail at a later time, you will receive the same error message as before: **Your message file could not be found.** For this reason, you should always answer **Yes** to convert your backup file.

In this lesson, you learned how to back up your message file and how to restore it if the message file becomes damaged. In the next lesson, you will learn how to send messages through Schedule+.

Scheduling Meetings with Schedule+

In this lesson, you will learn how to send messages through Schedule+.

What Is Schedule+ ?

Schedule+ is an appointment and task scheduler by Microsoft that is available separate from Microsoft Mail. (Schedule+ comes free with Windows for Workgroups.)

Schedule+ is an electronic day planner that you can use to schedule your appointments, meetings, and daily tasks. You can respond to requests for meetings sent by Schedule+ from within Microsoft Mail. Likewise, you can read replies to your own meeting requests as you would any other Mail message.

Sending a Request for a Meeting

Schedule+ contains several windows:

Appointment Book   This window displays today's appointments.

Message window   Similar in function to the Message window in Mail. Use this window to read and send replies to meeting requests.

Planner   This window displays your appointment schedule for several weeks. Meeting requests originate from the Planner window.

One at a Time, Please!   You can display only the Appointment Book or the Planner at any one time.

599

To send a request for a meeting:

1. Change to the **Planner** window (see Figure 26.1).

2. Select a time for the meeting.

3. If necessary, change the names of the attendees by clicking on the **Change** button. The Select Attendees dialog box appears. The Select Attendees dialog box looks and acts just like the Address window explained in Lesson 4.

4. From the Planner window, click on **Request Meeting**. The Send Request dialog box shown in Figure 26.2 appears.

5. Enter the purpose of the meeting in the Subject text box.

6. Enter your meeting request.

7. If you'd like to receive a written response, check the **Ask for Responses** check box.

8. When you are ready to send the request, click on **Send**.

Schedule+ sends the request for a meeting.

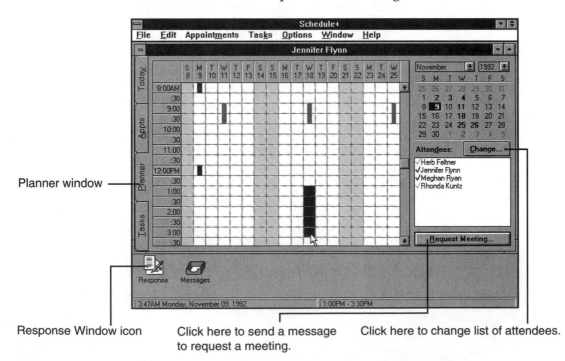

Figure 26.1 Send meeting requests from the Planner window.

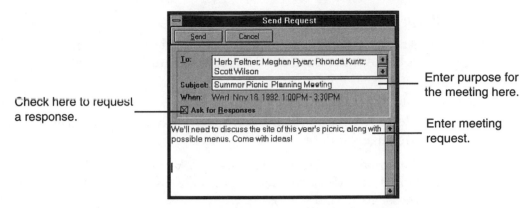

Figure 26.2   Type your request for a meeting into this dialog box.

Responding to a Request for a Meeting

Once a request for a meeting is received, it can be read either in Mail or in Schedule+. Reading the request is similar in both Mail and Schedule+:

1. Select the message from the **Message** window in either Mail or Schedule+. (In Mail, meeting requests look just like any other message.)

2. Press **Enter** to open the meeting request. The Meeting Request dialog box appears, as shown in Figure 26.3.

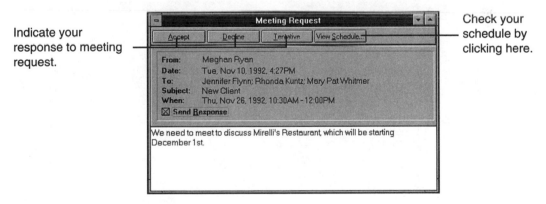

Figure 26.3   We request your presence . . .

To reply to a request for a meeting:

1. If necessary, you can access your schedule (even from within Mail) by clicking on **View Schedule**.

601

2. Select your response from the following option buttons:

   Accept Displays a check mark in front of the message in the Schedule+ Message window, or the word **Yes** in front of the message in Mail's Message window.

   Decline Displays an **X** in front of the message in the Schedule+ Message window, or the word **No** in front of the message in Mail's Message window.

   Tentative Displays a question mark in front of the message in the Schedule+ Message window, or the word **Tentative** in front of the message in Mail's Message window.

3. If a response was requested, a Response dialog box appears. Enter your response to the meeting request, and click on **Send**.

Reading a Response to a Meeting Request

Reading a response is similar in Mail and Schedule+:

1. Select the response from the **Message** window in either Mail or Schedule+. (In Mail, meeting responses look just like any other message.)

2. Press **Enter** to open the meeting response. The **Response** window appears, as shown in Figure 26.4.

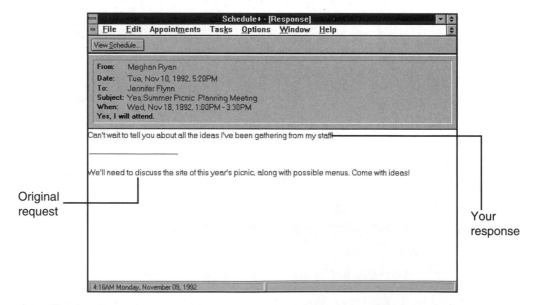

Figure 26.4 You can read the responses to your meeting request in both Mail and Schedule+.

In this lesson, you learned how Schedule+ can be used with Mail to schedule meetings with your co-workers. You should now feel comfortable using Microsoft Mail.

ACCESS™ 2

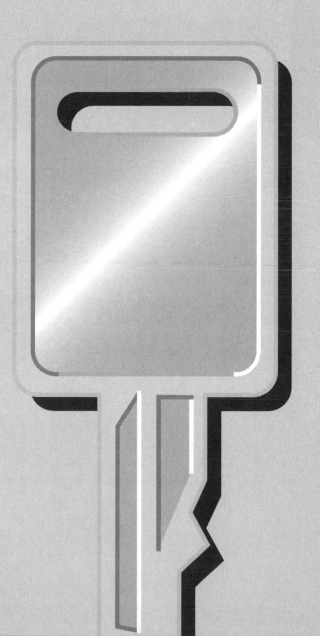

Getting Started with Microsoft Access

1

In this lesson, you'll learn about Microsoft Access and basic database concepts, as well as how to start Access, examine the parts of the startup screen, and quit.

What Is Microsoft Access?

Microsoft Access is a popular *database management system* (DBMS). You might think that a database program would be hard to use, but you are in for a nice surprise.

Microsoft took the anxiety out of learning and doing database management by creating an easy-to-use system called Microsoft Access. The program is so easy to use that you can be doing productive work in a few minutes, using your computer to organize, store, retrieve, manipulate, and print information.

With Microsoft Access you can:

- Enter and update your data.
- Quickly find the data you need.
- Organize the data in meaningful ways.
- Create reports, forms, and mailing labels quickly from your data.
- Share data with other programs on your system.

This section will show you how to use these Access features.

Basic Database Concepts

Before you start Microsoft Access, you should know some basic concepts. If you are new to working with databases, these definitions will help you:

Database   A collection of objects used to manage facts and figures. A database could be used for keeping track of tapes in a video tape library, controlling an inventory, working with a customer list, or keeping a Christmas card list. A database contains one or more tables, as well as other objects (such as reports). An Access database is stored as a single file.

Table   An object in a database where facts and figures are stored in a two-dimensional form, in rows and columns.

Field   A category of information in a table, such as an address, tape title, or customer ID. Fields represent the columns of a table.

Record   A collection of all facts and figures relating to an item in a table. Rows represent the records of a table.

Object   An identifiable unit in a database, such as a table, report, or form.

You can think of a database management system as a filing cabinet. Each database is like a hanging folder in the cabinet, with the various objects (including the tables) as manila folders in the hanging folder.

Starting Microsoft Access

Before using Microsoft Access, you must install it on your computer (see Appendix A at the end of the book for directions). Once Microsoft Access is installed, you should be able to start it from Windows.

Start Windows by typing **WIN** at the DOS prompt. Program Manager will start automatically. Click on the group icon that contains Microsoft Access to make it active. For example, if you installed Microsoft Access to the Microsoft Office group, click on the Microsoft Office group (see Figure 1.1). If the group is not visible, select it from Program Manager's Window menu.

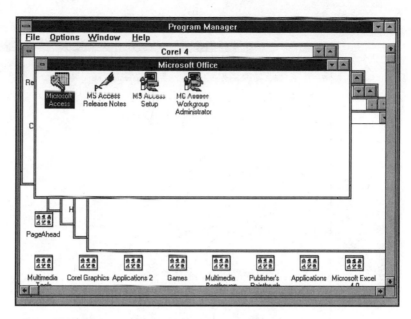

Figure 1.1 Find the Microsoft Access program icon.

Start Microsoft Access either of two ways:

- Double-click on the **Microsoft Access** icon.
- Highlight the icon with the arrow keys, and press **Enter**.

Microsoft Access will start, displaying the startup window. The menu bar will contain two options: **File** and **Help** (shown in Figure 1.2). The toolbar contains four active icons: **New Database**, **Open Database**, **Cue Cards**, and **Help**. From this startup window, you can create or open a database.

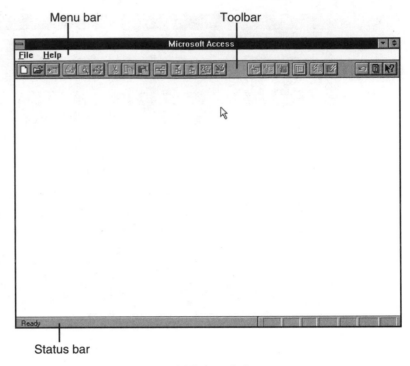

Figure 1.2 The startup screen of Microsoft Access.

Quitting Microsoft Access

To quit Microsoft Access, double-click on the **Control-menu** box, or press **Alt+F4**.

In this lesson, you learned some basic database concepts and how to start and quit Microsoft Access. In the next lesson, you'll learn about the main menu and some of its options.

The Startup Main Menu

In this lesson, you will take a brief look at the startup main menu options, learn how the menu bar works, get an introduction to the toolbar, and find out how to get help.

Introduction to the Menu Bar

Microsoft Access uses *dynamic menus*: that is, the options on the menu bar change depending upon how you are using the program. When you first start the program, there are only two options: **File** and **Help**. Once you open a database, the menu bar will change, and there will be more options.

New to Windows? If you are a new user of Windows and Windows applications, see the part of this book on Windows 3.1 for more information.

Using Shortcut Keys

As you learned in the Windows section of the book, you can often use shortcut keys instead of using the menu system. Access has a number of special keys that function as shortcuts for certain operations. For example, there are shortcut keys to cancel an operation, cut or copy text, and close the program. Table 2.1 lists a few of the most common shortcut keys.

Table 2.1 Microsoft Access Shortcut Keys

Key	Function
Alt+F4	Terminates Microsoft Access.
Esc	Cancels a menu, command, or dialog box.
F1	Initiates the Help system.

continues

Table 2.1 Continued

Key	Function
Shift+F1	Initiates context-sensitive help.
Ctrl+F10	Maximizes the document window.
Ctrl+X	Cuts data to the Clipboard.
Ctrl+C	Copies data to the Clipboard.
Ctrl+V	Pastes data from the Clipboard.
Del	Clears or deletes selected data.
Shift+F2	Zooms in.
Ctrl+F6	Cycles between open windows.
F11	Returns to the database window.
Shift+F12	Saves a database object.

Introduction to the Toolbar

Just under the menu bar is a *toolbar* with various *buttons* (icons) that can simplify tasks. Like the menu bar, the toolbars change depending upon the operations you are performing. When you first start Access, the Database Toolbar is on-screen, and there are four active buttons: New Database, Open Database, Cue Cards, and Help. The toolbar is shown in Figure 2.1.

New Database button   Help button

Open Database button   Cue Cards button

Figure 2.1 The Database Toolbar.

> **TIP**
>
> **Show Me Your Label** If you leave the mouse pointer on a toolbar button for a few seconds, a little label will pop up that tells you the button's name.

Getting Help

As with other Windows applications, you can get help at any time by pressing **F1** or by using the **Help** menu.

You can also use the toolbar to get help for objects that are on-screen. Simply click on the **Help** button, and then click on the part of the screen you need help with. For example, if you don't know what the binoculars represent on one of the toolbar buttons, you can click on the **Help** button and then click on the button in question. A Help screen pops up, telling you that if you click on the binoculars button, you can search for text.

Need Help on a Command? *Context-sensitive help* is a feature that gives you information on-screen about how to use the menu command that's currently highlighted. To use this kind of help, press **Shift+F1** when the command is highlighted (instead of pressing Enter to activate the command).

Another method of getting help is to use the Cue Cards that are a part of Microsoft Access. These electronic tutorials guide you through the various processes, such as creating a database. To use the Cue Cards:

1. Choose the **Help** menu.

2. Select **Cue Cards**.

3. Select the option you want help on (such as **Build a database with tables** if you need help creating a database).

The Cue Cards (shown in Figure 2.2) lie on top of the normal Microsoft Access windows. While you continue working with the program, the Cue Cards guide you.

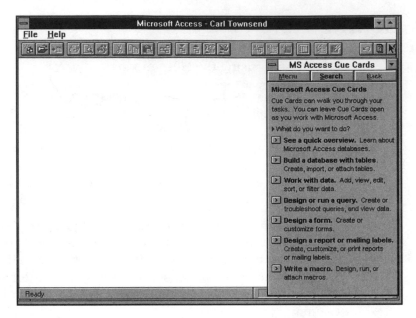

Figure 2.2 Getting help with Cue Cards.

In this lesson, you were introduced to the startup main menu options. You also learned how the menu bar works and how to get help. In the next lesson, we'll create a database.

Creating a Database

In this lesson, you will learn how to create a database for tables, reports, and other objects.

Plan Your Database

Suppose you've just been given the task of tracking an important mailing list for your organization: a prospect list for the salespeople. Microsoft Access is a good choice for managing this prospect list because it's easy to use, the salespeople will learn it quickly, and it has all the right features.

Your first step is to define a database. Once that is done, you can decide if tables, reports, forms, and queries are necessary. The prospect list would be a very simple database; a single table and a few reports would probably suffice.

Tables in Databases In this example, the prospects' addresses can be put in a *table*, an Access object that stores information in rows and columns. The table can then be stored in the same single database file as the reports and forms.

What Are Forms, Queries, and Reports? A *form* is any object you can use to enter, edit, view, or print data records. A *query* is an object used to retrieve specific information from a database based on a condition. A *report* is a collection of information organized and formatted to fit your specifications.

A database can evolve into a fairly complex structure, and it needs to be properly organized. Follow these general rules when you create a database:

- Look at the way the information is currently being managed, and decide if it is the best way.

- Define the new objectives, and build the database to meet these objectives.

- Avoid putting too much information in a single table.

Creating Your Own Database

Let's create a sample database for practice. Remember that you can store tables, queries, reports, and forms associated with the database all in the same database file.

To create a new database, follow these steps:

1. Choose **New Database** from the **File** menu, or click on the **New Database** button on the toolbar. The New Database dialog box is displayed (see Figure 3.1).

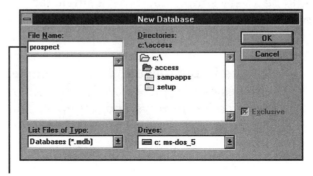

Enter the name of the new database here.

Figure 3.1 Entering the name of the new database.

2. In the File Name text box, type the name for your new database. (You can use up to eight characters, plus a three-character extension. If you don't type an extension, Access will automatically add the extension **.mdb**.) The default name is **DB1.MDB**, but you can give the file a more specific name. For our example, we'll enter **PROSPECT**.

3. (Optional) If you want to save the database in a different directory, select the desired directory from the Directories list box.

4. (Optional) If you want to save the database on a different drive, choose the drive in the Drives list box.

5. When you're finished, click on **OK**.

Once the database is created, a Database window appears on-screen (see Figure 3.2). You can use the displayed window to add tables, reports, and other objects to the database, or you can use any objects you've already created. The list box is empty because you have not yet created any tables, forms, or reports. Notice that you now have more menu options on the menu bar and additional active buttons on the toolbar.

The Database window

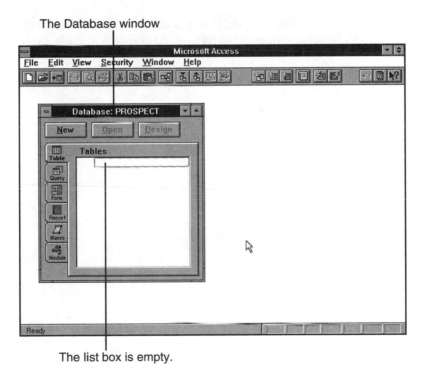

The list box is empty.

Figure 3.2 The Database window.

What Happened to Those Buttons? The Design and Open buttons on the new window are dim at this time because no objects have been created in the database yet.

617

Closing the Database

Closing the database ensures that all objects are properly stored in the database and returns you to the startup window. To close the database, choose **Close Database** from the **File** menu. The startup window appears again; if you want, you can open another database or create a new one.

Some Cautions About Closing By saving the database before you close it, you are ensuring that everything is stored on disk properly. You have to close a database before you can open another one, because only one database can be open at a time in the program.

In this lesson, you learned how to create and close a database. In the next lesson, you will learn how to create a simple table to hold data.

Creating a Simple Table

In this lesson, you'll learn how to create a simple table to hold your data.

Designing a Table

First, you need to define the information you want to put in the table. For now, let's look at a database for managing sales prospects. The database will have a single table with the prospects' addresses. What we really need to store now is the name, full address, phone number, a tickle date, a region code, and sales totals for the last six months.

Tickle Date   The *tickle date* is the date when the salesperson should call that prospect again.

Keep It Simple   Keep the database simple. Don't try to put everything you know about the prospect in the file. Decide what data you need to accomplish your purpose, and in what form it should be. Once you have started entering data, you can redefine the database structure as needed for additional data. It's still a good rule, however, to plan ahead as much as possible. It's easier to enter all data for a record at one time than try to add something to each record later.

When you design your table, identify some type of item in the table that will be unique for each record, such as the Social Security number, membership number, or model number for an inventory. Make this unique item the first field in the record; it will be used later as the *primary key*. Access uses the primary key field to *index* your database (see "Setting the Primary Key" later in this lesson). For our example, we'll use the first field to give each person an identification number. The first field will be our primary key field.

TIP

What's in a Name? Don't use a person's name for your primary key field. There could be two people in your database with the same name. Access won't allow two primary key fields to have the same information.

Creating a Table

Now let's create a table for our prospects. If you have already created a database using the steps in the last lesson, use these steps to open that database.

1. Choose **Open Database** from the **File** menu, or click on the **Open Database** button on the toolbar.

2. Choose the drive and directory, if necessary, and then choose the database from the File Name list.

3. Click on **OK**. The empty database window appears (see Figure 4.1).

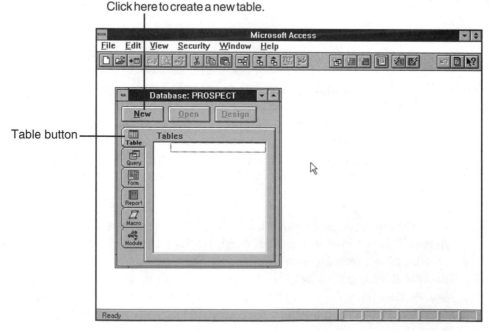

Figure 4.1 The Database window.

Creating a Database   If you have not yet created a database, create one (and name it PROSPECT) by choosing **New Database** from the **File** menu, typing **PROSPECT** in the File Name text box, and choosing **OK**.

Be sure the word **Tables** is displayed over the list window in the dialog box. If it is not displayed, click on the **Table** button at the left side of the dialog box (see Figure 4.1). To create a new table, choose the **New** button. The New Table dialog box appears. Choose the **New Table** button to create a simple table. Microsoft Access opens a new Table window in Design view (see Figure 4.2). You can use this window to create the structure of your table.

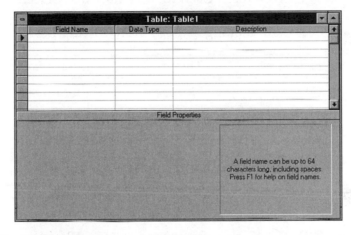

Figure 4.2   Design view for a new table.

Design View vs. Datasheet View   Design view is a view of a table, form, query, or report that permits you to modify its basic structure. Datasheet view permits you to view the data of a table, query, or form, but does not allow you to change the structure.

You define a table by telling Access what the structure of the table will be. The structure of a table is made up of *fields*. For each field, you must specify a field name (such as PHONE or LNAME) and a data type (such as

Text or Number). You can also enter a simple description if you want. Access supports eight data types:

- **Text**   Indicates text and numbers that aren't used in calculations.
- **Memo**   Indicates long text strings (multiple sentences).
- **Date/Time**   Used for dates and times.
- **Number**   Indicates numbers used for calculations.
- **Currency**   Means that the data is a currency value.
- **Counter**   Used for an integer which is incremented automatically.
- **Yes/no**   Indicates logic values that can be true or false.
- **OLE Object**   Used for an embedded object.

For our mailing list, use the following fields:

Field Name	Type	Description
ID	Number	Identification number
LNAME	Text	Last name
FNAME	Text	First name
ADDRESS	Text	Address
CITY	Text	City
ST	Text	State
ZIP	Number	ZIP code
TICKLE	Date/Time	Call-back date
PHONE	Text	Telephone number
REGION	Number	Region
SALES	Currency	Sales for last six months

To create the database structure, follow these instructions:

1. If necessary, move the cursor to the first field's text box, and enter a field name. (For example, enter **ID**.)

2. Press **Enter** or **Tab** to move to the Data Type column.

3. A default value of **Text** will be entered. If you want to use the Text data type, simply press **Enter** or **Tab** to move to the next column. If you want a different data type, click on the down arrow in the Data Type column, or press **Alt+[da]** to open the Data Type list box. For this example, choose **Number** from the list box.

4. If necessary, go to the last column and type in a description for this field. For this example, type **Identification number**.

5. Press **Enter** to go to the next row, and then type in the information for the second field. Continue until all fields have been defined.

Setting Field Properties

For each field in a table, you must set certain *properties*. You have already named each field; for now, the only fields for which you need to set properties are the format properties of the ID, ZIP, TICKLE, REGION, and SALES. The text fields do not need to be set in this example.

Property   A characteristic of an object, such as its size, color, or name.

To set the properties, follow these steps:

1. To set the ID field format, click on any box in the row that defines the ID field. The Field Properties box at the bottom of the screen will display the current field's properties (see Figure 4.3).

Click here to display a list of property options.

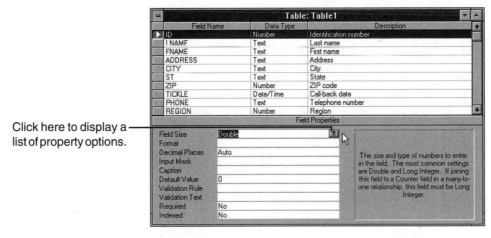

Figure 4.3   The properties of a field.

2. Click on the **Field Size** box, and an arrow appears. Click on the arrow to display your options.

3. Choose **Long Integer** to tell Access you will use whole numbers only.

4. Click on any box in the ZIP row, and change the field size to **Long Integer** by repeating steps 2 and 3.

5. Click on any box in the REGION row, and change the field size to **Integer**.

6. To set the TICKLE field format, click on any box in the TICKLE row, and click on the **Format** property box.

7. Open the list box, and choose **Medium Date**.

8. To set the SALES format, click on any box in the SALES row, and click on the **Format** property box.

9. If Currency is not the current format, select it from the list box.

Setting the Primary Key

For the next step, you need to set the primary key. The value in this field will be unique for each record, which permits faster access to the record. Microsoft Access does this by creating an index on the primary key field.

Indexing the Database   To organize or sort a table's records according to the content of one or more fields.

To set the primary key, follow these steps:

1. Make sure your table is in Design view. If it isn't, click on the **Design View** button on the toolbar.

2. Click anywhere in the row of the field you want to use for the index. For this example, click anywhere in the ID row.

3. Click on the **Primary Key** button on the toolbar. A key icon appears in the row selector area to the left of the first field (see Figure 4.4).

Design View button   Primary Key button

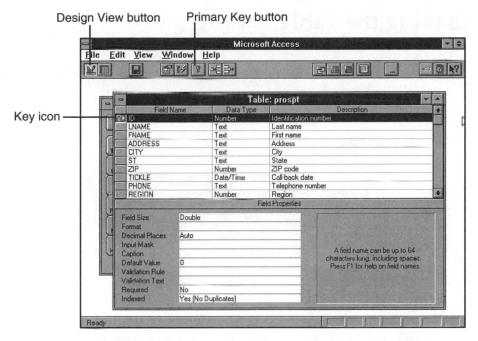

Key icon

Figure 4.4   Setting the primary key.

Row Selector   The small triangle to the left of the first field of the database is called the *row selector*. Clicking on any field in a row will move the triangle to that row.

If you try to save the table before you select a primary key, Access will ask if you want to create one before it saves the table. If you answer **Yes**, a new Counter type field will be created and used as the primary key field. If you already have a field with the Counter data type, it will be chosen as the primary key field.

Now, each time you display the table (as you would when switching from Design to Database view), it will be reordered by the primary key fields (in our example, by ID number).

Saving the Table

Once the table is finished, save it by following these steps:

1. Choose the **Save As** command from the **File** menu, or click on the **Save** button on the toolbar.

2. Enter the name for the table (see Figure 4.5).

3. Choose **OK**.

Figure 4.5   Saving a table.

Closing a Table

To close a table, choose **Close** from the **File** menu. If any changes have been made since you last saved the table, Microsoft Access will prompt you to save the table. You are returned to the Database window, and the new table is displayed in the list.

In this lesson, you learned how to create a table, set field properties, save the table, and close it. In the next lesson, you will learn how to create a table using the Table Wizard.

Using Table Wizard to Create a Table

In this lesson, you will learn how to use the Table Wizard to customize Access' sample tables.

What Is Table Wizard?

Access comes with several *Wizards* to help you create objects, such as tables, forms, and queries. The *Table Wizard* helps you create a table quickly by providing you with a list of sample tables. Table Wizard has over 40 sample tables, divided into two categories: Business and Personal. After you choose a category, use a list box to choose the table you want, and then use another list box to select the fields you want.

For example, say you wanted to create a table of all your friends' addresses and birthdays to use as an address list. Using the Table Wizard, you could choose the Friends sample table. A list box will appear, showing all the available field names that are associated with that table. All you have to do is select the field names you want to use, name your table, and set a primary key—and you're done! The formats for each field name are already set, and you don't have to change anything.

Wizards When you use a Wizard, you are basically just customizing a sample object (like a table or a form). The Wizard will lead you through a series of dialog boxes that ask you questions, allowing you to specify options. Once it has all the information it needs, the Wizard creates the table to your specifications.

Creating a Table

To create a table with Table Wizard, follow these steps:

1. With the **Table** button selected in the Database window, choose the **New** button.

2. In the New Table dialog box, select the **Table Wizards** button. The dialog box shown in Figure 5.1 will appear.

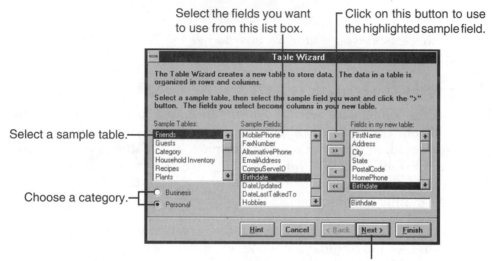

Select the fields you want to use from this list box.

Click on this button to use the highlighted sample field.

Select a sample table.

Choose a category.

Click on this button to go to the next dialog box.

Figure 5.1   The first Table Wizards dialog box.

3. Choose whether you want to use a table template from the Business or Personal list by selecting the appropriate option button. For example, to create a table for your friends' names and addresses, choose **Personal**.

4. Select the table you want to use from the **Sample Tables** list box. For our example, you would choose **Friends**.

5. Choose each field you want to use in the table by selecting it from the **Sample Fields** list box. Then click on the > button to move to the **Fields in my new table** list box.

TIP

A Moving Experience   Click on the >> button to move all the sample fields to the **Fields in my new table** list box at once.

Quick Removal If you decide not to use a field name once you've moved it to the **Fields in my new table** list box, you can easily remove it. Highlight it, and click on the < button. Or click on the << button to remove all the fields at once.

6. When you have selected the fields you want, choose the **Next >** button. A new dialog box will appear, as shown in Figure 5.2.

Type a name for your table here.

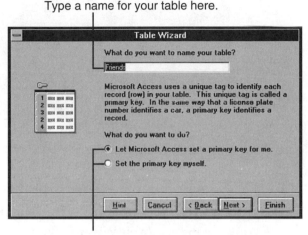

Tell Access how you want to set the primary key.

Figure 5.2 Customize your table further with the second Table Wizards dialog box.

7. Type in a new name for your table if the one provided is not what you want.

8. Choose one of the option buttons to tell Access how you want to set the primary key.

9. When you're finished, select the **Next >** button.

10. Depending upon the options you selected, you might need to answer more questions. If so, more dialog boxes will appear. Follow the instructions in the dialog boxes.

11. When you get to the final dialog box (shown in Figure 5.3), choose an option button to tell Access what you want to do next.

12. Select the **Finish** button to have Access create your table.

Displays the table in Datasheet view
so you can immediately enter records

Displays the table in Design
view so you can edit it

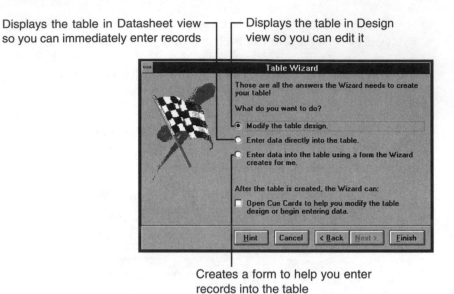

Creates a form to help you enter
records into the table

Figure 5.3 Tell Access what to do next.

This Isn't What I Wanted If you make a mistake when you're using the Table Wizard, don't worry. You can edit the finished table in Design view, just like a regular table.

In this lesson, you learned how to use the Table Wizard to customize an existing sample table. In the next lesson, you'll learn how to add records to your table.

Adding Data to a Table

In this lesson, you will learn how to add records to a table and print them.

Opening the Table

In the last three lessons, you created your database and added a table. Now it's time to place your facts and figures into their appropriate fields of the table. Every time you enter a complete row, filling all the fields, you have entered one complete *record* to the database.

Before you can add records to a table, you must open the database (if it is not already open) and the table. To open a database, choose **Open Database** from the **File** menu, or click on the **Open Database** button. Select the desired database, and click on **OK**.

Quick Return to the Window If a database is open, a Database window will be displayed. The title bar shows the name of the database. If the window is hidden under another window, use **F11** to quickly return to the open Database window.

When you have a database open (such as the one you created in earlier lessons), examine the Database window. Be sure the word **Tables** appears at the top of the list box. If not, click on the **Tables** button to the left of the list box. The list now displays the current tables in the database. Double-click on the name of the table you want, or select the desired table (such as PROSPT) and select **Open**. The table opens, showing empty rows and columns like a spreadsheet (see Figure 6.1). This is called the *Datasheet view*.

Datasheet View   A view of a table that displays the data in columns and rows, with the records as rows and the fields as columns. To change to Datasheet view from Design view, just click on the **Datasheet View** button in the toolbar.

Design View button ─┐   ┌─ Datasheet View button

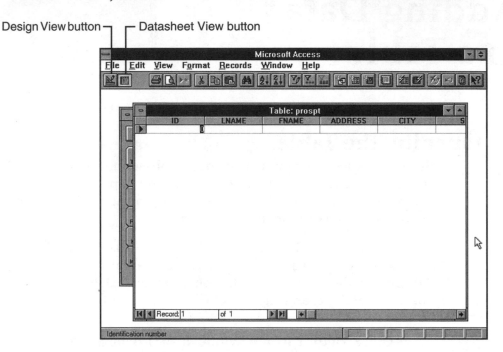

Figure 6.1   An empty datasheet for adding records.

Adding Records

If you have just created a table, there will be no records in the table. To add a record to the table, fill in the cells for the first row. Use the **Tab** key, the **Enter** key, or the arrow keys to move the cursor between the columns as you fill in the data. Pressing **Shift+Tab** moves you backward through the columns. After completing the entry of a record, you can press the **Tab** key to move to the first field of the next record and enter that record. Continue until you have added all the records you want to add (see Figure 6.2).

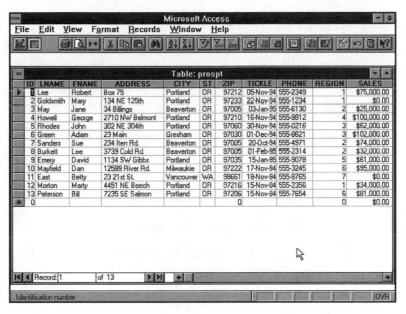

Figure 6.2 The datasheet after entering a few records.

Adding Records to Existing Records in a Table

If a table already contains records, any records you add will be placed at the end of the table. For example, open the PROSPT table you created in Lesson 3 (if it is not already open). At the end of the table, you will see an asterisk marking a blank or empty record. To add a record, you fill out this row, which in turn opens another record.

In the record selection area to the left of the first field, a right triangle marks the current record. If you start typing a new record without moving to the blank row, you will overwrite the data in the current record. If this happens, you can delete the new data by selecting it and choosing **Undo Saved Record** from the **Edit** menu. The new data is deleted, and the old data is restored. Close the table and database when you are finished adding records.

Saving Records

Microsoft Access saves your records to disk as you enter them. Each time you move the cursor to the next record, the program saves the record you just entered (or changed) automatically.

Printing a Datasheet

Sometimes, it's easier to look at your datasheet on paper than it is to scroll through it screen-by-screen on your monitor. You can print your datasheet by following these steps:

1. Make sure your datasheet is the active window.

2. Select **Print** from the **File** menu.

3. A dialog box appears, showing the options listed in Table 6.1. Select the print options you want.

4. When you're finished selecting options, click on **OK**. The table is printed.

Table 6.1 The Print Dialog Box Options

Option	Description
All	Print the entire datasheet.
Selection	Print only the selection you have highlighted.
Pages	Print only certain pages.
From	Use this box to enter the first page to print.
To	Use this box to enter the last page to print.
Print Quality	Enter a number, followed by **dpi** (dots per inch). A higher number means a better print quality.
Print to File	Check this box to print the datasheet to a file instead of to paper.
Copies	Type the number of copies you want.
Collate Copies	Have pages collated if you select more than one copy.

TIP

Print Preview If you want to see what your datasheet will look like before it's printed, select **Print Preview** from the **File** menu, or click on the **Print Preview** button on the toolbar. You can view different pages by clicking on the arrows at the bottom left of the window. To exit Print Preview, press **Esc**.

The Print dialog box lets you specify *what* you want to print, but you might need to change *how* your datasheet is printed. You do this from the Print Setup dialog box. If you select **Setup** from the Print dialog box or **Print Setup** from the **File** menu, the Print Setup dialog box is displayed. Using this dialog box, you can change any of the options shown in Table 6.2

Table 6.2 The Print Setup Dialog Box Options

Option	*Description*
Default Printer	Tell Access to print to the default printer.
Specific Printer	Tell Access to print to the printer of your choice.
Portrait	Print the datasheet across the shorter width of the paper (such as a person's portrait).
Landscape	Print the datasheet across the longer width of the paper (such as a landscape painting).
Size	Select the size of the paper to use.
Source	Specify whether you want to print from the paper tray or from your own paper (manual feed).
Margins	Specify Left, Right, Top, or Bottom margin sizes.
Data Only	Check this box to tell Access to print only the data on the datasheet (no embedded objects).

Can't Print? Access will display the **Print** command in the **File** menu only if you are in Datasheet view. To change to Datasheet view, click on the **Datasheet View** button on the toolbar.

Closing a Table

When you have finished entering data, you should close the table and database. This will ensure that everything is saved to the disk properly and no data is lost. To close the table, follow these steps:

1. Choose **Close** from the **File** menu. The table is saved to the disk and is no longer displayed.

2. When you are through with the database itself, close it by choosing **Close Database** from the **File** menu.

A Word to the Wise   Although Microsoft Access saves the records automatically as you enter them, a wise computer user will not trust this feature to ensure complete safety. You have no assurance that all your data is on the disk until the database is closed. If you plan to take a break from the computer, close the database; open it again when you return.

In this lesson, you learned how to add some records to a table, save the records, and print them. In the next lesson, you will learn how to edit your records.

Editing Records

In this lesson, you will learn how to move around in a datasheet, edit existing records, and move and copy data.

Moving Around in the Datasheet

Once your records are entered, you might discover a few errors that need to be corrected. Fortunately, moving around the datasheet is easy. You can use the shortcut keys in Table 7.1 to move the cursor.

Table 7.1 Moving Around with the Keyboard

Press	To
Tab	Move the cursor from left to right between fields of a record.
Shift+Tab	Move the cursor from right to left between fields of a record.
Arrow keys	Move up, down, right, or left.
PageUp	Scroll up through the datasheet one screen at a time.
PageDown	Scroll down through a datasheet one screen at a time.
Home	Move the cursor to the beginning of the current record.
End	Move the cursor to the end of the current record.
Ctrl+Home	Move the cursor to the first field of the first record.
Ctrl+End	Move the cursor to the last field of the last record.
Ctrl+PageUp	Move left one screen.
Ctrl+PageDown	Move right one screen.

You can also use the mouse to select any field of a record you want to edit: simply click on the desired field. You can use the scroll bars the same way you would use them in any Windows application (see Figure 7.1).

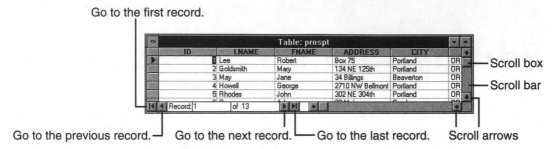

Figure 7.1 Use the scroll bars to move around the datasheet.

Editing Existing Records

To edit a record in a datasheet, first select the field in the datasheet you want to edit. Using the mouse, you can position the cursor anywhere in the field. Or you could use the keyboard to move to the field and do one of two things:

- **Replace the existing data** If the data in the field is highlighted, you can start typing. The highlighted data is deleted, and the new data replaces it.

- **Keep the existing data** If the data in the field is highlighted, but you don't want to delete everything, press **F2**; this lets you move around in the field with the arrow keys. When you're finished, press **F2** again.

Deleting Entire Records

If you want to delete an entire record, click on the row selection box to the far left of the record. An arrow appears in the box, and the entire record is highlighted. Select **Delete** from the **Edit** menu, or press the **Delete** key. A dialog box appears asking you to confirm your action. Click on **OK**.

Inserting a Record

Since Access sorts the database by the primary key field, new records are inserted in the proper sequence automatically. If you are using sequential numbers as your primary key fields, you have to renumber your records to allow for the new record (if it doesn't go at the end). If you have ten records, for example, and you need to insert a new record as number eight, you change the primary key fields in records eight, nine, and ten. Then you simply type a new record in the bottom row, using the number 8 in the primary key field. When Access saves the table, the records are in numerical order.

Copying and Moving Data in the Datasheet

You can use the Edit menu to simplify your editing by cutting or copying selected material and pasting it. Cutting a selection will move the data from the datasheet to the Windows Clipboard. Copying a selection will keep the data in its original place, as well as placing a copy in the Clipboard. To copy the data from the Clipboard, paste it to your datasheet.

Moving Records

Pretend you have a database exactly like the one in Figure 6.2. After typing the records, you realize that Marty Morton's ID number is actually 13, and Bill Peterson's number is 12. You could move Marty Morton's record by using the Cut command. Here's how:

1. Highlight the data you want to move. In this case, click on the row selection box to the left of the row to highlight Marty Morton's entire record.

2. Open the **Edit** menu, and select **Cut**.

3. A dialog box appears asking you to confirm your changes. Click on **OK**.

4. To paste the selection to a new location, first position the cursor in the correct row. In this case, move the cursor to the row beneath Bill Peterson's record.

5. Highlight an area that is exactly the same size as your selection. For this example, you would click on the row selection box to select the entire row.

6. Select **Paste** from the **Edit** menu.

To make your sample database correct, all you have to do now is change the ID numbers for Marty Morton and Bill Peterson.

Copying Records

Copying selected data is similar to cutting it. The only difference is that the data is not deleted from the original location. For example, seven of the people listed on the datasheet in Figure 6.2 live in Portland; instead of typing the city's name time after time, you can paste copies in each City field. To do this you would:

1. Highlight the data you want to copy. In this case, highlight **Portland** after the first time you type it.

2. Select **Copy** from the **Edit** menu. Access copies "Portland" to the Clipboard.

3. Position the cursor in the correct location. For our example, place the cursor in the City field.

4. Be sure that the area you select to paste the data to is the same size as the area of the data you copied to the Clipboard.

5. Select **Paste** from the **Edit** menu.

For our example, you could just select **Edit Paste** every time you have to enter "Portland"—as long as you don't cut or copy anything else to the Clipboard.

Duplicate Records?   If you are copying an entire record to a new location, be sure to change the data in the primary key field. You must have different information in each primary key field so Access can distinguish between records.

Appending Your Selection   If you want to paste your cut or copied data to the end of your datasheet, select **Paste Append** from the **Edit** menu. This automatically pastes your selection to the last empty record in your datasheet.

In this lesson, you learned how to move around in the datasheet and edit existing records. In the next lesson, you will learn how to edit and rearrange fields in the table structure.

Changing the Structure or the View of a Table

8

In this lesson, you'll learn how to modify a table's structure by deleting, inserting, and rearranging fields, and how to change the way the table appears onscreen.

Changing the Structure of a Table

Changing the structure of a table does not cause any data loss unless you delete a field or change the field properties to a format that doesn't support the existing data.

Safety First!   As a safety precaution, always save a database (back it up) before changing a table structure in the database. Do this by copying it to a backup floppy disk.

If you want to change a table's structure, first click on the **Design View** button on the toolbar to put the table in Design view.

Deleting a Field

You may decide you don't need a particular field anymore and want to delete it from the table. This will save disk space and simplify future data entry.

Fields Versus Records   Don't confuse the terms *field* and *record*. Fields are the pieces of information about each item in your table; they are stored as columns in the table. Records identify all the information about a particular item, and are stored as rows. All the information for Dan Mayfield, for example, might be stored as a single record (row). His address, city, state, ZIP, and telephone number are all fields in that record.

To delete a field, follow these steps:

1. If necessary, open the database using one of these methods:

   • Choose **Open Database** from the **File** menu.

   • Click on the **Open Database** button in the toolbar.

2. Choose the database file, and click on **OK**.

3. Click on the desired table name, and click on **Design**.

4. Click on the row selector for the row that defines the field to delete, or use the arrow keys and press **Shift+Spacebar** to highlight the row selector (see Figure 8.1).

Design View button

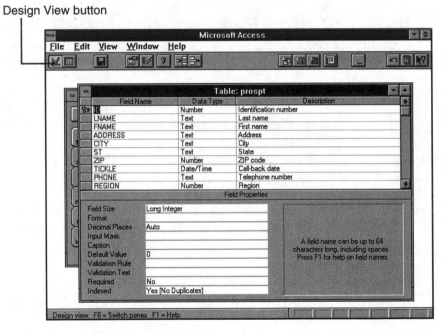

Figure 8.1 Table Design view.

5. Choose **Delete Row** from the **Edit** menu, or press the **Del** key.

6. Click on **OK** at the warning prompt.

The field and all the data in it are deleted.

Row Selector   The row selector is the triangle pointer in the space just to the left of the first column in the table.

Be Sure!   Be sure you have selected the correct field. Once you have deleted the field, all data in that field is lost. Data in other fields will not be affected. If you need to recover a deleted field, you must immediately choose **Undo Delete** from the **Edit** menu.

Inserting a Field

After you have created a table, you may want to add a new field. For example, after creating a database of a club membership, you may decide to add a field later that defines when the member first joined the club. Microsoft Access permits you to add new fields at any time without losing data in existing fields.

To add a new field:

1. If necessary, switch the display to Design view by clicking on the **Design View** button on the toolbar, or by choosing **Table Design** from the **View** menu (see Figure 8.1).

2. Click on the row selector for the row just below where you want to add the new field (or use the arrow keys to move to the row, and then press **Shift+Spacebar**).

3. Choose **Insert Row** from the **Edit** menu, or press the **Insert** key.

4. Define the new field by entering the field name, data type, and description (see Lesson 4 for more information).

Rearranging the Fields

There may be times when you want to rearrange the fields in a table. You may want to move a primary field (used for an index) so that you can use it as the first field, or (in our example database) you may want to move the phone number field so that it comes before the tickle field.

1. If necessary, switch the display to Design view by clicking on the **Design View** button on the toolbar, or by choosing **Table Design** from the **View** menu.

2. Select the entire row for the field you want to move.

3. Click on the row selector, and hold down the left mouse button. Then drag the row. When the row is where you want it to be, release the mouse button.

I Made a Mistake   If you decide the move is not what you want, you can undo the move by immediately choosing **Undo Move** from the **Edit** menu.

Changing the View of a Table

Changing the view of the table affects what you see in the Datasheet view, but doesn't change the basic underlying structure. For example, you can make a column smaller, but the structure doesn't change, and any data in the smaller column is not truncated.

Reordering a Field

Sometimes, you might want to change where a field appears in a datasheet without changing its order in the structure. For example, you might want to keep a primary key as the first field in the structure, but give it a more convenient location on the datasheet. To reorder a field position on the datasheet, follow these steps:

1. With the table in Datasheet view, position the pointer on the field selector (the area with the field name above the row). The pointer changes to a down arrow.

2. Click on the field selector to select the entire field.

3. Click on the field selector, hold down the left mouse button, and drag the column to the new position.

4. To deselect the field, click anywhere else in the datasheet.

Can't Undo   You can't undo a reordered field, but the process doesn't destroy any data. If you make a mistake, reorder the fields to return them to the way they were.

Resizing a Field or Column

Resizing a field's column width permits you to tighten up the view, which in turn lets you display more data at a time in the window. To resize the column width for a field, follow these steps:

1. Position the pointer to the right of the column you want to resize, on the line between the field titles. The pointer changes to indicate the border can be moved.

2. Drag the line until the column is the desired size.

You can resize a row in the same way, by dragging the line that separates the rows. Note, however, that resizing one row affects all the rows; they all resize at once.

Save Your Changes

You can use the **Save Table** command on the **File** menu to save the new layout. Once you have modified the database structure, choose **Close Database** from the **File** menu to save your changes.

In this lesson, you learned how to open a table, and how to delete, insert, rearrange, resize, and reorder fields in the table structure. In the next lesson, you will learn how to create a form.

Displaying Tables with Forms

In this lesson, you will learn how to create forms and arrange records in forms.

Introduction to Form Creation

Forms permit you to enter, edit, and display data a record at a time. If you use Datasheet view to enter records, usually all the fields are not visible at once; you have to scroll constantly as you add, edit, and view records. Using forms, you can see all of the fields of a single record at once. This simplifies data entry.

Microsoft Access includes a Form Wizards button to help you put together forms. This lesson shows you how to use it.

Creating a Form

To create a form, click on the **Form** button when the Database window is active. A list of all of the forms in the database appears. (If it's a new database, none are listed.)

To create a form, follow these steps:

1. Click on the **New** button in the Database window, and a New Form window appears.

2. Open the **Select a Table/Query** list box to display the tables from which you can build forms. In this example, use **PROSPT**.

3. Click on the name of the table for which you want to build a form.

4. Choose the **Form Wizards** button.

5. On the first Form Wizard screen, you are asked to choose an Access Wizard. Choose **Single-Column**, and then click on **OK** (see Figure 9.1).

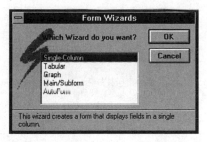

Figure 9.1   Choosing the type of form.

6. On the next screen, you are asked to select the fields you want displayed in the form (see Figure 9.2). Select the **>>** button if you want to move all your fields to the **Field order on form:** box on the right. Click on **Next >**. Another dialog box appears.

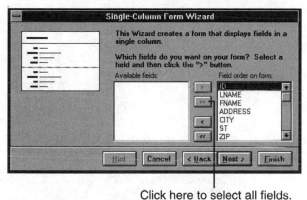

Click here to select all fields.

Figure 9.2   Choosing the fields for the form.

7. Figure 9.3 shows the third Form Wizard dialog box. Select a look for the form by choosing **Standard**, and then click on **Next >**.

8. On the next screen (shown in Figure 9.4), enter a title for the form, and click on **Finish**. Form Wizard creates the form and displays the table's first record in it (see Figure 9.5).

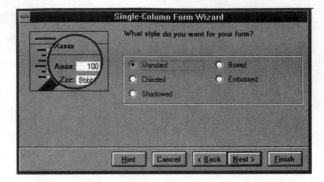

Figure 9.3   Choosing the type of format.

Figure 9.4   Entering the form's title.

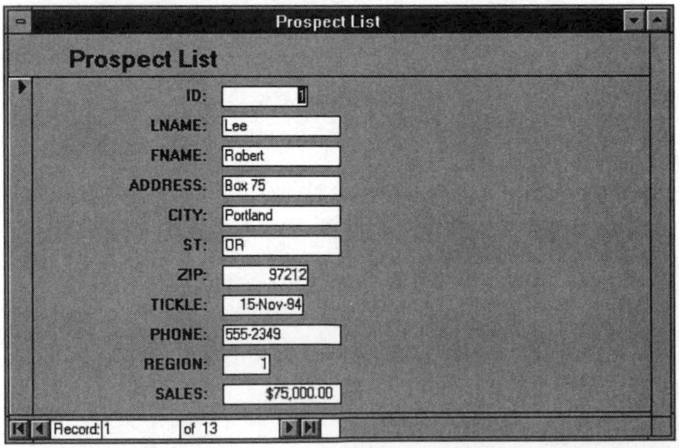

Figure 9.5   The final form.

Viewing Records with a Form

The form you have created can be used to display (view), add, change, delete, or print records. The various objects on the form are known as *controls*.

 Controls   On a form or report, a *control* is an object that displays data from a field, the result of a calculation, a label, graph, picture, or another object.

Areas of the form that are used for input (for text or numbers) are called *text boxes*. Labels identify each text box, as well as a title for the form. There may also be a *check box* on some forms for entering logical values. (The next lesson shows you other types of controls.)

To view a particular record, use the **Go To** command on the **Records** menu, or the navigation buttons at the bottom of the window. To return to a Datasheet view and see multiple records, click on the **Datasheet View** button on the toolbar, or select the **Datasheet** command on the **View** menu. Click on the **Form View** button (or select **Form** from the **View** menu) to return to the Form view.

Adding Records with a Form

Forms simplify adding records, as all fields of the new record are displayed at the same time. To add a new record with a form displayed, follow these steps:

1. From the **Records** menu, select **Go To**.

2. Select **New** from the list that appears.

3. Enter the data for each field. Press **Tab** to move the cursor forward between fields; press **Shift+Tab** to move backward through the fields. Or you can use the mouse to click on any field.

4. From the last field, press **Tab** to display an empty form for the next record.

 **Oops!**   Select the **Undo Current Field** command from the **Edit** menu if you need to restore a field. To restore a previously typed value, choose the **Undo Typing** command from the **Edit** menu.

Automatic Saving   As you enter or edit records, when you begin a new record, the previous record you entered or edited is saved automatically. You don't need to do anything else to save records as you enter them.

Saving the Form

Once the form design is completed, you should save the form if you intend to use it in the future. To save an open form, follow these steps:

1. Choose **Save Form As** from the **File** menu.

2. Enter the name of the form you want to save. (Avoid using the name of any existing table, query, report, or other form.)

3. Click on **OK**.

Printing Data with a Form

To print data using an open form, follow these steps:

1. Choose **Print** from the **File** menu.

2. Click on **OK**. The data is printed using the form.

 Print Preview   If you want to see what your form will look like before you print it, select **Print Preview** from the **File** menu, or click on the **Print Preview** button in the toolbar. To exit the Print Preview window, press **Esc**.

Closing a Form

When you are finished using a form, close it to remove it from the screen. To close a form, choose **Close** from the **File** menu. The new form's name will be on the list in the Database window.

In this lesson, you learned how to create a form using Form Wizard, and how to view a record in the form. In the next lesson, you will learn how to customize a form for your specific needs.

Creative Form Design

In this lesson, you will learn how to add, resize, and move the labels and text boxes on a form, and how to customize the text.

Modifying a Form Design

After you have created a form with Form Wizard (see Lesson 9), you may want to change the design. Microsoft Access makes this easy: you simply use the mouse to drag and resize.

To start redesigning a form, open your database, and click on the **Form** button in the Database window. The list of the current forms is displayed. Highlight the form you want to modify, and choose the **Design** button. The form opens in Design view (see Figure 10.1).

The Design View button is selected.

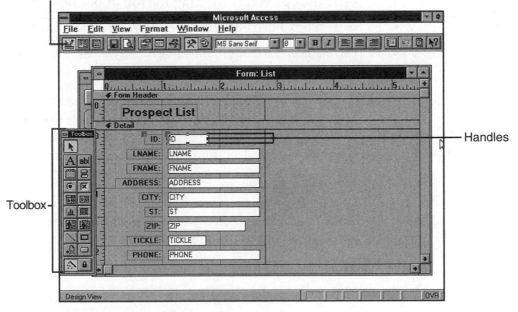

Figure 10.1 A form in Design view.

Notice the differences between this view and a normal form display. The title is now in a separate Form Header area, and an empty Form Footer area has been added. The labels and text boxes are in the Detail area. The toolbar is displayed by default, but you can change your options on the View menu so that the Field List or the Properties List is displayed. A *toolbox* is also displayed.

Toolbox   Notice that in Design view, a new window called a *toolbox* is displayed. It contains a special set of buttons that don't appear on the regular toolbar. You use these buttons to design forms. You can move the toolbox by dragging the top title bar, and you can turn it on or off from the View menu.

Resizing Controls

As you learned in Lesson 9, each object on the displayed form is called a *control*. In Design view, you can move and resize these controls and add new controls.

To manipulate a control, you must first select it. You select a text box with a label by clicking on the associated text box. The text box and its associated label are displayed with handles (see Figure 10.1).

- To resize the box vertically, drag the top or bottom handles.

- To resize a box horizontally, drag the right or left handles.

- To resize a box horizontally and vertically at the same time, drag the corner handles diagonally.

Aligning Your Work   You can use the rulers to align your work. The rulers should be displayed by default, but if they aren't, you can select them from the View menu.

More Than One   You can select more than one control at a time by holding down the **Shift** key as you select.

Moving Controls

Microsoft Access permits you to move a text box and its associated label together, or you can move each separately. To move them separately, select the control, and then drag the large handle in the upper left corner (this is known as the *move handle*). When you move the text box or label separately, the mouse pointer will look like a pointing hand.

To move the text box and label together, click on the control until the pointer looks like a hand with the palm showing. Now drag the text box and its label to the new position.

Keep Multiple Selections Aligned   To maintain the current alignment when moving multiple controls, select them together, and then move them.

Adding a Label

A *label* is simply text that is added to the form display information. The title that's already on the form is one type of label. You can add additional labels (such as your company name) to the form.

To add a label, use the special toolbox that appears the first time you open a form in Design view. (If it is not already displayed, choose **Toolbox** from the **View** menu.) Click on the **Label** button in the first row of the toolbox. Then click on the appropriate place, and enter the text for the label.

Customizing Text

You can modify any text by changing the font, size, color, alignment, and attributes (for example, normal, **bold**, *italic*). To change the appearance of text in a control:

1. Select the control you want to modify. If it contains text, the toolbar will display additional buttons for modifying the text (see Figure 10.2).

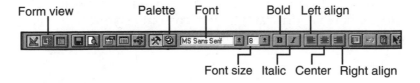

Figure 10.2   Modifying text using the toolbar.

2. To change the attributes, click on the **Bold** button or the **Italic** button on the toolbar.

3. To change the alignment, click on the Left, Center, or Right buttons on the toolbar.

4. If you want to change the font or font size, you have to set them from the toolbar. To change the font style, click on the arrow of the drop-down list box at the middle of the toolbar, and then click on the font. To change the font size, click on the drop-down list box to the right of the style box, and select the size you want.

After you have completed your work, resize the label to the new text by choosing **Size to Fit** from the **Format** menu. Now, you can modify the color of the text as needed. To set the color of the text, follow these steps:

1. Click on the **Palette** button, or select **Palette** from the **View** menu.

2. From the Palette window (see Figure 10.3), you can set the color of the text or you can set separate colors for fill and outline (simply click on the color of your choice). You can also set the appearance of the text (normal, raised, or sunken) and the border width.

Choose any button.

Click on a color.

Figure 10.2 The Palette window.

The buttons at the top of the Palette window control the appearance and border type. Leave the mouse pointer momentarily on any button for help on what each button does. (The status line in the main window gives even more information.) The color bars in the work area of the window change the foreground, background, and border colors. Again, for a more descriptive title, leave the mouse pointer momentarily on the bar.

In this lesson, you learned how to move and resize controls, how to add a label to a form, and how to customize your text. In the next lesson, you'll learn how to make a list box on your form.

Creating a List Box on a Form

In this lesson, you'll learn how to add a list box to a form.

Using a List Box

Sometimes, it's faster and easier to select a previously defined choice from a list box than to type in text. For example, in the sample database from Lesson 9 (which we'll continue to use in this lesson), all customers live in one of five cities. For the sake of the example, let's assume that all of your future prospects will also live in one of those cities. Rather than type in the name of the city each time (and take the chance of making a typo), you could create a list box that lists those five cities so that you can simply choose a city with one click. Access provides a List Box Wizard to help you create just such a list box.

To create a list box for your CITY field, follow these steps:

1. With the form in Design view, clear an area with sufficient room for the list box. In this example, we will create a list box for the city field, so delete the current city field (select the text box label, and press the **Delete** key).

2. Select each field below the city field (except for the State and ZIP fields), and delete them. (This is just to simplify our work for this example form.)

3. Move the State and ZIP fields down to provide more room for the City list box you will create.

4. Click on the **List Box** button in the Toolbox (shown in Figure 11.1).

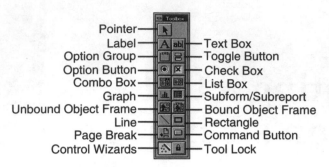

Figure 11.1 The Toolbox.

5. Your mouse pointer will look like a plus sign (+) and will include the List Box icon as you move it into the design area. (Don't hold the mouse button down, just move the mouse.)

6. When the pointer is positioned where you want to put the list box, press the left mouse button, and drag the pointer to ecreate the list box. The point at which you start to drag will be one corner of the list box; the ending point will be the opposite corner.

7. A List Box Wizard appears (see Figure 11.2). Click on the option specifying that you will type in the values (the city list) that you want, and then click on **Next >**.

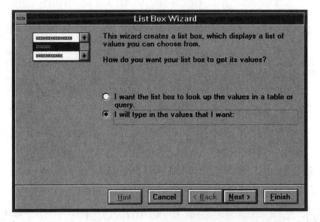

Figure 11.2 Defining the values.

8. In the next List Box Wizard window (see Figure 11.3), set the number of columns to **1** and enter the list of the valid cities you want to choose from. (For this example, type **Portland**, **Beaverton**, **Gresham**, **Vancouver**, and **Milwaukie**.) Then click on **Next >**.

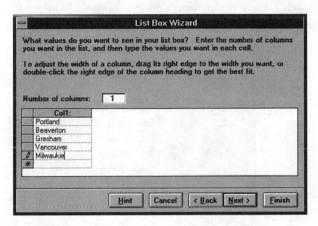

Figure 11.3   Defining the number of columns and the values.

9. On the next List Box Wizard screen (Figure 11.4), click on **Store that value in this field:**. Click on the arrow to open the list box, and select **CITY** for the field. Click on **Next >**.

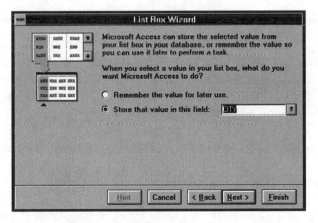

Figure 11.4   Defining the field for the value.

10. In the next window, enter **CITY** for the list box label, and click on **Finish**.

The new form is now displayed with the new list box. You can edit the form and move controls as necessary.

To see how your new list box looks in the form, click on the **Form View** button, or select **Form** from the **View** menu (see Figure 11.5). If the form doesn't look right, you can go back to Design view and change it. If you have scroll bars in your box and don't want them, you can make your list box longer by resizing it in Design view.

List box——

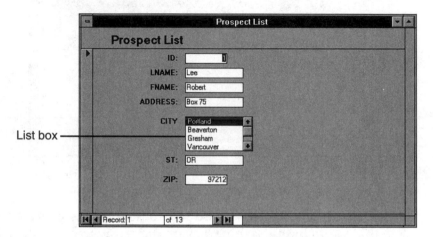

Figure 11.5 The finished form with the list box.

TIP

List Versus Combo Instead of making a list box, you might want to make a *combo box*, so you are not restricted to preset choices. A combo box lets you type a value or choose from a list. To make one, select the **Combo Box** icon from the Toolbox, and follow the steps for making a list box. With a combo box, your choices aren't displayed automatically; you have to select the down arrow button to see them.

TIP

Save It! Be sure to save the form if you want to keep it (choose **Save** from the **File** menu). Close the form when you are through using it by choosing **Close** from the **File** menu.

In this lesson, you learned how to add a list box to your form. In the next lesson, you will learn how to query your database for more information.

Getting Information from a Database

In this lesson, you'll learn how to query a database.

Introduction to Queries

Most of the time you will want to know some specific information when using a database. You won't want to look at the entire database—you just want specific data for making a decision.

The PROSPECT database for sales, for example, might contain hundreds of names, each with its own tickle date (a date that indicates when that person should be contacted again) entered from the previous call. Suppose, as a salesperson, you want only the names that have today's date as the tickle date. To do that, you can build a *query* to access the database and retrieve only the names that meet this criterion. Then you can print a report from the query containing only those names and phone numbers.

What's a Query? A query works much like a question directed at a database. In effect, it asks (for example) "Who are the prospects that have today's date as the tickle date?" The query has a *condition* built into it: "What records have a tickle date *equal to* today's date?"

Creating a Query

Now let's first create a query for the PROSPECT table. Then, we'll modify the query for using it to get today's prospects from the same table using today's date.

1. If the database is not open already, open it so that the Database window is displayed.

2. Click on the **Query** icon. The list window displays any current queries on the database. (In this example, there are none.)

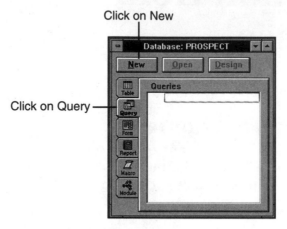

Figure 12.1 The Database window.

3. Click on the **New** button to begin creating a new query.

4. In the next window, you can choose to use the Query Wizard or to create a new query. Choose **New Query**. The Add Table dialog box is displayed (Figure 12.2) with a query grid behind it.

5. Select the table(s) you want to use for the query. (In this example, select the **PROSPT** table.) Choose **Add**. If you are selecting more than one, choose **Add** after each one.

6. After the last table is selected, choose **Close**. The fields of the table are displayed in a list box in the Query window. Any field that is used as a primary key appears in boldface.

7. Using the mouse, drag the fields you want to see in the query to the Field row of the QBE grid (see Figure 12.3). Place the fields in the columns in the same order you want them to follow the query. In this example, you would drag TICKLE, LNAME, FNAME, PHONE, and REGION one at a time to the Field row.

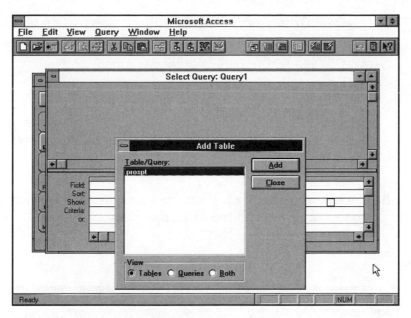

Figure 12.2 Adding the tables.

Datasheet View button

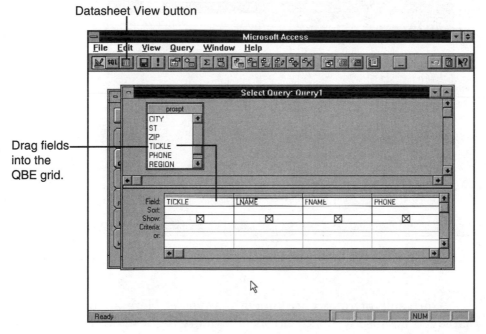

Drag fields into the QBE grid.

Figure 12.3 Drag the selected fields from the field list into the Field row of the QBE grid.

QBE Grid   As you create a query, you use a table called a *QBE grid* to define grouping, sort order, and criteria. QBE stands for Query By Example.

Add Fields Fast   You can also use the drop-down list in each Field cell to add a field. Click on the down arrow, and then click on the field name you want to use.

8. Click on the **Datasheet View** button to see the results of the query. Figure 12.4 shows the result of the query.

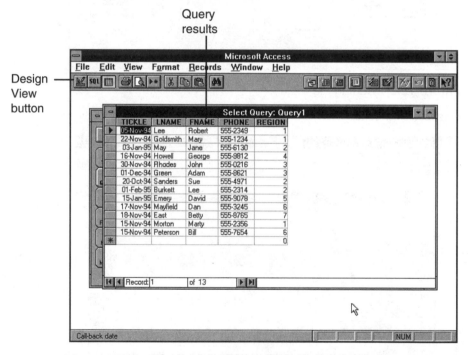

Figure 12.4   The results of the query.

The results of a query are known as a *dynaset*. Here, all the records are displayed because we made no specific query request; no condition was specified.

Dynaset When you select Datasheet view after you design the query, you will see a dynaset: a dynamic set of records that meet the requirements you asked for in the query. It is considered *dynamic* because the query results change every time you change the data. Each dynaset is temporary; it is not saved. Every time you query a database or change an existing query's design, Access creates a new dynaset.

Now click on the **Design View** button to return to Design view, or choose **Query Design** from the **View** menu.

Selecting Specific Records

Now, suppose we want only specific records from the table, such as those with today's date as the tickle date. To do this, you must specify criteria.

Criteria Criteria are conditions that a record must meet to be included in the dynaset. As Access creates a dynaset, it will include only the records that meet the criteria you set. In our example, there is just one criterion: the tickle date.

You can use the Criteria row in the QBE grid to specify the conditions for record selection. If today's date were November 15, 1994 and you wanted records for this date only, you could enter 15-Nov-94 as the criterion in the column with the field name TICKLE. Notice that after you press **Enter** to complete the entry, the date format changes. Pound signs (#) are added before and after the date. (If you were doing a text match, as with the LNAME column, quotation marks would appear around the text.)

Select the **Datasheet View** button again. Only those records with the November 15, 1994 tickle date appear in the dynaset (see Figure 12.5).

Specifying Additional Criteria

By adding and combining criteria in the Query window, you can create powerful queries that meet complex conditions. If you have specified criteria for more than one field (for example, November 15, 1994 for TICKLE and 1 for REGION), a record must meet all the conditions for each field before the query will include it.

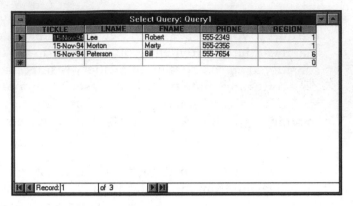

Figure 12.5   The final dynaset.

You can also specify that you want to retrieve any record that matches one of multiple conditions (an *OR condition*). Assume that you were leaving town for a few days and needed to take with you a list of prospects who would need to be contacted during that time. You could specify as a condition **>=15-Nov-94 AND<=17-Nov-94**. You could also specify as criteria a list of values using the IN function, as IN(CA,OR,WA) for the ST field. (IN is an operator that permits the entry, in this example, of any one of the values within the parentheses.)

Saving the Query

When you have finished designing your query, save the query by selecting the **Save As** command from the **File** menu. In this example, save the query as PROSPQ.

Beware of Table Names   When you save your query, *do not* use the name of any table in the database. If you do, saving the query overwrites the table, and you will lose all your table data. You will get a warning message, but it's easy to ignore the message—especially if you're in a hurry.

In this lesson, you learned how to query a database. In the next lesson, you will learn how to modify and print the queried data.

Modifying and Printing Queries

In this lesson, you will learn how to edit tables from a query, modify a query, calculate totals, and print the results of a query.

Editing Tables from a Query

When you run a query on a single table, you can edit the table directly from the displayed query. Display the query in Datasheet view and edit it as you would the original table. (See Lessons 7 and 8 for a review of editing tables.)

Can't Edit a Query? If two or more tables are linked in a query, there may be ambiguity regarding which table contains the data. In that case, Microsoft Access may not let you edit the data in the query (see Lesson 20).

Modifying a Query

Queries can be modified to include new fields, new criteria, or reordered columns. You can modify queries in Query Design view (Figure 13.1). To enter Query Design view, click on **Query**, select the query from the list, and click the **Design** button.

Selecting Columns

To add, delete, or insert columns, you must first select a column to specify where the action is to occur. To select a column, click above the column (in the *field selector*). When you position your mouse in the right spot, the mouse pointer changes to a down arrow. Clicking there highlights the entire column.

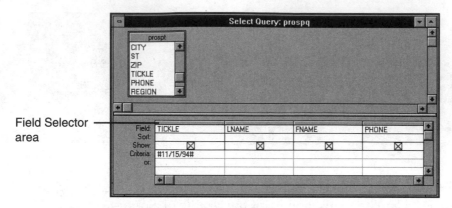

Field Selector area

Figure 13.1   The Query Design screen.

Field Selector   The cell area over the top cell of each column. When you click on this area, the entire column is highlighted.

Modifying the Criteria

You can modify the criteria at any time by editing the criteria row of the QBE grid. The criteria specifies the condition that must be met for inclusion.

Moving a Column

To move a column in a query, follow these steps:

1. Select the column of the field to move. (You learned to select columns earlier in this lesson.)

2. Drag the column to the new location with your mouse.

Deleting a Column

To delete a column in a query, follow these steps:

1. Select the entire column you want to delete, as you learned earlier.

2. Choose **Delete Column** from the **Edit** menu, or press **Del**.

Inserting a Column

To insert a blank column into a query, follow these steps:

1. Select the column to the right of where you want to insert the new column.

2. Choose **Insert Column** from the **Edit** menu.

3. Choose a field name from the drop-down list box in the top cell.

Resizing a Column

You may want to resize a column, for example, to get more data on the screen. To resize a column in a dynaset, drag the border of the field selector.

Hiding a Column

There may be times when you want to hide a column in a dynaset. For example, you may want to specify criteria for a field but prefer not to display that field in the Datasheet view. To hide a column, click on the check box on the Show line for that column. An **X** in the check box indicates that the column will be displayed. The X disappears from the box to show that the column will not be displayed in the dynaset.

Calculating Totals

You can also use a query to show totals. For example, assume the sales to each customer are added to the query, but you want to see only the total sales for each region. You would follow these steps:

1. Add only the fields necessary for the calculations. For our example, you would delete all columns except the REGION and SALES columns.

2. Click on the **Totals** button in the toolbar, or select **Totals** from the **View** menu. A new row called **Total** appears just below the Field row (see Figure 13.2).

3. Click on the **Total** row in the column you want to calculate. In our example, you'd click on the **Total** row in the **SALES** column.

4. Use the drop-down list box to select the type of calculation you want. In our example, you want the total sales, so select **Sum**.

5. To see the results of your query, click on the **Datasheet View** button, or select **Datasheet** from the **View** menu. In our example's table, the SALES column will show the total sales for each region.

Totals button

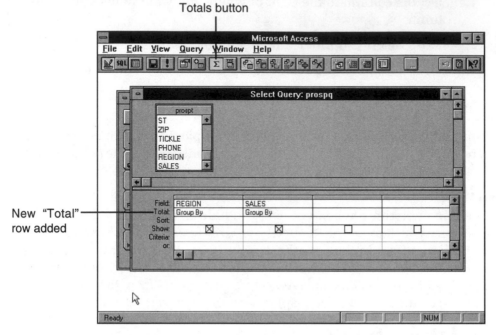

Figure 13.2 The Total row appears below the Field row.

Printing the Dynaset

If your query results are important, it's a good idea to have a printout of your dynaset (the query results). To print the dynaset, be sure the Query is in Datasheet view, and then follow these steps:

1. Select **Print** from the **File** menu.

2. Select any options desired from the Print dialog box.

3. Click on **OK** to print.

Print Preview   If you want to see what your dynaset will look like before it is printed, select **Print Preview** from the **File** menu, or click on the **Print Preview** button on the toolbar. You can view different pages by clicking on the arrows at the bottom left of the window. To exit Print Preview, press **Esc**.

In this lesson, you learned how to modify a query, calculate totals of columns, and print a dynaset. In the next lesson, you will learn how to find data using a form.

Finding Data Using Forms

In this lesson, you will learn how to use forms to find specific data in tables, and how to use forms with filters to create data subsets.

Tables, Forms, or Queries?

Using tables to find data has limitations. With a table, you can usually see only a few fields at a time. However, forms and queries allow you to get around the size limitations of a table. With a form, you can find specific data, create subsets of data, sort data to a specific order, and locate data that meets specific criteria.

Using an Existing Form To follow the instructions in this lesson, you'll need to have a form already created. If you haven't created any forms yet, turn to Lesson 8, and create one now.

Finding Data Using a Form

If you need to find data quickly and you don't want to take the time to build a query, use a form. You can do a simple search to locate the record you need. For example, suppose you need a telephone number for a certain prospect quickly. Let's see how to find it!

To find a value quickly, follow these steps:

1. Open the form if it is not already open. (In the Database window, click on the **Form** button, and then double-click on the form name.)

2. Select the field to search by clicking on the title of the field, or by pressing the **Tab** key until the field is selected. For our example, you would select the PHONE field.

3. Click on the **Find** button in the toolbar, or choose **Find** from the **Edit** menu.

4. When the Find in field dialog box appears, enter the data you want to find in the Find What text box (see Figure 14.1).

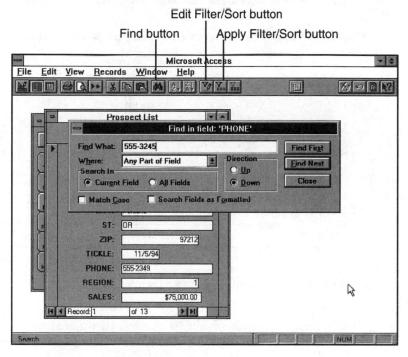

Figure 14.1 Finding data in a record.

5. Select the **Where** drop-down list, and click on an option. Not sure which one you want? They're listed in Table 14.1.

6. Click on the **Find First** button. Access finds the first occurrence of the data you specified.

7. If this is not the record you want, choose the **Find Next** button to move to the next occurrence.

8. When the search is complete, a dialog box appears, asking if you want to start the search from the top again. Choose **No**, and click the **Close** button.

Can't See Your Form? If you can't see your form because the dialog box is in the way, move the dialog box by dragging its title bar to a new location.

Table 14.1 Options for the Find in Field Dialog Box

"Where" lets you choose the location within each field:

Option	Description
Any Part of Field	Matches the data you specify in every occurrence.
Match Whole Field	Matches only the text you specify.
Start of Field	Finds only the matches that occur at the beginning of a field.

"Search In" lets you specify which fields:

Option	Description
Current Field	Searches only the highlighted field.
All Fields	Searches every field.

"Direction" specifies how to search the database:

Option	Description
Up	Searches toward the beginning of the table.
Down	Searches toward the end of the table.

The two remaining check boxes at the bottom set additional options:

Option	Description
Match Case	Finds only the matches that are in the same case as the data you specify.
Search Fields as Formatted	Finds matches based on how they appear on-screen, not the format they were stored in.

Creating a Filter

You might want to display all the records that contain certain information instead of viewing them one by one with the Find command. Or you might want to specify criteria in more than one field. To accomplish either one, use a filter to create a subset of specific data.

Filter A *filter* uses the data you specify to create a temporary datasheet of records (called a *subset*). A filter can be created only when you are using a form, never from a table or query.

Subset A *subset* is a group of records that contain the data you specified in the filter. A subset is similar to a query's dynaset.

For example, suppose you want to view a subset of the prospects in Region 1 from the PROSPECT database. Follow these steps to create a filter:

1. Open the form if it is not already open.

2. Click on the **Edit Filter/Sort** button on the toolbar, or choose **Edit Filter/Sort** from the **Records** menu. The Filter window opens (see Figure 14.2).

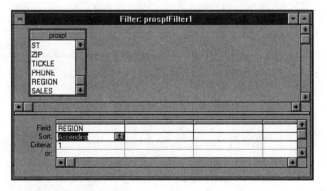

Figure 14.2 The Filter window.

No Calculations Allowed   Notice that you can define the criteria and select the sort order, but you can't perform calculations (as you can in a query).

4. From the field list, drag the desired field to the Field row. For our example, drag the REGION field to the first cell in the first column.

5. Enter the data you want Access to search for in the Criteria row. For example, you would type the number **1** in the Criteria row to tell Access to search for all of the REGION fields that contain the number **1**.

6. Open the drop-down list in the Sort row, and select the sort order. In our example, you would choose **Ascending** so the prospects would be in region order.

7. To see the subset, click on the **Apply Filter/Sort** button on the toolbar, or choose **Apply Filter/Sort** from the **Records** menu.

8. Click on the **Datasheet View** button to see all the records in the region you selected (see Figure 14.3).

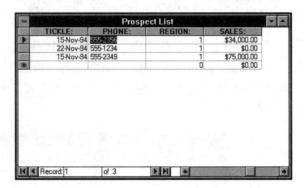

Figure 14.3   The results of using a filter.

Don't Panic!   Subsets, much like dynasets, are only temporary datasheets. When you create a filter, you are not changing your data in any way. Access is simply extracting the information you want from your table, and displaying it in a form that's easier to understand.

Saving the Results

Because subsets are temporary, they cannot be saved. However, filters that create subsets can be saved as queries. To save a filter, select **Save As Query** from the **File** menu when you are in the Filter window. Name your filter, and then press **Enter** or click on **OK**.

Naming Filters When saving the filter as a query, don't use the name of any existing table or query or the existing one will be overwritten.

Using a Filter Saved as a Query

After you have saved a filter as a query, you can open it from a form whenever you want. You can also open it as a regular query from the Query list in the Database window. To open a filter from a form, follow these steps:

1. Click on the **Edit Filter/Sort** button on the toolbar, or select **Edit Filter/Sort** from the **Records** menu.

2. Select **Load from Query** from the **File** menu. A dialog box appears.

3. Choose the filter you want to use, and click on **OK**.

4. Click on the **Apply Filter/Sort** button on the toolbar, or select **Apply Filter/Sort** from the **Records** menu.

In this lesson, you learned how to find data using the Find command and using a filter. In the next lesson, you will learn how to create and use indexes.

Indexing Your Data

In this lesson, you will learn how to create single field and multiple field indexes.

Indexes are used to access a specific record in a table quickly. If you have large tables, you will find that using an index speeds up the process of locating records. The index tells Access where to find the data in the table (as with an index in a book). You can then use the Find command to search within the indexed field for a particular value.

Unlike subsets and dynasets, you cannot see an index. It is not a tool for viewing data, it is simply a way for Access to find your data more quickly. For example, suppose you have a large table that stores records of clients. You search this table often for names of certain people, using the LNAME field. In this situation, using an index would allow you to find the data you need quickly.

Don't Slow Down   Indexes are saved along with the table, and are updated automatically when you make changes in the indexed fields. If you need to make many changes to data in an indexed field, remove the index (you'll learn how later in this lesson), update the fields, and then re-index. This is much faster than having Access try to update all of the indexed fields each time you make a change.

To create an index:

1. Click on the **Design View** button on the toolbar if you are not already in Table Design view.

2. Click on the field you want to index. Its properties will be shown in the window at the bottom of the screen. For our example, click on the **LNAME** field.

3. Click on the **Indexed** field in the Field Properties box.

4. Use the drop-down list box to select the conditions for your index.

In step 4, you can tell Access not to accept any duplicate values in the field, or you can specify that duplicate values are okay (see Figure 15.1). In our example, choose **Yes (Duplicates OK)** because there might be more than one customer with the same last name.

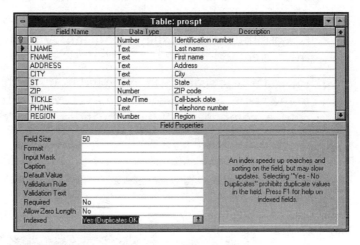

Figure 15.1   Creating an index for a field.

Primary Key Fields   When you create a primary key field (see Lesson 4), Access automatically creates an index on that field and maintains the index as you update the records in the table. The index property will be set for **Yes** (No Duplicates) so that Access can use the primary key field to distinguish between the records in the table.

Multiple Field Indexes

If you have a large table, you might search for records using criteria in two different fields. In that case, you should consider creating indexes for the two (or more) fields you search most often.

For example, our sample table from the last section contains names of our clients. If we have hundreds of records, chances are good that there are several people who have the same last name. If you are searching for a client named Susan Jones, it's easier for Access to find a specific match if you create an index on the FNAME field as well.

To create a multiple-field index, follow these steps:

1. Click on the **Design View** button on the toolbar if you are not already in Table Design view.

2. Choose **Indexes** from the **View** menu. A window appears showing the current indexes.

3. Enter a row for each field in the index, but include the index name in the first row only (see Figure 15.2). Microsoft Access treats all rows as components of the same index until it comes to a row containing another index name.

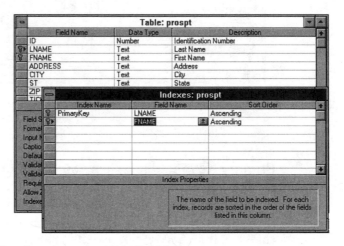

Figure 15.2   Creating a multiple field index.

4. (Optional) If you need to insert a row, click the right mouse button on the row above where you want to insert the new one. Then choose **Edit Insert Row**.

5. To save changes to the table or indexes, choose **Save** from the **File** menu.

Deleting Indexes

You can create as many indexes as you need, but remember that using them will slow down the process of updating your records. You should index only those fields you search often. If you want to delete an index for a field that you don't search often, change the Indexed property to **No** using the drop-down list in the Field Properties box.

To delete a multiple-field index, select the index in the Indexes window, and press **Delete**.

What Am I Deleting? When you delete an index, you aren't actually deleting any data. Your fields and the data in them remain exactly the same. You are simply telling Access that it doesn't have to remember where your records are for that field any more.

Searching for Records

Once you have created an index, you can use the Find command to search for the data you need. To find a record from a table in Datasheet view, follow these steps:

1. Click on the **Find** button on the toolbar, or select **Find** from the **Edit** menu. The Find in field dialog box appears.

2. In the Find What text box, enter the data you want to find.

3. Choose any of the options listed for the Find in field dialog box (for the list, see Table 12.1).

4. Choose **Find First**. Access finds the first occurrence of the data you specified.

5. If this is not the record you want, choose the **Find Next** button to move to the next occurrence.

6. When the search is complete, a dialog box appears asking if you want to start the search from the top again. Choose **No**, and then close the Find in field dialog box.

In this lesson, you learned how to use indexes. In the next lesson, you will learn how to create reports.

Creating and Using Reports

In this lesson, you will learn how to create a simple report from a table.

Reports are useful for communicating to people in an organized way. With Microsoft Access, the best ways to communicate your message is with a form or a report. Lesson 8 showed you how to use forms to communicate your message. In this lesson we'll look at using reports.

Which should you use? Forms are useful for doing simple reporting, as well as for viewing and editing your data. They are limited, however, in that you can't group data to show group and grand totals, you have less control over the layout, and you can't insert a report into a form. Reports can't be used to view or edit data, but allow you to have more layout control, to group data for totals, and to insert another report or graph into a report.

Creating a Report

Microsoft Access includes a Report Wizard feature that makes it easy to create reports from tables or queries. You will use it in this lesson to create a report from a table.

To create a report, open the database if it is not already open. (Select **Open Database** from the **File** menu, or click on the **Open Database** icon on the toolbar.) When the Database window is displayed, choose the **Report** button at the left, and then select **New**. You have your choice of using the Report Wizards or a Blank Report, as shown in Figure 16.1.

Figure 16.1 You can choose the Wizard, or choose to go it alone.

In the Select A Table/Query text box, click on the down arrow at the right. A list box opens, displaying available tables from which you can build reports. Click on the name of the desired table for the report. Then select **Report Wizards**.

The following steps walk you through creating a report with the Report Wizard:

1. On the first screen, select **Single-Column** as the Wizard you want to use, and then click on **OK**.

2. Choose the fields for the report or select >> to move all the fields to the Field order on report list box (see Figure 16.2). Then choose **Next >**.

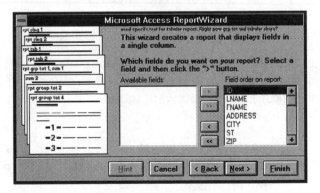

Figure 16.2 Choosing the fields to report.

3. Choose the field(s) you want to sort by, and click on **Next >**.

4. Choose the look for the report. For our example, choose **Executive** (see Figure 16.3), and click on **Next >**.

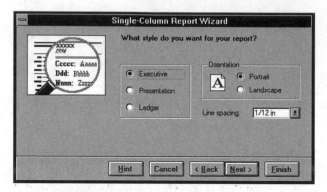

Figure 16.3 Choosing the style of the report.

5. Enter a title for the report, and then click on **Finish**. Report Wizard creates the report and displays a preview of what will print.

Previewing the Report

The preview mode gives you an idea of what the report will look like and the number of pages that will print before you actually print it. The pages will be magnified, and you can scroll through them using the horizontal and vertical scroll bars. You can use the Page buttons at the bottom of the window to scroll through the pages. The inside arrows move you a page at a time; the outside arrows move you quickly to the first or last page.

To see the entire page, move the cursor to the page (it becomes a small magnifying glass), and click. You can return to the magnified view again by clicking where you want to view.

Preview at Any Time   You can always return to the preview mode of a given report by choosing **Print Preview** from the **File** menu.

Printing the Report

You can print the report by choosing the **Print** button on the toolbar or by choosing **Print** from the **File** menu. A Print dialog box appears. Set the options you want, and click on **OK**.

Saving the Report

When you have created the report, you should save it. To save the report, choose **Save As** from the **File** menu. Enter the name under which you want to save the report (such as PROSPR), and click on **OK**. Do not use the name of any existing table, query, or form.

In this lesson, you learned how to create a report. In the next lesson, you will learn how to create custom reports.

Creating Custom Reports

In this lesson, you will learn how to customize a report form.

Modifying a Report Form

You can modify your report form in various ways. For example, you can move items to other locations, resize them, add labels, and set text attributes. To modify a report, follow these steps:

1. Open the database, and choose the **Report** button in the Database window. The list shows all existing reports in the database.

2. Highlight the report you want to modify, and choose the **Design** button in the Database window. The report is displayed (see Figure 17.1). It can be modified, much like a form.

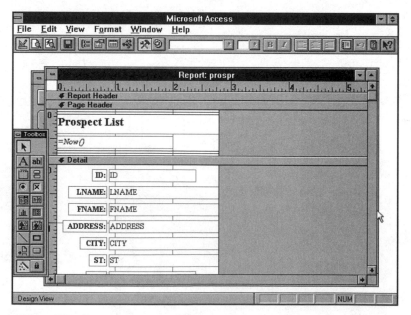

Figure 17.1 The Report Design view.

Resizing Controls

Each object on the displayed report is a *control*. In the report's Design view, you can move and resize the controls, as well as add new controls.

Control   An object on a report or form that displays the data in a field, a calculation result, specific text, a graph, a picture, or another object.

To manipulate a control, you must first select it. To select a text box with a label, click on the associated text box. The text box and its associated label will be displayed with handles (see Figure 17.2). The handles allow you to change the control in any way you like:

- To resize the box vertically, drag the top or bottom handle.

- To resize a box horizontally, drag the right or left handle.

- To resize a box horizontally and vertically at the same time, drag the corner handles diagonally.

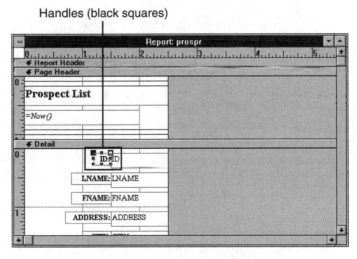

Figure 17.2   Handles surround the selected control.

Use the displayed rulers to align your work. You can select more than one control at a time by holding down the **Shift** key and clicking on them.

Moving Controls

Microsoft Access permits you to move a text box and its associated label together or separately. To move a text box or label separately, select the control, and then drag the large handle in the upper left corner. This handle is known as the *move handle*.

To move the text box and label together, click on a control. When the pointer becomes a flat-palm hand, drag the text box and its label to the new position.

 Use the Rulers The rulers can help with alignment when moving and resizing controls.

Adding a Label

A *label* is simply text that is added to the report at a later time to display information. The title that's already on the report is one type of label. You can add additional text, such as your company name, to the report. The label is not bound to any other control.

To add a label, you use the Toolbox. The Toolbox appears when you open a report in Design view; if it's not on-screen, choose **Toolbox** from the **View** menu to display it. Click on the **Label** button (at the left in the second row; it's the button with the large **A** on it). Then click in the report where you want the label to appear, and enter the text for the label.

Customizing Text

You can modify any report text by changing the font, size, color, alignment, and attributes (normal, bold, italic). To change the appearance of text in a control, follow these steps:

1. Click on the control you want to modify.

2. Click on any of the following toolbar buttons to customize the text:

Button	Function
B	Toggles boldface on or off.
I	Toggles italics on or off.

Button	Function
	Sets the text to left alignment.
	Centers the text in the margins.
	Sets the text to right alignment.
Times New Roma	Selects the desired font.
10	Sets the font size.

3. To set the color of the text, click on the **Palette** button, or select **Palette** from the **View** menu. From the Palette window (see Figure 17.3), you can set the color of the text, or you can set separate fill and outline colors. You can also set the appearance of the text (normal, raised, sunken) and the border width. Double-click on the Palette window's Control-menu box to close the window when you're finished.

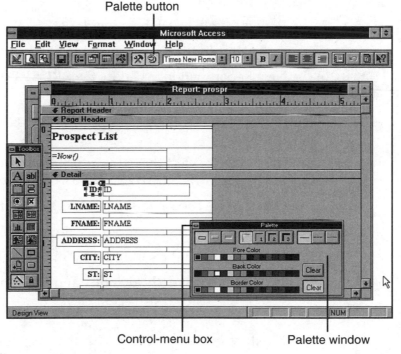

Figure 17.3 The Palette window.

4. After you have completed your work, choose **Size to Fit** from the **Format** menu to resize the label to the new text.

Toggle?   To *toggle* means to change between two alternating stakes. (A light switch toggles between on and off.)

Adding a Field to a Report

You can add fields to a report form after it is created. Open the report in Design view, and then open the field list. You can then drag fields to the appropriate place on the report.

Creating a Report with Grouped Data

You can use Microsoft Access to create reports with grouped data, showing subtotals and totals. For example, suppose you want to create a report showing sales by region with the grand sales total. You would use Report Wizard to create the report from the same table. Use these options for the Report Wizard:

1. Select **Report** from the Database window.

2. Click on the **New** button in the Database window.

3. In the New Report window, choose the **PROSPT** table from the list box, and then choose **Report Wizards**.

4. On the screen that selects the Report Wizard, select **Groups/Totals**. Click on **OK**.

5. On the next screen, select the fields to print and their order. Select **ID, LNAME, FNAME, REGION**, and **SALES**. Click on **Next >**.

6. On the next screen, choose to sort by **REGION**. Click on **Next >**.

7. On the next screen, choose to group as **Normal**. Click on **Next >**.

8. On the next screen, set the sort order to **SALES**. Click on **Next >**.

9. Set the look to **Executive** (the default), and click on **Next >**.

10. Enter the title, and choose **Finish** to see the report.

This procedure creates a report with the sales totalled by region, including a grand total.

In this lesson, you learned how to customize reports. In the next lesson, you will learn how to create mailing labels.

Creating Mailing Labels

In this lesson, you'll learn how to create and print simple mailing labels from your data in the database.

Creating mailing labels is an important part of using address lists effectively. For example, you could print labels from the PROSPT prospect list created in Lesson 5, and use them to mail brochures or letters to the prospects.

Mailing labels come in many sizes and types. Some labels are designed for sprocket-feed printers that pull the labels through. Other labels come in sheets and are designed for laser printers. Labels can also come in single, two, or three-column sheets. Microsoft Access is capable of printing addresses on a wide variety of label types and most common label sizes.

Don't Gum It Up! Use the proper labels for your printer! The adhesive gum used with standard peel-off labels cannot withstand the high temperatures of a laser printer. The labels can come off inside the printer and jam. There are special peel-off labels designed for use in laser printers.

Creating a Mailing Label Report

To make mailing labels, use Report Wizard to create a report in a mailing label format. You can save the report and use it again later.

Let's use the table created in Lesson 5 as an example. If you prefer, you can use any sample database with an address table (such as the Customer table in the NWIND database provided with Access). Follow these steps:

1. If the database is not already open, open it by selecting the **Open Database** command from the **File** menu or clicking on the **Open Database** button.

2. When the Database window is displayed, choose the **Report** button at the left, and then select **New**. The New Report dialog box appears (see Figure 18.1).

Figure 18.1   The New Report dialog box.

3. Open the drop-down list for the Select A Table/Query box. You'll see the list of available tables and queries.

4. Select the name of the table you want to use for the mailing labels.

5. Click on the **Report Wizards** button.

6. On the first ReportWizard screen, choose **Mailing Label**, and then click on **OK** (see Figure 18.2).

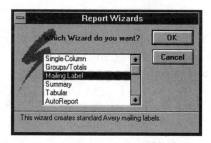

Figure 18.2   Choosing the mailing label report type.

7. In the Available fields list, select the first field you want to include on the mailing label, and then click on the right arrow button (>) to move it into the Label appearance box (see Figure 18.3).

Click here to move a field name onto the label.

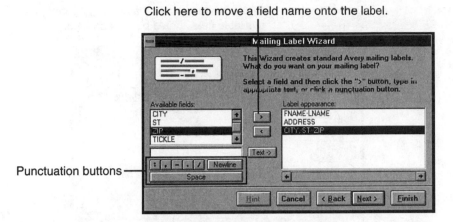

Punctuation buttons

Figure 18.3 Entering the mailing label design.

8. Use the Punctuation buttons to enter the punctuation desired after the field. For example, you might choose **Space** between the FNAME and LNAME fields, and then choose **NewLine** to start the ADDRESS on the next line.

What If I Make a Mistake? If you make a mistake, click on the left arrow button to move an entry back into the left-hand column.

9. Repeat steps 7 and 8 until the entire address appears in the Label appearance box. Then click on **Next >**.

10. To indicate how the labels should be sorted, select a field name in the Available fields box, and then click on the right arrow button (Figure 18.4). For example, you might want to sort by LNAME or ZIP. Then click on **Next >**.

11. To choose the size of the mailing label, choose the correct size from the list, and then click on **Next >**.

12. Choose the font and color for the mailing label, and then click on **Next >**.

13. On the last screen, click on **Finish**. Report Wizard creates the mailing label report and displays a preview of what will print.

Click here to indicate that the highlighted
available field should be the sort field.

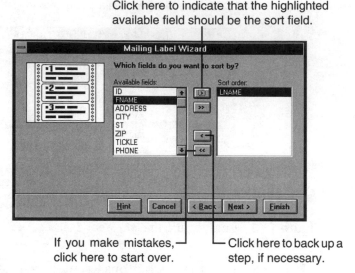

If you make mistakes,
click here to start over.

Click here to back up a
step, if necessary.

Figure 18.4 Choosing the sort order.

Previewing the Report

The preview mode gives you an idea of what the mailing labels will look like; however, this view of the labels will be magnified. You can use the horizontal and vertical scroll bars to scroll through them. Or you can use the page buttons at the bottom of the window. (The inside arrows move you a "page" at a time; the outside arrows move you quickly to the first or last label.)

To see the entire "page," move the cursor to the page (the cursor becomes a small magnifying glass), and click. You can return to the magnified view again by clicking where you want to view.

You can always return to the preview mode of the mailing label report by clicking on the **Print Preview** button on the toolbar or choosing **Print Preview** from the **File** menu.

Printing the Mailing Labels

You can print the labels by following these steps:

1. Choose the **Print** button on the Print Preview window, or choose **Print** from the **File** menu A Print dialog box is displayed.

2. Set the options you want.

3. Choose **OK**.

Saving the Mailing Label Report

After you have created the mailing label report, you should save it for future use. To save the report, follow these steps:

1. Choose **Save As** from the **File** menu.

2. Enter the name you want to use for saving the mailing label report. Do not use the name of any existing table, query, or form.

3. Click on **OK**.

In this lesson, you learned how to create and print mailing labels. In the next lesson, you will learn how to create graphs.

Creating Graphs

19

In this lesson, you will learn how to add a graph to a report.

Introduction to Graphing

Graphs show information in visual relationships and are especially useful for people who don't have time to read an entire report. A busy manager, for example, may find it quicker to look at a graph of sales by region than to decipher a statistical report.

Lesson 5's PROSPECT database shows sales by region, so this lesson will refer to it. (You can use any database, including the Access samples, to try the procedure; in that case, the database, table, and field names will be different.) First, we will create a query on which the report will be based. Then, we will create the report without the graph, using the Report Wizard. Finally, we will add the graph with the Graph Wizard.

Creating the Query

First let's create the query that shows sales by region. To open the database (if necessary), choose **Query** and **New** in the Database window.

1. Choose the **New Query** button in the New Query dialog box.

2. In the Add Table window, choose **PROSPT**, and click on the **Add** button.

3. Click on the **Close** button to close the Add Table window.

4. Scroll to find REGION in the list box. Drag **REGION** from the list to the first cell of the Field row of the grid.

5. Drag **SALES** from the list into the Field row of the grid.

6. Click on the **Totals** button in the toolbar (or select **Totals** from the **View** menu) to add a Total row to the grid.

7. The cell under the Field row's SALES cell now contains the words **Group By**. Click on this **Group By** cell to open a drop-down list box, and click on **Sum**.

8. Click on the **Datasheet View** button on the toolbar to verify the totals in a dynaset.

9. Save the query (as SALESQ for this example), using the **Save Query As** command on the **File** menu.

10. Press **F11** (or close the Query window) to return to the Database window.

Creating the Report

Now that this query has shown us sales by region, use Report Wizard to create a report based on the query.

1. Click on **Report** and then **New** in the Database window.

2. In the Select A Table/Query list box in the New Report dialog box, select the query you just created and saved (SALESQ).

3. Choose **Report Wizards**.

4. Select **Single-Column**, and click **OK**.

5. On the next screen, choose the field for the report, and click on the > button to move it to the right column. Or select >> to move both the fields to the list box. Then click on **Next >**.

6. On the next screen, choose the sort order (REGION) from the fields, and then click on **Next >**.

7. On the next screen, choose **Executive**, and click on **Next >**.

8. On the next screen, enter a title, and click on **Finish**. When the finished report is shown on-screen, scroll through it, and verify that the report totals are correct.

Adding the Graph

Now add the graph to the report by following these steps:

1. Set the report to Design view by clicking on the **Close Window** button on the toolbar.

2. Scroll down the Report window so that you have 2–3 inches of space under the footer section.

3. Click on the **Graph** button in the Toolbox (see Figure 19.1). If the Toolbox isn't showing, select **Toolbox** from the **View** menu.

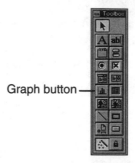

Graph button —

Figure 19.1   The Graph button in the Toolbox.

4. Using the mouse, drag to draw a control in the area below the report footer section for the graph. Make it about two inches high and six inches wide; use the rulers as necessary. (This will be the size not only of the control, but of the eventual graph.) When you complete the drag, a dialog box will appear (see Figure 19.2).

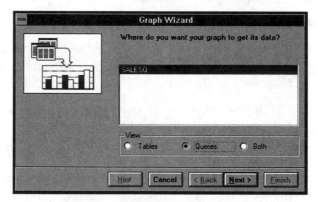

Figure 19.2   The Graph Wizard dialog box.

5. Click on the **Queries** option button in the View section of the dialog box. Then choose the query on which you want to base the graph (SALESQ), and click on **Next >**.

6. In the next box, select the field for the graph. Choose **SumOfSALES** and **>**, and then click on **Next >**.

7. The next box asks whether to link the graph to the data; choose **No**. This means the graph won't change if the table's data is changed.

8. Choose the **Add (sum) the numbers** option button, and then click on the **Finish** button.

Choose **Print Preview** on the **File** menu to see the report with the graph.

Editing the Graph

If you want to edit the graph, switch to Design view (by clicking on the **Design View** button). This will open the graph in Microsoft Graph, a modular program that comes with Access (and which resembles the chart mode of Excel, Microsoft's spreadsheet program). You can now add labels or titles, and even change the chart type, from the menu. To return to Access, choose **Exit and Return to Microsoft Access** from the **File** menu.

Printing the Report and Graph

When you are finished creating your report, you should save it (using the **Save As** command on the **File** menu). You can then print the report and graph by following these steps:

1. Choose the **Print** button on the toolbar, or select **Print** from the **File** menu.

2. In the Print dialog box, set the option you want.

3. Click on **OK**.

In this lesson, you learned how to create a graph to use with a report. In the next lesson, you will learn how to use macros to automate your work.

Automating Your Work

In this lesson, you will learn how to automate your work using macros.

After you have used Microsoft Access for a short while, you will probably find there are a few tasks you do repeatedly (for example, opening a form and going to the end of a table to enter records). Such an action can be automated so that a single command will set up a table for data entry. You can do this with a *macro*.

Macro   A series of actions that you program Microsoft Access to perform for you automatically when you enter a command.

Creating a Macro

Let's say that you want to create a macro to open a form, open a table, and display an empty form at the end of the table for data entry. Open the database, and then follow these steps:

1. Click on the **Macro** button in the Database window, and choose **New**.

2. Select **Tile** from the **Window** menu so that you can see the Database window and the Macro window at the same time (see Figure 20.1).

Macro Window   The Macro window is a two-column sheet in which you enter the actions you want the macro to execute. Many of the actions have *arguments*, which are additional information that you supply to specify how you want the action carried out.

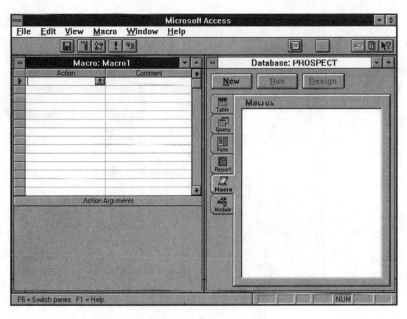

Figure 20.1 Database and Macro windows tiled so you can see both.

3. Click on the **Form** button on the Database window, and drag the desired form from the Database window to the upper left cell of the Macro sheet. **OpenForm** appears in the cell (see Figure 20.2).

4. Click in the cell directly under **OpenForm** on the Macro window, and then open its drop-down list. Select **DoMenuItem**.

5. In the Action Arguments area, click on the **Menu Name** field (currently containing Edit) and open its drop-down list. Choose **Records** as the Menu item. In the same way, set **Go To** as the Command, and **New** as the Subcommand. Figure 20.3 shows how it should look.

6. Save the Macro window using the **Save As** command from the **File** menu. Enter a macro name, such as PROSPM. Click **OK**.

7. Close the Macro window by double-clicking on its Control-menu box or by selecting **Close** from the **File** menu. The Database window should still be open.

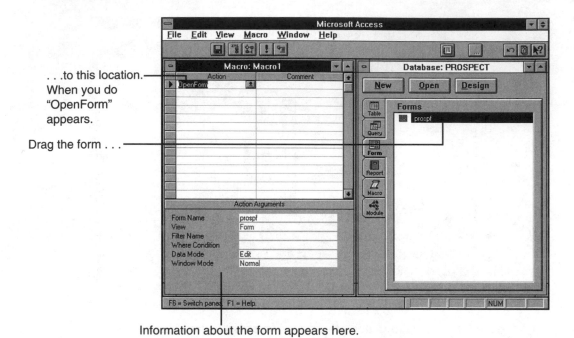

...to this location. When you do "OpenForm" appears.

Drag the form . . .

Information about the form appears here.

Figure 20.2 Entering the Action Arguments.

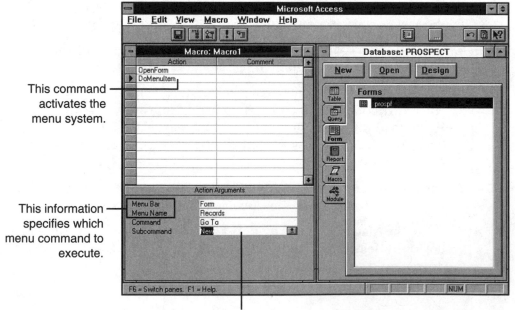

This command activates the menu system.

This information specifies which menu command to execute.

You can change each entry by clicking on it and using its drop-down list.

Figure 20.3 Editing the command arguments.

Executing the Macro

You have now created a macro and saved it. (A macro must be saved before you can execute it.) To execute the macro you have just created, follow these steps:

1. Choose **Run Macro** from the **File** menu.

2. Select the name of the macro.

3. Choose **OK**. Access runs the macro. In our example, it opens the table and form, and then displays the form positioned after the last record in the table, ready for a new entry.

There are also other ways of executing a macro. For example, on the Database window you could select the **Macro** tab and double-click on the desired macro. Another method you can use (when the Macro window is open) is to click on the exclamation point in the Macro window's toolbar.

Buttons for Launching Macros   You can also use buttons to run macros. For example, if you drag a macro name from the Database window to a form, you will see a new button on the form. You can click on this button to launch the macro. With this trick, you can use a macro to open a second form from the first one or to copy data from a previous form entry to the current form entry (such as a city or state).

More with Macros

Once you have had some experience with Microsoft Access, you can create macros for doing much of the routine work (for example, copying data from one form to another). Macros can do it faster, and help ensure that it's done correctly. For more help on macros, see the on-line help or your documentation.

In this lesson, you learned how to create and use macros in Microsoft Access. In the next lesson, you will learn how to share your data with other programs.

Using Data with Other Programs

In this lesson, you will learn how to share data between Microsoft Access and other programs you may be using.

Importing, Exporting, and Attaching

You may have already created data files in other programs, such as Microsoft Excel, Lotus 1-2-3, dBASE IV, or Paradox. You can use these data files in Access to build reports, print mailing labels, and do queries. You can also export Access data for use with these other programs.

- When data in an Access database table is converted to a format usable by an *external* program, this is called *exporting* the data. Access keeps the original file intact and creates a duplicate in a format suitable for the external program's use. The two files are not connected; that is, updating one does not update the other.

External Database An *external* database is one that is not a part of your open Microsoft Access database. You import data from or export data to an external database.

- When foreign data is converted to Access format for use in Access, you are *importing* the data. Access reads the file and creates a duplicate of it in its own language. Both files remain separate; updating one does not update the other.

- You can also *attach* an external database to a Microsoft Access database. This is slower than importing the data, but it enables you to view, edit, or report from the other program's data as though it were in Access format without actually converting it. In this case, there is only a single file; users of the other program can continue to use it, even while you are updating or reporting from its data in Access.

Exporting Data

When you export data, you are creating a file in the format of another program. Beginning with an open database (such as PROSPECT), let's try an example: exporting a table in the format of dBASE (a Borland database product). Follow these steps:

1. With the Database window active, choose **Export** from the **File** menu.

2. In the **D**ata Destination list box of the Export window, choose the destination format—for example, dBASE IV—as shown in Figure 21.1. Click on **OK**.

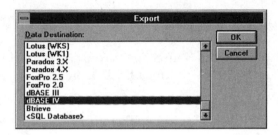

Figure 21.1   Starting an export.

3. In the Select Microsoft Access Object window, choose the table name from the list. For example, choose **PROSPT**.

4. Click on the **Tables** button in the View section at the bottom of the dialog box. Click on **OK**.

5. In the Export to File dialog box, enter the name of the destination file (see Figure 21.2). Select the drive and directory also, if necessary. Click on **OK**.

Enter the name of the destination file.

Choose a directory.

Choose a drive.

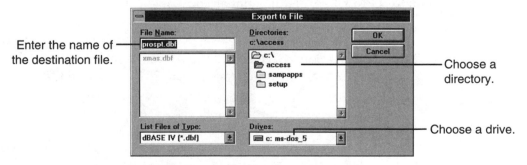

Figure 21.2   Choosing a name for the destination file.

The destination file is created in the desired format. In this case, the file PROSPT.DBF is created.

Importing Data

When you import data, you are creating an Access table from a file in another program's format. This file could be in any of several formats, including Microsoft Excel, Lotus 1-2-3, Paradox, dBASE IV, or an Access file from another database.

As an example, let's see how to import the file we just created. Open a database (such as PROSPECT) if one is not already open. Then follow these steps:

1. With the Database window open, choose **Import** from the **File** menu.

2. In the **Data** Source list box of the Import window, choose the type of input file to import. Click on **OK**.

3. In the Select File dialog box, choose the drive and directory for the input file and the name of the file you want to import. Select **Import**.

4. After importing, the screen will display the message **Successfully Imported** *xxxx*. Click on **OK** in the message box. The message will vary with the type of file imported.

5. Click on **Close** to close the Select File dialog box. The Database window will be displayed with the new table name.

Attaching Data

To use an external data file as if it were a table within Access, you can attach an external data file to an Access database. First, open the desired database (such as PROSPECT) if it is not already open.

1. Choose **Attach Table** from the **File** menu.

2. In the Data Source list box of the Attach window, choose the type of file you want to attach (see Figure 21.3). Click on **OK**.

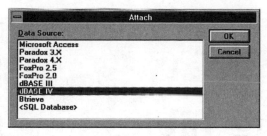

Figure 21.3 Choosing the type of file to attach.

3. In the Select File dialog box, choose the drive, directory, and name of the file you are attaching. Then click on the **Attach** button.

4. If there is an index file (or files), the Select Index Files dialog box will appear. Select any necessary index file if requested, and choose **Select** when finished.

5. Choose **Close** from the Select File dialog box.

The table is attached to your Access database. You can use it for reports, queries, mailing labels, or graphs as you would any other table.

Do I Attach, Export, or Import? Using attached tables slows Microsoft Access considerably, but they do make it possible to do your additions, edits, deletions, and reporting from a single file. This makes data control more reliable. Importing and exporting are best suited for moving data permanently between programs, particularly when the data is on different machines.

In this lesson, you learned how to import tables to, export tables from, and attach tables to Microsoft Access. In the next lesson, you will learn how to minimize data duplication by joining tables.

Joining Tables

In this lesson, you will learn how to join tables to minimize data duplication.

Why Join Tables?

Here's an example of a situation where joining two tables makes sense. In the database example used in these lessons, a REGION code identified the sales area for the prospects. It would be better to identify regions fully with text (such as Vancouver), but all that duplicated text would make the database's main table too large. It saves space to put the region's full identification in a separate table, give each region a code, and use the region codes in the prospect table. Then, we can join the two tables in a query and have the query use the region codes to display the text that identifies each prospect. Let's try it!

Create the Table

First create the new table for the regions.

1. Open the database, and click on the **Table** button if necessary. Then click on the **New** button.

2. In the dialog box that appears, click on the **New Table** button. Design view is displayed for a new table.

3. Enter **REGION** as a field name with a Number format.

4. Enter **REGION_NAME** as a field with a text format.

5. Select the **REGION** field, and in the properties for this field, click on **Format**. Set the Format to **General Number**.

6. Set the primary key by clicking in the **REGION** row, and then clicking on the **Key** button in the toolbar (see Figure 22.1).

Datasheet View button   Key button

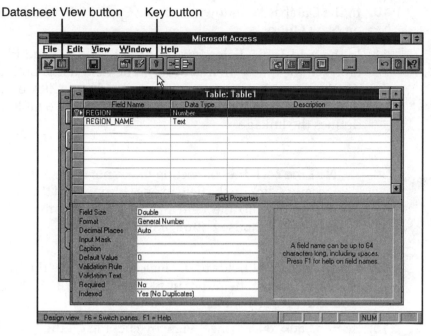

Figure 22.1   Select REGION as the primary key.

7. Save the table as REGIONS (using the **Save As** command from the **File** menu).

8. Click on the **Datasheet View** button to view the datasheet, and then enter the following data:

Under REGION	Under REGION_NAME
1	NE
2	Beaverton
3	Gresham
4	NW
5	SW
6	SE
7	Vancouver

9. Close the table to remove it from the screen.

10. In the Database window, select the **Query** tab. Choose **New**. Click on **New Query**.

11. In the Add Table dialog box, add the REGIONS and PROSPT tables to the query (in that order). The field list of both tables is displayed, with the primary keys in boldface. Click on **Close**. A line connects the two REGIONS fields in the two tables. This line defines the linkage.

No Line? If the connecting line is not there, you can create it easily. Click on the field in one column, and then drag your mouse over to the field in the other column. When you release the mouse button, a line appears.

12. Drag the desired fields to the Field row. Be sure the REGION and REGION_NAME fields are used (see Figure 22.2). Drag a few more from the PROSPT table.

13. Switch back to Datasheet view by clicking on the **Datasheet View** button.

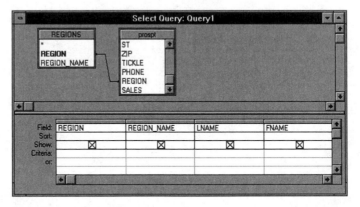

Figure 22.2 Linked tables in a query.

You will see that the link is correct, with each record showing the correct region name. If you save and close the query and table now, the link will remain. The next time you open the query, you will not need to re-establish the link.

Link Trouble?   Links can be a problem when you are editing a file from a query. If you need to do this and Microsoft Access won't let you, delete the link; re-establish it after editing.

Deleting a Link

To delete a link in Design view, click on the link to select it. Then press the **Delete** key. The linking line disappears, and the tables are no longer linked.

In this lesson, you learned how to create and delete links between tables. Congratulations! You've learned how to use Access to create databases, enter and edit data, build forms, use queries, and create reports.

OLE

Understanding Object Linking and Embedding

In this lesson, you'll learn some important OLE terms and learn the difference between pasting, linking, and embedding.

What Is Object Linking and Embedding (OLE)?

OLE (pronounced "oh-LAY") stands for *Object Linking and Embedding*. It is a Windows feature that enables the Windows applications that employ it to transparently share information.

For example, you might create a quarterly report in Microsoft Word that contains an Excel Chart and a list of employees created in an Access database. Each quarter, the Excel data in the chart and the employee list changes. When it comes time to generate the next quarterly report, you could try to find the most up-to-date version of the Excel chart and the employee list, copy and paste them into the report, or you could use OLE's linking and embedding features to automatically update the report with the changes made in each supporting document.

To understand how to use OLE you'll need to learn the terms listed below.

Compound Document   A document that contains links to other Windows documents. The linked parts are called objects. For example, a Word document containing a pie chart from Excel (an object) is a compound document.

Object   Objects are the pieces of data that you either link to, or embed in, a compound document. An object can be any size, from a small snippet of text to an entire multi-page spreadsheet. Examples include: a range of Excel cells containing numeric data, a company logo created in a drawing application, a sound clip created in Microsoft Sound Recorder.

713

Client Application   The client application is the application in which you're assembling the compound document. The client application receives objects created in other applications and places them in the compound document. For example, if you create a Quarterly Report in Microsoft Word that contains linked objects from Access and Excel, Word is the client application.

Server Application   A server application is a Windows application that created an object being linked to a compound document. For example, if you create a presentation in PowerPoint that contains an object created in Excel, Excel is the server application (and PowerPoint is the client application.)

Source Document   A source document is the document that contains the object you are linking. For example, if you are placing an Excel chart into a PowerPoint presentation, the Excel worksheet that contains the desired chart is the source document.

Destination Document   Destination document is another word for compound document. The destination document is the document into which the objects are placed (linked or embedded). For example, a Word document that contains an Excel chart (an object) is a destination document.

What Is Linking?

Now that you understand some of the terms associated with OLE, let's look at what linking (the "L" in OLE) entails, and examine some examples.

When a linked object is placed in a compound document, any changes you make to the object in its native application (the server application) are automatically made to the copy of the object in the compound document.

For example, let's revisit the quarterly report mentioned earlier in the lesson. In quarter 1, when the report is first created in Word, spreadsheet data from Excel and database data from Access are placed as linked objects in the report. Over the course of the quarter, changes are made in Excel and Access to the data. When it is time to assemble the report for quarter 2, the user simply opens the report in Word. The object links are still there, and the changed data from Excel and Access is automatically updated in the report. Figure 1.1 shows an example of some Excel data in a Word report.

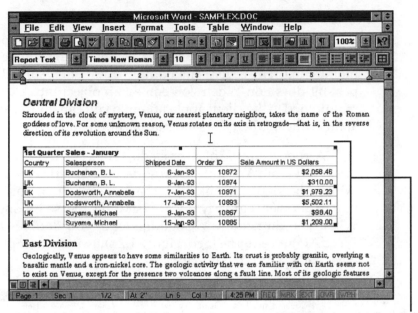

This table is actually a linked piece of an Excel worksheet.

Figure 1.1 An example of a compound document containing linked objects

One way to create links such as just described is with the Paste Special command on the Edit menu. It works a little differently from the regular Paste command on the Edit menu.

When an object is pasted into a document with the regular Paste command, the object is simply dropped in, with no information about its origin. In contrast, when an object is pasted into a document with Paste Special, several pieces of information about the object are stored as part of the destination document, including the source document's name and location, the server application, and the location of the object within the source document. This extra information is what makes it possible for the object to be updated whenever the source document is updated.

You'll learn the specifics about how to link objects in lessons that follow.

What Is Embedding?

When you embed an object, you insert a copy of it into your document, like the regular Paste command does. A link to the source document is not maintained. However, embedding does offer something that regular pasting does not. When you embed an object into a document, a link is maintained to the client application, so you can double-click on that object at any time to open the server application and edit the object.

A good example of an embedded object is a company logo created in Microsoft WordArt, embedded as part of a letterhead document created in Word. The logo is not likely to change very often, nor is it maintained as part of another regularly updated graphic file, so linking is not necessary. When you do need to change the logo, you double-click on it to open WordArt and edit the logo. Figure 1.2 shows an example of an embedded object in a Word document.

This logo is embedded.

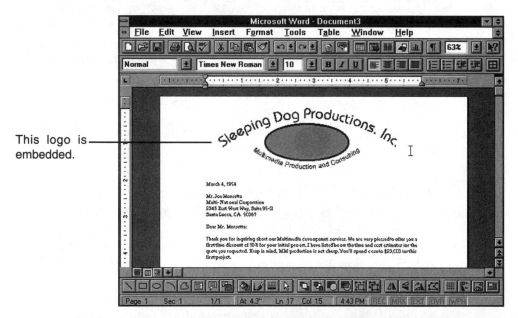

Figure 1.2   An embedded WordArt graphic in Microsoft Word.

As an embedded object, all the information about the logo is maintained in the letterhead document, so you do not have to worry about managing or locating a separate file for the logo.

The Paste Special command can also be used to embed as well as to link. You choose linking versus embedding by making the choice in the Paste Special dialog box. The Insert Object command can be used to link or embed as well. You'll learn more about these commands in later lessons.

In this lesson, you learned some important terminology you'll see repeatedly in the following lessons. In the next lesson, you'll learn the difference between Paste Special and Insert Object, two methods of linking and embedding.

Paste Special and Insert Object

In this lesson, you'll be introduced to two ways to create an OLE link: the Paste Special command and the Insert Object command.

Linking and Embedding with Paste Special

As you've learned in other sections of this book, Windows offers a simple cut-and-paste feature that enables you to cut or copy from any Windows program and paste your selection into any other Windows program. This is accomplished with the Cut or Copy command on the Edit menu and then the Paste command (on the same menu).

To create an OLE link (linked, embedded, or both), you also can use the Copy command, but instead of choosing Paste, you select Paste Special. This opens the Paste Special dialog box, which is used to inform Windows how you want the special linking or embedding to occur.

Exploring the Paste Special Dialog box

After you've Copied the desired object to the Clipboard, the Paste Special command on the Edit menu becomes available. When you select **Paste Special**, the Paste Special dialog box appears. Figure 2.1 shows the Paste Special dialog for Word. The following list explains the options found there.

Source   This is the name and location of the object currently in the Windows Clipboard.

Paste   Pastes the contents of the Window Clipboard into the document at the location of the insertion point. The link is not maintained.

718

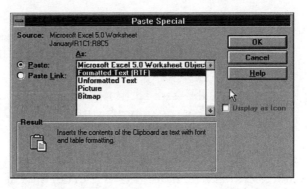

Figure 2.1   The Paste Special dialog box.

Paste Link   This option is available if the contents of the Clipboard can be linked to the destination document. With this option selected, a link is created between the source document and the destination document. If you have not saved the source document using Save or Save As, the Paste Link option is not available.

As   This section of the dialog box lists the possible formats the object in the Clipboard can be pasted as. The formats listed change depending on the object type. Some formats you might see include:

...Object   A type that ends with the word Object is a recognized OLE-capable format that you can either link or embed. If you want to embed, so you can activate the source application and change the object later, you should choose a data type that ends with the word "object."

Formatted Text (RTF)   This data type formats text as it is formatted in the source document. If the text is formatted as bold italic, it is pasted as bold italic. This format does not support embedding.

Unformatted Text   No formatting is applied to the object when this data type is selected. This format does not support embedding.

Picture   This data type formats the object as a Window metafile picture, but does not support embedding.

Bitmap   This data type formats the object as a bitmap picture, such as a Windows Paintbrush image. It does not support embedding.

Display As Icon   Selecting this option displays the pasted object as an icon of the object, rather than the object data. This option is only available if you have selected Paste Link. This is useful for pasting Sounds and MediaClips.

Result   The Result section of the dialog box gives a description of the outcome of the options you've selected in the dialog box.

Some Hints for Linking and Embedding

When deciding which options to select in the Paste Special dialog box, pay close attention to the notes that appear in the Result area. These notes tell you what will happen if you choose **OK** with the present set of options.

The type of linking, embedding, or pasting that is done depends both on your choice of **Paste** or **Paste Link** and your choice of type in the **As** list. Here's an example for a Bitmap picture cropped from Paintbrush:

Paste/Paste Link	Data type from As list	Result
Paste	Paintbrush Picture Object	Embeds but does not link
Paste	Bitmap	Neither embeds nor links
Paste Link	Paintbrush Picture Object	Links and embeds
Paste Link	Bitmap	Links and embeds

Edit It   When you double-click on a Paintbrush image in Word that is not embedded, instead of Paintbrush opening to edit it, Microsoft Draw opens (a simple drawing program that comes with Word).

Linking and Embedding with Insert Object

Another method of linking and embedding objects in a document is to use the **Object** command on the **Insert** menu. This command is useful if you have not yet created the object in the source application, or if you want to insert an entire document as your object (rather than a cut or copied piece of one).

Exploring the Insert Object Dialog Box

There are two tabs on the Insert Object dialog box: Create New and Create from File. Click on the **Create New** tab to view the options for creating a new object if you have not yet created the object you want to embed or link into your document. Figure 2.2 shows the Create New portion of the Insert Object dialog box. The following list explains the options found there.

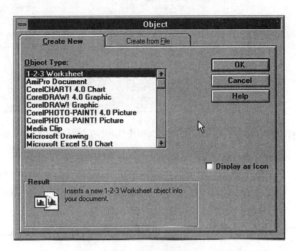

Figure 2.2 The Insert Object dialog box.

Create New   This file folder-like tab of the dialog box displays the options for creating a new object to embed into the destination document.

Object Type   This is a list of all the OLE-compatible applications installed on your computer. Selecting an object type of Microsoft Excel 5.0 Chart, for example, will start Excel so you can create a chart.

Display as Icon   Selecting this option causes the embedded object to be displayed as an icon when embedded, rather than the object itself.

Result   The Result section of the dialog box describes the results of the options you choose in the dialog box.

Click on the **Create from File** tab if you want to insert an existing file as the object to be linked or embedded. Figure 2.3 shows the Create from File portion of the Insert Object dialog box.

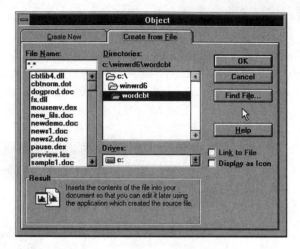

Figure 2.3 The Insert Object dialog box with Create From File options.

Create from File This tab changes the options in the dialog box so you can locate and select a file to embed in, or link to, the document you're working in.

File Name This list box displays the file names of the current directory listed in the Directories section of the dialog box.

Directories This list box displays the directories and subdirectories of your hard drive.

Drives This drop-down list displays the available disk drives on your system.

Find File Clicking on this button displays a file search dialog box, enabling you to search for a specific file name.

Link to File This option creates a link between the inserted file and the document you're working in.

Display as Icon Selecting this option causes the embedded or linked object to be displayed as an icon, rather than the object itself.

Result   The Result section of the dialog box describes the results of the options you choose in the dialog box.

Don't worry if you don't understand all these options immediately; they're covered in greater detail in lessons to come.

In this lesson, you learned about the various options available in the Paste Special and Insert Object dialog boxes. In the next lesson, we'll walk through the steps of creating a link.

Creating an OLE Link

In this lesson, you'll learn to create an OLE link.

One of the primary benefits of creating an OLE link is the ability to edit the linked object at its source (that is, in the original application and document it was created in) and have all of the destination documents that contain the linked object updated automatically. This lesson shows you, step by step, how to create a link between two OLE applications, using both the Paste Special and the Insert Object methods that you learned about in Lesson 2.

Linking with the Paste Special Command

Creating a link between two applications with Paste Special is quite similar to using the Windows cut and paste procedure, with a few additional options at the paste step.

What Are My Options?   The menu options for creating links between documents vary among Windows applications, or may not be available at all. Be sure to check your application's documentation if you find variances in the location or names of the menu options.

To create a link with **Edit Paste Special**, start with the server application (the application in which the object to be linked was originally created). For example, to link an Excel chart to a Word document, start in Excel. Here are the steps:

1. Start the server application, and create or open the source document (the document that contains the object).

2. If you create a new document in the server application, be sure to use **Save** on the **File** menu to save your document. You cannot link from a document that has not been saved.

3. Create the object to be linked if it does not already exist.

4. Select the object. The object may be text, a range of cells, a graphic, or database records.

5. Open the **Edit** menu, and choose **Copy**. The object you selected is copied to the Windows Clipboard.

6. Switch to Program Manager (press **Ctrl+Esc** repeatedly until it appears), and start the client application (the application into which you want to paste the object). Or if the client application is already open, simply switch to it with **Alt+Esc**.

7. If it is not already open, open the destination document (the document to receive the pasted object) in the client application.

8. In the destination document, position the cursor where you want the pasted (linked) object to appear.

9. Choose **Paste Special** from the **Edit** menu. A dialog box appears (Figure 3.1) showing the Data Types list of different formats in which the object can appear.

It's Not There! Some applications use slightly different wording for commands. If the Paste Special command does not appear on the Edit menu, use **Paste Links** instead.

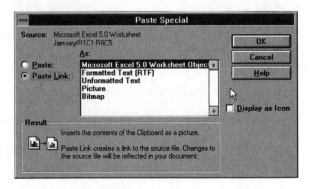

Figure 3.1 The Paste Special dialog box.

10. From the As list, select the data form in which you want the object to appear. Consult Lesson 2 to review the Object type options.

11. Click on the **Paste Link** button. Notice that the Result section of the dialog box describes the result of the options you are choosing in the dialog box.

12. Click on **OK** to paste the linked object into your document. The object is pasted into the destination document, and Windows creates an automatically updating link between the object and its source document.

Now, each time you update the information in the source document, the changes you make can be reflected in the destination document. The links you create can be updated automatically or manually. In the next lesson, you'll learn how to set the manual and automatic update options.

Linking with Insert Object

If you want to link an entire file to your document, such as a entire Excel spreadsheet, you can use the Insert Object command. It appears in the Edit menu of most Window's applications.

Unlike with Edit Paste, you do not have to open the source document to retrieve the object. You can perform the entire procedure without leaving the client application. Follow these steps:

1. Start the client application, and create or open the destination document. We'll use Microsoft Word as the Client application in this example.

2. Select **Object** on the **Insert** menu. The Object dialog appears (Figure 3.2), listing the OLE application Object types that can be inserted.

3. Click on the **Create from File** tab at the top of the dialog box. The dialog box changes to show a file name list box (Figure 3.3).

4. Select the name of the file you want to insert and link to the destination document. We'll use an Excel worksheet in this example. Navigate through the directories and subdirectories to locate the file if it does not appear in the current directory.

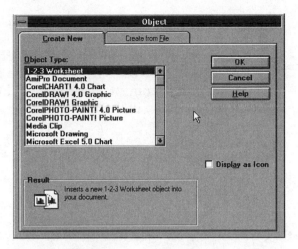

Figure 3.2 The Object dialog box.

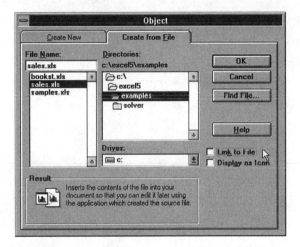

Figure 3.3 The Create from File options.

5. Click on the **Link to File** button. This will create an active link between the source file and the destination file. Notice that the Result section of the dialog box describe the results of the option you choose in the dialog box.

6. Select **OK**. The dialog box closes, and the source file is inserted into the destination document.

727

Whole Files Only Remember that using the Insert Object command to create a linked file links an entire file to the destination document. You cannot use this command to link an individual object, such as a range of Excel cells, to the destination document. Use the steps for Creating a Linked Object to link an individual object.

Now, the next time you update the source document that contains the data you linked, the file can be automatically or manually updated with the changes you make.

In this lesson, you learned how to create a link between applications. In the next lesson, you'll learn how to edit and manage your links between applications.

Managing OLE Links

In the lesson, you will learn how to edit, break, restore, lock, and unlock OLE links.

Editing Linked Objects

Once you have created a linked object, you may want to edit and update the information in the object. At this stage, you'll realize the full benefit of an OLE link, because you can edit the object one time and it will be updated in every document that it is linked to.

There are two ways to edit a linked object. The first is to start at the source document, using the server application to make changes to the object. The second is to start at the destination document and let the link information lead you to the correct source document and server application. With the second method, you do not have to remember the name of the source document or even what server application created it. Follow the steps below to learn how to edit objects using these two methods.

Editing from the Source Document

To edit a linked object starting from the source document:

1. Start the server application, and open the source document that contains the object you want to edit.

2. Edit and make changes to the object.

3. Save the document and close the server application.

4. Switch to (or start) the client application, and open the destination document. The changes should automatically be reflected in the destination document.

If the changes are not reflected, the document may not be set up to automatically update links. Skip to the "Managing a Link's Update Settings" section later in this lesson to learn how to update the links.

Now You See It, Now You Don't Some client applications let you edit or make changes directly to the object that is linked to the destination document without starting the server application. This can cause problems because the source document is not being changed, only the image of the object. The changes you make to the image will be wiped out when the object is updated via the source document. You will not have this problem with Microsoft Office products, but it may occur with other, non-Microsoft applications.

Editing from the Destination Document

Editing from the destination document is quick and easy, because you do not have to find and open the server application manually. To edit a linked object from the destination document:

1. From the destination document, double-click on the linked object you want to update. The server application starts and displays the source document. Figure 4.1 shows a linked Excel range ready to be edited in a Word document.

2. Edit the object in the source document. You can make as many changes to the object as like.

3. Choose **Save** from the **File** menu of the server application.

4. Choose **Exit** from the **File** menu of the server application. You're returned to the destination document, which reflects the changes you made to the linked object.

If double-clicking on the object does not start the server application, open the Links list dialog box by choosing **Links** from the **Edit** menu. Select the link you want to edit, and click on the **Open Source** button (see Figure 4.2). The server application will start and display the source document.

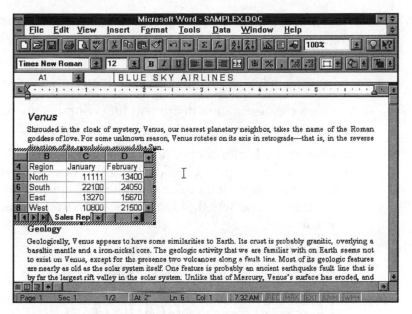

Figure 4.1   An Excel range linked to a Word document.

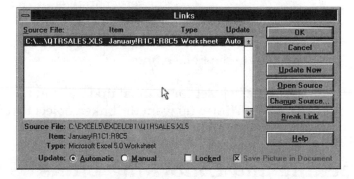

Figure 4.2   Another way to edit the object is to select it from the Links dialog box and click on the Open Source button.

Managing a Link's Update Settings

Once you have created a linked object, you can control when changes to the source document are reflected in the destination document(s). You can update a link manually or automatically. If a link is set to be updated manually, you must remember to follow the update steps each time you change the source document that contains the linked object.

With the automatic setting enabled (the default update setting), the changes you make to the source document are automatically updated each time you open the destination document.

To set a linked object to be manually updated, follow these steps:

1. Open the destination document that contains the object link you want to update.

2. Choose the **Links** command on the **Edit** menu. The Links dialog box appears (Figure 4.2). For the linked objects in your document, the list indicates the Link name, the path name of the source document, and whether the link is set to update automatically or manually.

3. Select the link you want to update.

4. Change the Update setting to **Manual**.

5. Update the link by clicking on the **Update Now** button in the Link list dialog box. The object is then updated with any changes that were made to the source document.

6. Click on **OK** to close the dialog box.

7. Choose **Save** from the **File** menu to save the document and changes to the link settings.

With the link set for manual update, you must repeat step 5 of this procedure each time you want the linked object to reflect changes made in the source document.

Locking and Unlocking Links

In addition to setting link update options to manual and automatic, you can lock a link to prevent the link from being updated when the source document is changed.

To lock and unlock a link, follow these steps:

1. Open the document containing the linked object.

2. Choose **Links** from the **Edit** menu. The Links dialog box appears.

3. Select the link that you want to lock.

4. To lock the link, select the **Locked** check box. To unlock the link, make sure the check box is empty.

5. Click on **OK** to close the dialog box.

A locked link will not be updated until it is unlocked.

Breaking Links

If at some point, you decide that you want a linked object in your document to remain fixed and no longer be updated by its source document, you can break (or cancel) the link. This does not delete or alter the object, it merely removes the background information that directly ties the object to its source document. The object becomes like any other object that was placed by Window's Copy and Paste operation.

To break or cancel a linked object, follow these steps:

1. Open the destination document that contains the object whose link you want to break.

2. Select **Links** (or **Link Options** in some applications) from the **Edit** menu. The Links list dialog box appears (Figure 4.2), showing linked object information.

3. Select the link name of the object you want to break.

4. Choose **Break Link** (or **Delete** in some applications). A warning box may appear cautioning that you are breaking a link. Click on **OK** or **Yes** to confirm your choice.

Restoring a Broken Link

It is possible to accidentally break a link to an object. If you move the source document from the directory in which it was saved when the link was created, or if you change the name of the source document, Windows will not be able to find it and the link is effectively broken. If this happens, and the link is set to automatically update, a warning dialog box appears telling you that the source document is missing or corrupted. To re-establish the broken link you must move the source document back to its original location, or tell Windows where to find the document in its new location.

To re-establish a broken link, follow these steps:

1. Open the destination document containing the object with the broken link. If you received an alert dialog box warning of the broken link, you have already completed this step.

2. Choose the **Links** command from the **Edit** menu. The Links list dialog box appears, listing the objects in the destination document that are linked.

3. Select the object whose link is broken.

4. Click on the **Change Source** button. A dialog box appears with a path name field of the linked object (Figure 4.3). The path name points to the location of the source document.

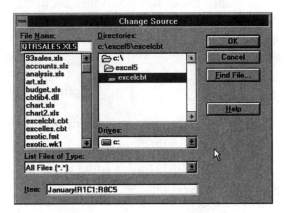

Figure 4.3 The Change Link dialog box.

5. Edit the path name or file name to reflect the new location or name of the source document.

6. Click on **OK** to complete the restoration of the link. The link is now re-established between the source and destination documents.

In this lesson, you learned how to share and dynamically update your documents. In the next lesson, you'll learn how to embed objects in OLE applications.

Embedding Objects in Windows Applications

In this lesson, you'll learn the difference between linking and embedding, how to embed an object in a Windows document, and how to edit an embedded object.

Understanding OLE Embedding

As you learned in Lessons 1 and 2, the procedure for embedding objects into your documents is essentially the same as that for linking objects, but the resulting connection between the source document and destination document is quite different.

Embedded objects are not linked to a source document. If you update the source document, any object in that document that is embedded in another document is not changed. The primary advantage of using embedded objects is the ease of editing the parts of a compound document. Use embedding instead of linking if automatic updating of objects is not required.

Embedded objects can be edited easily because they provide quick access to the application that created them. If you double-click on an embedded object, the application that created the object starts, allowing you to edit the object. When you're finished editing the object, you exit the application by choosing **Update** from the **File** menu. The application closes and you see the updated object back where you started.

Creating Embedded Objects

There are two ways to embed an object in a document. You can create the object in the server application and embed it in the destination document using the **Paste Special** command, or you can start at the destination document and choose **Object** on the **Insert** menu to launch the server application, create the object, and embed the object in the destination document.

Embedding with the Paste Special Command

The Paste Special command is useful to embed a portion of a document into another document. For example, you might want to embed a few cells from a large Excel worksheet into a Word document. (If you wanted to embed the entire worksheet, you would use the Insert Object command instead, which is covered in the next section.)

To embed an object with the Paste Special command, follow these steps:

1. Start the server application, and either open or create the document that contains the object you want to embed.

2. Select the object to be embedded.

3. Choose **Copy** from the **Edit** menu. The object is copied to the Windows Clipboard.

4. Start or switch to the client application, and open or create the destination document.

5. Place the insertion point where you want the object to appear.

6. Choose **Paste Special** from the **Edit** menu. A dialog box appears (Figure 5.1) enabling you to select the data type of the object to be embedded.

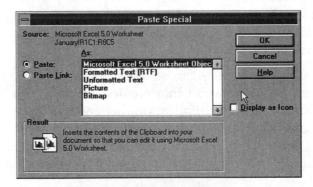

Figure 5.1   The Paste Special dialog box.

A Different Command   The Paste Special command's name varies slightly in some Windows applications. Be sure the command you choose allows you to select the data type of the object, and be sure *not* to select the Paste Link option.

7. Select the **Object** data type from the As list box (Microsoft Excel 5.0 Worksheet Object in this example).

8. Click on **OK.** The object is inserted at the insertion point and embedded in the destination document. Figure 5.2 shows the embedded object in the destination document.

9. Save the destination document. You can switch to the server application and either save or discard the source document. The destination document does not need the source document to maintain the embedded object (unlike a linked destination document that needs the source document containing the linked object.

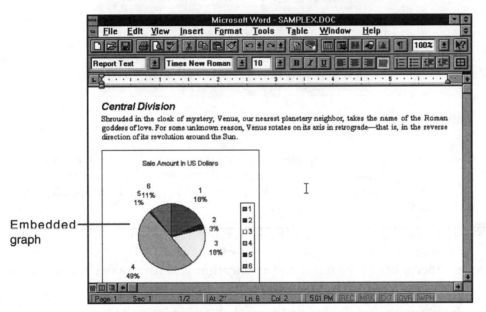

Figure 5.2 An embedded Excel 5 Graph in a Word document.

Embedding with Insert Object

If you have yet to create the object to be embedded, or if you want to embed an entire file, the Insert Object command is your best choice.

To create a new object, follow these steps:

1. Start the client application, and open the destination document. This is the document that you will place the embedded object into.

2. Choose the **Object** command from the **Insert** menu. A dialog box appears listing the server applications and object types that can be embedded in your document (Figure 5.3).

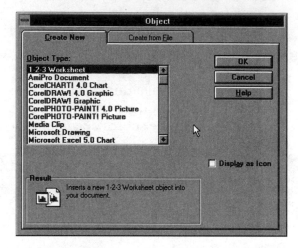

Figure 5.3   The Object dialog box.

3. Choose the server application you want to use, and click on **OK**. A special version server application starts, with the destination document still displayed on the screen. Figure 5.4 shows Microsoft Excel in a Word document.

4. Create the object using the server application's tools and commands. Notice that some of the menus and toolbar icons on the menu bar at the top of the application window have changed to those of the Server application's.

5. Once you've created the data, click on a portion of the destination document window. The server application closes, and the embedded object appears in the destination document. In some cases, you might need to manually exit the server application to return to the destination document.

6. Save the destination document.

   If you want to embed a file that you've already created, click on the **Create from File** tab at the top of the Insert dialog box. The dialog box changes to a file list box, where you can locate the file to be embedded.

Click on **OK** to insert the existing file in the destination document. Note that this option will only embed an entire file, not a individual object.

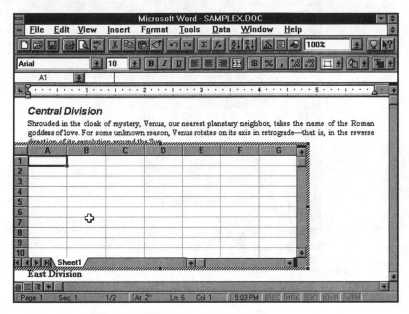

Figure 5.4   Microsoft Excel ready to create an object to embed in Word.

Editing Embedded Objects

Editing an embedded object is where the greatest advantage of embedding comes into play. You do not have to remember the name and location of the source document that you used to create the embedded object. You simply double-click on the object and the source application starts, allowing you to edit the object.

Follow these steps to edit an embedded object:

1. Start the client application and destination document containing the embedded object you want to edit.

2. Double-click on the object. The server application of the embedded object starts and displays the object (Figure 5.5). You can also choose the **Object** option that appears on the **Edit** menu to open the server application of the embedded object.

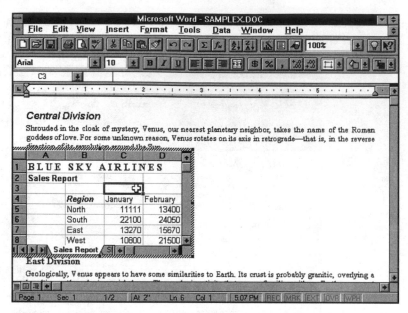

Figure 5.5 An Excel worksheet embedded as an editable object.

TIP

Modified Launch Some objects perform a function or action when you double-click on them. For example, Windows Sound recorder objects play a sound when double-clicked on. To edit objects like this, hold down the **Alt** key while double-clicking the object.

3. Edit the object using the server application's tools and commands.

4. Click on a portion of the destination document. The server application closes, and you are returned to the destination document. The embedded object reflects the changes you made. In some cases, you might have to select the **Exit** command to close the server application.

Converting the File Format of an Embedded Object

There may be a time when you need to edit a compound document containing embedded objects, but you do not have the same applications that created the embedded objects installed on your PC. For example, you receive a compound document from a co-worker that contains an embedded Excel object, but you do not have Excel on your PC, you use Lotus 1-2-3. Fortunately, you can convert the link information to change the server application of the embedded object.

To convert an embedded object to a different file format, follow these steps:

1. Open the document containing the object whose source application you want to convert to.

2. Select the embedded object.

3. Open the **Edit** menu. Select the last command on the **Edit** menu, **Worksheet Object** in this example. This command name changes, depending on the object type you selected in step 2. A submenu appears (Figure 5.6).

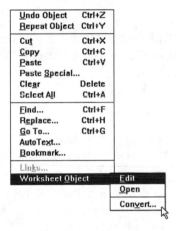

Figure 5.6 The Object Edit menu option on the Edit menu.

4. Choose **Convert** from the submenu. The Convert dialog box appears (Figure 5.7), displaying the possible Object types to convert the object to.

5. Select the Object type you want to convert the object to.

6. Choose **Convert To** to permanently change the object to the file format you selected in step 5. Choose **Activate As** to temporarily change all of the objects of the type selected to the file format you specified in step 5.

7. Click on **OK** to complete the conversion of the object.

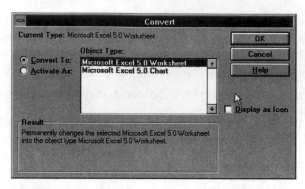

Figure 5.7   The Convert dialog box.

The next time you double-click the object to edit it, the application that you converted to will open so you can edit the object.

Update'em Now   If you install a new version of an application that was used to create embedded objects, you might have to use the Convert procedures in this section to update the objects to the new version of software.

In this lesson, you learned how to use OLE embedding to create a compound document that provides easy access and editing of objects created in different Windows OLE applications. In the next lesson, you'll learn to troubleshoot some common linking and embedding problems.

OLE Troubleshooting

In this lesson, you'll learn about some common linking and embedding problems and how to solve them.

Troubleshooting Linked Objects

Listed below are a few possible solutions to common problems encountered when working with linked objects and files.

Problem: The Paste Link button is dimmed out (not available) in the Paste Special Dialog box.

Solution: The source document that the object was copied from has not been saved. Return to the source document containing the object to be linked and use the **Save As** command on the **File** menu to save the document. Retry the **Paste Special** to create the link.

Problem: In Microsoft Word, confusing data is displayed in place of the object that was pasted in the document.

Solution: In Word, linked objects are not displayed if the Field Codes option in the Options dialog box is marked. To unmark the Field Codes option, open the **Tools** menu and choose **Options**. In the View option screen, uncheck the Field Codes option, and click on **OK**. The linked object will be displayed as it was created in its source document.

Problem: A linked object in a compound document is not updated when source file changes.

Solution: There are several possible causes of this problem. It is possible that the object is set to be manually updated. Follow the procedure for updating a link manually. The link also might be locked. Follow the steps in this section to unlock the link.

Another cause of this problem is a broken link. If the link is broken, an error message will be displayed, stating that the source document is missing or corrupted. Follow the steps in this section for restoring a broken link to re-establish the link.

Another possible cause of this problem is that no link was established when the object was pasted into the document. To verify that a link exists for the object, select **Links** on the **Edit** menu. If the Links option is available, a link exists for the object. If the Link option is dimmed, no link exists for the object. Repeat the steps for creating a linked object to create a link for the object.

Troubleshooting Embedded Objects

Listed below are a few common solutions to difficulties you may encounter when working with embedded objects.

Problem: Double-cicking on the object does not open its application.

Solution: The object was probably pasted into the document using the Paste command, not the Paste Special command. Or perhaps the Object Type selected in the Paste Special dialog box was either Formatted Text, or Unformed Text. These object types cannot be pasted as embedded objects.

Problem: An error message appears stating that The Server Application, Source File, or Item cannot be Found, when you select an object type from the Insert Object dialog box.

Solution: The application that creates the object type you chose is not on your hard drive, or its file name has changed. Try reinstalling the application to update Windows application list.

Problem: You are creating a new object to embed in a document, but cannot figure out how to return to the destination document.

Solution: The methods of closing the server application vary among Windows applications. Look for commands like **Exit and Return** on the **File** menu, or a small dialog box with a **Close Picture** button.

Installing Your Programs

The installation procedures for Windows and for the Microsoft Office products are not complicated. You simply insert the first disk into your floppy disk drive, issue the SETUP command, and follow the instructions on-screen. In this appendix, we'll walk through the installation of each product in case you need a little extra help.

It is always a good idea to make backup copies of your original program disks before you install them. Use the DOS DISKCOPY command (**DISKCOPY A: A:** or **DISKCOPY B: B:** for instance) or the **Copy Disk** command in Windows' File Manager (once you have installed Windows). Store the original diskettes in a safe place, and run the installation procedures from the copies.

Installing Windows 3.1

1. Insert the Windows 3.1 disk 1 into floppy drive A: or B:.

2. At the DOS prompt, type the drive letter of the drive you're using, followed by a colon (:), then press **Enter**. For example:

   C> A:

3. Type **SETUP** and press **Enter**.

4. Follow the on-screen prompts.

You can use the Express Setup or the Custom Setup option. It is recommended that you use **Express Setup**; this lets Setup do most of the work for you. The Setup program then installs the Windows files on your computer in the drive and directory you specify.

When the installation is complete, you are given the option to reboot your computer, restart Windows, or exit to DOS. To make sure all the changes made to your system are recognized, select the **Reboot** command button by clicking on it with the mouse pointer or pressing **R**.

745

Installing Word, Excel, PowerPoint, or Access

The instructions for installing Word, Excel, PowerPoint, and Access are the same. Just use the diskettes for whichever program you want to install.

1. Start Windows by typing **WIN** at the DOS prompt and pressing **Enter**.

2. Insert Disk 1 into Drive A: or B:.

3. Open the Program Manager **File** menu by pressing **Alt+F** or clicking on **File**. Select the **Run** command by clicking on it or pressing **R**.

4. Type **A:SETUP** or **B:SETUP**, and press **Enter**.

5. Follow the on-screen instructions. You can perform any of the following installations:

   - **Typical**   Installs Excel's most commonly used features. This is the recommended installation.

   - **Complete/Custom**   Installs all of Excel's features or just the features you choose.

   - **Laptop (minimum)**   Installs a trimmed-down version of Excel to conserve your laptop's disk space.

Installing Microsoft Mail

To install Microsoft Mail on a workstation, make sure that the server software has already been installed by your system administrator. *These steps are for workstation installation only.*

1. Start Windows by typing **WIN** at the DOS prompt and pressing **Enter**.

2. Run **File Manager** from the **Main** group.

3. Open the **Disk** menu, and select **Network Connections**. The Network Connections dialog box will appear.

4. In the Network Path text box, type the network path where the Mail programs are located (this information is available from your system administrator).

5. Click on the **Connect** button. You are now connected to the network directory which contains the Mail programs.

6. Click on the **Close** button.

7. Switch to the Network drive you just connected to by clicking on it.

8. Double-click on **SETUP.EXE** from the files list, and press **Enter**.

9. Type your full name in the dialog box, and click **Continue**.

10. Choose **Express** or **Custom Setup** (**Express Setup** is recommended.)

11. Enter the path where you want the Mail program to be located on your computer.

Using MS Office Toolbars

You have been introduced to several toolbars throughout this book. Microsoft makes great use of them, and through their consistency from program to program, they are easy to learn, recognize, and remember. This appendix will be a handy reference guide for you when you need a quick reminder of how to use the various toolbars you're encountering.

Remember, you can only access the toolbars with your mouse, and if you are ever in doubt as to what a tool is for, position your mouse pointer over it, and a description of the tool's function will appear in the status bar.

Word for Windows

Standard Toolbar

Icon	Name	What It Does
	New	Creates a new document
	Open	Opens an existing file
	Save	Saves the current document
	Print	Prints the current document
	Print Preview	Displays document in print preview mode
	Spelling	Checks spelling
	Cut	Cuts selection to Clipboard

Icon	Name	What It Does
	Copy	Copies selection text to Clipboard
	Paste	Pastes from the Clipboard
	Format Painter	Copies formatting from the selection
	Undo	Undoes the last editing action
	Redo	Reverses the last undo command
	AutoFormat	Automatically formats a document
	Insert AutoText	Creates or inserts an autotext entry
	Insert Table	Creates a table
	Insert Microsoft Excel Worksheet	Inserts a Microsoft Excel worksheet
	Columns	Changes column format
	Drawing	Displays the drawing toolbar
	Insert Chart	Inserts a Microsoft Graph chart
	Show/Hide ¶	Displays or hides nonprinting characters
100%	Zoom Control	Scales the editing view
	Help	Gives help on a command or screen region

Formatting Toolbar

Icon	Name	What It Does
Normal ▼	Style	Applies an existing style or records a style by example
Times New Roman ▼	Font	Changes the font of the selection
10 ▼	Font Size	Changes the font size of the selection
B	Bold	Makes the selection bold (toggle)
I	Italic	Makes the selection italic (toggle)
U	Underline	Formats the selection with a continuous underline (toggle)
≡	Align Left	Aligns the paragraph at the left indent
≡	Center	Centers the paragraph
≡	Align Right	Aligns the paragraph at the right indent
≡	Justify	Aligns the paragraph at both the left and the right indent
≝	Numbering	Creates a numbered list based on the current defaults
≔	Bullets	Creates a bulleted list based on the current defaults
⇤	Decrease Indent	Decreases indent or promotes the selection one level
⇥	Increase Indent	Increases indent or demotes the selection one level
⊞	Borders	Shows or hides the Borders toolbar

Excel

Standard Toolbar

Icon	Name	Description
	New Workbook	Creates a new workbook
	Open	Opens an existing document
	Save	Saves changes made to the active document
	Print	Prints the active document
	Print Preview	Displays active document in print preview mode
	Spelling	Starts spelling checker
	Cut	Cuts selection and places it onto Clipboard
	Copy	Copies selection onto Clipboard
	Paste	Pastes contents of Clipboard
	Format Painter	Copies and pastes formats for cells and objects
	Undo	Undoes last action or command
	Repeat	Repeats last action or command
	AutoSum	Inserts SUM function and proposes sum range
	Function Wizard	Displays the Function Wizard to insert or edit a function

continues

Standard Toolbar Continued

Icon	Name	Description
	Sort Ascending	Sorts selected rows in ascending order
	Sort Descending	Sorts selected rows in descending order
	Chart Wizard	Creates embedded chart or modifies active chart
	Text Box	Adds unattached text or a textbox
	Drawing	Lets you show and hide the drawing toolbar
100%	Zoom Control	Changes magnification of displayed document
	TipWizard	Shows or hides the TipWizard toolbar
	Help	Provides help on commmand or screen region

Formatting Toolbar

Icon	Name	Description
Arial	Font	Applies font
10	Font Size	Applies font size
B	Bold	Applies bold formatting to selected text
I	Italic	Applies italic formatting to selected text

Icon	Name	Description
	Underline	Underlines selected text
	Align Left	Left aligns text
	Center	Centers text in cells, text boxes or buttons
	Align Right	Right aligns text
	Center Across Columns	Centers text across selected columns
	Currency Style	Applies currency style to selected cells
	Percent Style	Applies percent style to cells
	Comma Style	Applies comma style to cells
	Increase Decimal	Adds one decimal place from number format
	Decrease Decimal	Removes one decimal place from number format
	Borders	Applies borders to the selection
	Color	Applies color to the selection
	Font Color	Applies font color to the selection

Mail for Windows

Icon	Name	Description
	Compose	Opens the Send Note form for you to compose a message

continues

Mail for Windows Continued

Icon	Name	Description
Reply	Reply	Opens a Send Note form with the sender already addressed
ReplyAll	ReplyAll	Sends a reply to everyone listed to the To and Cc boxes
Forward	Forward	Forwards a copy of your message along with your comments
Move	Move	Opens the Move Message dialog box
Delete	Delete	Deletes a message from the Inbox
Previous	Previous	Opens the message previous to the current one
Next	Next	Opens the message after the current one

PowerPoint

Standard Toolbar

Icon	Name	Description
	New File	Creates a new presentation
	Open File	Opens an existing presentation
	Save File	Saves the active presentation
	Print	Prints the active presentation
	Check Spelling	Checks spelling in the active presentation
	Cut	Cuts selection to Clipboard

Icon	Name	Description
	Copy	Copies selection to Clipboard
	Paste	Pastes contents of Clipboard
	Format Painter	Copies formatting of the selection to another object
	Undo	Undoes the last action
	Insert New Slide	Inserts a new slide after the current slide
	Insert Microsoft Word Table	Adds a Microsoft Word Table onto the slide
	Insert Microsoft Excel Worksheet	Adds a Microsoft Excel Worksheet onto the slide
	Insert Graph	Adds a Microsoft Graph onto the slide
	Insert Org Chart	Adds an Org chart onto the slide
	Insert Clip Art	Adds an image from the clip art library onto the slide
	Pick a Look Wizard	Helps to design a look for the current presentation
	Report It	Transfers to contents of the active presentation to Microsoft Word
33%	Zoom Control	Changes the scale at which you edit
	Help	Provides context sensitive help on different areas of the PowerPoint screen

Formatting Toolbar

Icon	Name	Description
[Arial ▾]	Font	Changes the font of the selection or sets default font
[44 ▾]	Font Size	Changes the font size of the selected text
A▲	Increase Font Size	Increases the font size of the selected text
A▼	Decrease Font Size	Decreases the font size of the selected text
B	Bold	Makes the selected text bold (toggle)
I	Italic	Makes the selected text italic (toggle)
U	Underline	Formats the selected text with a continuous underline (toggle)
S	Text Shadow	Adds a shadow to the selected text (toggle)
A	Text Color	Changes the color of the selected text
≡	Left Alignment	Aligns the left edges of each line of text
≡	Center Alignment	Aligns the centers of each line of text
≔	Bullet (On/Off)	Adds or removes the default bullet for the selected paragraphs (toggle)

Icon	Name	Description
←	Promote (Indent less) graphs	Unindents the selected para- one heading level
→	Demote (Indent more)	Indents the selected para- graphs one heading level

Drawing Toolbar

Icon	Name	Description
↖	Selection tool	Picks up the tool for selecting and editing objects
A	Text tool	Picks up the tool for creating text objects
\	Line tool	Picks up the tool for creating lines
□	Rectangle tool	Picks up the tool for drawing a rectangle
○	Ellipse tool	Picks up the tool for drawing an ellipse
⌒	Arc tool	Picks up the tool for drawing arcs
△	Freeform tool	Picks up the tool for drawing polygons or freehand lines
↻	Free Rotate tool	Picks up the tool which can rotate the selection to any angle
⬡	Auto Shapes	Shows or hides the AutoShapes toolbar (toggle)

continues

757

Drawing Toolbar Continued

Icon	Name	Description
	Fill (On/Off)	Adds or removes the default fill color from the selected objects (toggle)
	Line (On/Off)	Adds or removes the default line color from the selected objects (toggle)
	Shadow (On/Off)	Adds or removes the default shadow color from the selected objects (toggle)

Access

Standard Toolbar

Icon	Name	Description
	New Database	Creates a new database
	Open Database	Opens an existing database
	Attach Table	Creates a link to an existing table
	Print	Prints the active document
	Print Preview	Displays the document as it will look when printed
	Code	Opens Module window
	Cut	Deletes selection and copies to the Clipboard
	Copy	Copies selection onto the Clipboard
	Paste	Inserts contents of the Clipboard

Icon	*Name*	*Description*
	Relationships	Creates and edits relationships between tables
	Import	Creates a table or an object from an external source
	Export	Exports data or an object
	Merge It	Merges data with a Microsoft Word document
	Analyze It with MS Excel	Output and view the current object as a Microsoft Excel file
	New Query	Creates a new query
	New Form	Creates a new form
	New Report	Creates a new report
	Database Window	Shows the Database window
	AutoForm	Automatically creates a simple form based on the selected table or query
	AutoReport	Automatically creates a simple report based on the selected table or query
	Undo	Undoes the most recent change
	Cue Cards	Displays online coach to help you with your work
	Help	Get help by clicking on an area of the screen

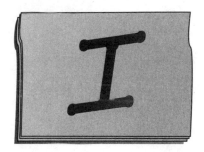

INDEX

Symbols

3-D charts, 346-347, 464-465
3-D View command (Format menu), 346, 464

A

absolute cell addresses, 296-298
Accept option
    automatic formatting, 199
    scheduling meetings, 602
Access, 607-610
    context-sensitive help, 613
    data
        compatibility, 702-705
        searches, 670-675
    databases, 607-608
        accessing, 659-664
        creating, 615-618
    forms
        creating, 646-648
        design, 651-654
        list boxes, 655-658
    graphs, 694-697
    help, 613
    indexing, 676-679
    macros, 698-701
    mailing labels, 689-693
    menu bar, 609
    queries, 665
    quitting, 610
    records, 637-640
    reports, 680-683
        customizing, 684-688
    shortcut keys, 611-612
    starting, 608-610
    main menu, 611-614
    Table Wizards, 627-630
    tables
        creating, 619-626
        inserting data in, 631-636
        linking, 706-709
        views, 641-645
    toolbar, 612
    toolbar icons, 609
accessing
    global user list (Mail), 524
    Help (Mail), 518

active window, 15
active workbooks, 264
Add (sum) the numbers option button (Graph Wizard dialog box), 697
Add Names button, 549
Add option (Spelling dialog box), 182
Add Table dialog box, 660, 708
addition, 292
address book (Mail), 551-553
    addressee selection, 524
    creating, 548-550
    displaying, 549
    names, inserting, 549
    postoffice address book, 552
    sending messages to personal groups, 558
    users
        deleting, 549-550
        inserting, 548-549
Address Book command (Mail menu), 548

M

X-Z